P9-AGA-407

The Compassionate REBEL

Energized by Anger, Motivated by Love

Interviews and stories written and compiled by

Burt F. Berlowe, Rebecca A. Janke, and Julie D. Penshorn

A Peacemaker® Products Publication

PO Box 248
Scandia, MN 55073-0248

www.peacemaker.org

Growing Communities for Peace gratefully acknowledges the support of the Hugh J. Andersen Foundation, the Bayport Foundation, the Margaret Rivers Foundation, and the Lifebridge Foundation, Inc.

Designed and co-published by Triangle Park Creative, Inc.
Minneapolis, MN • (612) 692-8560
www.TriangleParkCreative.com

 First Edition.

The Compassionate Rebel: Energized by Anger, Motivated by Love: interviews and stories/written and compiled by Burt F. Berlowe, Rebecca A. Janke, and Julie D. Penshorn; photographs by Todd Cota—1st ed.

p. cm
Includes bibliographical references and index.
ISBN 0-9646676-4-9

1. Human Rights—Literary collections. 2. Peace—Literary collections. 3. Self-realization—Literary collections. 4. Spiritual life. 5. Adoption. 6. Parenting. I. Berlowe, Burt. II. Janke, Rebecca A. III. Penshorn, Julie D.

PN6071.H784C66 2002 808.8'0353
QBI01-701050

Designed and co-published by Triangle Park Creative, Inc., Minneapolis, MN

Dedication

With love and gratitude, we dedicate this book to the compassionate rebels who shared their stories with us and to all those with stories we have not yet heard.

Thank you

Thank you to the many individuals who granted us permission to tell their stories and all the others who have believed in and supported this project along its extended path.

Table of Contents

Foreword

The compassionate rebel exists in all of us. Those featured in this book are ordinary people who have shared their stories and, thus, provided each reader with an avenue to uncover the compassionate rebel within himself or herself.

Our challenge, as we begin the twenty-first century, is developing ways to tell our own stories and bear witness to the stories of others, in order to create a more just society, where everyone can grow to his or her full potential. Our ancestral tradition of oral history as a method of creating culture is rediscovered as we read these interviews as spoken stories. Each story reintroduces us to important parts of our cultures and ourselves.

This book is a wellspring of hope. It challenges us not to be bystanders, but rather protectors of human rights in our daily lives. These life lessons provide an opportunity for us to travel to new places, see new perspectives, and acquire a new consciousness of the human experience.

What do the personal stories in *The Compassionate Rebel* have in common with our own life experiences? I hope that each reader will attempt to answer this question for him or herself. The commonalities are significant because they provide insights into us. Each connection may help us uncover what effective rebellion and true compassion are and lead us to what being "human" and "humane" really mean.

In every corner of the world, we continue to observe starvation, violence, discrimination, exploitation, murder, environmental atrocities, illiteracy, death from preventable diseases, homelessness, and war. *The Compassionate Rebel* provides us with an avenue for exploration of inspiring triumphs and courageous attempts to address some of these causes of suffering.

The Compassionate Rebel encouraged me to look at my life and reflect on additional ways I can make the world a better place. Yes, I understand that our suffering, oppression, and healing are connected. Yet, I benefited from the stories of others, as I found a renewed energy and compassionate voice from my youth saying, "That's just not fair. I'm going to . . ."

The compassionate rebels in this book continued learning from others while fighting against injustice. Whether or not these storytellers directly connected their actions to their personal or community values, they knew what action they must take and were driven to speak out. They not only realized what was and is "wrong," but also they related closely with their own and others' pain and struggles, and were mobilized to action.

After the atrocities of the Holocaust, a group of compassionate rebels gathered together with a commitment to creating a list of principles that every government, individual, and organ of society could agree upon as standards of values and behaviors for all. They succeeded in drafting *The Universal Declaration of Human Rights*, which was adopted by the United Nations General Assembly on December 10, 1948, and now represents a foundation for defining human rights today. We have been able to draft the document, now we need to affect the culture, so the goals of the document can be truly realized.

Why do some individuals rebel against injustice? Why do some individuals feel compassion on a very deep level? These two key questions have challenged me as a mother of two. I believe that we can learn many answers from our children.

Children show both their rebellion and compassion openly. They also know and value what is fair and just. Unfortunately, others too often role model hiding love and empathy, and accepting the injustice life deals them and others. *The Compassionate Rebel* provides amazing examples of people who have held onto these two human capacities: "compassion" and "rebellion." These rebels respected others' rights so intrinsically that their actions were passionate and persuasive without infringing on the dignity of other beings. These are the humane humans of the twenty-first century. These are my heroes.

Kristi Rudelius-Palmer,
Co-Director, University of Minnesota Human Rights Center

Introduction

Every day, the media take snapshots of our culture. And, though it is said that the camera doesn't lie, what we see is not truth. In fact, we are being lied to about something very basic: who we are. Because every picture tells a story, the way the camera is pointed matters. Huge sections of the story of "us" are not being documented.

In *The Compassionate Rebel*, we take the camera, literally and figuratively, into our own hands and point it at people whose stories depict the rest of who we are. Through interviews, stories, and photographs, we share with you a hidden culture, and our hope is to reveal it in its full power and beauty.

Compassionate rebels are role models for the masses and mentors for activists. They are producers of democracy, rather than embittered citizens. They teach us how to protest without violence, how to rebel without destroying, and how to say no without saying goodbye. Compassionate rebels bring to our viewfinder people who are exploring their anger, rage, and disappointment and seeking solutions to oppression, racism, abuse, troubled relationships, and economic woes.

Compassionate rebel Tom La Blanc does it by saying no to personal victimization and racism through building bridges between his Sioux culture and others in the States and Europe. Mary Shepard does it by using the power of her wealth to support grass roots movements. Rachel Hefte did it by standing against the U.S.-backed contras in solidarity with Nicaraguan peasants. Jim Lovestar does it by rebelling against the power of his childhood wounds and offering his compassion and energy to others through the "Men's Warrior" movement.

The stories of compassionate rebels delve deeply into issues of morality. With characteristic indignance, compassionate rebel Dorothy Woolfork said, "Don't ask me to fall in line. I don't fall in line. I do what's right."

Moral action is inspired by a deep-rooted sense of right and wrong, which can stem from a religious belief and/or a strong sense of fairness/justice. People on the right, the left, or the middle of the political spectrum can experience rage at immoral actions. This anger can be a powerful catalyst for action. Compassionate rebels use both compassion and anger in their efforts. They make a difference in their own lives, right where they stand.

The compassionate rebels in this book have found nonviolent solutions to personal, familial, national, and international struggles. They grappled with a host of obstacles as they pursued their dreams. You will relate to the multiple challenges each one faced, including child abuse, racism, isolation, hopelessness, lack of resources, and lack of support. Faced with injustice, the compassionate rebel is propelled to action.

Having moved from one millennium to the next, many of us are stirred by a yearning for deeper meaning and purpose in our lives. Perhaps we have made resolutions about creating a more livable world for ourselves or for others. Reflecting upon the past century, we know we can't continue the violence we inflict on each other and the earth, but we may not see our part in the solution. We may not know that none of the inequities in our society could exist without our complicity, that our society is out of balance largely because we, as individuals, are. The pain and suffering all around us are a reflection of our stymied consciousness and how gravely we are failing to love—to care.

We are well aware of great leaders or government programs that try to save us from ourselves, but we instinctively know that they are not enough. All is not well . . . a child is abused, someone is killed in a drive-by shooting, the store on the corner has been robbed for the fourth time, a hate-crime rocks the neighborhood, a violent shoot out occurs in an apparently tranquil school, a drunken driver leaves a brilliant teacher brain-damaged, a teenager has run away to escape from the war at home, the latest fight between husband and wife is heading them to the divorce court, and the list goes on. We want to scream out, "Enough is enough!" Cynicism, hopelessness, victimization, and treading the backwaters of bitterness are luxuries we can no longer afford.

Rebels, including children and adults, are often awake to injustice, but may use destructive methods when they try to right a wrong. They may be asleep to compassion, and thus create more suffering than solutions to problems. Many peacemakers, strong in compassion, feel they have fallen off the bandwagon if they voice their anger, frustration, disappointment, and/or outrage.

However, through our work as peace educators and activists, we became aware of others who managed to combine their rebellion with compassion in order to improve their lives and the lives around them. Once we knew what to look for, we began to find many of these individuals. We came to believe they represented a hidden culture. However, nowhere were their stories being told! No one had looked, as an anthropologist might, at these people. We decided we would. And along the way, we've learned that we discovered gold—in the form of hope for humanity. We found people who believe they can use their personal power to make a difference; who believe that dreams are not just to be dreamed, but also to be realized; who believe, like Denis Hayes, founder of Earth Day, that "there is no survival value in pessimism."

These representatives of this hidden culture, from all walks of life, are powerful examples of what can be done by the average person when the capacity for rage against injustice and capacity for love are fully joined. They have turned ugliness to beauty, loneliness to belonging, racism to interconnectedness, and conflict to harmony. They have said "no" to injustice and critically evaluated complex issues and/or shared power with those who previously had little, if any, voice or power. Because they feel their acts are so ordinary, they seldom talk about themselves—they go about their daily work and lives…until now.

Each one of the people you meet in this book was quite surprised that we wanted to interview him or her but didn't hesitate for one minute to share his or her story. As you read these stories, you will be moved by the power of their commitment, the strength of their rebelliousness, and the courage they demonstrate. You'll also see their gentleness and compassion. You will gain insights and courage as you take the next step on your personal journey.

These are ordinary, everyday people who understand their failures and inadequacies and do something anyway. They dispel the myth that people who work for social justice; create harmonious homes; have inner peace; interface and work with people of different cultures; and make the world a better place to live, work, and play; have some altruistic gene or are morally, socially, or politically gifted. No. They believe what they do, or have done, could be done by anyone.

Does every person have a compassionate rebel story in his or her history? We think so. In fact, we believe one way we create a culture of caring and action is by focusing on each other's compassionate rebel capacities and stories. This focus affects our realities.

We asked our compassionate rebels how they became what they are and how they have sustained their efforts. We wanted to know how people remained functional and created change when faced with any number of struggles. Each person had a unique answer, but there were some common elements.

- Compassionate rebels reflect the image of the Chinese character for power that has three elements: the first part is forward motion, the second is heart, and the third is goal or purpose. It is the combination of these elements that gives compassionate rebels the capacity to create the changes they want to see.
- Compassionate rebels reframe the problem: They ask the question, "What are we for?" rather than, "What are we against?" They move from a blame and shame approach to a positive, constructive one, wherein they can tap their creativity to find new possibilities.
- Compassionate rebels call up their anger to find renewed energy for their compassion: Compassion alone can sometimes yield few results and/or lead to compassion fatigue. Compassionate rebels use their anger to help them continue to work when perhaps they would just rather quit.
- Compassionate rebels harness their anger and temper it with compassion: They are willing to rock the boat, when necessary, to create space for diverse opinions to be included, yet they are willing to stand up and take action for their point of view.
- Compassionate rebels reflect before and after acting: In the reflection process, they determine the best possible action to take given their circumstances, resources, and power relationships.
- Compassionate rebels are willing to take risks: Societies typically resist dissent and discourage change. We learn that to change could mean death. So, we search for safety by sticking to the middle of the pack. Compassionate rebels risk living on the edge of the pack. They believe they demonstrate their compassion for the pack by seeking new frontiers. They don't stand by and say, "let someone else do it," or "let some new government program do it." Taking risks is essential for the survival of humankind. In fact, much of discovery has depended on being willing to journey beyond the known limits of the physical, psychological, or spiritual universe.

Many of our interviewees pointed out their inadequacies. We protested that there is no "perfect" person and no perfect compassionate rebel. Each act someone takes as a compassionate rebel

"They don't just ask for change; they act, for a change." *Rebecca Janke*

is an important contribution, indeed, a gift to society. The more acts of compassionate rebellion we commit each day, the greater chance we have of preserving, protecting, renewing, and remaking our society.

How to use this book:

We've been heartened by the response to *The Compassionate Rebel* and have been amazed at the wide range of ways people have been using this book.

Private and public middle schools and high schools have found *The Compassionate Rebel* to be useful in social studies, multicultural, English, and peace and social justice classrooms. In colleges, it has been hailed as a new and provocative curriculum for those who are majoring or minoring in peace studies or conflict resolution programs. In college writing classes, it has been used as a text for learning how to mine the stories that live within us.

Youth group leaders and camp directors have found that the stories serve as an inspirational guide to help young people find additional venues for community service. They also help youth reframe their personal struggles. Rather than succumbing to depression or lashing out at the world, youth can begin to see ways to tap into their creativity and resiliency and rise up to "right the wrongs."

People in correctional facilities, group homes, and treatment centers have found that the compassionate rebel stories validate the anger or rage they have felt, as well as provide intriguing insights about using anger as a constructive, powerful force to change the perceived injustices they have experienced.

Faith-based communities find it helpful to use *The Compassionate Rebel* as a reminder that "compassion in action" is central to living out one's spiritual values. Groups have formed study sessions to read the stories and reflect on how they can become more awake to the needs of others, confront their complacency, and be more courageous in their efforts to reduce the suffering of their fellow human beings.

Elders have recognized their own compassionate rebel stories and have enthusiastically responded to the idea of passing on their life's "learnings," not just their life's "earnings." The authors have put together a team of freelance writers who are available upon request to interview elders and capture their rich legacy. Growing Communities for Peace invite people to submit their stories for possible inclusion in future publications.

Community organizers and social activists use this book for moral support, buoyed by the knowledge that everyday citizens are taking action and finding creative ways to protest over local, national, and international issues. They are particularly pleased with the current and often difficult-to-find peacemaking resources that are included in the book. (Additional resources and resource updates are available at www.peacemaker.org.)

The Compassionate Rebel Response:

As authors or, as we prefer to call ourselves, story-carriers, our primary interest has centered on the belief that we have discovered a hidden persona. Our reference to looking at people's lives as an anthropologist might means that the more people we interviewed, the more we recognized a pattern of moral behavior. It was beyond what we expected. We interviewed fifty people and got fifty stories! What was this saying about who we are?

What is surprising is that the majority of the acts of compassion stemmed from anger. When we created the psychological free-space for people to talk about their lives as peacemakers and then worked backwards toward the catalysts for their actions, we found tremendous amounts of anger.

We have a nasty tendency, as humans, to blame ourselves and shame others rather than challenge the status quo and authority where and when it needs to be challenged. We wondered,

"Those who profess to favor freedom and drepreecate agitation are men who want crops without plowing the ground, they want rain without thunder and lightning. They want the ocean without the awful roar of its many waters. . . Power concedes nothing without a demand—it never had and it never will. Find out just what any people will quietly submit to and you have found out the exact measure of injustice and wrong which will be imposed upon them, and these will continue till they are resisted . . . the limits of tyrants are prescribed by the endurance of those whom they oppress."

Frederick Douglass

"Could it be that the powers that be have tapped into this tendency and manipulated our cultural self-perception to convince us that our anger is just *our problem*? Could it be that in this way they have found an effective and ingenious way to keep dissenters quiet so they don't challenge our traditions?"

In exploring the topic of anger further, we found that research shows anger is the first warning sign to let us know that something isn't quite right. And, the more we are being told to stop being angry, and our anger is not validated, the angrier or more rageful we seem to get!

We see this with children who no longer respond to traditional parenting roles. We see this with those who no longer are willing to take abuse from their batterer. We see this with lovers no longer willing to settle for a one-sided relationship. These people see injustice swirling around them, and nothing will silence them. They want to see something done and are willing to push the envelope if necessary. In the process, families are exploding.

What is encouraging however, is the vast numbers of people, all over the world, who are tapping into the compassionate rebel persona to address vexing personal and social problems. They are tired of violence and are devising creative, ingenious ways to solve problems differently. We profiled fifty such individuals in this book. You will see that not one of these compassionate rebels could have done what they did if they had silenced their anger.

Just being angry though, was not the solution to the problem. Their anger was what *propelled* them to action. When they acted, they also brought forth their compassion. They used anger as fuel to bring their compassionate responses to life.

Just as no two people are alike, neither are compassionate rebel responses. Using their unique personalities, temperaments, talents, interests, and passions, rather than a prescribed formula, they let their spirit and common sense guide them.

We struggled with ways to reveal and validate our true selves through our anger and found another key component was our bliss. Understanding anger and bliss together helps people access their own true selves in order to create transformative compassionate rebel responses.

Without understanding our bliss we can get caught up in what we are *against*, instead of what we are *for*. This negative approach doesn't result in positive, hopeful compassionate rebel responses.

We developed a fascinating process that helps people discover their own true selves through reflecting on their histories and focusing on early memories of injustice and bliss. From this reflection, they find the deepest roots of their anger and bliss and discover their personal metaphor. This helps them gain the insight to rewrite their futures. This process is part of our "Compassionate Rebel Response" workshops. It also is described for you at www.peacemaker.org.

Until you find your personal metaphor(s), we'd like to share with you the stories of the fifty people in this book. We hope you'll find examples and inspiration for your own journey.

"Metaphor is genius."

Aristotle

The Story-Carriers

Burt Berlowe is a freelance writer, journalist, educator, community organizer, and activist. He has authored several books, including: *Peaceful Parenting in a Violent World, The Peaceful Parenting Handbook, Dealing With Alcohol and Drug Abuse, Reflections in Loring Pond,* and *The Homegrown Generation*. His connections have led to many of the interviews for this book. Burt has served on numerous committees and action groups in his commitment to nonviolence and eradication of child abuse. He is known for his extensive volunteer work and his ability to add insight and leadership to grassroots community efforts.

Rebecca Janke, M.Ed., and **Julie Penshorn**, MBC, have done extensive writing together, including co-authoring several books: *Peacemaker's A,B,Cs for Young Children: A Guide for Teaching Conflict Resolution with a Peace Table, Six Keys to Participatory Leadership, Expanding the Circle: A Peacemaker® Teen Mentor Facilitator Guide, and Playing With Peace*. As co-directors of the non-profit organization, Growing Communities for Peace, they serve as consultants, workshop presenters, artists-in-residence, and curriculum designers. Information about these services and other peace education resources can be found at the Growing Communities for Peace web site at www.peacemaker.org.

Rebecca has served as a prekindergarten to grade six Montessori teacher. She is a peace education coach for families and a national keynote speaker. Largely because of Rebecca's extensive

Photo by Todd Cota

Authors Rebecca A. Janke, Burt F. Berlowe, and Julie D. Penshorn

reading, researching, and networking, we have been able to include several resources at the end of each story, thus providing readers with a path for continued learning and exploration. Rebecca is deeply committed to the practice of peacemaking education for children prekindergarten through grade twelve. Her seven-year-old granddaughter recently told her, "I'm going to help all the kids remember how to be peacemakers because I am the granddaughter of a peacemaker." The child's four-year-old sister followed that line with, "I'm a peace-a-maker, too!"

Julie coined the term "compassionate rebel" and has helped the book evolve. She sees compassionate rebellion as an artistic, full expression of life and humanity and tries to weave it into her equestrian work, music writing/performing, and her work with Growing Communities for Peace. Julie believes in the value of real human emotions and is acutely aware of the emotional effect of power inequities. She is deeply committed to helping people develop skills for "power with" relationships with animals or other people, rather than "power over" relationships. She, Rebecca, and Burt have developed a Compassionate Rebel Action Camp youth leadership model to honor the needs of young people to express their artistry and gain skills for rebellion with compassion. Julie is the producer of *The Compassionate Rebel* compact disc and has written and performed several of the songs.

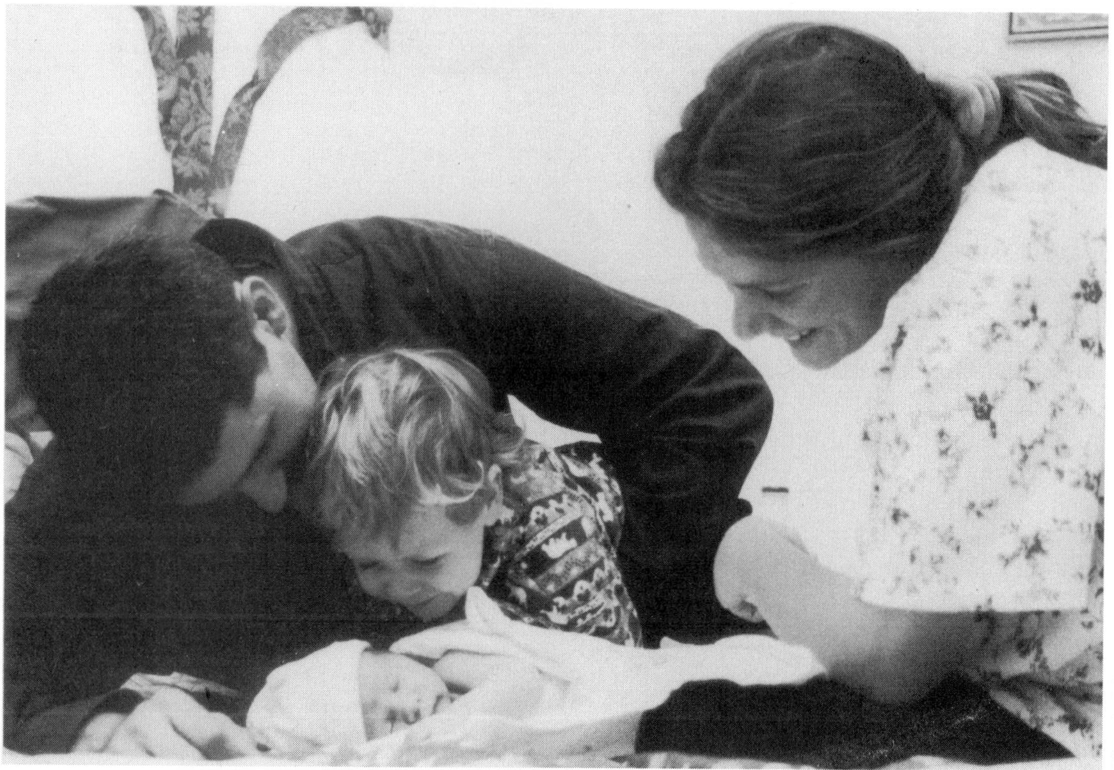

Photo by Marian Lucas

Photographer Todd Cota and his wife Debra share a moment with their two sons, Carsten and Aidan.

Todd Cota is a photographer, a teacher with a master's degree in education, a community activist, and most importantly a husband and father. With his wife Debra, he promotes attachment parenting. He has spent much of his life traveling, working, and photographing various cultures spanning North America, Europe, Africa, Asia, and the Middle East. Todd stated in a recent interview that, "Traveling has been a way for me to better understand my fellow humans and myself and has brought a deeper realization of the interconnectedness that is shared among all." As an educator, Todd is committed to creating a supportive, respectful, and tolerant community of learners. Currently, he is teaching at an innovative charter school located near Minneapolis, Minnesota.

Chapter 1

Brave New Warriors

Sheila Foster, Melvin Giles, Mike Boehm,
Dorothy Woolfork, Jim Lovestar

The term "warrior" has long been associated with violent confrontation and brutal conflict. Brave New Warriors do not use violence. Instead, when moved to anger over personal hurts or inequities, they catalyze changes in their lives and in systems. Their way of taking action is to use outrage, anger, and passion nonviolently. They are not powerless spectators, they are powerful initiators, who seek to protect and defend themselves and others from harm, wrongs, and injustices. As Brave New Warrior Melvin Giles said, "My role is to comfort the afflicted and afflict the comfortable." Through their personal growth, Brave New Warriors learn to heal their own lives, and ultimately, to impact the lives of others. They are aggressive but use their aggression wisely and effectively. Often, we view aggression as a way of being in the world that is just a step away from violence. A peace-loving person recoils when he or she is called "aggressive." Yet, aggression, in itself, is not violent. It can be a tool to prompt deep thinking and transformation. Without it, there may be no action.

Brave New Warriors show up! They appear at critical moments. They stand up when others are silent and express their outrage. They challenge the honesty of someone's position, ask for accountability, or encourage people to go further than they have gone before. They provide the necessary grassroots leadership for people to take charge of their own lives. Through their forthright actions, they focus on personal and communal health and well-being.

Finding the Magic | SHEILA FOSTER

by Burt Berlowe

Down deep inside. Locked in my pain
I remember where it came from
In your back room
In your back room
The shadows, the secrets,
Everything I had to hide
Wondered if I would survive.

—From a Sheila Foster song

"Happy birthday to me. Happy birthday to m . . ."

Sheila's voice cracked as she sang the verse, and a tear rolled down her soft, pink cheek.

Birthdays were supposed to be a happy time for little girls, but she felt no joy. She was alone in her room, seated on a soft cushion to ease the pain of the welts on her behind and the stiffness in her joints. In front of her, on a small table, was a pretend birthday cake made from a child's cooking set. Propped up near the table were a couple of her favorite dolls. They were the only guests at her eighth birthday party. From outside, the setting sun filtered through her window. Her special day was waning, and no one in her family had noticed. It seemed like all of her birthdays were that way.

Sheila tried hard to recall the few good times she had with her family, those rare moments when she experienced the joy of growing up. Instead, all that came to mind were images of terror and confusion—the familiar, heavy male footsteps cracking on the floor; the paddle looming overhead, her mother being knocked backwards, her brother being hauled off to the woods; her own sobs of "Daddy, please don't." The feelings of shame and violation followed her everywhere, especially in the solitary moments in her bed when her only comfort was a semen-stained pillow. Her home and her life seemed incredibly empty.

Sheila shook her head to make the bad memories go away. She didn't want to think ahead either.

"What was there to look forward to but more of the same?" she thought. "Please," she begged to no one in particular, "Isn't there some kind of magic that can make things better?"

"Happy birthday, dear Sheila."

Singing always seemed to help her release the hurt, so she struggled to finish the verse:

"Ha- aappy birthday to m-me."

Wiping away the tears, she leaned over and blew out an imaginary candle on the make-believe cake.

Sheila never really had a childhood. It was taken from her violently in the apparent calm of a quiet, rural Midwestern town. Her father's physical, sexual, and emotional abuse began when she was three or four years old and didn't let up as she grew. When she wasn't getting whipped or chided for never being "good enough," she had to watch as her dad took her brother to the woods and beat him up. Sometimes her dad would leave for weeks on end and then come home full of the drink and rage that turned him into a monster. When he was home, he would conceal his drinking. Young Sheila didn't readily make the connection between the alcohol and the abuse. She did know that his violence was random; that his anger could erupt at any time, that she could never know what was okay to him. It made her constantly tremble in his presence.

Sheila's mother, a teacher, was a silent partner to the abuse. Caught up in her own survival, she couldn't comprehend what was happening to her children. One time, as the family was about to leave on an outing, her dad and mom had an argument. He hit her a few times then pushed her down, breaking her ribs, as Sheila and her brother looked on. Scared out of their wits, the two kids grabbed their dog and fled to a friend's house a half-mile away, staying there until their parents called them back home. They told the friends what happened. Their response was, "It's your business. We're not going to get involved."

From the time Sheila was seven-years-old until about ten years ago, her father was in and out of prison for sexual misconduct, although he was never prosecuted for violations against her. On occasion, the family would visit him in the small, local jail where his furnishings were only a cot and a toilet. For Sheila, it was a time of mixed emotions: "My thought was, 'that's where he belongs,' and I was glad that he wasn't around me. I hated what he did. But there was always that fact that I was his daughter."

Sheila may have been most hurt by the subtle, yet insidious neglect. Birthdays were brushed aside as unimportant, forcing the children to celebrate by themselves. Her parents would only take their kids to the doctor for periodic checkups, never for complaints—not even when Sheila pleaded to be treated for painful childhood arthritis (that could have resulted in a permanent deformity).

As she grew up, Sheila was conditioned to keep "daddy's little secret." She and her brother were largely confined to their house, and kept from friends in whom they might confide. The family put on an impressive facade. They attended church and were active in it. They always got along in public. They seemed, for all appearances, like a stable family. It was painful for Sheila to keep the hurt inside and have no one with whom she could talk.

With her real world often unbearable, Sheila found herself in a frantic search for a different reality. "I sheltered myself from constant fear by reading a lot, losing myself in books, playing house, and pretending things were okay in an imaginary family," she says. "I had a big imagination where I lived. I had my own world inside that was good. Imagining a better reality is what pulled me through.

"I stayed away from home as much as I could and often thought of running away. I found opportunities to spend time with other adults I trusted instead of being at home. I threw myself into singing in the choir and working at church. I would go to church to meditate on how I was going to change things and how life could be different, trying not to think of what was bad, but of good things."

At times, Sheila tried to cry for help. Once, while on a youth retreat, she told a fellow student about her family abuse. But then she said what she had been programmed to say: "Don't tell anybody." She didn't really mean it. She wanted her friend to tell someone who might help. But her friend kept the secret.

By the time she reached high school, the pressure of keeping her secret became more than Sheila could bear. She stopped eating for two months and became anorexic. Her already small body grew slimmer until she weighed only 60 pounds. She was weak and bent on self-destruction. It was a desperate way to get attention. Certainly, she thought, someone would notice her bony frame and suspect that something was amiss. She finally grew tired of waiting for

Photo by Todd Cota

Sheila and her daughter Zoe make music together.

that to happen. "This isn't working," she thought. "I'm not getting anywhere, and it's taking too long. Is everybody so busy with their own things that there is no room to notice anyone else?" She ate her way back to normal, but the hunger for attention continued to eat her up inside.

With no one to turn to, Sheila found companionship in two old friends from her childhood: her faith and her music. In times of distress, she would sneak off to her church to pray alone for a way out or a way to cope. But even there she wasn't safe. She was sexually abused by both an adult church leader at a youth overnight and later, as an adult, by a priest she had gone to for guidance. Again, she kept the secrets from everyone. She almost left the church several times, but her faith made her stay.

Sheila's music was a way to release her emotions. Often, when she felt bad, she would huddle over her guitar and squeeze out the hurt with soulful songs about her faith, her lost childhood, and her hope for better times.

I have got the power
To be set free
Listen to me now
Break through the memories

Sheila's constant companions not only helped her survive, they bolstered her spirit and her independence. They gave her the power to break away from her past and her family. One day, soon after Sheila's high school graduation, the moment of rebellion came. She decided to leave home and move to St. Paul: "I jumped up and down on the bed and told my parents I was moving out. I think it was the only temper tantrum I'd ever had. They said they couldn't function without me—that I was the one who took care of the family. I said I didn't care what happened to them. I was leaving. And I did.

"I moved in with a friend and her mom and started my own life. Eventually, I moved into my own apartment for $200 a month. All I had with me was a sleeping bag, a pillow, and my guitar in a bunch of empty rooms. My parents begged me to come back home, but I wouldn't.

"I decided that I was going to live life and was going to make a difference—that if I made it out of this situation, I would work very hard to use my experiences to help others."

In the early 1980s, Sheila began keeping that promise to herself. She went to work as an advocate for battered women and kids at the Domestic Abuse Project in Minneapolis. Then she became a school bus driver. She did more than just drive the kids to school. She established connections with them, talking about what they did at school and home. She taught them good values, how to be nice to each other, and ways to resolve conflict.

In 1997, at 32, Sheila became director of children's and youth programs at St. Anne's Episcopal Church, nestled amidst woodlands in a tranquil suburban community called Sunfish Lake. The church's calming environs made it an ideal setting for her to heal others and be healed herself—to mend troubled young souls and nurse her own.

Working with kids within the confines of St. Anne's and on larger retreats, Sheila found ways to reach those who seemed unreachable, youngsters whose childhood, like hers, had been stolen from them through abuse, social deprivation, or family dysfunction. She initiated, organized, and attended statewide church retreats for youth, some of whom were in crisis, and was one of the founders and primary movers of the Children's Advocacy Network that operates through her affiliation with the Episcopal Church.

"We started out of a need to establish children as a church priority. We needed to set standards on how children would be treated and how to react to them, not just in the church but elsewhere."

Sheila has rescued many a childhood in the small, square, St. Anne's youth room. Inside the cozy space, several beanbag-cushion chairs lean against walls decorated with kids' artwork about peace, cooperation, and self-esteem. Signs lining the walls say, "Stay sober," "Discuss it," "No inappropriate behavior of any sort," "If you can't save yourself, you can't save others," and "You are entering a sacred and holy place." This is where troubled, confused or concerned youngsters come for help under Sheila's guidance.

In recent years, Sheila has helped conduct a week-long day camp for homeless children from the People Serving People (PSP) shelter in downtown Minneapolis. In 1998, the camp was held at St. Anne's as a form of retreat for the inner-city kids and their counselors.

The camp was designed as a youth outreach mission for senior high students in the state Episcopal Diocese. Its goal was to provide a camp experience for homeless children, ages five to ten years old, who attended a PSP learning center next to the shelter. It was also a way to help children stay busy for a week while their parents looked for housing or jobs.

She explains how the camp was set up: "We had a number of older youth, thirteen to fifteen years old, who came as counselors with their younger siblings. We made an extra tier of participation called 'helpers.' The counselors were mainly white suburban kids, fairly well-off, who had no familiarity or experience with anything like homelessness. But while the two groups seemed to be at either end of the continuum, they had a lot more in common than they knew. They both needed to have hope for a future that could be better.

"I told them, 'When you're young, there is a desire for magical moments, when all the bad things that may be going on have magically disappeared. It is my hope that you will be able to help transform your days at the camp into magic.'

"But for many of the young children, hope was an elusive concept. We tried to pair kids up with a specific counselor, so they could feel involved in a safe way and go at their own pace. Some wanted to participate. Others didn't want to do anything at all.

"Most of the children enjoyed the project and activities we planned, but there were some that weren't ready for it. We had children with many behavioral needs—some were very violent. As one of the camp coordinators, it was my job to help them find peaceful solutions to their conflicts. Some got really out of control. They had to leave the group for a while, talk rather than yell and scream, and gain control of anger and frustration before they could come back.

"With one particular girl, nothing seemed effective. I pulled her aside and asked what she would like to do, and she ended up helping in the kitchen with lunch preparation. She also liked helping with my two-year-old child, Toby. She felt important and needed by me if not by anybody else. Before camp was over, she gave me a door hanger with the message written on it: 'I love Toby's mom.'

"Another time, I had a young boy of about nine who had been having difficulty getting along with other boys. Another boy had made a crack about his family, which upset him. He responded by punching the other boy in the head. He was filled with rage. I took him to the 'quiet room.' I could tell he wanted to punch me as well. I just kept asking him over and over again, 'What did the other boy hurt? Did he hurt your body? What did he hurt?' In a few minutes, the climate in the room changed and he yelled, 'He hurt my feelings.' I asked him to yell it again a couple of times, then all of a sudden he just became limp and looked at me and said in a calm voice, 'I need to apologize.' So he went to the other boy and apologized.

"In addition to games and other standard activities, the children did unusual things like a scavenger hunt to find nature's beauty, Earth Dancing, and a magic pot activity. At the beginning of the week, we talked about magic and pretended to have a pot where they could put their (make-believe) piece of magic to offer to the group. When we closed the camp, a magician performed, reminding everyone to look for the magic within themselves and others. Then we passed the pot around again and the children said what magic they saw come out of the pot during the week and how that experience affected them. When the children told their stories, their faces lit up as they shared what a wonderful time they had had.

"Each counselor told a story of a different kid and drew out imaginary pieces of magic for each one. These previously downcast kids had the ability now to pretend and be playful. And the counselors benefited in enlarging their world—learning how other people live and recognizing that we all want the same things. They realized that if you take all the material things away, you're left with feelings and relationships and the need to figure out what's really important.

"When the camp ended, it was difficult for the kids to leave. There were lots of hugs from them as their message of appreciation. They kept saying they were coming back when they knew they weren't."

Live today and tomorrow
To heal yesterday . . .

Sheila Foster has finally found her childhood. After years of purposeful searching, it has come to her like magic, waving away the demons that had appeared up her sleeve all this time. This time it is not an illusion. It is as real as the smile of a child who has just discovered happiness.

She has reconciled with her family and her jaded past. "I met with my dad and a lot of healing happened," she says. "He was ashamed and apologized. I told him, 'You can never give me back what you took away, but I do forgive you.'"

She has helped her dad realize hope for a healthier future and has been trying to do the same for her brother who has spent time in jail for sexual abuse. She also confronted her mother with the realities she had previously denied. Sheila says, "My biggest personal accomplishment is that I helped my parents realize the healing that can happen when you peel off the cloak of secrecy."

Sheila uses her healing to help the troubled children she works with find the magic in their lives through her church work and her music. She plays in a band called Some Assembly Required, entertaining families and children wherever she can. She also helps plan and implement the annual Stand for Children event in Minneapolis.

Sheila has become a dedicated community mom, raising her own three kids peacefully with her husband, while watching over and mentoring other children in her neighborhood, mediating conflicts, and helping to establish safe houses where youngsters can go when they feel threatened. "What empowers me to do what I do, is the desire to make a better world for the children."

Finally, Sheila has broken through the walls of abuse by sharing her story. "I couldn't tell it until recently," she says. "Basically, I waited until my dad gave me permission. He said, 'You have so many stories, you should share them.' At first, I would try telling it in modified versions and would break down in tears. Then I discovered the magic in forgiveness. When I was able to forgive, I was able to tell my story. I hope telling it will help others find a way to their own healing."

Questions for Contemplation:

1. Sheila's forgiveness of her father took years. Have you identified ways in which your parents hurt you or failed you? Sheila claims to have benefited from forgiving her parents. What benefits do you think are possible when one chooses to forgive? What are your obstacles to forgiveness?
2. What do you think is valuable about magic in a child's life? How have you used "magic" to create a better world for yourself or others?
3. When you read about Sheila's abuse by a church leader and a priest, what thoughts came to your mind? How can we increase our attentiveness and act on our responsibility to protect and defend children?
4. Have you ever been asked to keep a secret like Sheila's friend yet felt it should not be kept secret? What did you do?

Resources for Reflection and Action:

Peaceful Parenting Handbook, by Joseph Cress & Burt Berlowe (San Jose, CA: Resource Publications, 2001).

The Seven Habits of Peaceful Parents: A facilitators' manual, by Joseph Cress & Burt Berlowe, (San Jose, CA: Resource Publications, 2001).

Crimes Against Children: Child abuse and neglect, by Tracee Bekalm (Philadelphia: Chelsea House, 2000).

Healing Words: The power of prayer and the practice of medicine, by Larry Dossey (San Francisco: Harper Collins, 1993).

The Optimistic Child: A revolutionary program that safeguards children against depression and builds lifelong resilience, by Martin E. P. Seligman (Boston: Houghton Mifflin, 1995).

National Committee for the Prevention of Child Abuse, 332 South Michigan Avenue #1600, Chicago, Illinois 60604-4357. Phone: 312-663-3520.

Stand for Children, 1834 Connecticut Avenue NW, Washington, DC, 20009. Phone: 202-234-0095. Learn how to start a Stand for Children event in your community or find out where the nearest chapter for you is located. The organization's purpose is to educate the public about what constitutes a safe and healthy community, to push forward local, state, and federal initiatives and to assist in making concrete improvements in communities everywhere.

Peaceful Love Warrior | MELVIN GILES

by Rebecca Janke

Believe the truth about yourself, no matter how beautiful it is.

—Melvin Giles

"Why is Melvin so insistent about meeting at this restaurant for his interview?" I asked myself as I settled into a sun lit booth by the window. "Why had he turned down my other suggestions that were more convenient for him? The menu doesn't feature African-American cuisine. I don't see any African-American staff . . ."

My wonderment deepened as Melvin came walking through the door with his friendly, warm smile and showered the setting in an unusual way with bubbles blown from a tiny bottle he wears around his neck. It wasn't the first time I'd seen him do that. The smile and the bubbles are his trademarks. As the director of the Catholic Charities Frogtown Center in St. Paul, Minnesota, he needs both to maintain his possibility-seeker personality, as he works with people to reclaim their community and sense of self. While many would become depressed, or mired in the surrounding muck of poverty and violence, Melvin is full of good cheer and hope.

"It's great to be back at this place!" Melvin said with gleaming eyes. "People wait on me right away here. They'll continue talking to me even when the place is full of white customers. There aren't many restaurants where that happens, so I appreciate it."

"My white privilege is coming home to roost again, Melvin," I said. "I never have to think about those things when choosing a place to eat."

"It's good that you realize the privileges you have. When people do, it means they're awake to what is going on in the world and can work to make it better for everyone," he said optimistically.

Photo by Todd Cota

Melvin Giles blows bubbles beside a multilingual Peace Pole.

"What forces in your life have awakened you?" I asked.

"Each year, my father, an old-time Baptist pastor, pointed out—as we tilled the soil for our garden—how plants have relationships with each other. He would say, 'By paying attention to these relationships, Melvin, we can plant in such a way to get the best yield.' All that time spent out in the garden with my dad has given me an abundance of nature metaphors. For example, when adversity or conflict come along, I become like the willow tree, bending in the wind to accommodate the force without being uprooted.

"One day, as I was reflecting on my planting days with him, I realized that people are a lot like plants. They need nurturing and supportive relationships, too. Plants need the light of the sun, but people need the 'light' of each other. The light we can provide for each other can come in numerous ways, but one of the most important ones for me is cheerfulness. Dr. Patch Adams is one of my heroes. Look at what he accomplishes with humor … he helps people heal their bodies, minds, and souls.

"My focus on healing and being playful comes from my mother. As she tucked me in at night, she would remind me to play with the angels as I said my prayers. I took her literally and played with them in my mind before I drifted off to sleep. She died before I was twelve, but in those few years together, she convinced me that we all have the ability to love, touch, and heal. Whenever I was sick, not only would she take care of me, but she would also send the love of Jesus through my body. 'I'm a channel for God's love and so are you, Melvin,' she would say.

"When I was sixteen my brother gave me the book called *As a Man Thinketh* by James Allen. It wasn't until my second year in college that the message of that book sank in: our thoughts bring on disease or ease. What we think is what we become. It was then that I decided to dedicate my thinking time to good thoughts. I knew my thoughts were critical in forming myself.

"The first visible sign I received for my life's work was given to me on a mountain in Korea. I had gone there in place of my father, who had become ill, to investigate the religious activities of Reverend Sun Yun Moon and try to determine whether or not his group was a cult (since they were recruiting many young people in our community). While I was there, a group of us went to the mountains to pray and meditate. Just as we were about to descend, a rainbow appeared. Witnessing its radiant light and reflecting on my meditation, I knew that when I got back home, I was to look for the rainbow symbol to guide me in my next career move.

"I found it on a building as I was walking along a street in Minneapolis, Minnesota. When I walked around to the front of the building it said, 'Life Force Massage Studio.' I was about to knock on the door when two women flung it open and welcomed me in. They became my massage teachers showing me how to enhance my natural gifts as a healer.

"I noticed two things as a healer: there are very few people of color in the healing community—which is sad since we have a lot to offer—and very few people want to touch and heal cultural wounds. African-Americans, Native Americans, and European-Americans have few, if any, opportunities to talk about our shared history in terms of how we've hurt each other and how we can move to reconciliation. We need to heal more than our bodies—we need to heal our hearts.

"Sometimes woundedness happens in the workplace. It happened when I served as a health educator with Catholic Charities. I had been invited by Howard University to travel to South Africa to study how Southern Africans were dealing with AIDS. I wanted to go so I could learn some cultural practices that could help our community. My request for travel expenses was denied. I had been so sure that they would give their stamp of approval that I had purchased a plane ticket early to keep airfare costs down. When they said, 'No,' I couldn't believe it. People are dying and we want to squabble over a few hundred dollars! Anger was coursing through my veins. Since I couldn't get a refund for my airfare, I decided to go at my own expense.

"I didn't want to make such an important a trip with the amount of anger I had, so I asked my co-workers and friends to conduct a healing ceremony with me. I appreciate the gifts and wisdom of other faiths such as Buddhism, Hinduism, and Native American spirituality, even though Jesus is my main man. I guess I'm a Baptist with a spiral twist. After smudging, prayers, and singing, I asked them to help me let go of the pain and anger in my heart so it would have room to expand again.

"I went to four African countries and felt the land speak to me. Many good meditations with people and by myself accelerated my healing process. I could feel myself being purified, and I knew I would come back transformed because I had spent time in the homeland.

"Three months after my return, I was offered a new position with my employer as the director of the Catholic Charities Frogtown Center. At first I hesitated. I have a participatory management style, not a top-down one. I didn't want to be put in a position of working in a way that would compromise the people I would be serving. Rather than ignore the offer, I told the management people I wanted to use a participatory leadership approach and be free to explore new ways of operating and serving in the community. They hired me and cut me loose.

"A year later, when we experienced one of our biggest years of violence, including the killing of a four-year-old girl, we decided to take a leap of faith and establish the center as a place that would promote peace. We defined ourselves as Peaceful Love Warriors.

"A Peaceful Love Warrior uses wisdom and makes sure to show up instead of waiting for someone else to take care of a problem. Rather than arguing about issues or decreeing a program, a Peaceful Love Warrior builds relationships with people so, together, they can discover ways to solve dilemmas. Peaceful Love Warriors share power and take time to listen to each other. We chose the word 'love' to remind ourselves to work in a loving way and the word 'peace' to remind ourselves that peace is the goal we are trying to achieve.

"Peaceful Love Warriors are courageous people who are strong enough to think that creating peace, creating community, embracing diversity of all kinds, and working together are possible. We are wise enough to know that celebration is an important part of life and peace, and we weave it into daily practice. We are courageous enough to take the challenge and engage in this adventure, not necessarily knowing the destination, but enjoying and learning from the journey.

"The children in our community resonated to the Peaceful Love Warrior concept. They have a desire to see themselves as powerful, capable, and contributing people. We printed hundreds of 'Junior Peaceful Love Warrior' cards for senior citizens, business people, and police officers to give to the children when they saw them doing something positive, kind, or peaceful. The children turned in their cards at the center for stuff that had been donated to us. We liked giving out the cards because it was a fun and easy way to build relationships with the children. It gave us hope to see the younger generation do what they could for peace. The cops liked it because it gave them an opportunity to knock down the barriers that existed between them and the kids. The young people liked it because they knew they were helping our community be a more peaceful place to live.

"The hardest task for me, when we began this work, was to talk with the police officers. It stems from having many encounters with them when I was a young man. My brothers and I were constantly pulled over and guns put in our faces—for no reason. Our white friends rarely experienced this.

"For example, shortly before this job started, my brother and I went to Chicago to visit some relatives. As we were driving away from our family's apartment, two squad cars pulled us over. The cops informed us that we were suspects in a robbery of a nearby grocery store. While they were going through all the stuff in our car, four more patrol cars pulled up. We were told to follow them to the crime scene.

"As we were driving, I remembered a technique that my grandmother and my parents taught me to do when you're in danger . . . 'Call upon your angels, and surround yourself and others in a circle of light and love.' So, for the entire ride, as we drove through the dark, rainy night, I asked our ancestors and guardian angels to come. I concentrated on sending the cops as much love and light as I could possibly muster.

"'Get out!' they said when we arrived at the crime scene. They motioned the storeowner over to the squad car.

"'Are these the men who robbed your store?' they asked.

"We couldn't believe our ears! If he said 'Yes,' our chances of tasting freedom again would be slim to none.

"I prayed the owner would speak the truth, and surrounded him in love and light.

"He peered into our eyes and said, 'No. These aren't the ones.'

"With this experience still fresh in my mind, you can imagine how my body tensed up when I walked across the street to introduce myself to the police officers as the new dude at Catholic Charities Frogtown Center. I did it anyway. I knew we had reached a milestone when, two years later, we had a peace ceremony at the police station and planted a Peace Pole.

"The Peace Pole is an international symbol of peace. It bears the message, 'May Peace Prevail on Earth,' in four different languages. It acts as a daily reminder of the necessity to work for peace. Over the course of a few years, some police officers became viewed as 'peace' officers because of the numerous ways we discovered to have positive relationships with each other.

"The Frogtown Community Center provides job training, career counseling, conflict resolution, temporary housing, and emergency food and clothing for those who are faced with unforeseen crisis as they work themselves out of poverty. The Peace Pole ceremonies have been instrumental in changing the face of our community.

"It is important to realize that an organization doesn't just plant a Peace Pole and have a party. The Peace Pole is used when a group wants to create a peace zone. The group defines what issue(s) they want to work on, whether it be racism, crime, fair wages, violence in the work place, or whatever else is interrupting peace. They have the ceremony to announce what they did to overcome their problem and celebrate their efforts.

"The Peace Pole serves as a tool for healing since different languages are written on each side of the pole to represent the languages of the people in the community.

"Preparing for the ceremony gives us lots of opportunities to have intercultural and interracial dialogues and begin the work of healing our cultural wounds. People begin to have deeper, more meaningful relationships with each other."

"What else do you live by as you work with others to create a more peaceful community?" I asked.

"The head to the heart is a very short journey when I move my hand from my forehead to my chest. But it can be the longest journey when we try to change the way we live and treat each other. I found that when we make a mistake in trying to make things better, it's important that we forgive ourselves, ask what we can learn from our experience, and take the next step necessary to move forward. When we hear ourselves say, 'I shouldn't be feeling this way,' we need to trust that the feeling is giving us important information. Last of all, when we remember that the relationship in front of us is always more important than the task, it's amazing what we can accomplish together."

The Relationship is More Important Than the Task

by Julie Penshorn

I was amazed at how angry he could be! "What kind of a boyfriend do I have anyway?" I asked myself. I couldn't believe he would resist my contribution to his project! He had decided to help around my ranch by building the fences. But instead of discussing where I wanted them and how high they needed to be for the use I intended, he just went ahead.

I'd been working in my basement office that morning—on this book. It was one of those breathtaking spring days in Minnesota, so I was grateful when writer's block gave me an excuse to take a break with a walk outside. I saw my boyfriend and his helper working on a paddock, and walked over to see how it was shaping up.

When I approached, I could see his face tighten. Instead of his usual smile of welcome, he was cool. I surveyed the string lines he had laid out in preparation for digging post-holes and then said, "This paddock needs to be bigger than that. Let's bring it out to the fence line on the East Side." Inside, I was wondering why he started the project without discussing the specific details with me. He had drawn a rough plan that we had discussed, but we hadn't actually stood out on the site and walked it out. We hadn't really mulled it over together.

When I made my comment, he hollered, "What is your problem? You are impossible to work for! No one could work for you!" and walked off the job! I tried to engage him in discussion, but his back was turned, and it was apparent from his body language that no further listening was going to happen. I was hurt.

Here I was, finding my thoughts weren't being considered. I hate being left out of the decision-making process. Plus, I felt frustrated that my boyfriend's time and effort had been wasted. I knew he wanted to be involved with the ranch, and it was important to him to make his own contribution. But I didn't realize it had to be a contribution totally void of my input.

Working with my co-author, Rebecca, has spoiled me. She is rarely defensive and always listens to my thoughts and feelings. We discuss many things. Over the years, our teamwork has become a much-valued aspect of our work.

Anyway, his helper and I continued on and finished digging the post-holes for the paddock.

Later that night, my boyfriend continued to walk around in a tight-lipped, sour-faced, manner. I finally coaxed him into a conversation. He told me he had begun to question the size of the corral as he was working on it. He was angry because I had interfered, not letting him fix his own mistake before anyone saw it. He felt he had lost face. He felt shamed and humiliated. He also was acutely aware of the fact that this is "my" place, not "ours."

I told him I had no intention of hurting him, only of saving him the time of redoing it later.

He said, "In your world, time may be the most important thing. In mine, it's not. Someone coming along and correcting my work, especially in front of others, is disrespectful. When someone disrespects me, I don't even want to contribute anymore. I've worked on my own for twenty years. In the past, I have worked for great guys but hated not having any say in the decisions that were made. I'm a guy who is happy working for myself. I don't mind talking about stuff, but then I need free rein. I can't stand it when someone is questioning my every move. It makes me crazy! Let me tell you something else . . . My dad knew how to treat me. He'd watch me make a mistake and he'd walk away. Then, later, after I'd fixed it, he'd tell me what a good job I'd done."

"So you'd just like me to walk away and let you screw up?" I asked.

"Yes," he answered.

This really went against my nature. I almost turn green when time and effort is wasted. However, when I feel like this, I know I have to look deeper to find a compassionate rebel solution. So I struggled and struggled.

Finally I got it. I was valuing the task too much. I was forgetting, "The relationship is more important than the task," as Melvin says. My boyfriend would rather save face than save time. Once again, I was reminded that I have only one perspective. Other people don't walk in my shoes nor do I walk in theirs. I had to smile, celebrating the gift of perspective that my relationship with this man so often provides.

Questions for Contemplation:

1. What person close to you offers you "the gift of perspective" thereby helping you see a different point of view? Of what value has this been to you? Do you find yourself resisting such offers? If so, how can you reduce your resistance? Do you find you value teamwork for its own merit, or do you prefer to work alone? Why?

2. What reaction did you have to Melvin's healing ceremony to deal with his anger? What do you find helpful when you have more anger than you can bare?

3. Melvin feared the police. Who causes the fear response in you? How could you overcome this fear? What have you tried? What have others suggested or tried that you would like to try?

4. If you were to have a Peace Pole dedication ceremony at one of the organizations with which you are involved, what peace goal would you like to see attained and celebrated?

5. Melvin believes, "When we remember that the relationship in front of us is always more important than the task, it's amazing what we can accomplish." Julie shared the story of a time she hampered the completion of a task by neglecting the relationship. In what ways has focusing on the relationship helped you and those around you?

Resources for Reflection and Action:

Cultures of Peace: The hidden side of history, by Elise Boulding (NYC: Syracuse University Press, 1999). Offers clear perspectives on how to fuel the process of peace among families, communities, and governments.

Building Communities from the Inside Out: A path toward finding and mobilizing a community's assets, by John Kretzmann & John McKnight (Evanston, IL: The Assets-Based Community Development Institute, 1993: Phone: 800-397-2282). Summarizes lessons learned by studying successful community-building initiatives in hundreds of neighborhoods across the United States.

The Courage for Peace, by Louise Diamond (Berkley, CA: Conari Press, 1999). Peacemaking is exhausting and courageous work. It demands that we hold the largest vision. Even in lands soaked in ancestral blood, healing can begin. Silenced voices can speak. Hearts can open.

The Four-Fold Way: Walking the paths of the warrior, teacher, healer, and visionary, by Angeles Arrien. The four archetypes present in virtually all shamanic traditions are detailed. They show us how to: 1) Access the human resources of power, presence, and communication 2) Become open to love, gratitude, acknowledgment and validation 3) maintain our authenticity while developing our inner vision and intuition 4) become open and unattached in order to recover wisdom and objectivity.

Peace Pole Project, 3534 Lanham Road, Maple City, MI 49664. Phone: 231-334-4567. Provides information about Peace Poles and how to order one with your choice of languages.

Gesundheit!, by Patch Adams with Maureen Mylander. (Rochester, Vermont: Healing Arts Press, 1993). Bringing good health to people, the medical system, and society through physician service, complementary therapies, humor, and joy.

An Instrument of Peace | MIKE BOEHM

by Burt Berlowe

Lord,
Make me an instrument of your peace.
Where there is hatred, let me sow love;
Where there is injury, pardon;
Where there is doubt, faith.
Where there is despair, let me bring hope . . .
And where there is sadness, joy . . .

—Peace Prayer of St. Francis of Assisi

Mike Boehm huddled up to the stove inside the primitive wilderness shack, letting the warmth wash over him. It was a cold winter night, and he felt lonely and restless. His seven solitary years in the cabin, to which he had retreated to soothe the pain of past and present injustices, had helped to mend some deep wounds, but there were times when he longed for the outside world.

In moments like these, he turned to some loyal companions. One of them, a violin, lay in a case by his side. He reached over and picked it up, cradled it on his shoulder, and guided the bow across the strings. Its distinct voice broke the silence in the still room. He was a novice on the instrument he had found in a trashcan a few years earlier. But the mere act of playing it made his blues go away.

In a flash, a resident squirrel, carrying a big nut in its mouth, scampered across the room and sat near Mike, listening to the music. During his time in the cabin, Mike had tended to animals that had no parents. He became their caregiver, raising them until they were old enough to go out on their own, and finding gratification in the nurturing they gave him in return. The squirrel bit into its nut, and the crunching sound mixed incongruously with the violin's scratchy tones.

As he held the violin in his arms, Mike's anger left him and he felt whole again. In time, Mike's violin became an instrument of peace, not only to him, but also to people worlds away from his rustic cabin in the woods.

Mike grew up a victim of war. The battleground was his home in Mauston, Wisconsin. The "enemy" was his father, whose weapons were fists and vicious words. Mike and his six younger siblings were all brutalized. The physical beatings weren't as bad as the mental and verbal bullets that ripped away Mike's youth. The stress from the abuse had devastating effects. He developed chronic stomach cramps and wet his bed intermittently.

By age eighteen, Mike was a full-blown alcoholic, wallowing so deeply in his own despair that he was unable to experience human relationships. He commented: "I had been reduced to an animal. I saw people in loving relationships and wondered what human being could live without the possibility of love, as I was. I was always focusing on just trying to survive and had not been introduced to the possibility of love. I was a fucked-up kid."

Throughout the years of violence by his father, Mike desperately clung to the hope of reconciliation. In 1967, he volunteered to serve in the military in Vietnam. "I wanted my father's approval even though he had abused me. I wanted to be wounded, seriously, but not too seriously, so that he would express his love for me.

"U.S. soldiers in Vietnam were conditioned to think of all Vietnamese as enemies. But, except for mortar and rocket attacks at night, I was not in combat. I grew to like the Vietnamese people I met and would sometimes eat with them rather than in the mess hall with the soldiers."

In the mid '70s, a few years after leaving Vietnam, while attending a tech school in Madison, Wisconsin, Mike began to question what really happened in the Vietnam War. Eventually, he grew remorseful and rage-filled over the destruction of the Vietnamese people. He was disillusioned and depressed about the effects that militarism and consumerism have on people around the world.

Confused and filled with unresolved anger related to his childhood trauma and his Vietnam experience, Mike decided to leave mainstream society. Grabbing a few of his most prized possessions, he retreated to the woods and built himself a shack. He vowed to stay there until he could find his way back, physically and emotionally. Shortly after moving into the cabin, he had a breakdown.

"The walls I had constructed around myself over the years, started coming down. I found myself having to deal with an overwhelming need for love and nurturing. I realized I had to change my pattern of reacting to life—that I needed to take control of my life.

"Though life in the shack was healing for me, eventually, I began to get restless. In 1990, I read an article in a magazine asking for volunteer carpenters to go to Puerto Rico to help rebuild after Hurricane Hugo. I went. While I was there, I started thinking about the possibility of using my carpentry skills in Vietnam. When I got home, I found out about an organization that gathered veterans and sent them to Vietnam to help build medical clinics. I signed on.

"I felt I had no trauma associated with the war and believed it was those 'other guys' who were in combat that had the problems. Eventually, it became obvious that this wasn't true. I was traveling with vets who had spent the past twenty years just trying to survive. Their pain was so intense. I talked to the Vietnamese people and heard their stories. I could hardly stand it! I remember lying on my bed in our hotel, thinking about the war and asking, 'Why was there all of that destruction?' I couldn't forget the pain we had caused. I became convinced that the people of America needed to become involved with the people of Vietnam in order for healing to occur.

"I didn't plan go to My Lai. The need to go just rose out of my stew of emotions as my personal response to the war. The massacre of Vietnamese civilians by American soldiers was, to me, symbolic of the tragedy of war—they just put them in the ditch and shot them.

"After we finished building the medical clinic, a few of us traveled by van to Hanoi, stopping at cities along the way. I insisted we stop at My Lai. There, I went into a clearing and played 'Taps' on my violin as a tribute to the massacre victims. We were all crying. My hands were shaking so badly I wasn't sure I could play at all. But I did, not knowing what it would lead to.

"When I got back home and the emotional dust had settled, I realized this kind of healing work was what I had been looking for all my life. About a year later, a woman from Global Exchange came to Madison and gave a slide presentation to those of us who were interested in Vietnam. They had a study tour to Vietnam during the fall of 1993, and one of the places women visited was My Lai. There, they received a request from the Vietnamese Women's Union, an eight-million-member grassroots organization, to fund a revolving loan fund project which helps women start small businesses. They asked us, a newly formed Madison-Indochina support group, if we would be interested in taking on the project. I met with the Women's Union for the first time when I returned to Vietnam in 1993. After a series of meetings, I delivered the requested $3,000. We raised $10,000 more later on.

Photo courtesy of Mike Boehm

Mike Boehm smiles for the camera with some of his Vietnamese friends.

"Earlier in 1993, while we were still raising the initial $3,000, Professor Nguyen Ngoc Hung, a North Vietnam army veteran, was scheduled to speak in the U.S. I brought him to Madison with my own money so that we could hear his side of the story. I found out that when Hung had been in Madison in 1990, local veterans brought him to the Wisconsin Vietnam Veterans' Memorial called the Highground. Hung went to the Dove Mound, burned incense and said a prayer for his younger brother who was missing in Vietnam. The experience was so powerful for the veterans present that a few days later a poem was written by one of them. The last line says: 'I looked into the eyes of the enemy and saw myself . . .' When I heard this story, I got the idea for a peace park in Vietnam that would fill the need for deep spiritual and emotional healing across countries.

"In 1994, I secured funds from Madison Friends, a Quaker organization. To my delight, the Vietnamese gave their support, too."

On November 11, 1995, Mike's dream became a reality. A Vietnamese-American Peace Park was dedicated at Song Mai Village, Bac Giang Province. Mike describes that historic ceremony:

"A delegation, composed of veterans and non-veterans, came from Wisconsin and other parts of the U.S. to participate in the dedication. We started the morning by spontaneously pairing off with Vietnamese veterans to plant trees. Following the welcoming speech by the People's Committee of Bac Giang came the spiritual focal point of the morning. David Giffey (a veteran and artist), who had been carefully instructed by a Native American spiritual leader, prayed to the four directions and to Mother Earth for guidance and blessing. To perform this ceremony, he was given a pipe made by this Native American spiritual leader. After the prayer, the pipe was filled with tobacco and passed around and smoked by the Vietnamese and American people. The prayer, in part, went like this:

"'Grandfather, Great Spirit, we ask you to look on the people of Vietnam and America as we share the dove of peace in a spirit of friendship, and to guide our steps on a bridge of understanding between our two nations.'

"Finally, we gathered to release ten white doves and to tie colored, braided threads around each others' wrists, a tradition of an ethnic minority, the Thai.

"We stood there on that hill—veterans, peace activists, farmers, government officials, teachers and children—all of us transformed by what we had done. After two years of hard work, we had created this physical manifestation out of a deep spiritual need between our countries—the need for healing, and most importantly, the need for hope.

"Les Herring, a veteran from San Francisco, spoke about the profound, life-transforming experience that we all felt that day: 'The day I stood on that knoll, planted my tree, and embraced my former enemy, I became whole.'"

Within a year of the dedication, Americans and Vietnamese planted three thousand fruit trees over some six acres in the Vietnamese-American Peace Park.

Eventually, the fruit trees will be harvested by local farmers who will then sell the popular oriental fruit called Litchi, benefiting the economic security of the village.

In March of 1998, the thirtieth anniversary of the My Lai massacre, a symbolic groundbreaking ceremony was held for a proposed park there. A two-story gazebo was completed and dedicated. Still in the works are plantings, fishponds, winding paths, meditation areas, and a children's play space.

The Peace Park has taken on a life of its own. In addition to the foreign delegations that visit, Vietnamese teachers bring classes there, and a local poetry society comes to the Tet festival to compose and read their work. A hill that is the focal point is being terraced, and a gazebo for meetings and meditation is on its top. A plaque presented by the U.S. ambassador to Vietnam hangs there.

Ground has also been broken in My Lai for a new twenty room school house to alleviate overcrowding in makeshift educational facilities (such as old rice storage warehouses with dirt floors and rough plank tables and benches). Mike also has been raising funds to help improve a local hospital's water filtration system, provide decent beds for patients, and bring electricity to residents' homes.

The Peace Park project has created opportunity for cross-cultural learning. Mike has taken photos and drawings back and forth between Madison and Vietnam. An eight-year-old from Madison best expressed the meaning of this exchange project. When asked if she had ever heard of the Vietnam War she said she had "but that was a long time ago. Now we can be friends."

Even as Mike's Peace Park project has been the impetus for a long-overdue healing of Vietnam War scars, it also has mended his own inner wounds and given purpose and direction to his life. He puts it this way:

"I see a parallel between my life and what is happening in My Lai today. I have been able to bring my life out of the ashes. There has been a change in myself I never thought possible when I was in the shack. It gives me something to live for, being aware that I'm working to right a wrong in my small way. I've never had a family of my own. This work is my substitute for having children. I have people that care for me and look after me that I can count on."

Mike has begun to take the Peace Park idea into other countries. He recently went to El Salvador to facilitate a meeting between the women of that country and those of Vietnam. The El Salvador-Vietnam project is a pilot. If it is successful, Mike hopes to invite women from Nicaragua, Cuba, and Bosnia to join the dialogue about the process of healing after war.

Meanwhile, Mike goes back to Vietnam every year to continue his work and to play his violin. When he visits My Lai, he envisions what the park and village will be like someday: abundant fruit trees swaying in the breeze, shaking their Litchi nuts towards the farmer's baskets; fish nets swishing through the gently flowing river; and the patter of schoolchildren's footsteps bouncing off the dirt roads. And somewhere in the distance, the echoes of violin music will still reverberate through the valley—a symbol of healing and peace for one-time enemies—and for the man who helped bring them together.

Questions for Contemplation:

1. Do you know anyone who has fought in a war? What impact did it have on them? How has it affected others?
2. Mike experienced "war" in his own home before the Vietnam War. What "wars" have you experienced? What ways have you found to help "make the peace?"
3. What have you found that gives your life meaning and purpose?
4. Mike continues to refuse to participate in those aspects of society that he finds intolerable. What do you find intolerable in society? Why is it intolerable to you? Have you stopped being a participant? What have you done?

Resources for Reflection and Action:

Building a Peace System, by Robert A. Irwin (Expro Press, Exploratory Project on the Conditions of Peace, 1601 Connecticut Ave., NW, 5th Fl., Washington, DC 20009. Distributed by the Talman Company, 150 Fifth Avenue, NYC, 10011, 1989). This book examines different visions of a warless world and suggests what trends and strategies could make peace a reality.

World Without Violence: Can Gandhi's vision become reality?, edited by Arun Gandhi (Daryaganj, New Delhi: Wiley Eastern Limited, 1994). This book is available through the M.K. Institute for Nonviolence, Christian Brothers University, 650 East Parkway South, Memphis, TN 38104. Phone: 901-725-0815. Arun Gandhi invited people who have achieved goals in life to share their thoughts about Gandhi's nonviolence and how to remodel our societies.

Nonviolent America: History through the eyes of peace, edited by Louise Hawkley and James C. Juhnke (Newton, KS: Mennonite Press, 1993). History is viewed from the perspective of the underdog focusing on events and forces that transform society peacefully rather than violently.

Choosing Peace, A Handbook on War, Peace, and Your Conscience, by Robert A. Seeley (Central Committee for Conscientious Objectors, 1550 Cherry Street, Philadelphia, PA 9120. Website: www.libertynet.org/ccco. Phone: 800-NOJROTC, 1994).

The Sound of the Violin in My Lai, (Video) My Lai Peace Project (My Lai Peace Project, 2312 East Johnson St., Madison, WI 53704. Phone: 608-244-9505). Website: www.Mylaipeacepark.com.

National Veterans for Peace, 733 15th Street NW, #928, Washington, DC, 20005. Phone: 202-347-6780. Website: www.veteransforpeace.org.

Art Without Borders. A humanitarian organization made up of volunteer members who carry out the mission of bringing art to victims of war. Members believe that art is the foundation for mental and emotional healing, and no less important than food or water. Email: ArtWB@yahoo.com.

My Lai Peace Project, 2312 East Johnson St., Madison, WI 53704. Phone: 608-244-9505. Email: vapp@igc.apc.org.

Nobody's Slave | DOROTHY WOOLFORK

by Burt Berlowe

Late on a hot, summer day in 1929, thirteen-year-old Dorothy Woolfork pushed her weary legs through scorched plantation fields, picking cotton as fast as she could, going row by row toward her day's goal. She dropped the cotton bolls in a cloth bag slung over her shoulder until it was full. Then she emptied the bag and started all over again. The Arkansas sun beat down mercilessly through her protective hat, baking her skin and soaking her blouse with sweat. Her back bent in pain, her fingers numb from the repetition, she had been in the field since sunrise.

A few yards away, Dorothy's dad was also moving along the rows, grabbing up cotton. As usual, he was ahead of his daughter. He wasn't intending to race her. Still, she struggled to keep up. Mustering up a belabored surge of energy, Dorothy made a final lunge to the end of the last row.

"I made it. Daddy, wait up. I'm comin'."

For a moment, Dorothy stood erect and heaved a big sigh. Then she trudged after her dad who was already a few steps ahead, going back to their house. She was anxious to get home and compare their pickings and, most of all, to receive a loving hug for a job well done. She knew it would make the pain go away. As she walked slowly out of the knee-deep cotton field, Dorothy held her head high. The bag weighed heavy on her small frame, but her spirit refused to kneel.

Today Dorothy Woolfork leans across the dining room table in her modest Minneapolis home, stretching her thoughts back through time. She rests one hand firmly on a trusty walking cane waiting nearby—a concession to years of back-breaking toil and struggle. But time has not softened her voice, nor quelled her passion.

"My family lived on a plantation farm in Arkansas, owned by stewards. My mother was a midwife. My father was a minister and had church meetings at our house. Everyone, white and black, respected him and called him Reverend Woolfork. We were sharecroppers (farmers who worked another's land for a share of the crop). Generations ago, my great-great-grandmother had been born into slavery.

"When I was thirteen, I saw an eleven-year-old boy picking cotton. My job had been taking water to the pickers. But I wanted to pick, too. My dad tried to discourage me because I was so young, but I kept saying 'I can do it,' and insisted. He finally let me.

"I liked to compete to see who could pick the most cotton in a day. I particularly liked to go out into the field with my father. I would race with him, but I wouldn't tell him because I knew I could never beat him.

"I worked in the fields every weekday from about 7:00 a.m. to 5:30 p.m., nine months of the year. I didn't earn much, but it was more than I made when I used to haul water. I never felt poor. I learned that poverty is a state of mind.

"My mother taught us all the right things about how to keep our dignity. She was a strict disciplinarian. My father always said he didn't want his daughters to grow up with men whuppin' 'em. 'Whuppin' was a common discipline of that time but he never 'whupped' us. If I did something wrong, he just said, 'Oh my baby,' and I would cry because it hurt me to hurt him.

"Early on, I learned to be independent, to think for myself and to speak my mind. As a youngster, I would occasionally go out with friends that were drinking but would always refuse any alcohol. When they accused me of being unsociable, I told them: 'Why don't you be sociable and respect my rights?'

"The Depression came, and a flood wiped out our sharecropper holdings. There were long soup lines at my school, where students and teachers waited with cups to be filled. My mother did sewing for the Works Progress Administration, walking eight miles to work each day, leaving at 6:00 a.m. and not returning until 7:00 p.m. Sometimes I stayed home and took care of my brothers and sisters.

"There was segregation then. Women still couldn't vote. Black men had to pay a poll tax to vote. Because they didn't want to pay it, few of them voted. When I went into a restaurant, I would have to sit in the back with the other blacks, while the whites sat in front. The same thing happened riding the city bus. And, of course, blacks and whites had separate schools. The whites had a school building and went year-round, while we had a combined church and school about as big as a house and could only go half a year.

"I didn't think we needed to be separated. I got along fine with whites. I didn't grow up hating anybody. I learned that we need to give each other respect and understanding. My mother said to me once, 'Never hand anyone a stick to hit you with. If you walk down the street and some fool on the corner starts arguing with you, if you argue back, then there are two fools there.'

"The whites I worked for didn't make me feel beneath them. And my parents taught me to never feel inferior to anybody. They wanted me to get a good education and become a teacher. At that time, it was a big deal for black people to be teachers. But I was only able to get through the equivalent of eighth grade, so I couldn't go to college.

"When I turned twenty-three, I decided to leave Arkansas. I had been picking cotton for about ten years and it was getting tedious. I wanted to do something more challenging.

"I thought if I moved north to Minneapolis, Minnesota, maybe I could get away from the oppression. But things weren't much better there. When you place people by race, some people end up in the wrong place. Many black women couldn't get work, and out of desperation, turned to prostitution. They wouldn't hire black schooteachers. I had a friend who couldn't get hired, and I told her that if I were looking, they'd hire me or I would raise heck. I wasn't mad at people, but I was mad at the system."

After arriving in Minneapolis, Dorothy took a job at a Chinese laundry. But when the owner put his groping hands on her, she left. She worked in a fabric company while attending an all-white cosmetology school.

Photo by Todd Cota

Dorothy Woolfork makes a point.

When she tried to get work as a beautician, she ran into more racism. "There were no black beauty operators in Minneapolis, and I found out why," she told me. "When I called, the white shops said they had openings, but when I went there, they said they were full. I said, 'I just called you two minutes ago and you said it was open.'"

Eventually, Dorothy landed a job at a beauty shop in a wealthy white community, becoming the first black beautician in the Twin Cities. In 1956, she opened her own salon, Dorothy's Beauty Shop, which she ran for several years. Financial necessity then forced her to work on a computer factory assembly line where the rows of parts floating by seemed like so many cotton bolls waiting to be picked and where the reward was a lower wage than that of her white counterparts.

In 1980, Dorothy retired and volunteered in civil and human rights organizations where she gained an award-winning reputation for her outspoken advocacy and mediation skills in personal and social justice conflicts. She received community service awards from the National Association for the Advancement of Colored People, (NAACP), Sabathani Community Center, the Harriet Tubman battered women's shelter, and the Council on Black Minnesotans. At eighty-three years old, she is still going strong, volunteering at the NAACP office and at a local social service agency providing services to seniors.

"I've been a fighter all my life," she says. "I'm not about to give up now. When I see something wrong, I have to do something about it. Marching in protests has never been my style. I prefer to work within the system. For example, when I was at a Crisis Nursery Center recently, I noticed the terrible time that white teachers were having in relating to kids of different cultures. I talked to the director about getting more minority teachers. But whoever the teachers are, parents need to work with them not against them. Instead of teaching the child to go to school to learn, parents call teachers 'racist' and kids go to school with anger. If parents are unhappy, they should write proposals to the school telling them what they want teachers and administrators to do.

"We're not doing well at teaching kids what's right. One kid went to school and when they asked him his name, he said 'motherfucker.' That's what his mother called him. We need to do more to help kids, to show them we care, to ask them what they want to be when they grow up, then to help them get there. For example: "I let kids of all races play in my backyard so they can have the experience of being with a black woman as well as each other.

"I receive many calls from young black men complaining about police abuse—how police pick them up (randomly), throw them up against cars, search them, and threaten them with jail time. It scares and intimidates them. I tell them, 'The police can't send you to prison. Only the court system can do that. So, why put yourself in harm's way by shooting off your mouth? Who has a billy club and gun? The police. Who has the authority? The police.' The system is racist. There is a pattern of discrimination there. But you have to prove you were discriminated against.

"I have written letters to legislators opposing proposals to build more jails in the state, suggesting instead, construction of a vocational training school for youth. Our prisons are overloaded with too many people in there for nonviolent things. It costs more to keep them in prison than to educate them. Loading them into jails hasn't solved anything, so let's give them opportunity.

"While serving on a Civil Rights Commission panel with three others, I handled a discrimination complaint by a black man who worked as a security guard for a local department store. The store manager made him follow other black people around the premises, looking for criminal acts or intent. When he wouldn't do it, he was fired. After he talked to me, he sued the store and won. Some people get on commissions and boards but don't make a difference. I was there to make a difference.

"There still isn't equality here. We don't have a black woman or man at the head of nothin' in Minnesota. They're always in a secondary position—fifth or seventh vice-presidents—paid like a good secretary. They're never the owners of the plantation. I call this phenomena 'plantation pockets.' We still have a plantation mentality in some parts of our culture. How far are we from slavery? Everything being done now to blacks has been done before. We've never completely moved away from it. It's just being done in a different, subtler way. We've still got a long way to go. I've got to keep going because there are so many things to be done to become one people—and too many people who are too chicken to do it.

"That's why I started volunteering at the NAACP. I believe the status quo will continue unless people take political power. I've worked with the political people—the congressmen, senators, and the mayor. You can't just complain or accuse them. You have to tell them what you want them to do, or they can't do it. If you never confront the problem, it never goes away.

"I don't spend time worrying about what's going to happen. I don't have time for that. I'm too busy doing things that are positive, making something better for someone else. I make a difference by telling people what the needs are and by believing in equal opportunity for everybody. All people are really the same—just give me the chance to be as good as I can be.

"I was at an event, and two black women with doctorate degrees who were speaking seemed to talk down to me. I told them, 'I don't feel beneath anybody. I know I'm as good as anybody else. So, let's treat each other with respect. I may not have a Ph.D., but I have common sense. We can get a lot done if we don't put each other down.'"

The feisty edge that has crept into Dorothy's voice reaches a peak and she thrusts a formidable index finger outward to make her point:

"I teach people to stand up for themselves wherever I go. I'm not afraid to think and speak for myself, and I teach others to do the same. I always tell people that you may not agree with me or like me. But that doesn't bother me. I don't believe anybody can stop me from thinking independently because I don't need their approval. I don't need to please anybody. Don't ask me to fall in line. I don't fall in line. I do what's right."

Questions for Contemplation:

1. Think of the first time you heard about skin color as a measure of a person's worth. What happened and what were you feeling?
2. Some European-Americans feel they are just "Americans." If you are a European-American do you know your ancestors' homeland and cultural traditions?
3. What were you told as a child about racism? How were you expected to deal with it?
4. What is one word, phrase, name, or statement that you never want to hear again about your racial or ethnic group? What has worked for you to derail racist remarks and actions nonviolently?
5. What are your thoughts about Dorothy's father's method of disciplining? What other nonviolent parenting strategies do you know to be effective?

Resources for Reflection and Action:

Race Manners: Navigating the minefield between black and white Americans, by Bruce Jacobs (NYC: Arcade Publishing, 1999).

Educators Healing Racism edited by Nancy L. Quisenberry & D. John McIntryre (Association of Teacher Educators, 1900 Association Dr., Suite, ATE, Reston, VA 20191. Phone: 703-620-3110, 1999). The authors challenge us to establish goals that go beyond accepting the "minimum standard" of teachers who are just tolerant, to graduating teachers who are antiracists and who are actively against bigotry.

Dealing With Differences: Taking action on class, race, gender, and disability, by Angele Ellis & Marilyn Llewellyn (Thousand Oaks, CA: Corwin Press, 1997). A dynamic kindergarten-to-college curriculum for achieving the goals of justice, equality, and peace.

Sojourner Truth, A Life, A Symbol, Nell Irvin Painter (NYC: W.W. Norton and Company, 1996).

Crusade for Justice: The autobiography of Ida B. Wells, Alfreda M. Duster (University of Chicago Press, 1970).

National Association for the Advancement of Colored People (NAACP), 1025 Vermont Ave. NW #1120, Washington DC, 20005. Phone: 202-638-2269.

National Urban League, 120 Wall Street, NYC, 10005. Phone: 212-558-5300.

National Political Congress of Black Women, 8401 Colesville Road #400, Silver Springs, MD 20910. Phone: 877-274-1198.

Martin Luther King, Jr. Center, Mansfield, PA 16933. Website: www.msfld.edu-stuaivmlk.html.

Facing History and Ourselves National Foundation. Website: www.facing.org. Reaches six hundred thousand students per year and provides services and resources for educators to encourage empathy and critical thinking, going beyond teaching children about historical events towards developing a sense of social responsibility. Based in Massachusetts, they also have a branch in Switzerland and are internationally very active.

Feeling the Fear | JIM LOVESTAR

by Burt Berlowe

"I can still feel the crush of his hand on the side of my head. I can feel the terror and powerlessness of a little boy who has no idea of what is going on …"

Jim Lovestar was about four-years-old when he first felt the terror. One evening, he was playing with some toys when his dad—a bitter war veteran given to drunken fits of rage—stomped into the room, nostrils flaring, saying nothing. As Jim looked up, bewildered, he suddenly felt the impact of his dad's brawny hand coming out of stony silence, smashing against his face, knocking him backward. Jim sat there, stunned and surprised, absorbing the blow. Even though the pain was hard to take, he held back tears, knowing it would not be manly to cry.

The abuse happened again and again throughout Jim's childhood. He yearned to be big and strong so he could fight back. He would watch in dismay as his dad destroyed himself with beer, tobacco, and a generally unhealthy lifestyle, compensations for a disappointing marriage and a misspent youth.

"My experience with my dad was betrayal. He was a very bright man who had great ideals but didn't practice them. He abused himself and others. I saw him smoking a lot, drinking a lot. He hit me more than once in an abusive way, not a corrective way. It's hard to remember exact incidents. My sisters have more memory of it than I do. I assume a lot of beatings I was given are still repressed. I remember I felt shame and blame that somehow I had done something to merit the abuse. I was taught to be strong and not to cry when I hurt.

"My dad's life was about force meets force. He had been at Guadalcanal, where he was part of a machine gun crew. He never talked about it; he couldn't deal with a war survivor's shame. He liked to talk about bar fights he had. He was proud of those.

"He went into the Marines as a robust, all-around college athlete but spent three years in a hospital bed with malaria he contracted at Guadalcanal. He had a lot of rage about that and he didn't know what to do with it—so he smoked, drank, and abused himself and us. He couldn't face the memories of the war's reality and the fact that he had wasted so much promise. He felt so powerless. I can't imagine how horrible it would be to live through what he did . . . Now I know he was suffering from post-traumatic stress disorder.

"The constant abuse took its toll on Jim. He grew up with a rage, fear, and distrust of men—feelings he kept largely to himself. Occasionally, at odd hours of the night, the lingering shadow of his past would sneak out of its private hiding place. Violent, frightful dreams would stun him like a slap in the face, and he would rise up in his bed and cry out in agony. One recurring dream went like this: "I'm in my parents' home and get into a discussion with my dad. It escalates into an argument, a shouting match, and then a fight where we are throwing each other around the room. My mom says, 'Don't do that in here. You'll break the furniture!' She pushes us out of the door. Then we're in the backyard, and I'm trying to hold him down, but he's such a strong man . . ."

The only way Jim thought he could get rid of the nightmare and reclaim his life was through brute strength. He grew to believe that if he were strong enough and smart enough, he could make it in the world. He joined the Marines, thinking that he could prove his manhood by going into combat like his dad. Instead, he was put at a desk job and never got to the front lines. He left, disenchanted with the military and its war-making machine. He subsequently went to college on the GI bill. The dreams bothered him all the way through grad school. It was the mid-1970s before Jim could finally begin to confront his demons.

"I was hitchhiking and went to a gathering of counterculture-like people in California. One man called a healing circle and invited me in. I didn't know him, but somehow I was able to tell my reoccurring dream. I acknowledged my rage towards my dad. Many of the people there responded to my story of never-before-revealed pain and suffering. That was the first door to my own healing. It was a transforming experience.

"A year and a half later, I went to a men's conference in Minneapolis and started going to a support group run by the Men's Center. It was one of the hardest things I had ever done, but my soul was telling me 'this is for you.' I remember being terrified as I went to the Men's Center, thinking if I sat in that circle with all those strange men something terrible would happen. The next week, I had the same feeling of terror and resistance to going, yet I left the group feeling safe and trusting. Finally, I was able to go to a meeting with little anxiety, and in fact, gained a sense of relief and release.

"In 1984, I went to a men's conference in Madison, Wisconsin, expecting it to be a celebration of manhood. Instead, the conference was planned and organized by self-proclaimed feminist men who were basically apologizing for having 'balls,' saying 'I'm ashamed to be a man.' It turned out that their real agenda was fear of dealing with women.

"While I was there, I met Bill Kauth, one of the founders of the Men's Warrior Weekend. He and I connected with each other. We recognized that we weren't interested in making either women or men the enemy, the good guys, or the victims. Instead, we wanted a model that supported men in healing within the company of men so they could then be with women and be equal, strong, and collaborative. I had decided that instead of raging against other men, I would create something that celebrated the beauty of men. I went to the board of the local Men's Center and proposed a Men's conference for the Twin Cities and offered to coordinate it. We had a wonderful conference. It was a celebration of men.

"Kauth came to the conference and invited me to one of the Warrior Weekends he was having in Milwaukee. He offered to give me my money back if I didn't find it to be a valuable experience. I said, 'If it's not what you say it is, I want you to listen to my criticism.' He eagerly agreed. I hitchhiked to Milwaukee to Warrior Weekend in November of '85. At the end of that weekend, Bill called and asked me if I wanted my money back. I said 'I feel more like a man than I've ever felt in my life.' Another door had opened for me. That was when I became part of the warrior groups.

"Over the years, as men have gone through the Warrior Weekends, they've connected with others who have been through it and have developed a tribal sense of mission and community service I just love. A third door of healing that opened for me was when I became a facilitator of Men's Warrior groups. As time went on, I got more and more involved in men's work with the Men's Center and other organizations, teaching health and wellness classes and workshops, and putting together men's conferences."

Photo by Todd Cota

Jim Lovestar engages in his daily yoga.

Yet another door opened for Jim when he became a Quaker. He found a connection of service between the Quaker and Warrior communities. The term "warrior" has traditionally had a violent connotation, being likened to battlefield soldiers and the like. But going back to ancient history, various native tribes have defined the word in a different sense, to mean protector and provider—also a contribution of the Quakers. In addition, like Jim, Quakers share a value of self-awareness, a key to becoming a New Warrior.

Warrior Weekends are intense initiations that take men away from their natural surroundings into safe places where they express, define, and support their inner feelings and help those around them do the same. The interaction-based Mankind Project that conducts New Warrior Training Adventures notes, "Men have always been warriors." They believe every man has his warrior side but that social forces pressure men to repress that part of them and substitute distorted expressions. The New Warrior, they say, is a man who has confronted this destructive manifestation and "has achieved hard-won ownership of the highly focused, aggressive, native energy that empowers and shapes the innemasculine self . . . the New Warrior is at once tough and loving, wild and gentle, fierce and tolerant. He lives passionately and compassionately because he has learned to face his own shadow . . ."

Stepping out from the shadow of his past has been a continuing struggle for Jim. Just when he thinks he has come to terms with it, it sneaks up on him again. "One day, I was at a meeting with men I know and trust and have a history with, when I felt the anxiety again. I said, 'What is this about?' I realized it had nothing to do with the present time. It was that old pattern of childhood, still alive after all these years. We had a custom in the group that we called 'checking,' where each member says how he's feeling. When my turn came, I admitted to these men that I was experiencing that same old fear. It was so powerful to say, 'Here is my fear for all of you to see. It's the same old pattern from the past.' There were no comments, as is the custom. The power of this circle of men was in being witnessed for who I am.

As a part of this healing process, I finally came to terms with my dad. As I look back, I am ready to embrace and forgive him. I now believe that my dream has helped me come to that place; to face my fear and hate of him and make me want to put my arms around him. I used to spend a good amount of time in my life blaming him for what he did. Now I feel his pain and have compassion for him."

Jim doesn't dream about his dad much anymore. But another type of terror haunts and heals him. "I have dreams of crying out. I assume it is unfinished business from my childhood. I realized that as a child, I had not been allowed to cry, that I had to hold it all in. This is the crying I had never been able to do as a child. For years, I have been trying to escape or avoid the shadow in my past. I have had a fear of being myself, of being human. The crying is finally allowing me to do that."

Jim spends much of his time these days collaborating in building the new men's movement with other compassionate and committed men. He teaches workshops for men, edits a New Warrior newsletter and does publicity for the network. He has recently started the Institute of Men's Health and Well-Being, that he runs out of his home. In addition, Jim uses his home-based massage business to help others find inner peace and power. "I'm not a healer," he says. "I am a channel for divine energy that I want to share. Through massage, I teach people that we all have the ability to give and receive nurturing touch. Anybody can serve anybody else with touch. Anybody can channel divine energy. It's more than just the province of clerics and saints.

"A few years ago I was experiencing a lot of fear about not having enough money. I prayed about it. My answer came when an inner voice asked, 'Are you doing my work?' I paused, reflected, and said, 'Yes.' I heard, 'Keep doing the work, and I'll take care of the money.' Within two days, I received an unexpected check in the mail.

When I worry about making money, I remind myself of the voice that said it would take care of the money. I pause, calm myself down and ask myself, 'Am I doing the work?' When the answer is yes, the worry is gone . . . I haven't missed a mortgage payment. I haven't been hungry or without a car. My physical needs have been met. So I just keep doing the work."

"I acknowledged my rage. It was the first door to my healing."

Jim Lovestar

Questions for Contemplation:

1. What deep-seated fears have you overcome in your life? What was helpful to your healing process?
2. What is your perception of a warrior? How do you think young men of today can learn to make the transition from boy to man/warrior, in a healthy way?
3. What has been your experience with men's groups?
4. What kind of livelihood appeals to you when you think about being true to yourself? What skills do you need to learn?"

Resources for Reflection and Action:

Boys Will Be Men: Raising our sons for courage, caring and community by Paul Kivel, (New Society Publishers, 1999). Drawing on decades of experience doing antiviolence work with men and teens, Kivel challenges the traditional training boys receive.

Lost Boys: Why our sons turn violent and how we can save them, by James Garborino (NYC: Free Press, 1999).

A Fine Young Man, by Michael Gurian (NYC: Jeremy P. Tarcher/Putnam, 1998). Gurian provides an insightful view of raising boys.

The Zen of Making a Living: A practical guide to creative career design, by Laurence G. Bolt (NYC: Arkona, 1993). This book is about finding meaningful work and helping to reduce suffering at the same time.

Domestic Violence: Guidelines for research-informed practice, edited by John Vincent & Ernest Jouriles (Levittown, PA: Jessica Kingsley Publishers, 2000). This book describes recently developed intervention programs that have been shown to be effective for reducing the incidence, severity, or impact of domestic violence in particular populations.

Right Livelihood information can be found on the Website: www.rightlivelihood.se.

Check out shadowwork.com for Shadow Work Seminars: Information on working with your shadow to enhance your personal growth and overcome obstacles.

For information on the New Warrior Movement, contact The Mankind Project, PO Box 230, Malone, NY 12953-0230. Phone: 800-870-4611, email: dhnwmtl@aol.com.

A Tribute to a Compassionate Rebel

By Rebecca Janke

Compassion for yourself and others leaves you
Open to searching your soul for the
Myriad ways you can nonviolently respond to the
Potholes of social injustice and everyday human struggles.
Anger, anguish, disappointment, and disgust
Serve as warnings—something is amiss in the sea of life.
Standing as a beacon of light in the darkness of suffering, you
Invite your rebellious nature to assist your heart
Over and over again.
New ways of being human are the treasures you discover,
Allowing you to deepen your relationships and giving others hope.
Tales of your legacy will be told for years as you
Experiment in creating a culture of peace.

Rebelliousness found a mighty reason for
Existing in you to serve the common good.
Bringing inspiration and insights, you choose to live
Expressively, and to act in your everyday life with your
Love and outrage, to make a difference where you stand!

Chapter 2

Bridge Builders

Ray Nelson, Ray Valentine, Jim Gambone, Loan Huynh, Vivian IronHeart, Larry Long

Bridge Builders are people who recognize that connections can be made in the most unusual of places. Since bridges span distances, they are symbols of peace, connecting oneself and the "other." Bridge Builders have used hope, determination, cooperation, conversation, conflict resolution, the arts, and intuition to build and sustain the bridges they have built between sometimes unlikely partners.

In this chapter Jim Gambone's and Larry Long's stories are about bridges between generations. Vivian IronHeart builds bridges between cultures. Loan Huynh builds bridges between immigrants and United States citizens. Ray Nelson and Ray Valentine build bridges between humans and animals.

Bridge Builders help others see the beauty in interconnectedness. They demonstrate uniqueness in their way of relating, their ability to overcome obstacles, and their capacity for forgiveness.

I Love You, Boy | RAY NELSON

by Julie Penshorn

It seems when people can't communicate with an animal, they figure it's the animal's fault. But I guess much of the time it's the person who isn't listening or isn't speaking the right language.

—Ray Nelson

In his flannel-lined blue shirt, jeans, and cowboy boots, Ray Nelson is the picture of rugged masculinity. Yet the sensitivity and compassion this man has for animals belies the hardened front. He's not a compassionate rebel by intellectual design. He just does what he thinks is right. Here is the story he shared with me.

"Standing in the vet's room, with its aluminum table and bare, white-painted walls, I could barely breathe. The lump in my throat made me want to throwup. My best friend for fourteen years, looking smaller in his old age, but still beautiful with his golden mane and auburn coat, lay on the table. He had just taken his last breath.

"I just said, 'I love you boy.' There was nothing else I could do. He was old. He was sick. But when he looked at me in that trusting way, while the vet gave him his last shot, it was just too much . . .

"After the vet left me alone with him, I couldn't help but notice the contrast: this barren room wasn't what he represented to me. He was about a ball found in the lush green grass of the springtime, a stick fetched from the sparkling blue of a lake, and a flash of color on white snow.

"All my friends knew he was special to me. They had heard the countless stories about him or seen him in action. They all knew that he, a dog with no professional training, could out-fetch and out-swim any competitor he encountered, giving his best and showing off—especially when it really mattered. When he was swimming against another dog, he'd raise those powerful shoulders up out of the water and look more like a miniature boat than a dog!

"I remember the day I bought him. He was the most attentive and friendly of the litter and turned out to be one of my best lifetime friends. I still accidentally call my current dog by his name: 'Dune.'

"The first nights he was with me, he was scared and lonely without momma, so he slept by my bed and looked for my hand hanging down. Then he'd nuzzle it.

"Dune seemed to understand English. I'd just talk to him. He knew lots of simple phrases like, 'Go eat,' or 'Get in the truck.' If I was talking and he heard certain words or phrases he'd heard before, he'd bring the object over to me. But I was amazed the day I had some friends over watching football on TV and we saw a commercial showing a golden retriever getting his master a beer. My friends asked if Dune could do that. I really didn't think he could, but I went in the kitchen and showed him the beer in the fridge and said, 'beer.' Then I went back and sat down (having left the fridge open). I said, 'Dune, go get me a beer,' and within a minute there he was holding a beer, mouthing it carefully. Of course everybody had to try it, so pretty soon we all had a cold one. What a dog!

"Dune was incredible, but he wasn't the only special dog for me. I also had a boyhood companion, Pepper, a Gordon Setter. My parents put him to sleep when I was ten. Although he was fourteen and sick, I was devastated, and angry that it was done without my permission. I refused to go to school for several days.

"Pepper was the first animal I loved. He gave me everything he had. One day, a German Shepherd strayed down our street. The Shepherd was in his prime. Fit and strong, he came toward me in a menacing way. Pepper, who was old and lame, came limping to my rescue. I had to use my Schwin's bike tire to help him by putting it between the Shepherd and my dog. Together, we won our first battle.

"I am a person who can't stand to see animals suffer—and I've seen a lot of people abuse their animals. When I was sixteen or seventeen years old I was at a party. A couple of popular guys were screwing around with a cat. They dropped him off the banister and then threatened to put him in the oven. I couldn't believe they had no respect for the people's home or the cat. I wondered, 'Who's going to stick up for that cat?' No one, even the girls, was saying anything. I decided I wasn't going to be quiet. I stood up—looked them in the eyes, and told them if I saw them touching the cat, I'd put them in the oven. We had a stare-down. Finally, they backed off and left. Everybody began to know me as somebody who'd stand up for things.

"Now I live here at the ranch where my girlfriend and I work with horses. We have one abused stallion that can be difficult. Before he came here, a trainer took a baseball bat to his hind legs, another confined him to standing in a small stall for months straight. Every now and then you can see the gentleness in him, but he sure likes to be aggressive. The other day, he charged at my girlfriend and me when he was stressed out by the commotion of our barn construction efforts. We recognize that he's very susceptible to stress and needs special care, so it helps us be more patient. It's amazing how much animals can communicate when we pay attention.

"We train horses in a gentle, respectful way at our place, Sunborn Stables, in Minnesota. We treat them as unique individuals. Each one has its own personality and its own needs.

"The other day, a two-year-old stallion came in for training. He was scared to death! We had to spend a lot more time on basics than we usually do, just to get his confidence up. The poor horse had a rope burn on a hind leg and several cuts on his nose that we figure were made with a chain. We heard that the trainer who hurt him felt he was untrainable because he had multicolored eyes! I guess she felt frustrated at not being able to read those eyes like she could read the eyes of other horses. It seems when people can't communicate with an animal, they figure it's the animal's fault. But I guess much of the time it's the person who isn't listening or isn't speaking the right language.

"I love the work we do with horses because I know they are being treated fairly. Since we can only have a few horses in training ourselves, we also teach others how to work with their horses.

Photo by Todd Cota

Ray Nelson demonstrates his bond with his dog, Tucker.

That's probably the greatest gift we give. When I look out my window and see all the happy critters, I feel at peace, knowing I'm part of the landscape here.

"Now, each night I check the horses, then I come in and go to sleep with my dog, another golden retriever named Tucker, at my bedside. His presence is a comfort. I know he's there for me, like I'm there for him and the horses. And sometimes I say, 'I love you, Dune—I mean Tucker.'"

Challenger | RAY VALENTINE

by Julie Penshorn

It was a hot, sunny, Colorado day. The expected afternoon shower had just moistened the roping arena, and the ropers and watchers were getting ready to resume the exciting sport of steer roping.

Each time a roper rode his or her horse into the box (the place where they waited until the steer was released), others watched. Many were anticipating the horse's full-speed departure from that box, with its rider spinning a rope in preparation, as rider and horse worked together to catch up to, and capture, the horns of the steer. Others, those who were more experienced, were watching to see the kind of behavior the horse exhibited in the box—was the horse acting crazy or well-mannered? Was the rider able to position him properly for a successful departure? Was valuable time wasted while the horse disobediently threw his head or jumped out too quickly? Rarely were words exchanged, as one cowboy after another tried to prove his skill at handling his horse and catching his steer. Honor was important, and giving opinions was rare.

But today was different. This day, a young man, Jim, riding a four-year-old horse, Lucky (in his first season as a roping horse and just learning how to do it), was having all sorts of trouble. Every time Jim would get into the box with his horse, he'd jazz him up with his spurs so that he'd come out fast. However, the horse was so jazzed he didn't know what to do anymore and was starting to lunge and plunge and rear and carry on.

Ray Valentine observed all this commotion. A seasoned roper and horse trainer, Ray was watching young Jim and his horse, and biting his tongue. Every time Jim went into the box, it got harder and harder for Ray to be silent. The horse was confused, overwhelmed, rushed, and distraught, and it was getting worse. His compassion for the animal finally got the better of Ray. He rebelled against the common courtesy of keeping his mouth shut, and said, "Jim, you're pushing that horse too fast. Give it a rest."

Photo by Julie Penshorn

Ray Valentine and a roping buddy are caught in action.

The next time Jim's turn came up, he did the same thing as every other time. Ray said to him, "Jim, get down off that horse." Now when Ray talks, most people listen. His often jovial stories and sense of humor brighten your day. However, he can also put an edge in his voice that makes a person pay attention. He's got the voice of Ben Cartwright, or maybe your dad when he's mad—it's the kind of voice that oozes power.

Anyway, Jim stopped in his tracks, looked at Ray, and then, eyes hidden under a lowered head and a broad hat-brim, he thought about what to do. It wasn't until Ray dismounted and started walking toward him that he made his decision. Jim dismounted and led his horse out of the arena, unsaddled, and left.

People buzzed about this for weeks, and from time to time you'll still hear the story at a roping practice. Ray had broken the standard cowboy etiquette, yet most were happy to see Jim challenged for abusing his horse.

Questions for Contemplation:

1. Do you think a person who cares about animals can eat meat or use leather products for clothing or shoes? Why or why not?
2. Ray Nelson's tone when he told the boys who were molesting the cat to stop touching the cat or he'd put them in the oven, was not gentle. Neither was Ray Valentine's. Do you think tough talk like that is ever warranted?
3. Both Rays were taking a risk when they used tough talk. What if words didn't get the cat abusers or the horse abuser to stop? What could be a nonviolent backup plan if the tough talk didn't work?
4. Have you ever experienced a situation wherein you felt your intervention was necessary in order to protect or defend an animal or a child? If so, what did you do? How did it feel to you while you were intervening? Afterward? What kind of feedback did you get from others (observers, your family, your friends)?
5. In what ways could you assist a child whose parent was abusing him or her in the grocery store? In what ways could you assist the parent? What relationship is there between helping the parent and helping the child?
6. Some people believe the sport of roping is too violent, though it began as a way for ranchers to catch and treat sick animals. What do you think? Why?

Resources for Reflection and Action:

Hey, Little Ant, by Phillip & Hannah Hoose. (Berkeley, CA: Tricycle Press, 2000). Recommended for children ages four through eight, this book tells the story of a young boy who is about to step on a tiny ant, when the ant pleads with him to reconsider.

Diet for a New America, by John Robbins. Graphically depicts some of the horror stories about meat production and gives rationale for becoming a vegetarian. Also points out a study that shows how prisoners who were paired up with an animal before their release showed a much lower recidivism rate. Research has shown that ninety percent of prisoners in this country abused animals as children.

The Man Who Listens to Horses, by Monty Roberts (NYC: Random House, 1997). Roberts is a horse trainer who uses the language he has named "equus." Roberts has figured out this horse language by spending years observing domestic and wild horses. He uses this language to communicate with and thus gently train horses.

Horse Sense for People: Using the gentle wisdom of join up to enrich our relationships at home and at work, by Monty Roberts (2001).

When Elephants Weep, by J.M. Masson and Susan McCarthy (1996). This book shows the richness of the emotional life of animals.

Stickeen, by John Muir (Berkeley, CA: Heyday Books, 1990). Muir's relationship with his dog, Stickeen, reveals the fundamental unity and sanctity of all living things.

The Latham Foundation, Latham Plaza Building, 1826 Clement Avenue, Alameda, CA 94501. Phone: 510-521-0920. Website: www.latham.org. The Latham Foundation publishes a newsletter called the Latham Letter which promotes respect for all life through education. In addition to their newsletter, they offer several books, including: Child Abuse, Domestic Violence, and Animal Abuse: Linking the circles of compassion for prevention and intervention, edited by Frank R. Ascioun, and Phil Arkow (1999); and Teaching Compassion: A guide for humane educators, teachers, and parents, by Pamela Raphael (1999).

Animal Production Institute. Website: www.api4animals.org, has worked to protect animals from cruelty and exploitation for more than thirty years. Phone: 800-505-4949. Call for a free issue of their full-color magazine, *Animal Issues*.

Gardens of Memory, PO Box, 1694 Lyons, CO 80540. Phone: 720-732-6095. Website: www.gardensofmemory.com. Gardens of Memory provides information about designing a memory garden and other nature-based ways to heal grief.

Generations Together | JIM GAMBONE

by Rebecca Janke

"It was one day, among many—a mixture of African, Italian, and Polish Americans sitting around the kitchen table, sharing their night dreams with my grandmother, Bessie, and anxiously awaiting her interpretation. Even though she spent the entire night on her knees scrubbing the marble floors of the Mellon Bank and Trust Company, she was never too tired to help her friends and neighbors increase their chances of winning the numbers game.

"My grandmother was the neighborhood bookie. She had developed a number code that coincided with people's dreams' symbols. She would give them those numbers to play.

"I actually learned how to read by studying her system which was recorded in her Dream Book. She served as the local 'social worker,' too . . . She took time to listen to the many problems that were shared around her kitchen table.

"My father, mother, and I lived with her because we couldn't afford a home of our own. When I was fifteen we finally had enough money to move out on our own. It was difficult for me. I missed the diversity of my grandmother's neighborhood. It felt odd to be living with only white, middle-class people. Though I did the best I could to make new friends, I found reading brought me the most comfort. The characters in books filled my mind in a familiar way—reminding me of the days at my grandmother's house.

"As time went on, I noticed and became particularly upset over the racial prejudice I witnessed in the suburbs of Philadelphia. It broke my heart and made me mad as hell. When I read Martin Luther King's book, *Letter from the Birmingham Jail*, I cried. I knew I had to do something.

"I asked the priest if I could give a speech to the men's group, which met on Sunday morning after mass. To my surprise, he said yes.

"However, I was completely taken aback, in fact, devastated, to hear the audience boo, not once, but several times during my speech. Even the priest and my dad were shaking their heads. It was bad enough to see anger on the faces of people in my community, but it pierced my heart to see the disappointment and anger in my father's eyes. It was so visceral. I felt like I was going to throwup. It enraged me to see the hypocrisy of these men. Where was, 'Love your neighbor as yourself?'

"My first impulse was to run away from home. But, being fifteen, I couldn't strike out on my own; plus I still wanted my dad in my life—after all, he was my dad. Remembering that Jesus was a change-agent, I committed myself to doing the same. I did what many people do with their first attempts to change minds: I argued my points with him—incessantly. Our kitchen table became a war zone, and we didn't resolve a thing.

"One night, at the height of showing him how deeply I felt about the civil rights movement, I shouted, 'I'm joining the Urban League!' Later that evening, he either feigned or actually had a heart attack. As I knelt at what we thought was his deathbed, he asked me not to join the League, and I promised I wouldn't. However, it didn't stop my resolve to work on what I thought was wrong.

"Because I was getting nowhere, I decided to beef up my intellectual muscles. The neighbor down the street had an extensive library in his basement and had, many times before, invited me to use it. I had been rather hesitant because he was an atheist. But now I realized that anyone who could defend his position as strongly as he did was somebody I could learn from. Between the access to his library and his willingness to argue and debate spiritual issues with me, I not only sharpened my intellectual abilities, but I became a skilled debater. So skilled, as a matter of fact, that I won a full scholarship to college.

"After graduating with a masters in Latin American Studies and Inter-American Diplomatic History, I served in the Peace Corps where I became even more convinced that we have a long way to go before we put our 'isms' to rest. After the Peace Corps, I went to the Highlander School in Tennessee to become more skilled in addressing racism and became personal friends with Myles Horton, the school's founder.

"To continue my quest, I went on to the University of New Mexico and got a Ph.D. in bilingual/bicultural education. I began to dream of developing a process that could help people of all ages and cultures dialogue, solve problems, and enjoy each other's company—like we did around my grandmother's table. Eventually, that process evolved into "Intergenerational Dialogue™."

"My first opportunity to use it occurred when a St. Paul, Minnesota housing cooperative was having a dispute. Apparently, one fall day, some children rode their bicycles in the vicinity of the senior high-rise. One of the children ran into a senior woman with his bike. The woman fell and became frightened. She told her friends about the incident, and uproar ensued, with residents of the senior housing unit and the neighboring family cooperative housing unit openly hostile toward each other.

"The management staff called me to do an Intergenerational Dialogue™. Only a small handful of people of various ages showed up, but because that discussion went so well, they decided to hold more meetings. After several meetings, the group began to realize that the reason they didn't care very much about each other was because they didn't know each other. They decided to sponsor a movie night once a month. On the first move night, over one hundred sixty elders, parents, and children showed up!

"Some of the elders ultimately helped form a grass roots organization called Generations Together, which is dedicated to bringing all ages together under the banner of respect, caring, and cooperation among generations. They have raised several thousand dollars to continue to improve the social and physical climate of their community.

"Since its inception, Generations Together has sponsored a spring cleanup, planted several flower beds around the community property, coordinated an intergenerational spring picnic at a local park, established a bike fix-it program and a bike rodeo, and maintains a community room, where the elders read to the children.

"To spread the techniques of Intergenerational Dialogue™, I authored a book called: *Together for Tomorrow: Building community through intergenerational dialogue.* My wife, Wendy, researched international standards of legibility and arrived at certain design considerations to make the book's print easier to read for the older eyes. An added pleasure in my life is to be married to someone who supports and adds to what I do.

Photo by Todd Cota

Jim Gambone is always at home when he's with a book.

"Years of aching over racism and ageism continue to propel me to go wherever I'm asked to facilitate dialogue groups. I can still see, in my mind's eye, people of all different ages and backgrounds sitting around my grandmother's kitchen table, sharing their dreams, working out their problems, and hoping for a better tomorrow. Now I feel it's my job to make that table available again. My grandmother would want it that way."

"The past is prologue. . . history is a deep, moving river of experience from all generations."

Jim Gambone

Questions for Contemplation:

1. What elders have had a strong influence in your life? How did they impact your life?
2. What experiences have you had regarding ageism?
3. What resources or interests do you have that could be shared with a neighborhood child?
4. What opportunities exist for elders in your community to connect to youth or youth to connect to elders? What have you noticed in the culture or your community that keeps generations separated from each other?
5. With many elders having scarcely enough money to squeak by, can we imagine ways to compensate them for their contributions? Could elder teaching and mentoring be a later-life career path—in schools, after-school programs and community centers? What are some ways we can send the message to elders that we deeply value them?
6. Jim Gambone believes that to solve the problems that society is facing today, input from every generation is necessary. What can your community, group, family, or organizations do to ensure that voices from all generations are heard when decisions are made?

Resources for Reflection and Action:

Together for Tomorrow: Building community through intergenerational dialogue, by Jim Gambone (Elder Eye Press, PO Box 142 Crystal Bay, MN 55323, 1997. Phone: 1-800-586-9054. Website: www.pointsofviewinc.com. Email: pointsofview@earthlink.net).

All Are Welcome: A primer for intentional intergenerational ministry and dialogue, by Jim Gambone (Elder Eye Press, PO Box 142 Crystal Bay, MN 55323, Phone: 800-586-9054. 1999. Website: www.pointsofviewinc.com. Email: pointsofviewinc@earthlink.net).

Re-firement: A boomer's guide to life after fifty, by Jim Gambone (Bloomington, MN: Kirk House Press, 2000. Phone: 800-586-9051).

Spiritual Eldering Institute, 970 Aurora Ave. Boulder, CO 80302. Phone: 303-449-7243. Publishes a quarterly newsletter with mentoring tips, resources, and retreat opportunities for elders.

Generations United, 440 1st St., NW, 4th Floor, Washington, DC 20001-2085. Phone: 202-326-5263. This organization focuses on bringing children, youth, and elders together by promoting intergenerational strategies, programs, and politics.

Grandparents and Books, Los Angeles Public Library, 630 West 5th Street, Los Angeles, CA 90071. Phone: 213-228-7482. Grandparents and other elders come to the library at the same times each week, becoming dependable, welcoming faces. They are trained in sharing books with children who use the library and giving them tips for finding high quality books. The Grandparents and Books Trainers' Manual is available at www.lalp.org.

Little Brothers: Friends of the Elderly, 954 West Washington Boulevard, 5th Floor, Chicago, IL, 60607. Phone: 312-829-3055. Little Brothers partners elders with visiting volunteers who share common interests.

Intergenerational Connections. Website: www.nnfr.org/igen. Includes information for those interested in community-based intergenerational programs. The links provide access to a wealth of intergenerational children's books, articles, position statements, videos, and study programs.

International Center for Education about Aging. Website: www.iceaa.org. The stated mission of this institute includes educating primary and secondary students about the aging process, to help them better appreciate older adults.

Generations Together. Website: www.pitt.edu/~gti. The site includes a solid overview of intergenerational programming, as well as some very helpful resources.

Elderhostel Intergenerational. Website: www.elderhostel.org/pubrel/igenfac.htm. These pages describe a variety of opportunities for older adults to partner with young relatives and friends, as part of the Elderhostel program.

United Generations Ontario. Website: www.intergenugo.org. In addition to program information, this site provides very helpful background information about intergenerational programming.

Sanctuary of Compassion | LOAN HUYNH

by Burt Berlowe

"Heroes, all of them—at least they're my heroes, especially the new immigrants, especially the refugees. Everyone makes fun of New York cabdrivers who can't speak English: they're heroes. To give up your country is the hardest thing a person can do: to leave the old familiar places and ship out over the edge of the world to America and learn everything over again different that you learned as a child, learn the new language that you will never be so smart or funny in as in your true language. It takes years to start to feel semi-normal. And yet people still come—from Russia, Vietnam, and Cambodia, and Laos, Ethiopia, Iran, Haiti, Korea, Cuba, Chile, and they come on behalf of their children, and they come for freedom. Not for our land (Russia is as beautiful) not for our culture (they have their own, thank you), not for our system of government (they don't even know about it, may not even agree with it), but for freedom. They are heroes who make an adventure on our behalf, showing by their struggle how precious beyond words freedom is, and if we knew their stories, we could not keep back the tears."

Garrison Keillor, 1988
Used by permission

Photo by Todd Cota

Loan Huynh, in her usual upbeat manner, gives advice to new immigrants.

"I remember being very frightened. The fear is still with me today."

Loan Huynh can never forget being a child of war. Three decades of time have washed away some of the harsh details but have not erased the pain.

When Loan was a little girl, the Vietnam War was all around her. The Vietnamese City, Banh Me Thout, where she lived with her family, was within striking distance of American bombing raids. She remembers lying in her bed trembling and softly sobbing at the sound of the explosions in the distance; afraid that one day a bomb would fall on her house. She would seek comfort in her parents' arms and try to understand when they explained what the war was all about. When her father was away on military intelligence missions, Loan would worry about his safety.

Loan and her family moved around a lot to get away from the encroaching conflict. But the war seemed to follow them wherever they went, and they had to constantly prepare for it.

"Our military-base-home had a long hallway like a courtyard," Loan recalls. "Mom made bags of rice and other essentials and my sister and I would practice running up and down the hallway with the items on the our back, so we would be strong and ready to flee when the war came closer."

One day, Loan's worst fear came true. Saigon fell in April, 1975. Terrified of what might happen, the family struggled to escape. They packed themselves and their possessions into a jeep and drove along the beaches of Saigon. But rather than avoiding the war, they were chased by it. Shells exploded around them, coming dangerously close, as they sped along the city roads. Loan cried all the way, hiding her hands in her face and covering her ears, terrified that they might not make it.

After driving all night, the Huynhs reached the boat the next morning. It was already packed with other fleeing Vietnamese, pushing and shoving to get on a small boat. When her feet plopped down on board the small ship, Loan heaved a sigh of relief. For a moment, the fear left her body and she thought about the trip ahead. But then she was transferred to a bigger ship, lifted high in the air above the water for several seconds. Loan was afraid of heights. As she was boosted skyward, she looked down at the sea far below and once again cried and shook with fear.

As the immigrant ship left the harbor, Loan looked back at her homeland one last time. Little did she know what a difficult time she would have putting Vietnam behind her.

America was not the "Promised Land" the Huynh family had hoped for. They had a hard time adjusting to the white, middle-class culture, complicated by the fact that they were on welfare and knew little English. Loan felt like she was once again in a battle zone, with bombs of culture shock exploding all around her.

"We felt shameful. We felt different. I cried and cried from a feeling of not belonging. It was difficult growing up knowing you didn't belong in any culture. I rebelled against my parents. They thought I was being too American. It was difficult for them when I was out roaming the streets or being with friends. They weren't used to that. I was caught between two cultures and didn't belong in either one."

To make matters worse, Loan and her family were targets of virulent discrimination. "Once we were stopped by some (African-American) girls. They harassed us, called us names, and threatened to beat us up. They pushed us around and stole some of our things. That was my first experience with racism. Another time, after we moved to Texas, some African-American women beat up my younger sister and broke her arm. They taunted her with comments like, 'What kind of shampoo do you use?' and 'You think you are so beautiful.' They also beat my aunt up because she was Vietnamese."

Considering that she was harassed by African-Americans in her childhood, it would seem natural for Loan to harbor resentment or revengeful racism. But Loan and her sisters were brought up to never hate anyone, to be able to forgive even those that have hurt you, and to treat others as you would want to be treated.

Buoyed by her parents' support and powerful inner strength, Loan grew up and learned to adapt to America. She studied international relations and became the first in her family to graduate from college, then the University of Houston Law School.

To help pay her way through law school, Loan worked at her parent's grocery store in Houston, Texas. For seven years, the store was a Huynh enterprise, providing jobs for the whole family. Her parents often worked twelve hours a day to keep it going. But the store was in a dangerous part of town and her dad was attacked several times by intruders. When Loan got phone calls in the middle of the night, it usually meant that someone had broken into the store. She was happy when it was sold.

During college, Loan interned in the U.S. Congress, a job that made her realize the value of public service. Then, once again, she became an immigrant, only this time she left her family. She moved to Minneapolis, Minnesota where she knew no one, in order to pursue a career in the nonprofit sector. She was guided in her job search by her war and refugee experiences. It was as if she were back on the boat. But this time, she was reaching out to help other fleeing immigrants come on board.

As the legal director of the Immigrant and Refugee program of Minnesota Advocates for Human Rights, and, more recently, as a private attorney, Loan has represented individuals seeking asylum and help adapting to U.S. culture. Her clients come from all over the world, including a large new wave of immigrants from East Africa.

Loan's clients are largely new refugees fleeing repression, torture, and other dangers in their home countries, only to find new difficulties here. When she talks about how America treats its immigrants, Loan's usually calm voice rises in anger:

"I'm outraged at recent changes in the immigration laws. They are atrocious, especially the 'expedited removal' proceeding, where immigrants who come to a port of entry without appropriate visas or other documents are detained and sent back to their country. Some can apply for asylum through a 'credible fear' interview. During this period, they are detained full-time in county jails or other detention facilities just like criminals.

"These laws were enacted because those people (immigrants) don't have a voice. They don't vote. They have come here to get away from torture. Yet they have to go to jail for months before we can even get a court date for them. They're no danger to the community. Yet they may share a cell with criminals while they are waiting for deportation. Some have families here. Sometimes mothers are separated from their children. Because we don't have appropriate facilities for children here, they're transferred to Chicago while their mothers are kept in jails . . . We need to change the laws so new immigrants are treated more humanely."

Loan has been extremely frustrated with how far we have to go to provide sanctuary for people. "For example," she relates, "In her home country, this woman was taken out in the streets, stripped naked, and whipped in front of her family by her husband. She came to the U.S., for help. She tried to get a divorce but needed permission of both families, which she couldn't get. She was in the process of applying for asylum. The culture in her country is that married couples should be together no matter what. She is seeking protection in the U.S. through immigrant status, so she will not be forced to return to her country. "We say we're concerned about human rights around the world," Loan says, "What about the human rights of this woman and others like her?"

Loan does what she can for these refugees. She counsels them, leads them through the minefields of the legal system, visits them in jail, empowers them to exercise their rights, and helps them to stay and settle in America. But, perhaps most importantly, she offers the safe, warm haven of her open heart—what you might call a "sanctuary of compassion."

"Peace is not an absence of war, it is a virtue, a state of mind, a disposition for benevolence, confidence, justice."

Benedict Spinoza

Questions for Contemplation:

1. What have immigrants told you about why they came to your country?
2. Have you experienced or witnessed any discrimination against people of immigrant cultures? What happened? How did you feel?
3. What ideas do you have for meeting the needs of those who already live in the U.S. while still responding to the needs of immigrants?
4. Do you have more bedrooms in your house than you need? What are your thoughts about being a host family to new immigrants? What would you need to know and what obstacles would you need to overcome?
5. What services exist in your community to help meet the needs of immigrants? What other services are needed?

Resources for Reflection and Action:

Generally Speaking: Asian-American perspectives on modernism and the American experience, journal edited by Danial Krotz (Mpls., MN: Centre for Asian and Pacific Islanders).

Immigration: A civil rights issue for the Americas, by S. Jonas (Wilmington, DE: Scholarly Resources).

The Uprooted: Refugees and the United States, a high school curriculum, by D. Donahue (NYC: Publishers Group West).

I Speak English for My Mom, by M. Stanek (Morton Grove, IL: Albert Whittman).

In Defense of the Skin, by L. F. Tomasi (Staten Island, NY: Center for Migration Studies, 209 Flege Place).

Lost on Earth: Nomads of the New World, by Mark Fritz (NYC: Little, Brown & Company, 1999). Pulitzer Prize-winning foreign correspondent Mark Fritz intimately tells the tale of an epic moment. Investigating the forces at play in the world and with compassionate insight into the human will to survive, Fritz shows us where these refugees come from, why they flee and what they encounter during their journeys. This is a remarkable account of the exodus that will affect us all for generations to come.

Resource Center for the Americas, 3019 Minnehaha Avenue, Minneapolis, MN 55406. Phone: 612-276-0788. This center has an extensive library and provides connections for people nationwide.

The Tomas Rivera Center, 710 North College Avenue, Claremont, CA 91711. Provides public advocacy and other work for immigrants.

Center for Migration Studies, 209 Flege Place, Staten Island, NY.

Northern California Coalition for Immigrant Rights. Website: www.205.149.0.20/~/cheetham/gnotts-1.

Lutheran Immigration and Refugee Service. Website: www.elca.org/dcs/lirs (Not for Lutherans only.)

Immigration and Refugee Services of America. Website: www.irsa-uscr.org.

All One Heart. 12240 Perris Blvd., Suite A-1414, Moreno Valley, CA 92357. Website: www.allone-heart.com. Provides resources for educating for tolerance in your community.

The Center for Victims of Torture. 717 E. River Road, Mpls, MN 55455. Phone: 612-626-1400.

The Compassionate Rebel

Song by Julie Penshorn

You're a compassionate person, but you have a rebel side.
You're brave enough to stand up. You don't just run and hide.
Life gives you many chances to make your voice heard.
You speak loud or you whisper, but there's value in your words.

You're a rebel, compassionate rebel.

Some try to change our rebels, some try to keep them down,
But your journey to your center, prepares you for each round.
It's a journey for a strong heart, a journey through the dark,
Take someone there with you if they're not afraid to start.

Being a rebel, compassionate rebel.

Oh it can be so lonely
Oh it can tear you up—
But you don't give up.

You're patient sometimes maybe, and then sometimes you're not.
You're working strong and subtle, you're working cold and hot.
You keep making connections, enhancing lives you touch,
On a path of heart and courage, you are offering so much.

You're a rebel, compassionate rebel.

Remembering Who You Are | VIVIAN IRONHEART

by Rebecca Janke

I'm always searching for the bridges that allow people to participate. Sometimes the most effective way to build a bridge . . . is to meet the basic physical needs of another human being.

—Vivian IronHeart

"I was nine years old when I left the Indian Reservation to help my sister take care of her children on the army post in Denver, Colorado. During my three-month stay, I noticed how equally everyone was treated. People from all cultures worked side by side. I was tired of standing outside and looking in, which is how I felt when trying to be with people off the 'res.' in other situations.

"Although I was young, I was already weary of the stereotype image portraying Indian girls as dumb, with nothing to offer. During my stay, I grew to believe that I had as much to offer as anyone else and I was as smart as anyone else.

"When I got home, I started reading everything about my culture that I could find at the school and town library. The more I read, the more convinced I became that my culture was rich beyond measure. I was excited that this was my heritage. However, I was left with one burning question: 'Where did this beautiful culture and all its traditions go?'

"When I asked my Dakota father about our lack of Indian cultural practices, he said, 'Your mother and I decided it would be best to raise our family without practicing our ways because we have been persecuted for our beliefs and traditions. We felt you children would be safer and have a better chance at life.'

"Not only was I angry and sad about losing our beautiful culture, but I was sad for my dad, who I knew longed to live his life differently. As he rose to go out and do the farm chores, my heart ached for him, for me, and for our people.

"Not too long after that conversation, his back gave out. All the years of farming had taken its toll, and he had to quit. To my surprise he started making pipes for Indian ceremonies and we started going to pow-wows so he could sell them. As he sat with the singers and drummers, my mother and I noticed how happy he was. The medicine men began to have great respect for him and searched him out. They would talk by the campfire into the early hours of the morning. As I listened, I learned things that I couldn't find in any books. My Dakota, German, Irish, Scottish mother made me beautiful dance outfits for the pow-wows. While I danced, she visited with the older women. We all loved being there and always stayed until the last person went home.

"When I graduated from high school, I wanted to go to college, but the guy I was dating at the time wanted to get married before he shipped out to the Vietnam War. I was reluctant, but my dad convinced me to marry him by saying, 'Maybe something will happen to him and you'll always regret that you didn't get married.' A few days later we were married and within a few months I was pregnant. I had our first child while he was overseas. When he came back I became pregnant again.

"He never was 'right' after he returned from the war. Drinking became his refuge. Hitting me one time too many was the reason for our divorce. Shortly thereafter, he had a nervous breakdown and was hospitalized. When he got out, he came to visit the children once in awhile. On his last visit, he told us he was going to California to join the Marines. He said, 'The armed forces is the only place I feel comfortable.' Several months later, we heard he went swimming while intoxicated and drowned. Meanwhile, I needed to take care of my children and get a job with more pay. I decided to go to college under the American Indian Education Act.

"Things were progressing well until my third year, when I started to do 'social drinking.' I liked how it made me feel, and before I knew it, I needed to drink. I spun out of control. I couldn't believe this was happening to me.

"I dropped out of college and moved to Minneapolis, Minnesota, where I got a job as a teacher's aide in a public school. I had settled for less than what I wanted, but this job afforded me the opportunity to bring Indian kids closer to their culture.This new work became my passion.

"Near the end of my first year, I decided I needed to put myself in treatment because I wasn't able to quit drinking on my own. My desire to be a better mom and a role model to the Indian students is what saved me, along with my supportive boss who gave me a leave of absence. For a year, I couldn't visit my parents because my father believed it was shameful to ask for help and felt I should just come home to achieve sobriety. They did give their support, however, by taking care of my children while I fought the battle of alcohol.

"After treatment, I returned to school, happy to see my Indian students. It distressed me that many of these kids knew little about our rich history and weren't practicing any of our traditions. Quite a few were not reading or doing well in school. As I began to share my cultural heritage, they began to talk about things they had never shared with anyone else. They were hungry for their identity, and being with another Native American helped them remember who they were.

"Since I was a teacher's aide, I didn't have full classroom responsibility, and it was disappointing to see teachers presenting diversity lessons just because they were part of their job descriptions. I took the Child Development Technician's test so I could be a paraprofessional and join the team in planning more cultural opportunities. I designed a Native American cultural studies elective. I taught kids the importance of keeping their culture alive and the reasons people developed their traditions. They began to understand how our rituals and ceremonies can sustain and nurture, especially in difficult times.

"The first thing I did in my class was to tell my students to go home and find out what tribe they belonged to. We studied all of them. I took the kids to pow-wows, had picnics in my backyard, and took them swimming. I wanted to open their eyes to the possibilities of the world, so they would become motivated to be the best they could be.

"I taught my seventh and eighth graders to read so they could explore their culture through the written word. Slowly but surely, they became smarter and prouder to be Native Americans. They were captivated by the stories I had heard from the medicine men. They learned about my

Photo courtesy of Vivian IronHeart

Vivian IronHeart models a traditional Dakota dress she made for herself.

grandfather's bravery when he risked his life to keep Indians from being slaughtered by leading them to Canada, and they learned that's why we have a large settlement of Dakota there to this day.

"Since I was teaching some things that weren't in the school's history books, the other teachers eventually reported me to the principal for 'making Europeans look bad.' When the principal came to observe my class for himself, I was tempted to go back to the history books for the day, but decided, 'the hell with it,' and proceeded like I always did—telling history from the Native American perspective. He observed the entire period, walked out, and didn't say a word. At the next staff meeting, he said he had been to my class and saw nothing wrong with what I was teaching and, furthermore, he didn't want to hear another word about it.

"Later, I became concerned that harsher punishment was given to Native American kids when they got into trouble for doing the same things other kids were doing. I knew something had to be done, so I made a proposal. I said I would write out behavior contracts with the children to hold them accountable for their behavior, but in turn I asked the other teachers to focus on helping them rather than simply punishing them. I soon earned a reputation for being effective with even the most rebellious kids. Over time, the staff was solving problems with kids instead of just sending them to the office.

"Leonard, one of the most rebellious students of all, showed such gentleness to the younger children when I gave him the job to tutor them in reading. The other teachers began to see him in a new light. Leonard began to see himself as someone who had something to give to his community.

"Because I've never been afraid to speak my mind, I'm in a good position to help people get closer to truth and see something different. I am able to build bridges between the minority and dominant cultures.

"It's important to help kids build bridges with each other. One day, I asked my black students why they were so afraid of Indians. It was obvious to me that they were by the way they were talking and acting. A black youth said, 'They are cold. They could kill you and not change the expression on their face.' We gradually broke down the stereotypes by creating honest dialogues and getting to know each other.

"Sometimes, the most effective way to build a bridge, I found, is to meet the basic physical needs of another human being. I had put up a sign reminding students to bring five dollars for our planned ski trip. Willie, as usual, gave a sneer and said he didn't want to go to any dumb ski party. The kids thought Willie was being his big bad ugly self again but I noticed he hadn't been wearing a winter jacket when he came in the building. I knew his mother was drinking again and that his father had long ago abandoned him. It was likely he didn't have a jacket to wear skiing. I couldn't blame him for his attitude. Who would want to admit such a reality? On my next payday, I went to the store and bought him a jacket, gloves, and scarf. I secretly put the bag in his cubby along with the five dollars. When he saw the bag, he told the kids he had changed his mind and thought the ski trip was a cool idea.

He was wounded from the poverty, alcoholism, and abandonment, but underneath he was like any other kid. He wanted to go skiing. He just needed the opportunity to participate.

"Unaddressed woundedness makes it hard to be a decent kid. Helping Indian kids find their identity as an Indian gives them strength. I tell them it is okay to be loved. Never be ashamed for who you are . . . that is what will hold you.

"Individual survival and cultural survival are hard work, and I'm very tired now. My hope is that the children I've worked with will take what was given to them and pass it on. I'm proud of my two nieces who have been interested in learning the Dakota ways and bringing them to their children and the community.

"I recently had the opportunity to become an adopted grandmother to a young Native American girl, who doesn't have any connection with her native culture. The circle of life goes on, as I continue to honor my father's dying wish, 'Pass the culture on, Vivian. Don't let it slip away.'"

Vivian IronHeart serves in a leadership role with the American Indian Advisory Council on Alcoholism and also started a Women's Talking Circle in her community so. As Vivian puts it, "We need to heal ourselves when life has been harsh." Vivian and some Indian women have reclaimed the "Maiden Ceremony" for the adolescent girls in their community. The women teach the girls Indian ways for a three-year period. At the end of their studies, the girls are taken to a high hill for their right-of-passage ceremony, fully aware of what it means to be Indian and what it means to be strong.

Questions for Contemplation:

1. With what stereotype images of your own or other cultures have you struggled? What have you found to be effective in building bridges of deeper understanding?
2. Have you experienced obstacles in practicing your traditions, language, rituals, or ceremonies? If so, what has helped you to overcome these obstacles?
3. What traditions, ceremonies, and rituals sustain and comfort you? What are you doing to pass them on to the next generation?
4. How can each tradition most effectively and most immediately demonstrate its respect for other traditions?
5. How are we to build urgently needed bridges between and among religious and spiritual traditions, communities, and leaders?

Resources for Reflection and Action:

Look to the Mountain: An ecology of indigenous education, by Gregory Cajete, Ph.D. (Skyland, NC: Kivaki Press, 1994). Dr. Cajete not only remains respectful of his traditions, but he outlines the urgent need for utilizing the indigenous worldview in contemporary society.

The Education of Little Tree, by Forrest Carter (Albuquerque, New Mexico: University of New Mexico Press, 1993). An inspirational, autobiographical remembrance of a young Indian boy that provides a fresh perspective for a mechanistic and materialistic modern world.

Culturally Responsive Teaching: Theory, research, and practice, by Geneva Gay (NYC: Multicultural Education Series, 2000). The author makes a convincing case for using culturally responsive teaching to improve the school performance of underachieving students of color. She demonstrates how Native American, African, Asian, and Latino students will perform better, on multiple measures of achievement when teaching is filtered through their own cultural experiences and frames of reference.

Lame Deer Seeker of Visions, by John Lame Deer (Washington Square, 1994). The personal narrative of a Sioux medicine man reveals his way of life, his role as a holy man among the Lakota, and his relationship with whites.

Multicultural Education: Issues and perspectives, edited by James A. Banks & Cherry A. McGee Banks (Needham Heights, MA: Allyn and Bacon, 1993). This book shows how to move beyond a "tourist" approach to multicultural education.

Grandmothers Wisdom Keepers. Wisdom Keepers, Box 20665 Knoxville, TN 37920. Phone: 423-573-4030. Provides mentoring program for girls ages six to eighteen, giving them the opportunity to learn the ways of Native American women and to pass on that wisdom to others through sharing and education.

Angeles Arrien Foundation for Cross-Cultural Education and Research, PO Box 1278, Sausalito, CA 94966. Phone: 415-331-1890. Fax: 415-331-5069. Integrates the wisdom of indigenous peoples into contemporary culture by honoring their oral traditions, arts, myths, and deep respect for nature. The foundation introduces activities that enhance creativity and creative problem-solving, develop communication and leadership skills from a cross-cultural perspective, and explore community building and multicultural conflict resolution.

Four Part Harmony | LARRY LONG

by Burt Berlowe

... Today, more than ever before, the troubadour's songs are essential to the survival of that part of us that is both universal and unique ... The troubadour must stay on the road, must come into a community ... and give it back its own character and experiences ... we need the troubadour to find songs in our lives. The troubadour ... will leave us changed in that we will be more ourselves than ever before.

—Madonna Hettinger, Assistant Professor of Medieval History, College of Wooster Ohio

On an early April day in 1968, youthful Larry Long burst through the door of his home, hungry for dinner and some family time.

Throughout his childhood, Larry had always enjoyed the hours he spent with family members. In grade school, he had worked part-time at his grandfather's fish market. He also helped his grandpa pass out Bibles on street corners and at front doors on the Eastside of Des Moines, Iowa. Sometimes Larry went on the road with his father, a traveling salesman, setting up coffee displays in corner grocery stores in Iowa and Minnesota.

Those happy memories had been tempered by violence and tragedy that had recently struck close to home during the turbulent 1960s: the rape and murder of an eight-year-old cousin, the loss of his father at when Larry was thirteen, the assassination of President John F. Kennedy, racial riots, Kent State, the Vietnam War—all of which filled Larry with confusion and anger. Two things had pulled him through those difficult days: his music and the quiet moments with his family. He was looking forward to both as he came home on that spring evening.

But Larry had barely entered the house when the loud blaring of the TV in the next room had caught his attention. Instead of being in the kitchen for the traditional family dinner, everyone was gathered around the set. Larry peered into the room as a somber newscaster repeated the words:

"The Reverend Martin Luther King was assassinated today while standing on a hotel balcony in Memphis . . ."

Larry listened in stunned silence. Although he was a white suburbanite, he had worshipped Dr. King and had been moved by his words and actions. He recalled storming to his room and picking up his guitar, his rage and sorrow pouring out with his furious strumming and singing. His spontaneous songwriting had helped him vent his deep sorrow that words alone could never express.

Larry's music was a way to soothe and release his complex feelings. It had been that way ever since he began sitting next to his mother at the piano while she played at their Baptist Church.

When he wasn't playing his own music, Larry loved listening to the Beatles, Tim Buckley, and Miles Davis, or spending time with Woody Guthrie's book *Bound For Glory,* which he read over and over again. That book changed his life.

"Woody struck me in a big way. He had been through a lot of hardship, yet he sang that we were bound for glory. He was always the optimist. I wanted to be like Guthrie, a troubadour, traveling around, singing songs for common people everywhere.

"I was moved by Martin Luther King because I was raised in a strong Christian family. I realized that you couldn't separate the teachings of Jesus from Dr. King. And what made King so powerful was that he took the principles from old biblical text and brought them into present-day practice. He made people feel that they were on an ancient mission of justice motivated by faith. He pointed out that you can't separate people's faith from their actions. King touched me as a child. He still does."

The teachings of Guthrie, King, and Jesus shaped Larry's beliefs and actions. He practiced their principles of peaceful protest while he was still in high school. In 1969, a devastating flood hit the St. Croix River near Afton, Minnesota. The town needed help sandbagging the shores. Larry and 100 students ignored the admonitions of their school principal, cut classes, and traveled in vans to the flood area to help battle the waters. When they returned, the principal kicked the project organizer out of school and threatened to do the same to the rest of the group.

"We did a twelve-hour sit-down strike in the principal's office and vowed to stay there until the student organizer was readmitted. We contacted the mayor of Afton and told him we were going to get kicked out of school for saving his town. He contacted the governor, who in turn contacted the principal and convinced him to readmit our student organizer. It was my first taste of effective nonviolent action but not my last."

Larry became a conscientious objector, refusing to go to war. He not only counseled others contemplating the draft but he made friends with

Vietnam veterans, "who came back from the war and wanted to make a difference in the world."

Larry ultimately chose to make a difference, too, through his music. One particular song he wrote and recorded became his signature statement on peacemaking:

If someone strikes, I won't strike back
If they strike again, I will not attack
I'd rather talk than hear bones crack
I don't believe in violence...

Living in Minneapolis, Minnesota, Larry became concerned about the welfare of the Mississippi River. After joining Pete Seeger on the Hudson River on a sloop called the Clearwater, he became inspired to organize people to save his own river. He had learned a lot from Pete's efforts. With the help of other singers and community members, Pete drew attention not only to the river's environment, but also to its cultural history through song, poetry, and storytelling.

Pete began by picking up cans and cigarette butts along the banks of the mighty Hudson. It wasn't long until he was reaching underneath the legs of local fishermen to get at the litter. Soon, the fishermen stopped fishing and started picking up garbage, too. Without saying a word, everybody started pitching in until that small stretch of river was cleaned up. Seeger's actions, based upon principle, and the belief in the common good, affected Larry's work back home.

Larry and some friends started the Mississippi River Revival, a series of hometown festivals that

Photo by Andrew Goetz

Larry Long

combined celebration with environmental awareness. "We used festivals to organize people to do cleanup," he recalls. "One summer, we had twenty festivals. A bunch of us at the Revival hauled hundreds of thousands of tons of trash off the river and recycled it. Our work contributed to creation of the Minnesota's Clean Rivers Act.

"Little did I know then how rivers would continue to be places to work for peace. Because of my work on the revival, I was invited to go on a peace cruise on the Mississippi and Volga Rivers (in the former Soviet Union) with a United States Navy admiral, Russian cosmonaut, and clergy and laity from both sides. I was a cultural ambassador for the United States. We sang along the way and came off the boat singing. Afterward, I realized that I was part of some very important efforts, from helping to restore the Mississippi to helping put an end to the Cold War.

"It was elsewhere along the river that I discovered a deeper meaning to my work. I was broke, so I went down to Nashville to peddle songs. There, I met Dr. Jack Shelton, a university professor and Methodist minister, who organized health and food fairs in Alabama. The group he was with hired me to help the farmers organize so they could sell their products directly and get fair market value. We thought church parking lots would be the perfect place to display produce, but the churches were resistant. I believed that all I had to do was convince one local minister to open his lot, play my music while the farmers sold their goods, and the rest would take care of itself. Sure enough, soon, all the church parking lots in town were opened. With no middleman, the farmers were finally able to get fair prices. If it weren't for music, it wouldn't have happened. Music has this incredible power. When used at the right place and right moment, it creates a world of possibilities where none existed before."

Once again, Larry was inspired to write about his experiences:

Food Fair
Where the farmers and the people
Don't need a middleman.
Food Fair
Where the farmers and the people
Work together hand in hand . . .

"Because of the success of the food fair organizing, and my work with school age children in Woody Guthrie's hometown of Okemah, Oklahoma, I was hired by the University of Alabama to work with their PACERS Small Schools Cooperative program, called 'Better Schools Building Better Communities.' The cooperative included twenty-seven public schools in twenty-four rural Alabama communities. Our goals were to develop new and improved curricula for rural schools, help the children connect to others in the community, and develop a deep connection to a 'place.' I got to use all the components of my previous work: education, community organizing, and celebration.

"Four groups were necessary to achieve our goals—elders, students, teachers, and residents of the community. To begin, I asked the local elders to visit the classrooms. They told their stories as well as talked about the skills they had needed in order to make their lives work. The children, teachers, and I then turned the information into songs that honored the elders. Students gained a better understanding of their community and developed relationships and attachments to the elders that they didn't have before. History came alive. Through the face-to-face conversations with elders, students became more aware of how people dealt with difficult challenges. Students also gained a new feeling of competence from creating quality music and poetry. Much of what we did was recorded on the compact disc, *Here I Stand: Elders' Wisdom, Children's Song*.

"The children's work was presented to the rest of the community through performances in schools, churches, and town halls. We had huge celebrations—it was not uncommon to have five hundred to one thousand people show up.

"One student in the town of Sunshine, Alabama, who had been struggling with drugs and been kicked out of school, became part of our group. Once he became connected to the elders and got involved in creating music and poetry, he turned his life around.

"In doing this work, I know I'm part of something sacred, something much greater than myself. The work brings together everything I have ever done, and everything I have ever believed in—it gives me hope."

The impact of these songs was summarized by one of the elders, Lewis Martin, Jr. of Camp Hill, Alabama. He said, "I never would have dreamed that I would've seen the day in the days that I'm in now to see how young people could go back and make a song out of what I said the other day. And I'm glad that God has saw fit for our young peoples, black and white, (to find) a better way in the world today. I'm just so happy I could cry."

Through his work, Larry has helped build bridges between generations; between war veterans and peace activists; and between people of different cultures, complexions, and economic classes.

"I was considered a protest singer for decades. I sang at a lot of rallies about problems in the world. I marched against the Vietnam War (although not against the veterans who fought it). I wrote songs to help stop a high voltage power line from being built through central Minnesota. I rode shotgun on a family farmer tractorcade to Washington, DC, singing all the way, to draw attention to the farm crisis and help pass federal legislation to insure fair prices for those who produce our food. One time, when I was on trial for civil disobedience, I started singing on the witness stand. The judge said, 'There'll be no singing in my courtroom.' I spent the following weekend in jail, reading Gandhi.

"I no longer consider myself a protest singer. I work to affirm the best of who we are as people, not the worst. For one to learn, one must question. The best way to teach and to learn is to question. To simply protest is reactive. How long can you be against something before you destroy yourself? The problem with political movements is they're so rooted in the negative. I'm more interested in the positive—in what's proactive. We have to create, with intention, models of compassion that can be replicated by others.

"The model I developed, 'Elders' Wisdom, Children's Song', is, by intention, intergenerational and culturally rooted in the belief that in order to build community, one must first listen to the stories of those who came before, while working to create a better world with and for the children.

"After all, the co-op farm movement, the labor movement, and the civil rights movement all began with and were sustained by stories of injustice that were handed down through generations. These stories prompted people to action."

It was during a recent trip to Montgomery, Alabama, that Larry found his way back to Martin Luther King. He was staging a concert where students were performing music pieces based on elders' stories. Trusty guitar cradled in his slender arms, a harmonica slung around his neck, his brown cowboy boots stomping the floor, Larry embraced and engaged the crowd. At the end, everybody joined hands singing.

Afterwards, Joe Nathan, visiting from the Center for School Change at the University of Minnesota, spoke to Larry. He quoted from King's "I Have A Dream" speech made in Montgomery—the part where King dreams of a day when black boys and girls would be holding hands with white boys and girls. "It was at that moment, that I realized what happened that day," Larry says, "We were the fulfillment of the King prophecy."

"Music is an integral part of life, not separate from it, but an extension of it. It's also a way to learn and discover."

Larry Long

Questions for Contemplation:

1. Larry plays guitar to soothe his troubled mind. What constructive activity provides a refuge for you?
2. What part, if any, have you or your family played in antiwar or civil rights protests?
3. Larry says, "Our consumer-based culture is based on separating people from so many things—their faith, their cultural upbringing, their class. I believe all people need to connect. By stepping outside of that culture, we can link people with their roots and with each other." Do you agree? What are some benefits of stepping outside of the "consumer-based culture?" What are some ways you can do so?
4. Larry believes in the power of stories to make connections across generations. What is a story about yourself you'd like to share with others? What can people learn about you from your story that they didn't know before?
5. Larry says he's not a "protest singer" because protesters are against something. He doesn't want to focus on what he's against, but rather, what he is for. What have you been against? How can you reframe it into a statement of what you are for?

Resources for Reflection and Action:

Elders' Wisdom, Children's Song, by Larry Long & Jim Fanning (Tuscaloosa, AL: Pacers Small Schools Cooperative Program for Rural Services and Research, 205 University Blvd., Box 870372, 1999). This curriculum guidebook for elementary teachers helps students learn to celebrate their community and life in it, get to know local elders, and work with their creativity to write and perform music.

Larry Long has also recorded *My House is Your House* (Washington, DC: Smithsonian Folkways Children's Music Connection, 1998), *Run for Freedom, Sweet*, (Thunder, Cambridge, MA: Flying Fish Records, 1997), *Here I Stand, Elders' Wisdom, Children's Song*, (Washington, DC: Smithsonian Folkways, 1997), *Living in a Rich Man's World*, (Minneapolis, MN: Atomic Theory, 106 W 49th St., Minneapolis, MN 55400, 1995).

Troubadour, CD recording (Cambridge, MA: Flying Fish, 1992), and *It Takes a Lot of People*, CD recording (Tribute to Woody Guthrie), by Larry Long (Cambridge, MA: Flying Fish, 1988).

Everybody Says Freedom, by Pete Seeger and Bob Reiser (NYC: W.W. Norton, 1989). This is a classic portrait of the music of the civil rights movement. Through moving photographs and interviews with leaders of the movement, we discover how song inspired a generation of courageous black and white Americans to join hands in guiding a multiracial society.

Rise up Singing, by Peter Blood (Highlander Research and Education Center, 1959 Highlander Way, New Market, TN, 37820. Phone: 865-933-3443). Consists of lyrics, chords, and sources for over 1200 songs that work especially well in group singing. Good music for promoting social justice.

A Public Peace Process: Sustained dialogue to transform racial and ethnic conflicts, by Harold Saunders (NYC: St. Martin's Press, 1999). Those who believe that something more, something different, something radical has to be done in order to move us away from approaches to addressing human interaction that do not get at the roots of the issues will find support and real how-to information.

My Backyard History Book: an activity-filled resource guide for third through sixth graders. (City Lore, 72 East First St., NYC 10003). Encourages an intergenerational approach to learning about the past.

Chapter 3
Community Workers

**Mona Satre, Cindi Claypatch,
Donald Jackson, Jim Janke, V.J. Smith**

Community Workers are compassionate rebels who address the root causes of violence through championing such issues as fairness and justice, health, and community safety. They work on a grass roots, interpersonal level with others and often help people use their strengths in a collective manner. Some, like V. J. Smith and Mona Satre, work in their home communities, while others, like Cindi Claypatch and Donald Jackson, work in communities that they had to make their own.

Acutely aware of people's suffering, they may take up the torch for better access to health care (Cindi Claypatch), safer streets (Donald Jackson or V. J. Smith), more support for teens (Mona Satre), more humane environments (Jim Janke), or other issues. Community workers help people build relationships. They are known for becoming part of the community through their long years of service. They are good at continuing to support people as they make their way from a place of struggle to one of empowerment.

Community Workers tend to approach the "impossible" with undaunted passion. They are convinced that there is a way! Through their efforts, many more citizens are empowered so they, too, can speak up and contribute their talents. Some pursue issues of social justice by helping with grassroots organizing alongside people who have traditionally been underrepresented, while others work behind-the-scenes. Community Workers recognize that families or individuals can't do it alone. They may provide support, much like a member of the extended family, or they may help people make connections to others who can give them the support they need. They frequently work with powerful people in the community—not in opposition to them—recognizing that those people are part of the community, and part of the solution, too!

Destined for Greatness | MONA SATRE

by Rebecca Janke

Everyone has the power for greatness, not for fame, but greatness, because greatness is determined by service.

—Martin Luther King, Jr.

The smell of the Fireman's Corn Roast called eight-year-old Mona and her friend from their play. "Let's go eat," said Mona, anxious to bite into the hot buttered corn. The two girls ran as fast as they could to the firestation yard.

The man at the entrance gate told her, "I'm sorry, young lady, you can't eat with us. Your dad isn't a fireman."

"Ok-a-y," she said, choking back the tears.

"I'll see you later," she said to her friend. It hurt to be excluded, but it distressed her even more that her dad was so different from the rest of the dads in this small, rural Minnesota Norwegian community. He hadn't joined any community organizations and refused to attend gatherings of any kind.

She knew it would do no good to complain when she got home since he had made it clear, time after time, he wasn't about to sit around and chit-chat with people when he could be working on more interesting things such as restoring old artifacts for the museum he wanted to build. She longed for a father who was "normal." Being left out or showing up without him was not her idea what a family should be.

Even though Mona didn't have the kind of dad she thought she wanted, his desire to build a museum from scratch impressed her. She also enjoyed the stories he shared at the kitchen table about philosophers, theologians, outstanding ordinary people, and leaders. However, it was hard to deal with the embarrassment when one old contraption after another for the museum found its way into the back yard for everyone to see.

Mona probably could have learned to live comfortably with her dad if it hadn't been for the men in town who harassed and ridiculed him. Their daily teasing and taunting of him angered her to the bone. She begged him to move to a bigger town where nobody would know them.

He just quietly shook his head and said, "I could never leave this place."

When she asked her mother why her dad couldn't pack up and move, she was shocked by the answer.

"This harassment is nothing compared to the pain he experienced in World War II," she said. "He identified and bagged dead bodies of soldiers before they were shipped home for burial. He got to the point where he couldn't take it anymore. Knowing that each soldier was somebody's dad, husband, son, brother, or uncle became too much for him to bear, and he had a mental breakdown. He was given a medical discharge and sent home. Ever since then, all he's ever wanted to do was to stay put. He has a real fear of ever being away from home again."

With this stunning bit of family news, Mona decided the only way she could cope with the stigma of being in a "weird" family—by everyone else's standards—was to earn recognition on her own.

"Since my dad had been a stellar student all the way through school and had completed a double major in math and business at St. Olaf College, I figured maybe I was smart, too. Starting in seventh grade, I decided to try for the 'A' Honor Roll. I made it and continued to do so every quarter thereafter all the way through my senior year. I went out for all sorts of extracurricular activities, but it was music and my high academic honors that made me stand out in a crowd. I was selected as the school pianist, won one musical award after another, and served as the church organist. Every time I was written up in the local newspaper for my academic or musical achievements, it served as proof, as far as I was concerned, that we were a family that deserved respect.

"My dad beamed with pride to have an accomplished daughter. 'You're destined for greatness,' my dad would often say. 'You are using your mind and talents in ways that other great people have done.'"

As Mona blazed her way to success, she didn't want her dad's tormentors to think she aspired to their definition of "normal." She also didn't want to snub radical kids and do to them what had been done to her father, so she hung out with the "hoods," as well as the "normal" kids.

"I discovered that the 'hoods' were a lot like dad. They questioned life and they weren't interested in going along with the flow," she said. "I felt at home with them.

"I'm particularly glad that my mom provided me a tremendous amount of freedom during this time. I was never told I couldn't hang out with this or that person," said Mona. "Everyone was deserving of empathy and understanding in my mother's eyes. Her ability to walk in another person's shoes made anyone I hung out with interesting to her. Along with my own self-imposed agenda of not wanting to get in trouble and bring shame to myself or my family, she knew I could be trusted to do the 'right' thing, no matter what situation I was in.

"In addition to the free rein, she created opportunities for me to perform my music in public, which helped build my confidence. She offered my musical talents to the nursing home, women's groups, and gatherings of relatives. She had made certain I received the best piano instruction available in Southern Minnesota, even though we had little money. (All the extra funds we had went to building the museum.) She recruited the area's most gifted piano teacher to give lessons in exchange for letting eighteen paying students come to our house every week. Mom told me that all her life she had wanted to learn to play the piano, but her family was too poor and she was regulated to playing the imaginary keys on a windowsill . . . a window with no curtains. She was bound and determined that was not going to happen to her children.

"Even though my dad couldn't attend many of my performances, because crowds made him nervous, Mom always came. After each performance, she would smile from ear to ear and say, 'I'm so proud of you, I could just bust my buttons.' With my parents' support and encouragement, I felt I could do anything. Neither one of them gave me a sense that any of my endeavors were expected. They put no pressure on me. If I failed, I knew it wasn't going to change their love for me.

"When I graduated as the valedictorian of my class and gave the address to a packed auditorium, it was a bittersweet experience. It was the one event that my father would have attended, in spite of his fear of crowds. Unfortunately, he had died of a heart attack the summer before my senior year. The tears flowed when I looked out at the crowd and saw the empty chair next to my mom. 'This one is for you, Dad,' I said to myself.

Photo courtesy of Mona Satre

Mona Satre pauses en route to Sturgess, SD.

"Graduating as valedictorian was the culmination of years of work to prove our family was deserving of respect, but I was exhausted from all my years of effort. Then I met Kenny. He was a breath of fresh air—the most carefree person I had ever met. He wasn't the least bit concerned with what other people thought of him. He was busy enjoying who he was. I found myself spending more and more time with him and gave up a four-year college scholarship to marry a man, who, by small-town standards, was radical.

"However, he was radical in an enjoyable way. One minute he was driving his Harley and hanging out with the biker crowd, and a few days later he was in a business suit making a presentation to top business executives regarding a new grain bin dryer system he had invented. He used humor as effectively as a machinist uses a precision tool, and no matter whom he was with, he could get them to laugh and forget about any of their troubles.

"Even though some his biker friends looked meaner than hell, I didn't hesitate to hang out with them. My years of hanging out with the 'hoods' prepared me for stepping outside the box.

"Kenny couldn't believe that the valedictorian found him worthy, but what I saw was raw intelligence and one of the most well-balanced, mentally healthy people I had ever met. I was ecstatic to be released from my serious self and be surrounded by friends, who would come from far and wide to just sit around our kitchen table, tell stories, and laugh late into the night. He helped me to loosen up and develop a sense of humor. Kenny volunteered to be on all sorts of community committees. We went to the corn roast every year because he was a fireman!

"The birth of our son, Ryan, and six years later, the birth of our daughter, Mandy, made our family complete. Since I had given up on the idea of going to college and becoming trapped in my previous competitive world, I joined Kenny in his work with his grain bin dryer invention. During our test runs, we were able to save tons of grain from spoiling and were on the verge of changing the grain bin drying industry. Our lives were full to brimming and I couldn't have been happier—until the middle of one night when everything came to a crashing halt.

"It was June 10, 1989. A loud knocking on the door woke me from a sound sleep. I was frightened and rolled over to ask Kenny to answer it, but his side of the bed was still empty. 'Where is he?' I thought. 'It's late. Why isn't he home yet?' When I opened the door and saw the police officer and town minister, I instantly knew . . . he wasn't home because something was wrong, very wrong.

"'I'm sorry, Mona. Kenny has been killed while riding his motorcycle,' the minister said.

I remember screaming as I collapsed onto the floor.

"The day of the funeral, the church was packed with people from every walk of life, with several standing outside. I felt so weak from grief that I didn't know how I was going to make it through. Then, I heard the rumbling of Harleys in the distance and within minutes several big strong bikers surrounded me and walked me to the front pew. Kenny had been a tremendous leader, friend, husband, and father—there are no words to describe the sadness that enveloped us.

"As the military gun salute went off to honor Kenny as a Vietnam vet, and one person after another looked at me with tear-stained cheeks, I wondered why his life was snuffed out instead of that of the drunk driver that hit him. I was filled with rage at the injustice of it all, but the sadness of not being able to share my life with him took over my entire being.

"After the funeral, I made my way back home where the bikers had a spread of food prepared for us. A soft, misty rain began to fall. While we were reminiscing about Kenny's life, someone said, 'Mona, it stopped raining. Come and see the double rainbow.'

"Everyone who saw it came away with the same message . . . he was letting us know that he had made it to the other side. His mother had committed suicide when he was eighteen to end the pain from a severe illness, and it looked like his rainbow was tucked right under hers. It came down into the ditch where he had been killed. The rainbow made us all smile, in spite of our grief, because he had always joked that when he died it would be his job to man the stream of light that prayers travel on because of his electrical engineering skills.

"Within days, my loneliness became overwhelming. Although I was glad both kids were in school and was relieved of attending to their needs for a few hours each day, it drove me nuts to be in the house alone. Sometimes I would hear a sound that sounded like Kenny was coming home, and then I would go through the trauma all over again realizing, 'No. He's not coming home. He's never coming home.' To keep from losing my mind, I turned to an old friend—my music. Even though I had my music by day and my kids by night, I still found myself contemplating suicide.

"Just when I didn't think I could stand the pain any further, the school from which I had graduated as valedictorian, was listed for sale. My dad's love for preserving old things surfaced in me. I purchased it with the intent of creating the community's first teen center. Even though I was mired in depression, I had been noticing that more and more of the kids in our community were resorting to drinking and drugs for entertainment. With Ryan about to turn thirteen, I wanted to do something that would lessen the chances of him dying. I knew I couldn't face another death. I felt teens needed a place to hang out, enjoy their music, and be themselves. I was determined it wasn't going to be a goody-two-shoes place. I knew the radical kids wouldn't show up and it was they that traditional programming leaves out whenever the community steps in to help kids.

"The one thing that I've learned over the years is that radical people, whether kids or adults, don't want to be part of the mainstream. They don't fit in and they don't want to fit in. I wanted the center to be a place where they would be accepted for who they were and I was convinced, that, as my dad used to say, they would 'rally to greatness.'

"Kenny began to appear to me in dreams and say he was proud of my efforts and that he would do everything he could do to help me. At first, I was frightened that he had found a way to communicate, but it turned out to be so comforting that I didn't want his visits to end. Each time I ran into an obstacle, he would come and give me a message, or just the right people would show up. Somehow, within a few months the teen center was up and running.

"I combined the image of the rainbow at his funeral with our mission to be a bridge to radical kids and named our organization 'Rainbow Bridge.'

"Ryan was old enough to be involved in the business-end of things and learned right alongside me how to make presentations to the community, do marketing calls, order equipment, book bands, run sound and lighting equipment, and be a DJ. Mandy was busy running around and playing in our old abandoned building and helping make it sparkle and shine. We slowly became a functioning family again with a reason to get up in the morning.

"The fear that many community members initially voiced about having 'those kind of kids' hanging out in a large group crumbled when we were able to report that not one fight had erupted nor had one arrest been made in our first six months. Most adults are afraid of at-risk teens. They don't know how to be with kids who are radical and fed up with the system. The more adults don't listen, pay attention, or take them seriously, the more they act out with rage, or succumb to depression, bulimia, anorexia, or suicide.

"Luckily, I had all the years in the biker world to prepare me for outrageous clothing styles, pierced everything, and threatening looks. As a matter of fact, people who are intent on being themselves have come to fascinate me. Consequently, I was able to get things out of those kids that they had never given to other adults. They knew I understood their need to be different.

"There are lots of kids who don't feel connected to their community, but they do have dreams. When they pursue their dreams in a healthy way, they can find an alternative connection to the mainstream. When I asked the kids what they wanted to name the center, they unanimously chose 'Utopia.'

"I believe that instead of trying to reroute these kids, we need to follow their path. At Utopia, we didn't deny who they were. Kids learned that it was a place that took them seriously. For example, when a group of teens approached the city council to help them build a skate park, they were denied. They came to Utopia and, together, we built one. They worked hour after hour and night after night. We went on to serve as hosts for skateboarding championship games.

"When Josh, our eighteen-year-old night manager, learned that eleven-year-old Tony, who came to the skatepark often, was struggling with cancer, he took it upon himself to call the national skateboarding champions in California and asked if they would come and do a fund-raiser. Josh had dropped out of high school after school authorities constantly hounded him not to be carrying a backpack. They had heard he was carrying a weapon, but when they searched him, they found nothing. It was bad enough that he had to carry his supplies by hand, but when he was told that he would not graduate, he knew they didn't have his best interests in mind. After dropping out, he got up an extra hour early and drove to an alternative school in another city. He graduated right on schedule.

"Here was a guy the community didn't have much time for, yet his heart was full of determination and compassion to make Tony's last days as meaningful as possible.

"The California skateboarding champions made a detour trip to our small town, on their way to Japan to film a commercial. They spent the entire evening giving Tony and all his friends one of the best skateboarding performances they had ever seen. Tony watched in amazement, as they raced up the ramp 'getting air' while the oxygen tank on his now frail body gave him his air. The next morning, the team came to take Tony out for breakfast and gave him a top-of-the-line skateboard. When it was time to say goodbye, Tony's father looked at Josh with tears in his eyes and said, 'Thank you, Josh, for making my son's dream come true.'

"Tony continued to deteriorate and was up to twenty cc's of morphine per day to combat the pain. The end was near. One day, he walked into the family kitchen, sat down and announced to his dad that he wanted to go to Utopia one more time.

"'Tony, how is that possible? It's so difficult for you to breathe,' his father said with grave concern.

"'I can do it, Dad. Look at me,' and he ran around the kitchen table five times.

"When Tony arrived, the kids all took turns sitting with him on the couch and sharing the latest news of their teen world. Tony was grinning from ear to ear . . . happy to be back among the swirl and whirl of his skateboarding friends.

"A few weeks later, we lost a major gambling site that helped fund our center. We had no choice but to close the doors of Utopia—after a six-year presence in the community. As I made the final preparations to close our doors, I thought, 'Wouldn't it be ironic if Tony died today? I opened the center because of Kenny's death . . . would I be closing it on Tony's day to die?' Later in the day, I learned that just as I had been walking out the door and turning the key, Tony died.

"The day of his death I cried all afternoon, not only because we had lost Tony, but we had lost a place that had meant the world to Tony and all the other kids. Tony wasn't the first person we had supported during our stay. The kids always had a way of sniffing out who was suffering or struggling in some sort of way and then finding ways to lift them up or try to help remedy their plight.

"Through my tears, my fathers' words came back to me, 'You are destined for greatness.' And then I realized my greatness lies in my ability to see greatness in others when some believed there was none. For me, it isn't about becoming famous . . . it's about positioning my life to help young radical kids tap into their greatness. I've witnessed the power of their ideas, anger, creativity, and compassion. I believe they have important things to say and offer, and we shouldn't be crushing them into compliance. They are compassionate rebels in the making and are destined for greatness, too."

Questions for Contemplation:

1. In what way(s) are you or someone in your family "different?" How do you stand out from the crowd? What greatness would you like people to see in you?
2. Mona has strong opinions about at-risk youth and insights about how to listen to them and work with them to help them reach their potential. What "insights" do you have that you would like to bring forward?
3. How do you react to radical youth? Why? What could you offer in terms of support?
4. Mona lost both her father and husband. Whom have you loved and lost? What impact did this have on you?
5. Do you believe that someone who died can communicate with you? What comforting messages or "help" have they provided?

Resources for Reflection and Action:

Sitting in the Fire by Arnold Mindell (Portland, OR: Lao Tse Press, 1995). One of the worlds' most gifted group facilitators shows how attention to power and rank helps build sustainable groups/communities. His groundbreaking approach demonstrates how to stay centered and further the group's/community's development while sitting in the fire of conflict and diversity.

The Power of Their Ideas by Deborah Meier (Boston, MA: Beacon Press, 1995). Meier pledges her faith "in the extraordinary untapped capacities of all our children" and shows why a new and different form of public school is no longer a luxury.

A School for Healing: Alternative strategies for teaching at-risk students, by Rosa Kennedy and Jerome Morton (NYC: Peter Lang, 1999). This program won the best-practice award for those working with at-risk youth.

The Disciplined Mind, by Howard Gardner (NYC: Simon and Schuster, 1999). Not only for educators but also for all those interested in the human mind, behavior, morality, and social well-being of adolescents.

New Moon Magazine: The magazine for girls and their dreams (Duluth: New Moon Publishing, PO Box 3620, Duluth, MN 55803). This magazine is for young women who wish to be leaders. Website: www.newmoon.org.

The Center for Emerging Leadership, 4658 Cascade Beach Road, Lutsen, MN 55612-9519. Website: www.emergingleadership.com. For women leaders.

Giraffe Project, PO Box 759, Langley, WA 98260. Phone: 360-221-7989. Their Heroes Program is a k-12 character education curriculum that teaches courageous compassion and active citizenship by telling students the stories of real-life heroes. Website: www.giraffe.org.

Hear My Story

By Julie Penshorn

You want me to change and you tell me I must
I'm such a rebel; I'm causing a fuss.
You want me to stop but you really don't know
How inside my heart is churning, burning,
Inside my heart is aching, breaking.
I can't change. I can't change!
Listen to me when I say,
"I can't change."
'Cause no one has taken the time or the care,
No one has made the space anywhere,
No one has offered the listening ear
Loved without judging and held me near
So I say: "I can't change."
But then, I have a story to tell,
I have some hurt deep inside.
I have a story; I'm living with history,
So listen, don't talk, don't fix (It's a story!)
Compassionately, I will tell my story
Then I'll decide, how I change.
Shhh! Please, just listen.

Peace from the Inside Out | CINDI CLAYPATCH

by Burt Berlowe

You must give birth to your images. They are the future waiting to be born . . . fear not the strangeness you feel. The future must enter into you long before it happens.

—Rainer Maria Rilke

Cindi Claypatch cautiously walked toward the community center in the middle of the low-income housing project in north Minneapolis. As she looked at the rundown, dingy neighborhood around her, she felt apprehensive, as well as excited, about what lay ahead.

Bleak brick buildings grimaced at each other across narrow, untended streets. A few children of color ran barefoot amidst broken bottles and debris—supervised minimally by parents who snuck an occasional peek from behind a half-open curtain.

Once occupied primarily by African-Americans, the Glenwood-Lyndale community had become home to many new Asian immigrants. Its resident families were poor, undereducated and, in many cases, struggling to adjust to a different culture. Although their two-story rowhouses almost hugged each other, next-door neighbors often seemed distant from one another, isolated from any sense of community and frightened of the hazards of the street.

As she moved past the shabby rowhouses, residents slammed their doors and drew their shades. Those she met turned away or simply frowned and looked past her. Cindi shuddered at the challenge confronting her, a middle-class white woman, hoping to have a positive impact in this deprived multicultural neighborhood.

Photo by Todd Cota

Cindi Claypatch shares a smile with Glenwood-Lyndale children.

To counteract her anxiety, Cindi called upon her trusty secret tool. She greeted each suspicious stare with an engaging smile that beckoned others to her side and assured them that everything would be okay. The smile warmed her face, radiated through her, lifted her spirits, and quickened her step.

The warmth and self-confidence that emanated from Cindi that day came from deep inside—a product of her past experience and beliefs. "I come from a family that values love, common sense, and responsibility," she says. "My parents said, 'We were poor in money, but rich in love.' There was a real family feeling we had growing up. My parents created an incredible feeling of love and support. Mom believed that you had to let go of things that bothered you, that we all have an internal power that is there when we need it.

"We were taught to believe in ourselves, to be good listeners, to value people rather than money, and to stand up for what we believed in, while trusting our internal power to be there when we needed it. Because of that, I was free to question things, including our Catholic religion. I was not afraid of saying or doing what was on my mind.

"In junior high, I followed peer pressure and dabbled in drugs for a while. I soon questioned my own ethics and quit using, only to later struggle with a co-dependent relationship with a chemical abuser. After that, I went to the northern part of Minnesota to live in a cabin and learn to fend for myself. I always had a sense of wanderlust, of wanting to know about other places and cultures."

Upon her return to Minneapolis, Minnesota, Cindi found her calling. While working with people with chemical addiction and mental illness, she became concerned that, "No one knew where to put people who didn't fit into traditional therapy programs." She was also angry that most programs focused on a 'sickness' model rather than a 'wellness' model. She wanted to try an approach called the Health Realization Model, which presupposes that a person's mental status can create and shape how they perceive reality. It assumes that if people have a good feeling about themselves, and can clear out the 'static in the attic' (calm their minds), they can rise above their circumstances, put the past in its place, leave it there, and become new and better people. Her commitment to this radical approach put her at odds with mainstream psychology.

When she applied for the job of Health and Wellness Program Specialist at the Glenwood-Lyndale Community Center, Cindi thought she would finally have a chance to implement the Health Realization Model. But instead of being hired immediately, she encountered some reluctance. Some of her interviewers wondered how she expected herself as a white, middle-class woman to work effectively in a community dominated by minorities on fixed incomes. She responded, "When you have an understanding that connects people at the core, it doesn't matter what the differences are."

But being hired was only the beginning of Cindi's struggle to adjust and be accepted. "When I first came here, it was tough," she now recalls. "Gangs were active in the area. Buildings were run-down. It felt so unsafe that I carried mace on my key chain. It appeared the residents had very little trust in the Glendale-Lyndale Community Center staff. They had seen many staff come and go with their ideas for 'fixing' people rather than dealing with their potential."

At first, residents hesitated to come to Cindi's Health Realization parent groups. When they did, it was always with a dose of skepticism. As her students got to know her better and realized the benefits of Health Realization, she won their trust and confidence, and they allowed her to work with them.

Cindi's leadership and persistence influenced Glenwood-Lyndale to renew itself from within. The Community Center where Cindi works has been an integral part of the neighborhood's about-face, turned from an aging, neglected facility into a gleaming model of freshness and vigor. It is the focal point of the neighborhood with its plethora of youth and family programs, a gymnasium, classrooms and theater space, and a state-of-the-art multicultural clinic that provides English interpreters to eighty-five percent of its clients.

In the community around the GLCC, programs have been designed to meet residents' needs—with impressive results. Members of the growing Asian population have planted two large community gardens. Special events draw up to two thousand people. Crime is down and reporting of it is up. Cindi feels safer now in this neighborhood than in most others. "People here watch my back," she says.

On the particular day that I trailed Cindi through her adopted neighborhood, signs of its notorious past were hard to find. Residents were perched on steps, playing in peaceful yards and streets and busily mixing among one another. Cindi was very much part of the action—greeting and speaking to people, sometimes in their own foreign language, interacting with kids, sauntering easily past open doors and windows, joking with a black man about a neighborhood fish fry, and, of course, wearing her magnetic smile.

Our tour ended in the massive Southeast Asian community garden, where vegetable plants sprouted like the neighborhood's new beginning. Gazing into the distance, Cindi mused: "We're planting seeds for people to experience more power, to locate peace from the inside out rather than trying to find it outside themselves. As a result, we can build community together."

As a way to directly demonstrate the results of her work, Cindi took me to one of her teaching rooms to meet some of her clients. Seated together in a semicircle, they each told a story of transformation:

Nancy Vang is a Cambodian mother of six children who came to the U.S. from Laos in 1979 and to Glenwood-Lyndale in 1984. She lived there for eight years before buying a house in another community.

"I always thought I had to be in control of my kids and my husband, that they would do what I asked them to do—that I could have my way with them by showing my anger or displeasure with them, instead of dealing with the real issue. For example, my eight-year-old would get scared of stories or events. He would come to me frightened in the middle of the night and bother me about it. I would scream at him to 'leave me alone and get back to bed.'

"The Health Realization Model helps me to deal with my eight-year-old better. I explain to him the cause of his fear and help him trust that everything will be okay. My new attitude is helping my children do better in school and have respect for others.

"Although I recently moved out of the neighborhood, I still work at the GLCC as an interpreter and help plant the community garden. And my kids still use the center. When we first moved to the neighborhood, it wasn't safe. Kids couldn't go out and play. Things are better now."

Gwendolyn McCraven is an African-American single mother of four, who now works as an administrative assistant at the Glenwood-Lyndale Community Center.

"I used to get overly angry with my kids. The Health Realization Model helps me stay connected to my kids and to know when to calm down.

"As an example, one day I picked up my five-year-old daughter at day care. I walked in and said, 'Let's go now.' She refused to go. What could I do? I didn't want to drag her out. Instead, I said, 'I'm going to wait in the car, and you come when you're ready.' I went to the car and opened a book to read and there she was. She made her own decision. Before, I might have said, 'Why are you doing this to me?' Now I realize that the incident wasn't really that bad. I also was raised in an old belief system that included spanking. Now, I do things in a different way. The model has also helped me with a difficult relationship with my husband. I realize that everybody is born with wellness in him or her. We just have to find it."

Rita Hutchinson is an African-American single mother and grandmother who moved into a single-family home in 1997 after 13 years in Glenwood-Lyndale.

"Before I learned the Health Realization Model, I was addicted to crack cocaine and used marijuana and alcohol. I would go around the neighborhood in black leather, smoking a joint. I didn't have a relationship with my kids. I didn't listen to them. And we never came to the community center.

"When Cindi first came here, we thought she was the police looking for crack. We would close our shades and doors and hide 'til she went by. But we noticed that she was always smiling. I thought she was crazy.

"The only reason I went to Cindi's training was to find out what was her song and dance. I said to myself, 'What's this white woman doing coming into our community telling us what to do?' I actually wanted to make her leave. But in class, she treated us like human beings, not as a problem. I went there in a low mood. Everything seemed personal. I found out that when you're in a low mood, you don't have to let yourself get down. Before, I couldn't stand me. I couldn't look in the mirror at myself. Now I love me. I realize that beauty comes from within. I've stopped hanging with the wrong crowd. I've stopped using drugs. I have a beautiful relationship with my kids. I've learned to listen to them. I don't react to them out of anger. I calm myself down first, then go back and discuss the issue. I accept them for who they are. Before, I never wanted a house. I was on AFDC. But I made up my mind I wanted something better. People notice and say how I've changed. I used to be shy and quiet and didn't trust people. Now I always have a smile and a greeting for everyone. It's because Cindi didn't give up on us."

In 1999, the year after our interview with Cindi, a new, dramatic ending to her story unfolded. Much of what Cindi and the GLCC had done to turn around the community was bulldozed away.

As the result of a massive city renewal project designed to deconcentrate poverty, the 73 acres of public housing surrounding the Glenwood-Lyndale Community Center was razed, it's residents relocated across the Twin Cities. Only a few high-rises remain intact in the immediate neighborhood. All of the town homes that housed Cindi's largely Southeast Asian clients were taken down. "There were between two and thirteen people living in each of those homes," Cindi says. "That's thousands of people displaced." Without its client base, the center, along with other neighborhood social service agencies, faced an uncertain fate.

But even though the GLCC's clients have moved away from the neighborhood, many continue to frequent the center. Most of the center's programs are continuing, including the Health Realization project and the community garden. "We have more business than we even had before," Cindi says, the smile still in her voice. "People are searching us out."

Questions for Contemplation:

1. What strengths do you see in yourself? How do use them to help yourself through troubled times?
2. Think back on the last time you handled a conflict with the use of shaming or blaming. What language could you have used instead?
3. Who has helped you solve some of your problems? How were they helpful?
4. What works for you to calm down when you are angry, distraught, or anxious?
5. Cindi treated people with dignity no matter what their situation. What behaviors make you feel you are treated with dignity and respect?

Resources for Reflection and Action:

Pedagogy of the Oppressed, by Paulo Freire (NYC: Continuum Publishing Company, 1995). Freire's work is based on the conviction that every human being is capable of looking critically at the world, and, provided with the proper tools, can transform their world. He offers a revolutionary pedagogy.

The Common Vision: Parenting and educating for wholeness, by David Marshak (NYC: Peter Lang Publishing, 1997). David Marshak's pioneering, highly original study introduces some of this century's most astute explorers of the human spirit, whose insights pose radical questions about modern understandings of education.

Happiness is a Choice, by Barry Neil Kaufman (NYC: Ballentine Books, 1991). A moving exploration of the healing power of compassion and caring. Affirms the unlimited potential of the human spirit and offers hope to those who have been challenged by adversity.

You Already Know What to Do, by Sharon Franquemont (NYC: Jeremy Tarcher/Putnam, 1999). Intuition is a sense, just like sight or smell, a perception that brings you information. Your gut is "intelligent." It knows things ahead of your rational mind. Research shows that we intuitively know what isn't working "best" for us and that we have the power to heed this inner advice. This book tells you how to bring this power into your body, mind, and spirit.

D.J. of the Streets | DONALD JACKSON

by Burt Berlowe

His real name is Donald Jackson. But everyone calls him D.J. He has traditionally spun his lyrics of peace over the cluttered airways of diverse and deprived core neighborhoods. His "beat" is the inner city with its mean streets, crowded apartment buildings, and busy community centers.

D.J. has worked in Phillips and Elliot Park, two of the most violent Minneapolis, Minnesota, communities, where crime has run rampant, especially in one area that residents call "a war zone." He has wandered that area often, looking for trouble and staring it down. He is at his best one-on-one: confronting, assisting, and challenging aimless inhabitants of street corners and sidewalks. It is dangerous work, but D.J. has a gift for it.

"I was born in Kansas City, Missouri, in a rough part of town. It was very segregated. The only white person was a cop or an insurance salesman—that kind of thing. Not many stores were owned by white people. I grew up with disrespect for and fear of white people. I did some crazy things. Then, when my brother was arrested, Mom pushed me to leave town. She was afraid I would end up in prison, too.

"I moved to Minneapolis, thinking I would become my own boss, own my own business, and with my wealth, help others. Well, I did have a couple of businesses, but they didn't work out. One day, I said to myself, 'If you're not going to have a million dollars, you should do something else.'

Photo by Todd Cota

Donald Jackson (center) interacts with Alliance Apartments residents.

"So, I got into show business and became an Eddie Murphy look-alike. While auditioning for an amateur showcase, I met some frustrated kids. I thought, 'Maybe I can provide something for these kids.' I asked them what they wanted to do. They said they wanted the opportunity to do something they could succeed in. So I formed Youth Performing Arts on Wheels, offering performance opportunities for kids. I worked with kids and critiqued what they did. We made a forty-eight-minute crime prevention video on the choices kids make. We got some funding and distributed a hundred copies of it. In the process, I had to work with people of all races. At first, I was reluctant to work with people of different cultures, but my anger over racism, poverty, and violence helped me overcome my fears. I figured the only way change could ever be made was to walk the talk. To get myself further involved, I became a crime prevention coordinator.

"I get involved with kids to keep them out of prison. I go out on the streets, find and talk to kids, and sometimes I ask them to sign up for specific programs. I just give them alternatives. Something other than what they've got. Sometimes it helps, sometimes it doesn't.

"A white kid was in a foster home because his parents were using [drugs], and he was on the edge. I made a connection with him and got other people to give him support. He went on to graduate from high school and took video production and public speaking classes.

"I have a lot of street savvy. I know what's going on out there. I believe we were put here for a reason and mine is to help inner-city kids be a part of positive, healthy change in our society and community."

As the brash leader of the Phillips Peace Initiative, D.J. worked with neighborhood block clubs; built coalitions of businesses, institutions, and residents; recruited volunteers; organized marches, rallies and youth events; and pressured public officials to take action. He has more recently transferred his people-talents to the corridors of Alliance Apartments, a low-income housing project in Elliot Park, where he works as a tenant advocate and organizer.

One of D.J.'s most noteworthy peacemaking endeavors began during the frigid, waning hours of 1995, a year of record violent crime in Minneapolis. He led a group of neighborhood folks in a march to reclaim their neighborhood. Police cars with lights flashing and a lit-up fire truck joined in. Car horns blared through the chilly air. A city council member chanted out a call for peace. Leaflets and handshakes were distributed on the streets and through lowered car windows. "Today is the day we start all over again," D.J. announced at that event. "We're going to make some noise, talk to strangers, shake some hands, and show people that this a thriving, hopeful community."

At D.J.'s behest, January of 1996 was declared "peace month" in the neighborhood, and marked the beginning of a yearlong campaign to reduce crime. D.J. secured an eight-foot long wooden rod and converted it to a peace staff that has become a symbol of the neighborhood's violence prevention efforts. The staff was then transferred each month from one Minneapolis neighborhood to another, marking the beginning of peace month in that new community. The project came to be called "Peace in the Hood" and it spurred other Minneapolis neighborhoods to initiate related events in their communities. To get the word out, D.J. helped the kids publish a special edition of their newspaper, *Youth Speak* and distribute twenty-five thousand copies around the city. "Peace in the Hood" won D.J. a city role model award.

Perhaps D.J.'s most unique "Peace in the Hood" activity took place in the gym of the Phillips Community Center. It was called the Hip-Hop Tip-Off Basketball Tournament—a combination of hip-hop dancing and playground basketball. It was hoped that participating in more constructive activities through organized events would help keep kids off the streets.

As pubescent girls danced to hip-hop rhythms, two competing teams—one consisting of highschool dropouts—took to the gym floor. The thumping instrumentals synchronized with the pounding of basketballs and the rhythm of scrambling gym shoes. The plethora of Michael Jordan wanna-bes in baggy pants, sweats, and assorted T-shirts dashed and darted the length of the court, occasionally flying through the air to swish or bank baskets. The game had an aura of safe, structured aggressiveness that contrasted with the uncontrollable feel of the streets outside.

Spliced in between the musicians' sets was a ceremony that included passing the peace staff from this neighborhood to the next one. D.J. handed the staff to Christine Faber of the nearby Little Earth of United Tribes housing project, saying these words into the microphone, "We are spreading the peace to other neighborhoods. We are sharing the message of peace."

As the gym clock crept toward 9:00 p.m., the basketball tourney ended, and the winners marched to the mike to receive Olympic-like pendants as awards. D.J. was beaming as he touted the youths' talents and announced that the Phillips Community Center hopes to have similar nights on a regular basis as a way to continue to keep kids off the streets and out of trouble. He was obviously pleased. "This is why I don't have a real job," he said. "I love doing this."

Then, as the well-planned event wound down, a young black girl standing in the area spontaneously asked for a hand mike. She cupped it in her fingers and held it to her mouth. Without musical accompaniment, she sang the words of a popular song of that time from the sound track of a basketball cartoon film called *Space Jam* that starred Michael Jordan—a song that had become an anthem and a metaphor of hope and courage:

I believe I can fly.
I believe I can touch the sky.
I think about it every night and day
Spread my wings and fly away
I believe I can soar
See me running through that open door
I believe I can fly . . .

The lyrics floated through the gym, bringing a hush to the crowd and a pause to people's steps. Even as the young vocalist ended her rendition, the song went on, picked up by some youth milling in the center's entryway, then by a group of the basketball players hanging out in the parking lot. The words froze for a moment in the cold air before soaring into the night sky.

"The future is not a result of choices among alternative paths offered by the present, but a place that is created . . . created first in the mind and will, created next in activity. The future is not some place we are going to but one we are creating. The paths are not to be found, but made, and the activity of making them changes both the maker and the destination."

John Schaar

Questions for Contemplation:

1. What is your neighborhood like? What problems does it face?
2. Are you ever afraid to venture out into your neighborhood?
3. What are your neighborhood's strengths?
4. What experience(s) have you had that helped you believe, "I can fly?"
5. How did D.J. use compassion and rebellion in planning and carrying out his event?
6. Does D.J. and the work he has done inspire you? Why or why not?

Resources for Reflection and Action:

Violence: Reflections on a national epidemic, by James Gilligan, M.D. (NYC: Random House, 1997). Gilligan unveils the motives of men who commit horrifying crimes, men who will kill others and destroy themselves rather than suffer a loss of self-respect. With devastating clarity, Gilligan traces the role that shame plays in the etiology of murder and explains why our present penal system only exacerbates it.

Violence Unveiled: Humanity at the crossroads, by Gil Bailie (NYC: Crossroad Publishing Company, 1997). Winner of the Pax Christi USA Book Award. A synthesis of cultural history, including scripture, current events, literature, and cultural theory. The book's scope, insight into the roots of violence, and final message of redemption and hope reflect a truly innovative Christian cultural critique.

Fist, Stick, Knife, Gun, by Geoffrey Canada (Boston, MA: Beacon Press, 1995). The author's vision for a changed future for violent inner-city youth is backed up by descriptions of his acclaimed and innovative programs for children and their families. His is a vision that includes governmental, community, and personal innovation and bravery.

All Kids Are Our Kids: What communities must do to raise caring and responsible children and adolescents, by Peter L. Benson (San Francisco, CA: Jossey-Bass Publishers, 1997). Presents a compelling and creative vision for promoting the positive development of youth and, in so doing, provides decision-makers with a powerful means to develop new policies and programs that can enhance the life chances of youth.

City Kids City Teachers: Reports from the front row, edited by William Ayers and Patricia Ford (NYC: The New Press, 1996). This book dispels the terrible rap city kids get. It speaks hard truths to anyone that will touch or be touched by the jagged edges of urban kids' lives. It gives a voice to these kids, as well as to their teachers, who know better than anyone does the vitality and promise of their students.

Office of Juvenile Justice and Delinquency Prevention (OJJDP). The OJJDP provides grants and funding information, programs, resources, calendar of events, statistics, and access to publications online, dealing with delinquency prevention, gangs, violence and victimization, and substance abuse. Website: www.ojjdp.ncjrs.org.

Life Pieces to Masterpieces. A program that uses art and meditation as tools to rescue boys from the violence of Washington, DC's, worst housing projects. Website: www.lifepieces.org.

Acting Out of Character | JIM JANKE

by Julie Penshorn

A successful marriage comes from falling in love many times with the same person.

—Anonymous

Working in a small office provides opportunities those larger offices with cubicles and closed doors do not. I sit next to co-author Rebecca Janke every day, working to fill the pages of this book. Frequently, we share our family stories—our miseries, our dilemmas, our personal struggles, and our triumphs. Over the years, I've listened to Rebecca's stories about her husband and their evolving relationship. They've struggled, as has any couple, as they've changed and grown as individuals.

Rebecca and I find we can best support each other when we have personal struggles or conflicts with our loved ones by trying our best to illuminate the loved one's point-of-view. This challenges us to see beyond our current perspectives, to stretch beyond where we can comfortably reach, and to really hear what our conflict partner is trying to say. We often challenge each other with the words, "What would be a compassionate rebel response to that dilemma?"

Our families, too, have heard that question. They have listened as we read some of the stories in this book to them. And sometimes, they demonstrate their own compassionate rebellion. Such was the case with Jim Janke, Rebecca's husband, not too long ago. He had ventured forth and rebelled against his conservative, don't-rock-the-boat upbringing by stepping outside of his box. He had taken a risk and strode into the trenches to reach out to a work colleague.

Photo by Todd Cota

Jim Janke

Jim, who is a professor, had come home on a cold, Minnesota evening after his day at the office. He was distressed because the rumor mill was buzzing about his colleague Michael. He heard that Michael's staff was meeting behind his back and making plans to find jobs elsewhere. They claimed the office had become an unsafe place to work due to his recent bizarre behavior and even had an evacuation plan so they could get out of the building at a moment's notice. Jim couldn't believe Michaels behavior was 'bizarre.' In fact he had always liked and respected him.

The staff said he had been extremely short-tempered—yelling and ranting about things with a wild look in his eyes, making decisions unilaterally, missing work without letting anyone know why he was gone, and keeping his door closed for hours on end. When he'd come out, he'd scowl and give people a nasty look. The staff reported him to the district manager, but nothing was done. Instead, they were told not to worry because Michael's behavior was related to a health problem. The staff wondered if that response was simply a case of management not wanting to go through the legal hoops to let him go. Health problem or not, they wanted something done about it. They were angry and frightened.

Jim said the last time he and Michael talked, Michael indicated how disgusted he was with the uncooperative behavior of the staff. He told Jim he had tried everything to get them to work together better. Michael requested, and was granted conflict resolution specialist support, not once, but three times. Even the experts had no impact in helping turn the office around.

Michael's office has had a reputation for years as a difficult work environment. Jim was worried that maybe it had finally reached a crisis level, but yet he also thought maybe it was just more of the same and he should let it go at that.

As Rebecca kept me posted on this story, she reported that Jim seemed resigned to let it go. He felt he couldn't really do anything about it, especially when the conflict resolution specialists couldn't help the situation. Plus, Jim hated conflict and would sooner have spikes put under his fingernails than purposely put himself in the middle of someone else's dilemma. So, I was really surprised when she relayed, a few days later, that Jim had taken further steps to right this situation.

Jim had been at a district-wide meeting, and purposely sought out Michael to spend time with. When he got home he told Rebecca about it:

"I thought I'd hang out with Michael and see for myself if he was acting bizarre in any kind of way. He seemed fine to me, so I took it upon myself to call our district-manager. I told him what was being spread around in the rumor mill and expressed my concern."

I could just imagine how Rebecca's jaw must have dropped. In their twenty years of marriage, Jim had been a kind and compassionate man to his family, but to put himself at risk and become involved in something that was none of his business was very unusual.

She asked him why he did that. Jim's answer was: "I've known Michael for several years, and I couldn't just stand by and watch all this turmoil and suffering. Plus, the other employees seem pretty miserable . . . At any rate, the district manager was angry at first and treated my call as just another complaint about the 'office from hell.' But then I told him this was serious and not just a bunch of people with their undies-in-a bundle. I told him it had reached a point where several employees were looking for new jobs.

"It was then that the district manager confided that Michael has a brain tumor! I was just sick when he told me. Evidently, Michael wanted to keep it a secret. Now I don't know if that'll be possible. Anyway, the district manager thanked me since he didn't realize how serious the situation had become, and assured me he'd talk with Michael on Monday."

I phoned Jim to find out what ultimately happened. He told me that the district manager negotiated with Michael to step aside as office chair so he could just focus on his regular job and getting well. It was a relief to Michael because he's a responsible person and has a hard time saying no to additional tasks. Michael is now experiencing less stress and there is no more talk of people quitting.

Jim's actions not only saved the county from having to replace employees and helped Michael regain some balance in his life, but also endeared him to Rebecca. She was exhilarated hearing about her husband's efforts to make a difference. She told me, "I felt so proud of him! It was like falling in love all over again! There's nothing sexier than a man who stands up for what's right in a positive, nonviolent way."

"I feel the capacity to care is the thing which gives life its deepest significance."

Pablo Casals

Soggy Shoes and Socks

By Julie Penshorn

The other day, my boyfriend, Ray, refused to eat dinner because I insisted he and his helper take their shoes off before coming inside. They'd been out in the muddy trenches laying water lines that day, and their shoes were filthy. What I didn't know, and only found out the next day, was that the helper, Pat, was very self-conscious about taking off his boots. He was sure his feet would be smelly and dirty after being in the wet trenches, and he had told my boyfriend that he didn't want to take them off. Complying with Pat's wishes, my boyfriend was unaware that I was trying to comply with someone's wishes, too—my mother's.

I knew that it was important for my mother to keep the floor clean. She had just mopped it, and she had given up her entire day to help around the house and prepare a hot, delicious home-cooked meal. The last thing she wanted to see was a muddy floor. I felt I needed to protect her feelings and support her efforts, so I stubbornly insisted that they both take off their shoes.

My boyfriend stormed out before we could find a mutually satisfactory solution and took Pat home. My mother, father, and I ended up with a lot of leftovers and plenty of frustration.

Looking back, the obvious solution would have been a change of venue. We could have eaten in the garage, on the deck, on the front steps, but no one's creativity kicked in. There were so many emotions flying—things were happening so fast—a creative solution momentarily eluded us.

It's the deep roots of guilt that most often subvert our most creative compassionate rebel responses. It's the "I shoulds:" "I should eat dinner with the family. I should take off my boots. I should be grateful for the efforts made by my mother." When a person is faced with a "should," sometimes rebellion runs blind. Things become unbalanced. In this case, both of us were hot and our compassion was unilateral—not for everybody. If we had taken time to think before we acted, we would have been able to see a solution that demonstrated compassion for everyone involved.

So, was Ray's a compassionate rebel response? Well, yes, I'd say so. Even though there was room for improvement, I was proud of him for standing up for his helper. This event reminded me how caring he is, and thinking of it helps me remember that, in some situations, we're compassionate rebels-in-the-making. It's our sometimes-halfway, sometimes-incomplete efforts that will evolve into our greatest achievements. There is no effort too flawed. No attempt unworthy of celebration. When we celebrate our baby steps, our larger steps will follow.

Questions for Contemplation:

1. How do you feel when gossip is being spread around in your work or school environment? What have you found to successfully address it?
2. Have you been prompted to stand up for a co-worker or family member? What happened? Have you stood up for someone at the expense of another? If you were to re-role-play the situation, what would you do differently so everyone in the situation would feel your support? What stops you from supporting a co-worker or family member who is struggling? What obstacles do you need to overcome to lend your support?
3. What types of "right action" have caused you to fall in love all over again with your significant other?
4. Describe one of your best working environments. What made it that way?
5. Julie's mom came over to help cook and clean so Julie and Ray could concentrate on their yard work. Who helps you out when life becomes overwhelming or extra demanding? What do they do that you find helpful and supportive?

Resources for Reflection and Action:

Nonviolent Communication: A language of compassion, by Marshall B. Rosenberg (Del Mar, CA: Puddle Dancer Press, 1999). The techniques in this book can help individuals break patterns of thinking, depression, and violence and improve the quality of their relationships.

Working with Emotional Intelligence, by Daniel Goleman (NYC: Bantam Books, 1998). Goleman describes how workplaces have been transformed into cohesive, trusting, communities through the development of individuals' competencies in areas ranging from self-confidence, empathy, and communication to conflict management, understanding diversity, and awareness of political and social networks.

Resolving Identity-Based Conflict in Nations, Organizations, and Communities, by Jay Rothman (San Francisco, CA: Jossey-Bass Publishers, 1997). Conflict can either destroy or create. Identity conflicts are passionate and volatile because they strike at our core. Though often impervious to traditional methods of conflict management, identity-based conflicts provide adversaries with dynamic opportunities for finding not only common ground, but higher ground than either party could have found on its own.

The Global Brain Awakens: Our next evolutionary leap, by Peter Russell. (Palo Alto, CA: Global Brain, Inc., 1993). He tells the story of our evolutionary journey so far, and points out that the growing complexity we see in society "reveals three important areas of growth in terms of evolution: a diversity of human beings; an elaborate organizational structure, parallel to that observed in all other living systems; and a communication and information-processing capability approaching that of the human brain. Society would appear to be completing the prerequisites for the emergence of a new evolutionary level."

Who We Could Be at Work, by Margaret A. Lulic (Newton, MA: Butterworth-Heinemann, 1996). Anyone who has been part of corporate America can relate to these stories and inner questions about how to encourage each individual's wholeness in mind, body, spirit, and emotion in the workplace.

The Heart Aroused: Poetry and the preservation of the soul in corporate America, by David Whyte (NYC: Doubleday, 1994). Explores the personal dilemma experienced by many of us who choose to earn our living in the corporate world. Each day, we come home a little richer in our wallets, and a little poorer in our souls. Gives readers some valuable perspectives, together with implied questions to help us resolve workplace dilemmas.

Random Acts of Kindness Foundation, 1801 Broadway, Suite 250, Denver, CO 80202. Phone: 800-660-2811. Email: rakinfo@actsof kindness.org. Website: www.actsofkindness.org. Contact them for further information regarding the Random Acts of Kindness Week, the second week of November.

Mad Dad | V.J. SMITH

by Rebecca Janke

"V.J Smith, get in the car. Let's go!" said my stepfather.

"I hopped my nine-year-old body into the car and away we sped into the dark, damp evening. He dropped me off at what I thought was a community daycare, and I was glad to have an opportunity to play with some other kids. It sure was better than staying home and watching him beat up my mother one more time. My evening of reprieve turned into a living nightmare when no one came to take me home. I couldn't believe it. 'It must be some horrible mistake,' I thought. 'No one would forget their kid. Where is my mom? Maybe she was in a car accident. Maybe she was beat up too bad to get here. Maybe she's dead. Maybe he killed her.' My mind was reeling. What was going on? 'Mom! Mom! Mom! Where are you?' I silently screamed as I tried to go to sleep in a strange bed.

"Day after day went by and she never came and neither did he. I learned that I was not at a daycare center after all, but at a boys' detention center. Some of these boys were bad, really bad, but I couldn't figure out what I had done to be here with them. There were sixty-two of us and we all had to share the same bath water, which was totally disgusting. However, a year later when my mom showed up, I was so disgusted and angry with her that when the judge asked me if I wanted to go back and live with her, I said, 'NO!' The judge honored my decision and I spent the next seven years living in one foster home after another.

"On my high school graduation night, I scanned the crowd to see if anyone was there for me. No one. . . Again no one came for me. Even though I had left the foster care system when I was a senior in high school and lived by myself in a hotel, I thought somebody who knew me would show up. 'People don't just forget about a kid on a night like this,' I thought. I couldn't believe it! In order to get through the ceremony I imagined the entire audience had come to congratulate me.

"You can imagine how thrilled I was when one of my foster brothers introduced me to some of his 'friends.' For the first time, someone was there for me . . .never mind that they were part of the Black Mafia. I did everything they told me, was good at it, and soon moved up the ranks to top leadership. It didn't phase me whatsoever that people were violently hurt under my direction. My callousness and ability to outrun the police kept me at the helm for fifteen years.

"Cocaine trafficking and hustling allowed me to flash thousands of dollars in front of my girlfriends' faces. One girlfriend along the way was the most negative person I had ever met. To get away from her negativity, I went to the bedroom, played my music and pretended that I was a disc-jockey. A friend of mine encouraged me to try DJ-ing at a local stage. The crowd loved me. All I ever knew before was how to traffic and hustle. Now, newfound skills were emerging. One night, a guy in the audience from the radio station asked me if I would like to host a radio show. I thought it would be a perfect cover for me so I could continue my illegal activities. We called it 'Late Night Love.' To my surprise, I began to get all sorts of fan mail. In no time at all, we were on the top of the radio shows! The show received an award from the mayor and he even proclaimed a day named V.J.-DJ in my honor.

"My way of life slowly began to unravel when I met a lady who was straight. When she asked me out, I thought we were going to have a night of sweet love. Much to my surprise, she pulled up in a church bus and yelled for me to climb aboard. Before I knew it, I was in the middle of a church hall helping serve supper to those who were gathered for a night of worship. Even though it was far from what I had imagined, the evening was warm and wonderful. I found myself going back week after week because it felt good to be there. Little by little, my own faith began to grow, even though sometimes I would come to church drunk.

"It began to bother me to sell drugs to people who were deteriorating from their long-endured habit. Instead, I wrote them a check. The more my heart began to soften with my growing faith, I began to realize that being loved and giving love was what I wanted more than anything. I got married and tried to turn my life around. One night, looking into my stepson's eyes, I imagined him in a few short years asking me, 'Dad, what kind of work do you do?' Deep down I wanted to be able to tell him something good about myself. However, I began using more drugs than I was selling. I spent less and less time with my stepson. When a drug deal went bad and I was unable to pay, I became suicidal. My wife helped me to decide that the best thing to do was to leave town and be serious about carving a new life for ourselves. So, we went to Kansas, and I got off drugs.

"I worked at a box company and shined shoes. We were able to make a go of it. Because we wanted to go back to Minnesota, we decided to save up money to pay the drug dealer off. As soon as we got back, I enrolled at Minneapolis Community College and worked at Northwest Airlines. All the leadership skills I had developed in the Black Mafia were now put to use on campus as the president of the African-American Student Association. One of the committees that I chaired, the Phoenix Group, did grassroots organizing to secure housing for homeless people. Eventually, I was hired to provide community events for the people who had secured housing. With my DJ background, you know we had a good time. The community became my extended family.

"However, there are many forces that threaten families. My wife and I heard the gangbangers roll past our windows and gunshots going off in the dark. We could smell the dope being peddled down the street. The life I was finally able to leave behind was taking place right outside my front door. It was time to fight for my community. I prayed about what to do and laid awake for hours every night hoping an answer would come. Within a few days, a friend of mine told me about a national organization called 'MAD DADS' which mobilizes strong, drug free men of faith to reclaim their neighborhood one child at a time.

"I quickly recruited a handful of volunteers for a local chapter, raised a first-year budget of $2,000 from private donors, and started 'walking the streets' again. The fathers behind MAD DADS represent a rebirth of community spirit and hope for a safer neighborhood for ourselves and our children. The inner-city has traditionally lacked strong, visible male involvement that is both positive and proactive. Each time we street

V. J. Smith relaxes in the Mad Dads office.

rebels go out at night on Street Patrol and give of our time to mentor a troubled youth or young father, the community becomes a little stronger. We believe that real fathers are needed on the street to parent youth who have never experienced the love of a father. As a leader, my life has shifted to protect and strengthen families.

"People ask me if I'm ever tempted to go back to the world of drugs, violence, and wild women. Sure, there are some friends waiting for me to come back to my old way of life. They think this is just a temporary thing with me. I live by the motto, 'Stay away long enough to be strong enough.' Where you put yourself makes a lot of difference.

"I also believe that those who have a loving

relationship with their mother and/or father need to cherish it. I wish more than anything that I had that. And I believe that kids need parents who care. Don't let your child grow up hearing, 'You ain't got no mama, what's the matter with you?' or 'Your daddy don't want you.' Don't ever let your child hear that."

Janet Reno, U.S. Attorney General, recently presented V.J. with a 1999 Ameritech Award of Excellence in Crime Prevention, given by the National Crime Prevention Council, which is made up of U.S. law-enforcement officials. The prestigious honor was bestowed on only six other individuals nationwide. V.J. also received a proclamation of support and thanks from Minneapolis Mayor Sharon Sayles Belton. He has also organized a values-sharing group called "Block on Block Love," designed to promote peace, health, and community giving.

"There is hope for a violent man to be someday nonviolent, but there is none for a coward."

Mohandus Gandhi

Questions for Contemplation:

1. If you were to take the worst thing that happened to you in your childhood and work for its eradication, what possible career or volunteer choices surface?
2. V.J. developed his DJ skills in order to get away from a negative-thinking woman. What is something you do to reduce your stress? Can you develop it as a talent?
3. A growing faith was the catalyst that steered V.J. into a different life. Who or what has been pulling at your heartstrings that opens you up to being a more loving person? How can you continue to put yourself in the presence of this force?
4. What national or local organization brings relief to an issue that was difficult for you to bear as a child? What can you do to support it?

Resources for Reflection and Action:

Violence Unveiled: Humanity at the crossroads, by Gil Bailie (New York: Crossroad Publishing Co., 1995/97). The book's scope, insight into the roots of violence, and final message of redemption and hope, provide a truly innovative Christian cultural critique. Winner of the 1996 Pax Christi USA Book Award.

Reclaiming Youth at Risk: Our hope for the future, by Larry K. Brendtro, Martin Brokenleg, and Steven Van Bockern (Bloomington, Indiana: National Educational Service, 1990). Strategies for creating a "reclaiming" environment wherein the needs of both the young person and the society are met.

World Without Violence: Can Gandhi's vision become reality? edited by Dr. Arun Gandhi (H.S. Poplai for Wiley Eastern Limited, 4835/24, Ansari Road, Daryaganj, New Delhi 110 002, 1994). Available through M. K. Gandhi Institute for Nonviolence, Christian Brothers University, 650 East Parkway South, Memphis, TN 38104. Phone 901-725-0815 or fax 901-725-0846. World leaders share their commentaries on peace and justice.

Spiritual Parenting: A guide to understanding and nurturing the heart of your child, by Hugh and Gayle Prather (New York: Harmony Books, 1996). Offers a radically new way to approach parenting—as a spiritual task. The authors offer ways to keep this essential focus amid the bewildering complexities involved in guiding children toward adulthood.

To start a chapter of MAD DADS, write to 3026 4th Avenue South, Minneapolis, MN 55408. Phone: 612-822-0802.

Chapter 4
Persistent Protesters

Carol Kratz, Tumblin' Tumbleweed, Sunshine, Jim Anderson

A willingness to take risks is always a prerequisite for change because the conventions, the constancies, are so deeply ingrained. —Nobel Peace Prize recipient Oscar Aria

Persistent Protesters are compassionate rebels who have a global worldview and find fulfillment in a lifestyle that includes speaking out, demonstrating, and/or nonviolent resistance. Their ability to see how one struggle is related to another helps them build alliances across issues. They believe they can make a difference and that their role is to be present. They believe, "If I don't do it, who will?"

Though they count on the support of those who share their points of view but do not actively protest, Persistent Protesters often develop a close-knit community with those who stand beside them. This is especially valuable, since they often have to be away from home and family to do this work.

We met with a group of Persistent Protesters who gathered to save an area in Minneapolis, Minnesota, from freeway development. They originally called themselves the Park and River Alliance and were joined by activists affiliated with Earth First and the Mendota Mdewakantan Dakota Native Americans. They came together because the Minnesota Department of Transportation was planing to do a major expansion of Highway 55, known as Hiawatha Avenue, which would cut through a major city park, take out family homes and destroy a sacred Native American site.

They knew they would have to stay weeks or possibly months to see this vigil through, and on August 10, 1998, they set up Camp Two Pines on the southwestern edge of Minnehaha Park. There, on government-owned land, they established a communal village, the Minnehaha Free State. Basing their work on the principles of nonviolence and group consensus, they vowed to stay until the road development was stopped and the sacred site was returned to the Native American, from whence it originally came.

We interviewed four of the "Stop the Reroute" protesters at their camp site. Here are their stories.

Leaving Home Behind | CAROL KRATZ

by Burt Berlowe

Each house along the road has many stories. Those stories, those people, have become a part of me. They are also a part of you.
—Deb Kratz, daughter of Carol and Al Kratz

Mother Nature is at home in Carol Kratz's backyard. The urban wilderness surrounding her modest house is home to the small birds and animals that flit, hop, and scamper along the edges of Minnehaha Park. The lush, serene parkland has been her neighbor for almost half a century. But someday soon, if plans proceed, Carol's house will become a footnote in local history, as a busy concrete highway turns the greenery to gray dust, and scatters her animal family to the wind.

Carol waxes melancholy as she leans back in a lawn chair in her yard beneath the glare of the setting sun. In front of her, campfire smoke and the scent of sage curl upward. Teepees, a few vacant houses, and a village of protesters flank her. Behind her, a squirrel dashes into the sheltering arms of a two hundred-year-old oak tree.

"I call this 'living in the country,'" Carol says, scanning the yard wistfully. "It reminds me of my childhood home on a farm. I've lived in the country pretty near all of my life. When my husband and I first moved here in 1966, we were one of forty homes on Riverview Road. Ten years later, the Minnesota Department of Transportation (MNDOT) started ripping out houses to make room for a proposed ten-lane highway. The park board stopped the project because they didn't want the highway running through the park. But now people have gradually moved out since MNDOT condemned and bought their homes. Originally,

Photo by Michael Bayly

Carol Kratz

four of us were holdouts. Finally, one woman, getting nervous, voluntarily sold her house, and now there are three. All of us got condemnation notices saying we had to be out."

During much of her adulthood, Carol kept to herself and away from social or political activism. But in 1996, with the pressure growing for city intervention on her property, she decided to act. "We went to a meeting with our alderperson," she says. "They were trying to ram this highway thing down our throats again. It was a horribly cold night. Out of the sixty, ten of us organized and started the Park and River Alliance. We got over seven hundred signatures opposing the highway. Stop the Reroute spun off from that. We have worked hard to get politicians to understand why it's a bad idea to put a highway or light rail system in here.

"When Earth First, an environmental activist group, came to me and said they wanted to take on this issue, we were grateful to get added support. Right away, they occupied the three houses that were to be destroyed. To prevent the wrecking crews from working, one Earth Firster chained himself to a house. Another dug in behind a house with his arm locked down. Without Earth First and the Dakota tribe, we would never have gotten the kind of attention we're now getting for our efforts."

Carol joined the cause, doing what she could between caring for her ailing husband and fighting for her home. She cleaned up around the sacred fire, flyered cars, protested at the state capitol, visited with passers-by and lifted lagging spirits. "At times, we thought this was a hopeless cause," she says, "but then we would get another surge of energy that kept us going.

"It wasn't until 1997 that I found out that the spring next to Camp Two Pines, Coldwater Spring, is an ancient spring that was part of the first Native settlement here. It's believed by them to be the center of creation. The Native people had the land taken from them in the 1800s with a promise to get it back. But they never have."

Carol pauses and points to the nearby sacred fire, which has burned since day one of the encampment and says, "The fire department threatened to put it out. We convinced them not to do it.

"Some people think that the protesters here are just a bunch of Hippies. That's not true. People in the encampment are incredibly friendly and dedicated. Most are working and have homes. They are giving up a lot to stop this highway. They are literally putting their lives on the line. It really amazes me. I love each and every one of them for their dedication.

"I have lived a sheltered life and didn't know such committed people were out there acting on their beliefs. I've loved every minute of being a part of this community. These people have been good to me. I've grown so close to them.

"I've hung on as long as I could because this is my home. I've got such an attachment to this place. Look at the wildlife here and right beyond those trees is Minnehaha Park, the last urban wilderness left in the city. It's so beautiful. That's why I'm making this last-ditch effort to save this place."

The month following our interview, Carol's home became a footnote in history. The Kratzes—the last actual residents on the reroute site—lost their fight to save their home of thirty-three years, packed their belongings, and moved away. It was an agonizing family affair. Carol helped her ailing husband on with his coat. Their children Greg, a former antiwar protestor and daughter Deb helped move their parents' lifetime of goods onto the truck. Later, she recalled how a friend from the Mendota Mdewakanton tribe had helped her mother let go of her home, saying: "Carol, you held them off long enough for us to come. We will take over this battle that you have fought for so long."

Even though Carol no longer lives at Camp Two Pines, she is not far away physically or emotionally. She remains in touch with her old neighbors and is still active in the cause. Two years after her eviction, she is upbeat about her experience with the Free State:

"I lost my home. I lost my old oak tree and the beautiful area in which I lived. But this I have learned: I have not lost because there is still a loving community that grew out of the struggle. I have not lost because of the self-respect we all gained from the Highway 55 protest.

"I think back and ask myself, 'Was it worth all the stress to fight for something I strongly believed in?' Of course the answer is, 'Yes.' I would do the same thing again."

"Courage is contagious. When a brave person takes a stand, the spines of others are stiffened."

Billy Graham

Questions for Contemplation:

1. Do you believe governing bodies (i.e., cities, counties, and departments of transportation) should consider individuals' interests when making decisions about the path of a new road? Does your answer change when history, tradition, and/or religion are part of the reason for people's desire to preserve the existing situation?
2. Have you ever participated in a protest? Why did you do it? Did you feel your efforts were productive? Would you do it again? Would you be willing to be arrested?
3. More and more, we are experiencing conflict between the desire to protect the environment and increased energy and transportation needs. What ideas do you have for resolving this ongoing conflict?
4. Have you ever lost your home, neighborhood, or a "sacred" site? What happened and what kind of impact did it have on you?
5. Who has given you support when you've had a crisis? What did he/she/they do?

Resources for Reflection and Action:

Thinking Like a Mountain: Towards a council of all beings, by John Seed (Gabriola Island, BC: New Society, 1988). A book of quotes and theories about our interconnectedness with all life and the impact we have on one another and on the Earth. A thought-provoking book.

Talking Leaves (Deep Ecology Education Project, 1430 Willamette St., Suite 367, Eugene, OR 94701). A global journal of ecology and activism. Send for a free sample.

The Persistent Activist, by James Downton Jr., and Paul Wehr (NYC: Westview Press, 1997). Draws on in-depth interviews with long-term activists. Their stories reveal how commitment to a social movement is created and sustained.

Widening Circles: A memoir, by Joanna Macy (Gabriola Island, BC: New Society Publishers, 2000). One of this era's greatest eco-philosophers, Buddhist scholar, and deep ecology activist recounts her adventures of mind and spirit in the key social movements of our time.

Putting Earth First | TUMBLIN' TUMBLEWEED

by Burt Berlowe

In the summer of '98 a Tumblin' Tumbleweed blew into Camp Two Pines and settled for a while. It came in the form of a twenty-three-year-old vagabond protestor whose real name is Bob. He wouldn't tell his last name, only that he now calls himself Tumbleweed. As we talked, he reclined on a patch of open space between the street and the woods of Minnehaha Park.

Tumbleweed, given this name because he makes a habit of "rolling around" where controversy is blowing, has been a protester since grade school, stemming from a childhood love affair with nature. It happened when he went to visit his grandparents in Virginia. "It was beautiful country for a kid from the city," he says. "The mountains blew me away. As I hiked through them, I started thinking that what it all comes down to is the planet—keeping things in the world intact."

By the age of twelve, Tumble was into "making a better world." He found vehicles in political music and anarchism, and the antiwar, pro-choice, and animal rights movements.

One of his strangest rebel activities took place during his school's homecoming week. The school had always had a homecoming queen but never a king. As a humorous protest, some friends nominated him homecoming queen. They made "Bob for Queen" stick-up notes, cups, and T-shirts. Amazingly, he won the election.

School officials tried to void his victory and told him not to come to school or the homecoming rally. In response, three hundred to four hundred students walked out, protesting the school's action. "Because of what we did," he chuckles, "the school now has a homecoming king."

After graduation, Tumbleweed kept meeting people who shared his concern about the earth. He eventually joined the environmental activist group, Earth First, in their antilogging campaign of old-growth forests in Oregon.

"We faced local, state, and federal opposition, but after we set up camp we made connections with mainstream community groups to help them understand what is at stake when we lose old-growth forests. We were able to stop the logging only temporarily, but I was happy to be playing a part in putting the Earth first."

When Tumbleweed no longer had a reliable vehicle, he rode buses and trains to places of protest. "I want to hop the trains again sometime. They have that nomad kind of feel. It's like poetry, the wheels 'chug chug chugging.' Jazz music is based on the sound of the train, all the different sounds at once in their own rhythm, kind of like the universe."

Before arriving at Camp Two Pines, Tumbleweed was in jail for trespassing and resisting arrest at a department store in Cincinnati, Ohio, where he was opposing the use of fur.

With his past experience, Tumbleweed helps organize and coordinate the Hwy 55 protest, including the protesters' nonviolent direct action, the lobbying of public officials, media communication, and legal action activities.

"If the bulldozers come, or when Minnegasco comes to shut off the gas to the homes we're occupying, I'll be giving orders as to what to do so we can stay in control in a peacekeeping way. We have to stop this project," Tumble says. "We will stay here until they drive us out or until we stop their road. If they evict us, we'll just keep coming back."

The Two Pines Community has come to be like a one big family with rules, relationships, struggles, and mutual objectives. "We all have our lives," Tumbleweed says. "We're not just activists. We have problems like everyone else, but we work at maintaining our relationships with each other. We have a men's and women's support group that meets regularly. People have their own rooms in the occupied houses and there are basic ground rules: No drugs, alcohol, or violence, and all dogs on a leash. We respect each other and contribute together.

"This is the greatest thing I've ever been involved in. You've got ecosystems' preservation, urban sprawl and development issues, land rights issues, and native sovereignty issues. Our community spirit keeps it going. These are some of the best activists I've ever worked with. This is a living community—rebellion in action. It's a beautiful thing to be here with these people.

"Home is wherever I am at the time. I now consider this my home. That's why a lot of us are so deep into this. It's not just about stopping a road and saving a park and sacred sites. It's about defending homes, people, plants, and animals. I don't know how anybody could be against this."

Along with the presence of camp activists, the protest has received support from a larger community of people who regularly visit the site, including college students from around the state and interested passers-by. Many visitors bring donations of food, clothing, blankets, or other staples. Some volunteer chunks of time. Others find unique ways to take a stand. Tumbleweed tells a story as an example: "Two days ago, a road construction crew came by here and saw what was happening. After finding out what we were doing, a couple of the older guys said they didn't want to work for the company that was going to be destroying the site and would quit their jobs in protest. That's the kind of thing that keeps me going. If those guys are willing to give up the work they've had their whole lives for this, then I have to stay."

Tumbleweed hopes that the Minnehaha Free State protest will be a catalyst for other such efforts around the country. "As a forest activist, I believe that the best way to preserve the wilderness we have left is to start reclaiming our cities and our streets, moving back to inner cities and making them communities—not just neighborhoods in stress, but communities like this. What if this happened all over the city, the country, the world? What if, as we walked down the street anywhere, we saw people sitting around just having a good time talking and eating together? We need to be sustaining communities, planting community gardens, and putting some wilderness back into the cities."

When he wants some solitary time, Tumbleweed likes to walk down to the nearby riverbluffs and wade into the shimmering water. "The water is always flowing, always changing, never the same," he says. "It's like the universe and the train wheels."

Those nature treks remind him of a long-range goal. "I'm saving money to buy some land in the Midwest to farm. I have the same dream as everyone, having a house with a white picket fence, well maybe a purple picket fence. But I want to be self-sufficient, to grow my own food, make money on my own terms, and sustain myself. I might get land

Photo by Michael Bayly

Tumblin' Tumbleweed

in southern Illinois, Wisconsin, or the North Woods of Minnesota. Or I may come back here. It's good to know I'll always have a place to come back to. I'd like to take a break from activism work and be by myself for a while. But I'll probably get caught up in something and be right back at it again. I'll stay in a place for a while and get a job there. Eventually, I may go somewhere for good. Who knows what will happen after this?"

Late in July, 2000, following a street demonstration against a genetics conference in downtown Minneapolis, the FBI, DEA (Drug Enforcement Agency) and Minneapolis police raided the Sister Camelot House, a nonprofit free food distribution group, allegedly connected to the genetic conference protest, on the pretext of searching for drugs. They arrested eleven people, beating some of them in the process.

According to an account of the raid, one occupant of the house was ordered to lie down on the floor, then was kicked repeatedly in his face until he stopped moving. When he didn't immediately respond to a police demand, they shoved their knuckles into his throat and continued kicking him. When he requested first aid, he was laughed at. Later, he was taken to a hospital emergency room for treatment before having to stand trial. His real name is Bob. But everybody calls him by his nickname: "Tumbleweed."

"Stand upright, speak these thoughts, declare the truth thou has that all may share. Be bold. Proclaim it everywhere. Those only live who dare."

Lewis Morris

Questions for Contemplation:

1. When you hear the word "protester" what images come to mind?
2. Do you think Tumbleweed and other persistent protesters make an important contribution to society? Why or why not?
3. The concept of "earth first" is central to Tumbleweed's philosophy. What ideas do you have for putting earth first and meeting the needs of people?
4. How should cities prepare and respond to protesters? What nonviolent protest strategies have you seen or do you know about that you think were effective?
5. What ideas do you have for making inner cities more attractive places to live?

Resources for Reflection and Action:

Naming the Moment: Political analysis for action, by Deborah Barndt (Jesuit Center for Social Faith and Justice, 947 Queen Street East, Toronto, Ontario, M4M 1J9 Canada, 1991). Shows how to move through the four cyclical phases of political analysis for action, which are: identifying our interests and ourselves, naming the issues and struggles, assessing the forces, and planning for action.

Counting our Victories: Popular education and organizing, by Denise Nadeau (Repeal the Deal Productions, 707 12th Street, New Westminster, BC, Canada V3M 4J7. Fax: 604-522-8975, 1996). Helps grassroots groups build their organizations and continue to work in coalitions with other groups.

Powerful Peacemaking: A strategy for a living revolution, by George Lakey (Gabriola Island, BC: New Society Publishers, 1987). Proposes a five-stage strategy for nonviolent revolution.

Earth Poems: Poems from around the world to honor the Earth, edited by Ivo Mosley (NYC: Harper Collins, 1996). Makes a fine reference book for people putting together rituals or seasonal celebrations.

Earth First! Website: www.earthfirstjournal.com. A grassroots environmental movement.

Earth Action. Website: www.earthaction.org. A coalition of eighteen hundred citizen groups in over one hundred fifty countries that provides action alerts on issues regarding the protection of the planet.

Organizers' Collaborative, PO Box 400897, Cambridge MA 02140. Phone: 617-776-6176 or go to www.organizenow.net. The subscriber's list, org-c@topica.com, comes out once per week and covers the use of the Internet to foster communication and collaboration among social change activists. To subscribe, just send a blank e-mail message to org-c-subscribe@topica.com.

Sustain. Website: www.sustainusa.org. Information on regional transportation issues, genetic engineering, and organic agriculture.

Livable Communities. Website: www.epa.gov/livability/. The EPA's Livable Communities site has a comprehensive list of links to EPA programs and resources related to livable communities.

League of Conservation Voters, 1920 L St., Suite 800, Washington, DC 20009. Phone: 202-785-8683. Website: www.lcv.com. Support environmental groups and let every candidate in your area know that, in future elections, your votes will go only to politicians—from either party—who share your desire for a safe, healthy, diverse, and sustainable environment.

Making Change at a Moment's Notice |

SUNSHINE (CARI CAMILLE WITCHER)

by Rebecca Janke

> *I have learned to accept the fact that we risk disappointment, disillusionment, even despair, every time we act. Every time we decide to believe the world can be better. Every time we decide to trust others to be as noble as we think they are. And that there might be years during which our grief is equal to, or even greater than our hope. The alternative, however, not to act, and therefore to miss experiencing other people at their best, reaching toward their fullness, has never appealed to me.*
>
> —Alice Walker

At the time this story was written, Sunshine was twenty-years-old and a student at the University of Wisconsin in Menomonie, Wisconsin. When she heard that Highway 55 was going to be rerouted, she temporarily suspended her college education and became part of the longest protest encampment in Minnesota history. Various people from all over the country had come to prevent the destruction of this Native American sacred site, the residents' homes, and the park. I met with her on a cold November day, wondering how these dedicated people were going to keep warm with winter around the corner, and no resolution in sight.

I don't scare easily, but I had to admit I was glad to be escorted into the area by a friend of her family. I could feel the polarization in the air the minute my feet stepped on the premises. Everyone's eyes reflected a determined stance as well as caution. I could feel the unspoken question, "Who are you?" But when I was introduced as a person who wanted to write Sunshine's story, the faces softened.

Sunshine and I were given two chairs in front of the burning fire so we could talk privately. Even though they didn't have much to offer, their fire was an unspoken message of hospitality. As she adjusted her shivering body nearer the flames, several others went off to finish winterizing their tents. I was acutely aware that a confrontation with the police could happen at any moment and found myself sitting on the edge of my chair. I wondered what strategies these people had developed for coping with such tension on an ongoing basis. What drives people to live like this?

"Sunshine, what brought you to this place? You're not sure where your next meal will come from. It's cold. You have no idea how long this protest will last. You are away from family and friends. Help me understand what this is all about," I asked.

"My mom taught me how to be a nonviolent protester," she said. "She and her husband have worked on various peace issues much of their lives. For the past four years, we've gone to the U.S. Army School of the Americas, better known as the 'School of Assassins,' to protest its activities. During the Gulf War, my mom took me to my first antiwar demonstration. I was eight years old. I loved being there, holding my candle and singing in the street, and believing my presence was going to make peace happen. I loved being part of changing things.

"In addition to being an active protester, my mom was always making donations to peace organizations and telling me about the work they did. Some of the social justice workers met at our house. I was intrigued with their stories and would gladly help my mom and stepdad prepare for their visits.

"I also was exposed to all sorts of ideas as I sifted through the books in my parents' library. Whatever they didn't have, they helped me find at the local library. Whenever I had a question, my mom always took the time to explain it and show me how it connected to other things in the world around me. As a result, I've always had clear ideas about what is just and unjust. I have developed a passion and an adventuresome spirit for learning.

"We raised a lot of our own food and the land became our spirituality. I know what the land has to offer when it is loved and nurtured—not only food, but also beauty. I've learned to live lightly on the Earth. It distresses me when the Earth is forced to lay down its life for one more paved road. My family's spiritual tradition has always been to have reverence for the Earth and to respect the cycle of life.

"When I heard about the reroute of Highway 55," she continued, "I had to come. This situation isn't going to wait. My college degree can. My classes in history, anthropology, and Spanish will be there when I return. This is not lost time for me because each time I'm involved in a protest, it sharpens my knowledge about what is important to study."

"What is it like to be here?" I asked, now that I understood why she came.

"I'm amazed at the kindness of the people. They give everything they have. I'm very touched by that. Their energy and commitment have helped sustain me. There are a lot of supporters who can't join us because they have jobs and families that prevent them being here, but they have been so generous in bringing us supplies and food. It's their way of paying us for being here and doing the work they feel needs to be done. When we put a sign by the road stating what supplies we need, within a few hours they are here. Some people give us encouragement by driving by and waving and smiling, while others stop and visit for a while. They go home and tell their friends and drum up more support. It all adds to keeping our spirits up to hang in here for the long haul.

"Every now and then, the land will speak more loudly in one place than it does at another, and this is one of those places. There is something special about it that you can feel through the soles of your feet. AIM, the American Indian Movement, is here because this land is sacred to them. I can see why. They believe that the area by the four Savannah Oak trees and natural spring is where the creation of the world began. I'm not Native American, but I can feel the sacredness of this ground. To have a place like this in the middle of a large metropolitan city is a miracle.

"What is the greatest cost you are paying to be here?" I asked. "It definitely doesn't offer the comforts of campus life."

"I miss my family, yet I just can't get up and leave and go spend the weekend with them. I know they are all sitting around a warm kitchen table, laughing, having fun, and telling stories. Being away from a loving family is painful. My relationship with my young nephew, whom I dearly love, has been put on hold. I've given up my health insurance because I'm

Photo courtesy of Sunshine

Sunshine paints a banner at Camp Two-Pines.

no longer a student, and I'm living in a city, which I said I would never do. It's hard on my soul to be here.

"When I had a boyfriend in college, it wasn't quite as hard to be away from home. However, it didn't take me long to realize that it is going to take someone special to be my boyfriend or husband—someone who can support me in my activist work. My previous boyfriend couldn't handle my activism, and I found his apathy disgusting. Whenever I protest, I'm reminded that I narrow my chances of finding my special someone."

"How do you keep going?" I asked. "Each day

that you sit here is another day gone by without earning money. At some point, don't you need something that isn't provided by sympathizers and supporters?"

"I ignore consumer needs as long as possible. You need to remember that I grew up knowing how to recycle everything and how to live lightly on the Earth. These are good skills to have in a situation like this. When I can no longer do without something, I waitress for a while or work at a food co-op for a few hours to make a little change. This lifestyle leaves me free to go where I'm needed."

"Your nickname is Sunshine. How do you manage to exude the feeling of sunshine when you have sacrificed so much to be here?" I asked.

"It's a wonderful emotional experience to be with people who are trying to make a difference. It gives me great joy to do this kind of work and be with these kinds of people. It would break my heart to just stand by.

"The '60s were more than drugs. They were a time of great social transformation. I don't understand how people of today can just sit and do nothing. I'm glad I'm not like that. History shows that it has always been small groups of people who make a difference and change its course. Knowing that I am making a difference and getting a message out is enough to put a smile on my face. What we do gets people to think. They may not agree, but at least they are thinking, and that makes them responsible for their decisions. Because of us, others are not making their decisions blindly."

"Will you feel your time has been wasted if this protest is not successful in halting the highway development?" I asked.

"Even if Reroute 55 goes through, something phenomenal has happened here. Earth First, an environmental group, and AIM, have had a long history of not getting along and have always worked separately from one another. With such a long extended stay, they have found ways to bridge their differences. With our new combined leadership, we can now be stronger when we are called to action the next time. No matter what happens, we have already been successful in creating peace between these two activist groups. I'm glad I was here to be part of it," she says with a smile that does indeed spread sunshine through the chilly air.

Sunshine eventually did return to her family where she helps tend her mother's nursery business and works at the local food co-op. She plans to transfer to the University of Wisconsin at Eau Claire, to major in Spanish, and is contemplating going on to law school. She feels these skills will be useful in future activism work in Central America, where she wants to help farmers maintain control of their land.

"What we do gets people to think. They may not agree, but at least they are thinking, and that makes them responsible for their decisions."

Cari Camille Witcher

Questions for Contemplation:

1. What cause or volunteer work have any of your family members pursued? How did it impact your life? Would you continue in their footsteps? Why or why not? What would you do differently?

2. Sunshine told me it would take seven Earths to support the lifestyle of Americans if everyone in the world were to live a similar lifestyle. Can you imagine modifying your lifestyle to live more lightly on the Earth? What might you do? What is a practical first step?

3. How might religions engage with government, business and commerce, education, and the media to ensure that the sacredness of the Earth is recognized and understood as a religious and spiritual reality?

4. Fran Peavy, a community organizer, believes that people aren't apathetic but choose not to get involved because they care very deeply and don't want to be disappointed, or they can't face the pain a particular issue brings up. What are some ways to deal with the pain and suffering one is likely to encounter as an activist?

5. Activists have strong opinions. What do you do when working with someone who has a strong opinion that's different from yours?

Resources for Reflection and Action:

Truth or Dare: Encounters with power, authority, and mystery, by Starhawk (San Francisco, CA: HarperCollins, 1987). Starhawk's brillant examination of the nature of power offers creative alternatives for positive change in our personal lives, our communities, and our world.

Soul of the Citizen: Living with conviction in a cynical time, by Paul Loeb (NYC: St. Martin's Press, 1999). Offers an antidote to the twin scourges of modern life: powerlessness and cynicism. He teaches us that everyone can work for social justice and claim their right to participate as an active citizen.

Pioneers of Change: Living experiments in creating a humane society, by Jeremy Seabrook (Gabriola Island, BC: New Society Publishers, 1993). Explores the work of the recipients of the Right Livelihood Award who have generated an amazing array of coherent, sustainable alternatives to destructive industrialism.

Ecological Education in Action: On weaving education, culture, and the environment, edited by Gregory A. Smith & Dolafruz R. Williams (NYC: State University of New York Press, 1999). Looks at the value of traditional and localized knowledge in fostering deeper personal identification with a landscape, and the essential connection between ecological sustainability and activism on behalf of social justice.

Stand Up/Speak Out (Video). Two grassroots advocacy groups, Parent Advocates for Youth and Youth Making a Change, develop their own voices and successfully utilize the arts and skills of political advocacy on behalf of families and children in their neighborhoods. Presents enthusiastic and committed women and teens discovering skills such as what it takes to get your voice heard, how anger can be used in a controlled and effective way, how to present your message quickly and decisively, and persuading public officials to meet with you. Contact the Video Project, 200 Estates Drive, Ben Lomond, CA 95005. Phone: 800-4-PLANET.

Sage Foundation, 744 West Hastings St., Suite 410, Vancouver, BC, Canada, B6C 1A5 Phone: 605-699-6298. Distributes a curriculum call Destination Conservation that helps faculty and janitorial staff plan conservation programs. The first year of a three-year program involves training staff in energy, solid waste, and water conservation; the second year emphasizes implementation; and the third year focuses on school energy audits.

Redefining Progress, 1904 Franklin St., 6th Floor, Oakland, CA 94108. Phone: 510-444-3041. Website: www.rprogress.org. This public policy research organization created a new model for measuring national social health that factors social costs and benefits into the GDP (Gross Domestic Product) equation. It starts with the same accounting framework as the GDP but makes some crucial distinctions: It adds the economic contributions of household and volunteer work and subtracts factors like crime, pollution, and family breakdown. The Ecological Footprint monitors the impact of human resource use, or consumption, on the earth, and The Satisfaction Barometer monitors people's contentment with their social and civic lives.

Alliance for Sustainable Jobs and the Environment. Website: www.asje.org.

Stoking the Fire | JIM ANDERSON

by Burt Berlowe

> *It may be that some little root of the of the Sacred Tree still lives. Nourish it then, that it may leaf and bloom and fill with singing birds. Hear me, not for myself, but for my people; I am old. Hear me, that they may once more go back into the sacred hoop and find the Good Red Road, the shielding tree.*
>
> —Black Elk

Inside a large white teepee in the midst of the Minnehaha Free State, Jim Anderson is hunkered down for the long, harsh winter. "My ancestors have been through thousands of winters and they didn't have a Tom Thumb nearby," he says, pacing the earth floor, "I have a World II oil-burning furnace and plenty of blankets. I'll be warm enough to stay here."

Jim is preparing for a new, increasingly difficult phase in the lingering occupation. He has already sacrificed much to be here: his job, time with his family, the privacy and comforts of regular life. Now the cold weather is on its way, bringing with it not only chill and snow, but also the ominous threat of a surprise police raid, rumored to be coming at any time.

Still, Jim and his fellow squatters show no signs of packing up. He points to a staff leaning against a canvas wall of his tent that was made by members of the Dakota community. "There's a lot of different stories about this land," he muses. "A lot of history told by our elders."

The power of that heritage can also be found a few feet from Jim's teepee. There, smoke rises continually from the hallowed blue flame of the sacred fire abutting the Native-American sweat lodge. That fire and what it represents, burn deep within Jim's soul, fueling his sense of history, his passion, and his reason for being at Camp Two Pines. This land once belonged to his ancestors, and it still bears their footprints. He is there to repeat an old tradition: protecting Indian territory from hostile invaders.

Jim has become more than just a member of this unique tribal community. He is—in a manner of speaking—its chief. As cultural co-chair and historian of the Mendota Mdewakanton Dakota Community, he has become a primary leader of the effort to stop the highway. Since he lost his job because of his protest work, he spends virtually all of his time at Camp Two Pines. His cluttered teepee serves as a command post for the campaign, with a cell phone, a VCR, a tape deck, and a collection of videos of the site. It is a busy place, abuzz with the chatter of constant visitors and the duties of running the camp. Between frequent interruptions, Jim explains what brought him here and what prompts him to stay:

"Our Dakota Community is a group of two hundred sixty adults from seven Native American families that had their origins in and around the town of

Photo by Todd Cota

Jim Anderson takes a break near the sacred fire.

Mendota at the confluence of the Minnesota and Mississippi rivers. It is where I learned what it is to be an Indian. One of my great-great-grandmothers bought land in Shakopee. My granddad wouldn't bring us kids there because there was so much prejudice and hatred. When he was in a car accident, they wouldn't take him to the hospital in an ambulance because he was an Indian.

"Most of our land in Minnesota was lost to white squatters. All our people were kicked out of this place and assimilated into white society. We lost our culture. My great-grandmother had her language beaten out of her. Her hair was cut and she came back and wrote stories saying she wasn't Native anymore.

"This area was the first white settlement in this country in the 1820s. Before that, it was a camping site for the Dakota Tribe. Under its ground are Indian artifacts, and growing on it are clusters of trees that are sacred to the Dakotas, as well as Camp Coldwater, a bubbling ancient spring that's been called 'the cradle of Minnesota.' We know that the spring contains medicine water and that people have been healed by it. We know our people came here and used this water and that it also restored the military men at Fort Snelling and their families that camped here into the nineteenth century. Immediately north of the spring is the last stretch of natural Oak Savannah trees on the Mississippi from its headwaters to the Gulf of Mexico. These are sacred trees where the Dakota and Chippewa tribes camped.

"I prayed for the power to help the people. An elder heard my prayer and said, 'Get up and do what you pray to do.' We sang in a circle, smoked the pipe, and prayed to the sacred trees. A couple of days later, a cousin of mine had a willow staff he prayed with. Every time he touched the sacred trees with it, he saw a flash of light.

"When I went down to the sacred area and looked over a cliff. I heard a chanting: 'Hun, hun, hun.'

"I never saw anyone. I heard the chanting three times: 'Hun, hun, hun. Hun, hun, hun. Hun, hun, hun.'

"I looked around but saw no one. I believe it was our ancestors, calling out to us to stay here."

Native Americans have been a powerful presence at Camp Two Pines. They have held powwows, parades, and other events on and near the site. Nearly every day, they have gathered around the sacred fire for meditation, drumming, and celebration. "The fire protects us," Jim says. "We light it for protection. We will keep it going no matter what—until they come in and put it out.

"Drumming is a key part of these rituals. Our drum is the heartbeat of our people. Not having it would be like a Christian church without a Bible. The first night we drummed, eight squad cars showed up because of the neighbors' complaints. They think it's a war drum. We need to get them educated that it doesn't mean war, but peace."

In lieu of taking me on an actual tour of Camp Coldwater, Jim plays a video he made in which he is walking around a desolate space, gesturing, and speaking emphatically. "This is what the park is going to look like if the highway goes through. Our sacred land is going to be desecrated worse than it has been already. These are the trees they're talking about tearing out. They're located in the four directions. Our spiritual leaders have told us that these are sacred trees. They are where our people would come and fast for four days and nights of their vision quest. There were dance circles here. The Savannah tree area is where our people used to camp. The trees grew together in the center to make an altar. This is our church.

"We've been called here for a reason. When I come here, the hairs on my hand try to come out of me. This place has touched me spiritually like no other place I've been. I'm here to help in any way I can."

The Free State's Last Stand

At 4:30 a.m. on a bitterly cold December morning in 1998, an army of over six hundred law enforcement officers stormed Camp Two Pines in the largest such action in state history. Bursting out of the back of Ryder trucks, they raided the remaining houses on the campsite, wielding guns, pepper spray, and bolt cutters in an attempt to evict the squatters. More than thirty protestors were arrested just before bulldozers flattened the homes. Several of the demonstrators suffered injuries, reactions to the pepper spray, and inadequate medical attention. A Native American's drum and a photographer's camera were taken away and broken. Tents and teepee poles were loaded into the trucks. Police dismantled the sweat lodge. A teepee, furniture, and other objects were consumed in a large bonfire used by the troops to warm themselves. The raid cost Minnesota taxpayers approximately $332,000.

The day after the raid, the reroute opponents were back at the site, announcing they would fight on. In a ceremony led by Jim, red cloth with tobacco offerings was tied to trees and shrubs, and a ceremonial fire was reignited. A banner saying, "The spirit is never crushed," waved from a tree. A group of Earth Firsters chained themselves to one of the four sacred trees two blocks south of the original encampment, alternating shifts to avoid frostbite. Eventually, the camp was rebuilt on a new site closer to the four trees and Coldwater Spring.

Just four days after the raid on their camp, the Dakota tribe and four individual protesters filed state and federal lawsuits seeking new environmental impact studies. An archaeological study, done by a city-hired company, denied the presence of Indian artifacts on the site, ignoring the testimony of several Native American elders. But the protesters kept on. One group fasted for several days. A young girl, protesting in a tree, was unable to eat because officials prevented her friends from handing her food. Several protesters chained themselves to trees and lay in front of bulldozers. As a way of expanding their base, the rerouters established an alliance with North Minneapolis housing activists and the two groups held a downtown march and rally. As its ranks grew, supporters vowed not to be moved.

In the fall of 1999, the Minnehaha Free State held a first anniversary celebration in their new encampment by the four sacred trees, adding to their record as the longest standing American urban environmental protest ever.

I found Jim and Tumbleweed at the anniversary party. Both had had been arrested recently for their protesting but had their charges dropped. Considering what they had been through in the past year, they seemed remarkably upbeat.

Tumbleweed said, "What we have accomplished here in one year is truly amazing. We now have hundreds of people with us. If nothing else, we have used this protest as a basis for education."

Jim added, "There must be some forces on our side for us to still be here. We can't match the strength of the opposition. But we will fight them with the truth."

A few months later, on another chilly afternoon, the occupation of the disputed site ended when police arrested over thirty protestors, while state workers chopped down the four oaks.

This time, there were no blaring sirens or surging officers with pepper spray. Instead, police in riot gear waited quietly for an Indian ceremony to finish before moving in. The trees came down only after transportation officials took time to remove ceremonial eagle feathers that had been recently tied to the top of the oaks. (In Dakota tradition, the feathers offer protection and cannot touch the ground). As police cleared the encampment, a sweat lodge, several teepees and parts of cut-up oak trees were returned to the Dakota Indians. Negotiations prior to this day had led to a compromise that left the Native Americans with at least remnants of their sacred site.

On the morning of this last stand, Jim Anderson sat with a remaining group of demonstrators huddled around a campfire and told them to be proud of what they had done. "We have done all that we could," he said softly. "It's not you that should be ashamed."

Jim was admittedly exhausted from the long struggle. Yet he vowed that the fight against the highway project would continue, now focusing on saving Coldwater Spring from possible environmental damage. "The spring is even more important to us than those trees," he said, "That's what we're going to fight for now."

And, indeed, that fight has gone on. The Stop the Reroute group changed its name to the Preserve Camp Coldwater Coalition. They won a significant victory by convincing MNDOT to alter its road construction plan slightly to avoid damaging the spring. They have been working with state and federal agencies to seek historic site designation for the area as a way to further protect it. Jim has led an effort to save a building on the Bureau of Mines property for use as a Native-American interpretive and education center. All of this, plus numerous pending lawsuits, prompted Jim to say recently, "The Highway 55 protest is not over."

Winter is once again settling on the former protest site. But this time, the howling cold faces little challenge as it sweeps across the open land. Where the blue flame once burned, there are only ashes, where the burr oaks stood, only stumps. The communal village has been disbanded; its once-proud occupants scattered to the four directions, rolled away like so many tumbleweeds.

But for those of stout spirit, hope still burns. They have not gone away, but have merely moved down the road a bit. They gather from time to time around the sacred spring seeking the strength to continue. They pray, chant, and play their drum, competing against the roar of the invader's machine once again taking over their land.

Questions for Contemplation:

1. What piece of land is special to you? Why?
2. Jim prayed that he could be helpful in some way. An elder told him to get up and do what he prayed about. What would you end up doing if you did what you prayed about?
3. What important things have you learned from your elders?
4. The protest group continually modified their efforts as first the houses, then the trees were destroyed. Finally, they had some success as they convinced MNDOT to alter the highway route to save Coldwater Spring. They also are working on a Native American interpretive and education center that otherwise wouldn't have emerged as an idea without the protest. What kind of constructive action have you seen that emerged from a negative or threatening situation?
5. After reading these stories has your view of nonviolent protesters changed? In what way?

Resources for Reflection and Action:

The Sacred Run, a film by Dragonfly Films, 4312 St. Dominique, Montreal, Quebec H2W 2B1, Canada, is a feature documentary about The Sacred Run event organized by Native American Indian leader, Dennis Banks. First Nation peoples from Canada, the United States, and Japan, joined by individuals from thirteen countries, traveled four thousand km along the Sea of Japan on a spiritual run, to carry the message that all life is sacred. Phone: 514-282-4569.

In the Absence of the Sacred: The failure of technology & the survival of the Indian Nations, by Jerry Mander (NYC: Sierra Club Books, 1992). Encourages us to take a fresh look at age-old Native attitudes toward life and economics and reclaim these values to save ourselves from destruction.

Hidden Heart of the Cosmos, by Brian Swimme (Maryknoll, NYC: Orbis Books, 1996). Swimme offers his readers a cosmology based on the latest science on one hand, and ancient wisdom and traditions of sacredness on the other.

Awakening Earth: Exploring the evolution of human culture and consciousness, by Duane Elgin (NYC: William Morrow, 1993). Elgin maintains that two views of evolution are dominant today: materialism (where matter is considered the primary reality) and transcendentalism (which emphasizes rising above the material world). But these old approaches no longer work in isolation from each other. A third, co-evolutionary view is emerging that integrates East and West, viewing reality as comprised equally of matter and consciousness in a mutually supportive spiral of development.

The Great Work: Our way into the future, by Thomas Berry (NYC, Bell Tower, 1999). Berry acknowledges that indigenous civilizations and cultures have governed our sense of the sacred and that we will never be able to function without these traditions. However, added to these older traditions, something new is happening. He says we are entering the Ecozoic Era—an era of an ever-renewing, organic-based Earth community. He urges us to take action during this brief period, this moment of grace, so we can succeed in reversing the destruction to the planet.

Remembering

Song by Julie Penshorn

It's late at night. I'm falling asleep
But in my mind are the moments I want to keep
Remembering, remembering.

I want to celebrate our day together
Just a bit of time we shared.
I want to thank you for holding me like
Your heart was full of love and care—
Full of love and care.
I know your story and you know mine.
Sometimes they put us on the
firing line
When we're remembering,
remembering.

I hate to hurt you, but I still do
It's so hard to love you like I know I need to.
Guess I'm not remembering, remembering.

I want to celebrate our day together
Just a bit of time we shared.
I want to thank you for holding me 'cause
Your heart was full of love and care—
Full of love and care.

Chapter 5

Carol Banister, Paul Cotton, Robert Hesslund, Manfred and Truan Schonauer, and Vernon Patterson

Gift Givers make contributions to their families and to society by using their unique talents in ways that enrich the lives of others. Some use the arts, some use their advocacy skills, and others use their workplace or home to make their contributions. Gift Givers have a deep commitment to the common good and share their resources abundantly.

Gift Givers seem to have a boundless capacity for giving. In fact, in some cases their lives depend on it. For example, Paul Cotton, verging on personal destruction, found new reasons to live as he recognized his importance as a giver of music and as a grandfather. Robert Hesslund, in the depths of depression, was able to find peace when he understood how his son's death was an important contribution to life.

Gift Giver Carol Banister believes: "Everybody has something to give. Sometimes it's as simple as just being there when someone needs you. My simple rules for myself are, take the best that was given to you, add your unique gifts and personality, and offer it. Hang out with people with guts. Get close to the situation and feel it. Try different methods to find what works. Don't worry about one way or one philosophy. Experiment. Be compassionate. Be strong . . ."

Taking Care of Family | CAROL BANISTER

by Rebecca Janke

In 1968, Carol and Fred Banister, white, educated, and financially secure, made a decision that would change their lives forever. The young couple, already blessed with a son and daughter of their own, decided to expand their family through adoption. They knew there were children who desperately needed homes because Carol volunteered at the Sutter Street YWCA in San Francisco, California, that provided services to young pregnant girls of color. "

At Sutter Street's YWCA, Carol saw pregnant girls, ages ten to sixteen, every day, few of whom had the means to care for their babies once they were born. Carol had specifically chosen to contribute her time to nonwhite girls because, "It angered me that the lack of services provided to young moms of color caused many of their babies to be born with health problems that could have been prevented. To make matters worse, due to the economic disparities between white and blacks at that time, there were very few families of color who could even afford to adopt."

Carol's sensitivity to racial inequities was sparked while she was still in elementary school. As a second generation American of Swedish, Welsh, and Scottish descent, she grew up in an Italian-American, Catholic neighborhood in New Hampshire. Swedes were considered to be on the very bottom rung of the social ladder, or so she thought, until she saw how poorly the other kids treated a new African-American girl.

"I became radicalized at the age of ten," she said with fire in her eyes. "I was incensed that this African-American girl was teased and tormented and no one did anything about it. The only power I had was to be her friend, and that's exactly what I did.

"I think I got my sense of fairness and justice from my mother," Carol said. "As the sole breadwinner for our family, she wanted to be an underwriter at the insurance company where she worked and was told that they only put men in those positions. Instead of accepting the status quo, she raised enough challenges to become New Hampshire's first female insurance underwriter.

"Years later, my strong commitment to fairness was further fueled by Professor Robert Reuman, one of my college teachers, and by St. Alban's Church that provided support for social activists. Because of my professor's commitment to social activism, we were exposed to the voices of people who have been silenced throughout history. Under his tutelage, we learned how to speak out and protest when injustice reared its ugly head. He led by example.

"I began to associate with activists on a regular basis and continued to learn nonviolent direct-action strategies. Any shyness I still harbored from my youth vanished. My soul felt free! No longer did I feel like I would be relegated to being a spectator to injustice. I was becoming a person who had the power and skills to stand up to it. I became a social activist. I was unstoppable and gave my time and energy to one community project after another. This kind of lifestyle suited me just fine, but I did wonder who would want to live with me. Though I was independent, strong, and needed my space, I didn't envision living my life as a single person.

"I was very fortunate to meet Fred. He was attracted to my strength of convictions and sense of rebellion to injustice. He's very much the same way. He even agreed to have the same number of kids—two biological ones and two adopted ones!

"My activist background was a real asset to my volunteer work. Working with the director provided further opportunities to learn about the subtle but effective ways of using power. I watched her do things that most other people would say, 'It can't be done . . . the obstacles are too great.' She, Elaine Wolfe Grady, was a wonderful role model.

"What started out to be a volunteer job, soon presented Fred and me with a chance to adopt a child—Daniel. He was six weeks old when the San Francisco Welfare Department placed him with us. He had been born to an Irish mother and an African-American father who had a hint of Native-American blood. His mother was in no position to care for him, his father was nowhere in sight, and there was no family of color on the list to adopt him. Fred and I put forth our names and, within a few weeks, our daughter, Tracy, and our son, David, had a new baby brother."

Carol and Fred were prepared for raised-eyebrows from family and friends, but were crushed when Carol's father disowned them for adopting Daniel. Her brother Charles was cool at best. But members of the racially mixed church gave them great support.

"My dad wouldn't have anything to do with Daniel. In some ways, I could understand it because he grew up during a time when whites and blacks kept to themselves. But it still hurt. We loved Daniel, and we wanted him to have the love a grandfather could give him. Even though we lived in two different states, we went home once a year. We didn't want Daniel to lose any more family than he had already.

"Rather than accept my father's rejection, I continued to call him and tell him how much I loved him. I sent pictures of our growing family and when the children got on the phone, Daniel was always included and cooed and babbled to Grandpa. Slowly, my dad developed a soft spot in his heart for Daniel, just in time for us to adopt our second African-American child, Val.

"I was volunteering at Lutheran Social Services when we learned about her. During her ten years, she had been so severely abused and neglected that her hair had completely fallen out, she was dangerously underdeveloped, and she had several types of infections. She had no extended family that was in any shape to take her in, and, because of her age, she would most likely not get adopted. Fred and I agreed to take her.

"When my grandfather met her, he took to her immediately. Perhaps it was because he could relate to her story. As a young boy, he had come with his parents from Wales and settled in North Dakota. He hadn't been abused, but both his parents died when he was nine and he knew what it was like to have no family. To survive, he went from barn to barn to keep warm and have a place to sleep. He got handouts here and there until a Native American family befriended him. With Val, he felt he had the opportunity to return the gift he had been given. He showered her with love and attention.

"Fred and I were soon appalled, however, at how society treats black boys compared to white boys. By now we were living in Minneapolis,

Photo by Todd Cota

Carol Banister rests on a meditational maze.

Minnesota, and chose to live in the inner city so that Dan, Val, Tracy, and David could live in a diverse neighborhood. One night, someone broke into our house. When the detective arrived to do his investigation, he singled out Dan. 'Did one of your friends do this?'

"Dan was kicked out of Boy Scouts over a behavior that white boys had also done without any repercussions. In his teens, Dan was frequently pulled over by the police even though he hadn't done anything wrong.

"One day, Dan was in the park, waiting for some of his friends, when two white men who had recently been released from prison assaulted him. They began by hurling racist remarks, and then they started pushing, punching, and kicking him. Dan knew tae kwon do and was able to make a few moves to defend himself. But if it hadn't been for David coming along just then and saying, 'Hang on, Dan. I'm going home to call the cops!' we think they would have killed him, as their racial hatred was so intense.

"We discovered with each incident that we needed to be advocates for our black children in ways that never even came up with our white children. Every time something happened that we felt was racist, I marched right into the office of the person in charge and demanded that they apologize and do what could be done to repair some of the harm they had inflicted. It takes a lot of energy to confront racism from the subtlest form to the most blatant. It gets so you have to choose your battles.

"A lot of people don't believe we have a serious racism problem. That's because much of it happens in subtle ways. Unless you live it, it is easy to miss. It is there. I've seen it with my own eyes. I've watched it reflected in the sad and angry faces of my children. So, I began telling our story of racism to all sorts of people, including the media.

"Fred and I gave our best to our children, but I have always believed, if possible, that children should be adopted by people of their own culture. Kids need their culture as much as they need their parents. When they are stripped of one, they shouldn't automatically be stripped of the other. Dan has written articles supportive of interracial adoption. However, he stresses that the family must be willing to provide contact with people in school, the neighborhood, and with friends that reflect the child's culture.

"Dan didn't really blossom until he was in a predominantly black school. As Dan says, 'Until I got there, Mom, I didn't feel like I belonged anywhere when I was away from home. I was too dark to be white and too light to be black. There was nobody I could relate to.'

"I encouraged him to join the basketball, track, and football teams at his new school so he would have black as well as white coaches. After going to summer basketball camp, he made the team and eventually became a tri-sport athlete, excelling in basketball, football, and track.

"Dan went on to attend UNC-Charlotte on a division one basketball scholarship. For Val, help came too late. Even though we helped find and reunite her with her seven siblings, finding them and providing a stable family was not enough to make up for those first crucial ten years. As an adult, Val is still struggling to put her life together. She has made some decisions that have worked against her. However, we are proud of her continued efforts.

"We need to change our focus from adopting kids to adopting families. Many families could stay together if they had some temporary help to get on their feet. Now that our children are grown, Fred and I have used the extra space in our house to be part of the movement that's heading this way in our country. Some families just need to stay a few weeks and others need to stay for six months.

"In cases when parents are not able to keep their children, even if they had support, more effort needs to go into reducing the cost of adoption. Kids need to go to same-culture homes whenever possible and, when not possible, into homes that are willing to keep them connected to their culture.

"When we adopted Dan and Val, there was no training at all to help parents of children of a different culture. We had to learn so much on our own. We now share that knowledge with adoptive parents."

Being acutely aware of justice issues, Carol works on a human rights commission board in Minnesota. She is working to ensure that people have equal access to services, as well as equal pay for equal work. She advocates for family preservation laws that help families stay together. She also advocates for affordable housing for families and provides consultation services to fledging grassroots nonprofit organizations working towards eradicating injustice.

"All my life I've been acutely aware of injustice. It's important we don't underrate ourselves and think we have nothing to offer. Things can change. My dad did. We all fail and we all have shortcomings, but we must never quit trying to take care of the human family."

Questions for Contemplation:

1. Think about a recent racial inequity or demonstration of bias that you witnessed. What was your physical response? Where in your body did you feel it? What effect did it have on you? What effect did it have on the other people involved?

2. Carol and Fred think it makes more sense to adopt a whole family to help its members get back on their feet emotionally, financially, and/or physically. Does this make sense to you? Why or why not?

3. What would you like to see happen that would help families be healthy and stay together? What gifts and talents do you have that you could share with a family that would help ease their burden and help them stay together?

4. Carol had an interesting way of reacting to her father's rejection of Dan. What have you found to be effective in dealing with parental rejection of your endeavors?

Resources for Reflection and Action:

Rules for Radicals: A practical primer for realistic radicals, by Saul Alinsky (Vintage Books, 1989).

Kinds of Power: A guide to its intelligent uses, by James Hillman (NYC: Doubleday, 1995). Shows how power can be used in ways that are psychologically healing, personally fulfilling, and organizationally effective. Explores twenty different kinds of power and offers practical approaches.

Grassroots and Nonprofit Leadership: A guide for organizations in changing times, by Berit Lakey, George Lakey, Rod Napier, & Janice Robinson. (Gabriola Island, BC: New Society Publishers, 1995). Weaving together theory, experience, and context, this book clarifies the nature of power and leadership, the stages of social movements, and the social environment in which change organizations exist.

Fundraising for Social Change, by Kim Klein (Berkeley, CA: Chardon Press, 1996). Tells you how to set up your office, keep records, and what to do if you are a brand new nonprofit. It is perfect for organizations wanting to become financially self-sufficient.

Next Steps in Parenting the Child Who Hurts: Tykes and teens, by Caroline Archer (Jessica Kingsley, 1999). Archer sets out to provide adoptive and foster parents with an understanding of the complex range of difficulties with which their children may struggle as a result of their early adverse experiences. She helps parents to make sense of the frequently perplexing behaviors of the hurt child within their family.

Lifebridge Foundation, Inc., PO Box 793, Times Square Station, NYC 10108. Phone: 212-757-9711. Fax: 212-757-0246. Email: LB457@aol.com. Website: www.lifebridge.org. Lifebridge Foundation, Inc., was established in 1992 for the purpose of supporting organizations and individuals who through cultural, educational, and or scientific means are dedicated to creating bridges of understanding among all people by bringing to realization the concepts of one humanity and the interconnectedness of all life. They support groups and individuals whose innovative projects foster transformative action in a changing world.

Women Against Racism, 130 N. Madison, Iowa City, IA 52242. Phone: 319-335-1486. A multicultural group of women working to dismantle racism and other forms of oppression at the personal and institutional level.

Council on Interracial Books for Children (CIBC) 1841 Broadway, NYC 10023. Phone: 212-757-5339. Provides resources to counter racism, sexism, and other forms of bias in school and society through its filmstrips, newsletter, curriculum materials, and children's book bibliographies.

Marching to the Beat of a Different Drum | PAUL COTTON

by Rebecca Janke

As soon as my business partner Julie and I coined the phrase "compassionate rebel," I started seeing them everywhere. I noticed the man who dared to playfully distract someone else's crying child in the grocery store. I sat with a teacher, who insisted on adding social responsibility as criteria for a high school investment class, even though it narrowed investment opportunities. I saw a woman who told a young man at a sandwich shop, "Stop hitting your girlfriend even if you think it's funny. She's asked you three times to quit. Listen to her." It even happened one evening when my husband and I went out to enjoy a reggae band.

As I watched and listened, I began to suspect that the drummer was a compassionate rebel. I didn't know why he moved me so powerfully. It might have been his aura of kindness. It might have been the street-wise look in his eyes. It might have been the way he moved when he played his music . . . I didn't know what it was, but I decided to find out.

I approached him backstage, introduced myself, and boldly announced, "I'm writing a book about compassionate rebels." During my brief explanation of the book I relayed that I'd like to interview him.

His fellow musicians interrupted with, "Paul's definitely a compassionate rebel."

Paul smiled, and said, "I'll be at the library doing some research on Wednesday. How about we meet at three?"

When I arrived at our scheduled time, he welcomed me as if the library were his home. As he escorted me through one corridor after another, I couldn't help but think how odd it was that he wanted to meet at the library. I was even more curious when I saw his mile-high pile of neatly stacked papers and books. "What was he doing that required such effort?" I soon learned he was studying the great works of other musicians for a visiting artist program that he was doing at one of the local schools.

When I inquired about his long-term relationship with the library he said, "I've been coming here every week for about forty-five years. My mom died when I was four. My father couldn't fight the pain of her death very well, even though he was a professional fighter. He took me to live with his mother, whom I adored. She included me in everything she did, even when it came to hanging out with her friends. It was so enjoyable that I chose to spend my time with her than with other kids.

"When I wasn't busy, I preferred to read, write, and play music. The problem was that we were so po'r we couldn't afford the second 'o,' let alone a bunch of books. When I discovered the library, I couldn't believe the amount of reading material that was available to me! I loved it. When I was older and school became boring, I skipped classes and came here. In the library, I'm exposed to the greatest minds in the world.

"I didn't intend to work with children in schools as a visiting artist. Originally, I wanted to be a teacher to help make school a more interesting place—like I wished it had been for me. I got a lot of encouragement from people to pursue a teaching degree since there is such a shortage of African-American teachers. My wife's family, though, had a completely different opinion. Her family didn't see how I could possibly provide for their daughter and grandchildren with a teacher's salary. They wanted me to get a real job so I could earn some real money.

"Money isn't the most important thing to me. I used to think that as long as I had a clean suit, my drums, and food to eat, that that was all I needed. At that time in my life, idealism and hope fueled me for the future. I didn't want 'things'—not anything more than I needed to live. I wanted my dream. I decided to pursue teaching, even without their blessing. However, the financial and emotional strain took their toll, and my wife and I ultimately broke up. It was excruciatingly painful.

"As I neared graduation, my dream of becoming a teacher came to a screeching halt. I enjoyed the kids during my student-teaching experience and they enjoyed me, but I was appalled at the discipline methods that were used. Kids were being yelled at, told what to do every minute of the day, and expected to toe-the-line or else. I knew I couldn't be a 'chair and whip' teacher—it wasn't how I wanted to live my life with kids. I never have and never will be comfortable with mean-spirited approaches with people.

"I put the brakes on my teaching career, so I could do some soul-searching to figure out what my path was going to be. I remembered that my grandmother used to say, 'Paul, you are good at your music. You have real talent for it.'

"I already had noticed how making music soothed me, and sharing it felt good, but I had to take care of my ex-wife and children. So I played in a band and made enough money to help them financially. The other guys in the band would get a motel when we were on the road, but I would sleep in the car so I would be able to send money home.

"About that time, a friend encouraged me to become a visiting artist in the schools. Music gives kids a safe and interesting place to share who they are, explore different identities, and celebrate their uniqueness. I found that the kids would tell me things that they had never told anyone before. As an artist-in-residence, I wasn't expected to play the heavy. I could concentrate on reaching kids and giving them new worlds to explore. In addition to teaching in the schools, I started teaching privately and sometimes through music stores' lesson programs. I'm good at teaching; it's my gift, and I want to give it away. The kids love me—and it doesn't hurt that I play a mean set of drums either.

"In my free time, I mentor kids one-on-one. There are some kids who don't want to, or aren't ready to do anything to better their lives. I don't spend my time there. I mentor kids who are ready to do the work, to move forward, and need help getting there. That's what I'm good at. I read everything I can about maintaining a positive attitude, especially Tony Robbin's material. It fits my style to work with motivated kids. There are other people who are good at mentoring kids with an 'I don't care attitude.' I leave it up to them to do what they do well.

"Several years ago, my self-made world came tumbling down. I lost my beloved grandmother. It

Photo by Todd Cota

Paul Cotton makes music to soothe his soul.

had always been just her and me. She was an anchor for me—an emotional center.

While my grandmother was hospitalized, I stayed with friends. One was a wonderful lady that I got very close to. Eventually, I knew I wanted to be with her the rest of my life. We actually were looking at houses and had a date set to be married. Then, just as I was ready to head off to play music on a cruise ship, she told me she had breast cancer and couldn't go along. It was serious—so bad she was determined to rebuild her relationships with her children and focus on healing her past, rather than building her future. She didn't know how much time she'd have and didn't want me to have to suffer through her deterioration. She broke off our relationship. I went on the cruise ship. Just a month after I returned from the ocean, she passed on.

"Between her death and my grandmother's death, I just didn't care what happened to me. My spirit was wounded. I was self-destructive. I was drinking and doing drugs, trying to escape. But I was still working. I still had my students. When I was giving lessons, I was okay. It was when I was alone, thinking, that I couldn't stand it. Finally, I tried suicide—twice.

"During the depths of my despair, I met a local minister when I was walking around in a fog one day. I knew him from the neighborhood and knew people who went to his church. That particular day I really needed someone to talk to, so I asked if I could make an appointment to see him. The first thing he asked me was, 'Are you a member of my church?' That alienated me forever from being a churchgoer, although somehow it didn't affect my faith. They say, 'What doesn't kill you makes you strong.' At the time, this was a serious blow to me. I was desperate, on the edge. However, his rejection made me angry. My anger made me stronger, and more determined to find my own spiritual relationship with God and a purpose for my life.

"A close friend who is a social worker helped me reclaim my life when she gave me a book of poetry: *There Are Men Too Gentle to Live Among Wolves*, by James Kavanaugh. She knew I wasn't a fighter and thought this poem would help me find my place in the world. For the first time, I felt my spirit of gentleness was no longer 'wrong'—my gentleness, my 'compassion,' as you say, is needed in the world. Kavanaugh helped me see that I was critically important, even if it didn't seem like it right then. It was like reading the Bible (in fact easier). I felt that this man's poetry saved my life. It's what made poetry really important to me. Kavanaugh had been a priest, and he had so much compassion and knowledge. He seemed so real, so sincere.

"Through Kavanaugh I was reminded how things can be said through music and poetry. I did a lot of writing. (It seems I'm most creative when I'm miserable.) The arts provide a universal language. A good poem or a good song can move a person into realms that can't be experienced any other way. So I continue to teach, and continue to write and play music.

"I share my poems with the kids in my artist-in-residency work, for I know they are suffering losses as well and that nobody is talking things through with them if they are not in some sort of counseling program or support group.

"After a couple years of the blues, things finally turned around for me. I'm more at ease and at peace with my life now, partly because I recognize I have a purpose in life. I have a job to do that no one else can do. I am a grandpa. No one else can have the job of being grandpa to my children's children. They need me. My conclusion about life is that the important things for me are my music and my granddaughter. It's funny, because I'm now in the place where my grandmother was with me ... life comes full circle!

Questions for Contemplation:

1. Paul's depression lifted when he was giving to his students and caring for his granddaughter. His giving gave him a reason to live. What experiences have you had in giving to others? How did it affect you?
2. Who has been a "pillar of strength" in your life? What did he or she do to make you feel loved, cherished, and valued?
3. Ask yourself regularly: Who needs me as a mentor? Who is watching how I live and the choices I make—and who needs me to affirm, challenge, and inspire them?
4. A poem changed Paul's life. What poem, song, or piece of music has had a profound impact on you and why?
5. Is there anything that bothers you about public school education? What would you like to see done differently?
6. Have you lost a best friend or lover? If so, what was helpful to you when you were grieving?
7. Paul gave the gift of connectedness to his granddaughter that his grandmother gave to him. What gift has been given to you that you find yourself now giving to others?

Resources for Reflection and Action:

There Are Men Too Gentle to Live Among Wolves, by James Kavanaugh (Steven J. Nash, 1991). An outstanding book of poetry.

God Lives: From religious fear to spiritual freedom, by James Kavanaugh (1994). Kavanaugh's compelling journey from priest to poverty to best-selling author and poet has been referred to in many of his other works, from *A Modern Priest Looks at His Outdated Church* to *America I Love You but Not like I Used To.* In this book, Kavanaugh again writes about his life, but this is an intense focus on Kavanaugh's revelation that the God he grew up with is indeed dead and there is a different God, a God within each person, that lives.

Man's Search for Meaning, by Viktor E. Frankl (revised and updated edition, Washington Square Press, 1998). Living in a German concentration camp, Viktor Frankl came to several conclusions about life and man's reasons for living.

I'm Only Bleeding: Education as the practice of violence against children, by Alan A. Block (NYC: Peter Lang Publishing, 1997). A passionate indictment of contemporary schools, where children become alienated from their own bodies and their creative potential. Block insists that we throw away the fixed curricula, universal standards, and intensive surveillance of children.

Kids Grieve, Too!, by Linda Goldman (Three videos available from KidsPeace, 1650 Broadway, Bethlehem, PA 18015-3998). Today's world is filled with a multitude of loss and grief issues that our children must face. Such a concept is a new paradigm replacing an older one in which the grieving child was the exception. The implications are far-reaching. Provides words, techniques, and resources needed to be able to communicate with children about death and other loss-related issues.

New Dimensions: A quarterly journal of the Mentoring Institute. A division of Big Brothers/Big Sisters of Greater Saint Louis, 4625 Lindell Blvd., Suite 520, St. Louis, MO 63108. Good resource for mentoring information.

Everybody Wins! This nonprofit organization runs a Power Lunch program in twenty-five cities, matching kids who need help reading with employees who are willing to tutor once a week during their lunch hour. Phone: 212-219-9940.

Strengthening the Circle of Life

ROBERT HESSLUND

by Rebecca Janke

The bumper sticker on a car at a pow-wow caught my eye: "My Child Strengthens the Circle of Life." As I looked at my five-year-old granddaughter, Chantelle, sitting next to me in the car, I reflected on the statement. Before the day was over, these words would hold much more meaning for me.

"Nana, let's go look at the Native American dolls," said Chantelle, who is part Native-American. I had brought her here hoping to find opportunities for her to make connections with that part of her culture. We went to the craft booth and were mesmerized by the hundreds of dream-catchers hanging from the ceiling. Gradually, we found our way to the dolls. She picked one up and hugged it in such a way that I knew she saw herself.

When we went to pay for it, I couldn't help but comment to the owner what a special world he had created with his display of dreamcatchers.

"Yeah," he said. "Some people like it, others don't. I sold a lot of stuff at the last pow-wow, but not much at a conference I went to earlier this summer.

"How come?" I inquired.

He looked around the booth, saw that his partner had things under control, and said, "Do you have time for a story?"

"Sure," I said, my curiosity piqued.

"The best way I can describe the tone of the conference is to tell you about a six-year-old boy who wanted a leather pouch with an animal printed on it. A relative bought it for him. Twenty minutes later he was back with his parents who insisted he return it. They were fundamentalist Christians and believed that the doll was evil because it had an 'animal spirit.' As the boy's eyes met mine, I could see he was embarrassed, sad, and disappointed. Most of the people there were Christians and were skittish about our booth.

"Thinking about that young boy, though, brought back memories of my childhood," he continued. "My father had never been part of my life, and when my mother's drinking and prostitution began consuming her days and nights, I was taken out of our home and put into a Christian foster home. It was just as well. I was tired of having to compete for my mother's attention. I hoped a loving family would adopt me.

"As the days, weeks, and months dragged on, it was apparent that no one wanted me as their son. I thought it was because I wasn't good enough. So, for the next several years I tried to get good at everything. I excelled in school and participated in every extracurricular activity I could. I went to church every Sunday and was the best-behaved boy in the bunch. Still, no one ever came for me.

"By the time I was eighteen, I was bitter and disillusioned. I figured that if this was how a loving God and Christianity operated, I didn't want any part of it. I shed Christianity and took up drinking. I vowed that I would never seek out anyone again. I stayed that way until my own son was born. As I looked into his eyes, his tiny soul touched mine. I loved him with all my being.

"As much as I tried, I wasn't able to regain my sobriety until he was eleven. When he was twenty-three, I was horrified to learn that he was drinking, but yet I understood the forces that can drive a man to drink.

"One night, he either tripped or passed out, on a step leading to the basement. When he landed, he hit his head and went into a coma. His neurosurgeon said, 'There is little chance your son will survive. If he does, he'll probably be a vegetable or have a complete personality change, more than likely a violent one.' A few days later, when I didn't think it could get any worse, they told me he was brain dead.

"'How could this be?' I wondered. He was the one person who had filled my heart, and now he was gone. I felt I was breaking into a million pieces.

"I knew my son would want to donate his organs. He was always generous, and his organs could help about one hundred people. However, I didn't want anyone else to pull my son's life support plug. I knew I had to do it.

"After I mustered up the courage to pull his life-support plug, I went to my car and decided to head for the nearest bar. Sobriety wasn't worth maintaining, not with this kind of pain. As the engine roared and died down to a quite hum, I could hear my car radio. Not wanting to listen, I was about to turn it off when I heard Robert Schuller saying, 'When your disappointment bears understanding, you shall have peace in your heart.'

"Instead of going to the bar, I decided to drive out to the country. I was determined I was going to sit there until my disappointment bore understanding—not really believing I would ever feel any relief from the pain that engulfed me. No bolt of lightning came out of the sky. No great bird of peace descended on my shoulder, but after several weeks of meditating on Schuller's words, I slowly began to realize that my son had strengthened the circle of life. My understanding came when I realized that each one of the one hundred people who had received a part of his body probably had about two hundred people who loved them, and could still love them, because my son's organs had kept them alive.

"In that instant, I could feel the love of those twenty thousand people. I knew then that my son's life had been for the greatest purpose of all . . . love. Not only had he lived for me to love, but also he'd lived for the 100 organ recipients and the 20,000 people who loved them. They were all impacted by his life."

"I'm number twenty thousand and one!" I said somberly, and thanked him for sharing his story. "By the way, is that your bumper sticker on the car in the parking lot that says, 'My child strengthens the circle of life?'"

"No. But that is a good one," he answered. "I would like one for my car."

As Chantelle and I were about to leave, he said, "Here, take this dreamcatcher. See the hearts around the rim? I give these away free to anyone passing by who has children. It's a reminder to celebrate the children who come into our lives."

"But mister, I've got a sister. Can she have one too?" asked Chantelle.

"Of course," he said, and handed us another one. She and I gave him a hug in gratitude.

As we walked away, hand in hand, I thought how natural it was for Chantelle to think of others. I imagined how her gifts to the world would unfold. When we knew she was coming into our lives, although our daughter was only fourteen at the time, my husband and I were devastated. Life had not gone according to plan with us either. But here, a few years later, with a strengthened family, and Chantelle tugging at my hand, I, too, had found ways to give that I didn't know I had within me. But that is another story.

As Chantelle ran to give her sister her dream-catcher, I made a mental note to check "donor" on my driver's license the next time I renewed.

Photo courtesy of Robert Hesslund

Robert Hesslund

Robert died in October 2001, from cancer. His story lives on and continues to strengthen the circle of life . . . and my granddaughter and I remember.

When Shall We Have Peace?

by Julie Penshorn

The other day, right after I had been reviewing some new research on bullies for my job as co-director of Growing Communities for Peace, my son came home from school and was very aggressive toward me. I said, "Stop talking to me that way! I don't like it!" and left the room. A few minutes later he came upstairs to apologize.

He said, "I'm sorry, Mom, but I'm just a bully."

I was horrified! In going over all the characteristics of bullies and victims in my mind, I saw my son having more than one of them. Then, as the responsible person I am, I could see how perhaps I was a role model for him. My son might construe my strong behaviors as bully behavior. I was devastated because I have such a commitment to nonviolence, and I know how horrible bully behavior can be.

So I yelled, "Well, if you're going to be a bully, just stay away from me! I don't like hanging around with bullies," and I went to my room. My son, frustrated by that last, very separating and hurtful comment, came after me.

I said, "Do I have to leave the house to get any space? I just want to be alone right now," and I tried to leave the house. He stopped me in the entryway.

"Mom, it's just that I always want to be a bully in school. But I can't because they won't let me, and I won't have any friends if I do. So I hold it in all day long, and when I get home, I just have to let it out!"

"Wow," I thought, "How insightful of my ten-year-old boy. But, how scary that he feels like he's always repressing his urge to be a bully. What is that all about?"

The next day, I asked him if we could talk. He grudgingly agreed, and over dinner I said, "Tell me more about being a bully. What do you mean?"

"Dana, in my classroom, always bugs me so much and I want to hurt her and I can't, so I just hold it all in. She gets away with treating me mean, but anytime I do one thing to her, I get in trouble," he complained.

I responded, "Tell me a time that she bugs you so much that you want to hurt her."

He thought silently. It looked like he was having a hard time deciding which story to tell. I said, "Tell me what happened today."

"Okay. Today, at recess, I'm playing football with the guys and Dana comes up behind me. Right before I throw the ball (I'm quarterback) she says, 'You suck,' to me. So, of course I throw the ball really bad. Then, I go to throw the ball on the next play, and she does the same thing again!"

I said, "Collin, it doesn't sound like you're being a bully to me. Sounds like you are being bullied, and you're angry at the unfairness of the situation. Sounds like you want to rebel against this injustice."

"Yeah, I do," he whined tearfully, "But I can't, because I'll get in trouble. It's just so unfair!"

"I didn't mean rebel in a hurtful way. Can you think of a way to rebel in a way that doesn't hurt anyone? Maybe talking to her more, or becoming friends with her, or something?"

"No way, I hate her!"

"Okay, let's look at this a different way. What benefit could she have in your life? What can you learn from her?"

"Nothing. She's a bully," he persisted.

"Okay, here's a question for you. Remember the other day when you went to the Twins game with the boys and you were all heckling the pitchers on the other team when it was their turn to pitch?"

"Yeah."

"Well, do you think they threw the ball badly every time you said, 'You stink!' or something like that?"

"Well, no."

"Of course not. They learned how to shut their mind to the mean things that people say. They developed a skill of focusing so intently that nobody can distract them. That's a good skill for a ball player like you, right?"

"Yeah, but she just makes me so mad!"

"Well, of course she does. Maybe she's in your life to help you learn to shut out hurtful things that aren't true. Maybe her presence can teach you how to be a strongly focused quarterback or pitcher."

"Well, maybe," he said, pondering.

"Collin, I'm glad we got to talk about this because now I realize that you're not a bully. I got scared when I heard you say you were a bully yesterday! I know you're not 'always a bully' like you said, and, I'm sorry I freaked out. I was not thinking straight because of all the infor-

mation I had just been reading. I overreacted because I was letting you put a label on yourself. I'm sorry."

"Okay Mom." We hugged.

As I was thinking about this incident, I remembered a time when my son's school had a speaker who talked about ADHD. Shortly thereafter, more kids than ever were being labeled ADHD! Likewise, when I read the bully research I was ready to label my son.

Every child is in the process of growth and change. Giving up on them and/or labeling them negatively can encourage more of what we don't want.

What if we could embrace all our little "bullies" and our "ADHD" children as gifts in our lives, finding in them the buds of compassionate rebellion and nurturing them?

We celebrate and honor Robert Hesslund because he sought understanding in his misery and looked for meaning in his life. We celebrate him as a compassionate rebel working to find his personal peace and reminding us that children are precious gifts. Our job as teachers and parents is getting to know our children as we search through the disappointments they can bring to our lives, so we can spot their beginning compassionate rebel strengths. Going beyond the superficial and the obvious to the underlying and the profound is, in itself, a compassionate rebel gift. That's one gift I want to give to my son.

Questions for Contemplation:

1. Have you discovered an insight or strength within yourself during a time of crisis? What was it?
2. What is one thing that has deeply disappointed you? What did you do to cope?
3. What were you told about other people's religions as a child? How does that play out in your life today?
4. What have you done to steer away from a self-destruct mode when you have been seriously disappointed with something?
5. What traits in children or you might be budding compassionate rebel skills? How could they be nurtured and channeled in ways that enhance life?

Resources for Reflection and Action:

Amazing Grace: A vocabulary of faith, by Kathleen Norris (NYC: Riverhead Books, 1998). Struggling with her return to the Christian church after many years away, Kathleen Norris offers believers and doubters alike an illuminating perspective on how we can embrace ancient traditions and find faith in the contemporary world.

Winning a Day at a Time, by John Lucas with Joseph Moriarity (Center City, MN: Hazelden Books, 1994). A tremendous collection of stories by one of the foremost drug counselors in the country and a former NBA star and coach.

The Power of One: Authentic leadership in turbulent times, by Sharif M. Abdullah (Gabriola Island, BC: New Society Publishers, 1995). Abdullah shows how, by rethinking our assumptions about power and leadership, ordinary people can create a society based on love, compassion, sustainability, and authenticity.

Peace Is Every Step: The path of mindfulness in everyday life, by Thich Nhat Hanh (NYC: Bantam Books, 1992). Contains commentaries and meditations, personal anecdotes, and stories that encourage the reader to work for peace in the world as he or she continues to work on sustaining inner peace.

Midwestern Prevention Project, Mary Ann Pentz, University of Southern California, 3414 Topping Tower, 1441, Eastlake Ave., MS-44, Los Angeles, CA 90033-0800. Phone: 323-865-0325. This program decreases the rates of onset and prevalence of drug use in young adolescents, as well as in parents, by combating destructive community influences.

Walk On | MANFRED AND TRUAN SCHONAUER

by Rebecca Janke

Once in awhile, we get to experience things that are so far removed from the ordinary that we can't help but sit up and take notice. Such was the case when I discovered the Pipe Dream Center. Nestled among pine trees on a winding country road, this quaint structure has been transformed from a two-room schoolhouse into a vibrant, cozy haven for the arts. Its owners are Manfred Schonauer, a German immigrant, and his wife, Truan.

Manfred, known for his astounding musical versatility, could fill concert halls playing his five different keyboards at the same time, or playing his B3 organ while wailing away on the saxophone or flute. Truan, called the "Erma Bombeck of the North," because of her quick wit and interesting stories, could fill any well-known comedy club.

During my monthly two-hour drive to get to this magical place in the woods to enjoy live music and some of the most amazing talent I've ever seen, I often wondered why Manfred and Truan chose to do this out in the middle of nowhere. When I asked, they obliged my curiosity and shared their story over warm banana bread in the kitchen.

Manfred was born into a musical family. His father, Joe, a professional musician, taught young Manfred how to read music before he was allowed to play the piano. Joe, a World War II veteran, tried providing for his family by traveling up and down the Rhein River in Germany with his wife and two small boys, playing night clubs. It was difficult. The pay wasn't that good, they had to stay in one-room efficiency apartments, and they could never stay in one place long enough to put down any roots. Even with all the obstacles of this gypsy lifestyle, Manfred could see how much his father loved music and he fell in love with it, too.

Eventually, Manfred and his brother had to stay at an orphanage for a while until the family became more financially stable. He developed compassion for his older brother and the other kids as they struggled with the emotional trauma of being away from their families while their parents were trying desperately to recover from the war. His intense dislike for authority figures to this day stems from the adults in the orphanage who represented a force that kept him away from his parents.

At age sixteen, now reunited with his family, Manfred announced he wanted to become a professional musician. "No son of mine is going to have a gypsy life," his father retorted. "I'm going to make sure you get a real job."

Manfred's father got him an apprenticeship as an import/export clerk. "Whatever you did in Germany as an apprentice, usually was your job for life," said Manfred. "The thought horrified me. The rebel in me came out, and I quit and took a job in a piano factory tuning pianos. It was the closest thing I could find to a musical career. The job lasted two years and ceased when my boss caught me playing the pianos more often than tuning them!

"So I put an ad in the trade papers. I accepted jobs as a keyboard player that were the farthest away, rather than the ones paying the most, because I wanted to see the world and learn from other great musicians.

"A lucky break came when I was invited to join an Italian band that got a two-year engagement in the United States at Mickey Rooney's Downingtown Inn and Golf Club.

"When we arrived in New York, I had just three dollars in my pocket, but I immediately looked for the best jazz and rock-n-roll teacher I could find. This was my chance to study where jazz was born! I found one of the greatest, Bernard Peiffer, a French immigrant jazz pianist. I studied with him for two years and still harvest from his teachings today. It was largely Mr. Peiffer's encouragement that motivated me to get a Green Card and stay in the States. I met and married my first wife, who I thought would be my partner for life. I was ready to be a musician who would provide for his family just fine.

"I worked with a trio, but it became very frustrating having to rely on others and hold a band together, so I decided to create a one-man act. I added instrument after instrument to my keyboard and vocals. I got booked right away."

Playing successfully all over the Twin Cities of Minneapolis and St. Paul, Minnesota, Manfred developed a weakness for parties—anytime, anywhere. His marriage fell apart and he became an emotional wreck. "I was so devastated," Manfred said, "that any woman wanting to go out with me soon lost interest after I went on and on about my misery."

"Fortunately, a woman in the neighborhood offered me a platonic friendship. She and her married friend, Truan, slowly pulled me out of my doldrums. Truan could make us laugh harder than I've ever laughed before. When I went on the road again, I lost track of her.

"A few years later, when I was putting away my instruments at a piano bar, who should appear from the kitchen, but Truan! 'Truan, what are you doing here? I thought your husband didn't want you out this late at night.'

"Ex-husband!" Truan exclaimed. "I left him. Why else do you think I would be cooking in someone else's kitchen?"

Truan was born to a cranky, moral Lebanese mother with high standards, and a father who had an amazing ability to laugh amidst adversity. They were as poor as church mice, but she and her two brothers learned creative ways to entertain each other and take care of themselves.

"We couldn't afford to buy a new pair of shoes when we got holes in the soles," said Truan, "so my brothers and I designed colorful, elaborate patches. They were such a hit in the neighborhood that even the rich kids wanted them instead of going on their customary trip to the shoe store.

"My parents were likely the most opposite people on this earth to marry and have children. Mother taught us work ethics, cleanliness, how to sit up straight, keep your elbows at your sides, and never chew with your mouth open. Dad played the accordion and harmonica, and sat in the sun with an onion bag on his baldhead to get reddish-tan squares. He would poke two holes in a piece of white bread and stare at us and then exclaim, 'Did I ever tell you how much I love you?' His devil-may-care attitude enraged Mother, and she would come out with the broom. We kids would say that Mom had the fastest broom in the west," Truan chuckled.

"Dad got crippled from a work accident and Mom had to work two jobs sometimes to keep the family intact, plus take care of Dad. It was at this time that I think my Mom pretty much thought life sucked."

Truan feels this odd combination of parentage made her and her brothers rebels. They worked when other kids horsed around, but in their fun times, they took scripting from their father and were the craziest kids in the neighborhood. To this day, all three of them are highly creative artists, actors, and writers with a different twist on life.

Photo courtesy of Manfred and Truan Schonauer

Manfred and Truan Schonauer

Truan escaped poverty when she married into a family with old money and plenty of proper etiquette. She and her husband had two sons and two daughters, but all was not well.

"It just seemed there were too many 'rights' and 'wrongs' being in such a proper, prestigious family.

Eventually, I thought I would explode from all the expectations. My husband even stuck a daily accomplishment list to the refrigerator door that I was supposed to complete. I wondered how could I get much of anything done with a babe in my arms, one clinging to my leg and another one in my belly! I continued to feel inadequate until my dearest friend, Sandy stopped by one day. She knew my frustration had been mounting. She looked at the list, shook her head, put it in her mouth and ate it! I knew then that I was free to be myself, and that's just what I did.

"My dad's playfulness cropped up in me and, while the more 'normal' neighborhood women were hanging wash on the line and getting their lists done, I put on a Gypsy outfit and went to the kids' elementary school and told stories. I had a clown outfit made up and marched in local parades. I dressed up at Halloween and trotted along with the kids. I rode an Indian pony to the grocery store and to church. I chained myself to a tree along with a friend to save it from destruction and wrote poetry every day.

"Eventually, I either became too much for my husband or he became not enough for me. We divorced. Reality hit hard. It was time to put the clown suit away and find a job. I was an excellent cook and ended up cooking in the very restaurant where Manfred was playing."

Over the next few months, Manfred and Truan renewed their friendship and in the process discovered they were soul mates. They soon became a family. As they worked hard to make ends meet, they were fueled by the dream of someday having an entertainment place of their own where Manfred could create and play original music, and Truan could do humorous skits and poetry readings. Little did they know it would be a journey of several years, and impact the lives of hundreds of people.

"We thought we finally found our place when we leased a bar with an option to buy," said Manfred. After putting a lot of our funds into it the option fell through, and Truan and I had forty dollars between the two of us."

Manfred went back on the road until he learned that he had developed throat nodes. This forced him to quit singing and return to writing music. Influenced by German artists like Klaus Schulz and Tangerine Dream, he started to write and record his first electronic music, Opus I, II, and II.

In the meantime, he earned money by bartending, and Truan started up a cleaning service for homes and businesses. To keep her sanity, she wrote a weekly article for the local newspaper called "Tossed Salad." With her Erma Bombeck style, she shared the trials and tribulations of their family. "It sure was more fun than cleaning toilets," she laughed.

This went on for several years until one day when Manfred was watching a PBS feature on a Modern Dance Performing Arts Center located in a nearby one-room schoolhouse. They decided that's the direction they wanted to take. The children had all left home. It was good time to pursue their dream again.

For two years, they drove around every weekend looking for an old schoolhouse. They finally found one for sale but it was going to take a huge amount of blood, sweat, and tears to make it presentable. For the down payment, they sold almost all their earthly belongings. "I didn't even keep the ironing board!" said Truan.

During the winter, they found time in their off hours to scrape the old tin ceilings and plaster walls. They named their place the Pipe Dream Center and were ready for business in the spring.

"When we opened our doors, the first few concerts were a shock to the audiences. People expected Mozart, Beethoven, and pop music that they had heard Manfred play in the bars. His music at the Pipe Dream was so far out it scared some people. Others were spellbound.

"That is when the rebel in me cropped up again. I continued to play only original music," said Manfred. "Those who were spellbound kept coming back, but we were concerned about the people who felt uncomfortable with us."

"We did anything and everything we could think of to let people in the community know we were safe and good people," said Truan. We went to every graduation, baptism, confirmation, and funeral we were invited to. We helped people chop wood for the winter, jump-started dead batteries, and shared food from our garden. People began to trust us and, slowly but surely, our place began to fill up with the locals, and, to our surprise, with people who lived hours away.

"Children wanted to learn how to play like Manfred. Soon, we were full during the week with piano students. Manfred was asked to give lessons to handicapped children in their homes since he believes music provides helpful therapy for kids. Parents were ecstatic that their child, who they thought could never play, got to play after all.

"In the beginning, it was tough because the repairs on the building sucked up any and all money we made. Chopping and stacking the tons of wood needed to heat the place added an additional, almost insurmountable, challenge. However, so many people came forward to help that the word 'compassionate' is almost inadequate to describe them," said Truan with tears in her eyes.

"We thought we were finally coming around the bend financially. Then the mortgage broker called to remind us of a balloon payment of five thousand dollars due in two weeks. We didn't have the money and didn't know what we were going to do. When I get stressed, I start to clean," said Truan. "I cleaned more vigorously than usual and came across an old box of papers that I had been carrying around for years as we moved from place to place. As I sorted through the old papers, I found an insurance policy. Curious to see if it had any cash value, I couldn't believe my eyes when I saw the amount—five thousand thirty-one dollars and twenty-three cents!

"At 1:00 p.m., the day our balloon payment was due, we walked into the mortgage broker's office, gave him five thousand dollars, and the building was officially ours."

Because Manfred and Truan worked so long and hard to make their dream come true, they decided to open up the Pipe Dream Center to other groups who were just getting a start or needing space. Tai Chi classes were offered. Local quilters and artisans were able to have the space for demonstration events and shows. A local women's discussion group helped ease the isolation rural women face. It even became a favorite spot for small informal weddings and a neutral meeting space for social action groups.

Manfred continues to study music, recently finishing a class at the University of Wisconsin on counterpoint and composition. He has produced music for films, made a CD, and enjoys adding new or ancient instruments to his monthly concerts. He is not seeking fortune and fame. "I want to reach out and put the arts in the rural area," he said. "Life is all about reaching out to each other. Music is a tool for that. Here, I know I am with people who care for each other. I am more grateful for that than having my name in bright lights.

"We get so many messages in our culture that we have to be this way or that way, but I'm glad that Truan and I stuck it out to just be ourselves. We've created something really beautiful here. Even during the cold winter months, concert night and boogie night bring people from miles around. We fire up the potbelly stove, hang backdrops that Truan creates, light candles, and look forward to seeing all the people that we consider our extended family.

"I've always had a hard time with authority figures, and have thought of myself as a rebel (so did others). But over the years, I've come to realize that we've put a lot of compassion into our rebellion. It was through our compassion that we were able to make a commitment to providing a service to people instead of just finding money and self-gratification in being entertainers.

"The most important thing about compassion is sharing it through human connections," said Manfred. "Truan and I talk to every single person who comes through the door. Often, people who are going through a rough experience find comfort sitting around the kitchen table with us while having a cup of coffee or tea, and maybe a good cry. Hugs are commonplace, and personal letters go out on a weekly basis.

"Coaching others out of their fears of performing and giving them a safe place to try their skills has allowed us to see torrents of creativity unleashed. That's a wonderful thing to watch and be part of."

Traun said, "We will never be financially secure or be on the cover of *Time* magazine, but the wealth we have accumulated in our hearts and the peace we have attained is spiritually more valuable than anyone can imagine."

Walk On

Among the Lakato is a concept, spelled "wakan"
In English letters
Walk on.
In English it is often translated as
All things are sacred or "It is a sacred place."
But in Lakato, it is not so. It is an attitude
And a worldview, not translated in words,
But all is sacred and nothing is not sacred.
Walk on
Martin Luther King said it, too.
Walk on.
He said, "Church is a not a place you come to.
It is a place you go from."
Walk on.
And so it is for me, the Pipe Dream Center.
It is not a place to go from
Walk on.
Yet it is not a place to leave,
But to take with.
Walk on.

—Jon Bell, written in honor of the Pipe Dream Center

Questions for Contemplation:

1. Humor is one of Truan's traits that Manfred so admires and benefits from. What is one trait that you so appreciate in your significant other and why is it helpful to your relationship?
2. Manfred and Truan worked a long time to make their dream come true. What is a dream of yours that you would like to pursue even if it takes a long time to achieve?
3. Which one of your talents could be turned into a gift of service to others?
4. Instead of just working to make a living, how could you make more of a human connection with others through your work?
5. Describe a time when you rebelled against the status quo because you knew it was time to offer up something new.

Resources for Reflection and Action:

About EOS (CD) by Manfred Schonauer. (Comstock, WI: Cosmic Plasma Publishing Co., 1997).

Ripple from Zambezi: Passion entrepreneurship and rebirth of local economy, by Ernesto Sirolli (Gabriola Island, BC: New Society Publishers, 1999).

Women Who Run With the Wolves: Myths and stories of the wild woman archetype by Clarissa Pinkola Estes (NYC: Ballentine Books, 1992). Full of wonderful, passionate, poetic, psychologically potent words and images that inspire, instruct, and empower women to be true to their own nature and be in touch with sources of creativity, humor, and strength.

To Love and Be Loved: The difficult yoga of relationships, by Stephen and Ondrea Levine (Louisville, CO: Sounds True. Website: www.soundstrue.com, 1999). Calls for deep inner work, both with self and with your beloved. With each listening, your hearts will become more uncluttered, your relationship more inclusive of compassion for self and other. In short, this is a life-changer.

The New Couple: Why the old rules don't work and what does, by Maurice Taylor and Seana McGee. Relationships have endless potential to bring joy and suffering to our lives. Our relationships initially seem to offer us joy, but then time and life set in and maintaining these joys becomes much more difficult. Shows how our challenges can help us lift our relationship to a higher level including focusing one's life priorities, expressing emotional integrity, and supporting each other in finding your mission in life.

Music for People, PO Box 397, Goshen, CT 06756. Phone: 860-491-4511. Founded by cellist and improvisator David Darling, their philosophy states that music is a natural creative expression available to everyone.

Music Therapist for Peace, PO Box 743, Cathedral Station, NYC 10025. Phone: 212-865-6895. Website: http://pages.nyu.edu/ˆboxill/mtp.html. Founded for the purpose of furthering peace on all levels of human existence through methods unique to music therapy. Networks with music therapy professionals worldwide and has initiated a project called Students Against Violence Everywhere, which is designed to reduce violence in schools.

Dreams of an Average Man | VERNON PATTERSON

by Burt Berlowe

Behind the open horizontal window that overlooks the Merwin Drug Café in North Minneapolis, Minnesota, Vernon Patterson flips an egg over-easy on the skillet then turns to take in his miniworld. Peering intently from under his cook's cap, he scans the familiar and new faces, dreaming up the verses that will intertwine the present with the vivid memories of his past:

I've lived the life from Pimp to Preacher, and at the age of forty,
I find myself the teacher.
Possessed with knowledge, I must confess. I'm just like all the rest.
Trying to make it day to day, hoping to keep the pain away.

In the section of Kansas City, Missouri, where Vernon Patterson grew up, family and community were important as a way of dealing with hardship. His mother had ten kids during two marriages and often times worked long hours just to make ends meet. This meant less time to be with her children, making moments of togetherness rare and precious. Young Vernon didn't always get along with other members of his family, but he was particularly close to his mother. Each night, he would wait anxiously for her return, no matter what the hour.

"When I was eight years old . . .my mom worked day and night, and I didn't see much of her. So, I got to the point where I would stay up until she got home, so I could have at least a few moments of my own with her.

Photo by Todd Cota

Vernon Patterson works at the Merwin Drug Cafe.

"It's five minutes until midnight, I'd better hurry, the bus will be here in a flash, and she'll have to walk home by herself. Boy, it's cold out here tonight, I better run. Whew! Sometimes this one block seems so long. There's the bus lights coming down the hill. I'm counting the streets by name: Montgall, Chestnut, South Benton, Bellafontaine.

"Oh wow, there she is!

"Hi, Momma!"

"Boy, what are you doing up so late?"

"I just wanted to walk you home."

"The neighborhood that I grew up in was a predominately black 'hood,' so my little world was pretty comfortable. My aunt introduced me to the civil rights movement when she invited me along to march with Martin Luther King in Selma, Alabama. That's where I picked up my desire for social action. I learned that you had to understand your history to understand your present. The music of that time preached unity. James Brown's new hit was 'Say It Loud, I'm Black and I'm Proud.' It was the start of a new era. It was okay to say that you liked yourself even though you were black. I decided that no matter what they would call us, I would always be a black man.

"When I was fourteen years old, there were so many things that changed my life, it would be hard to mention all of them at any one time, but a lot of dreams for my future were formed during that year.

In my youth, Aretha sang, and Lou Rawls would tell the stories.
In my youth, the church bell rang and God was in his glory.
In my youth, friends were friends and we never had to wonder

Because we saw the sun but we also heard the thunder . . .

"It was 1968. I was in Fellowship Baptist Church praying and singing, 'Father please teach me what I need to know in order to do what you have in store for me.' The next day, I met Pete and Gary O'Neal of the Kansas City Chapter of the Black Panther party, and began my education in being black in America.

"In 1969, I was arrested during the riots in Kansas City. After that, black unity was broken, much like the Hebrew children after they had crossed the Red Sea."

You can't have this
You can't do that
Like yesterday
If you're black
Get back.

"The day after Dr. King's assassination, I walked into Central Junior High with tears in my eyes and anger and confusion in my heart. I met up with some friends in the halls and the question was, 'What are we going to do?'

"I suggested a protest march down to City Hall. With those words, I was more or less drafted into leadership and everything mushroomed into pure hell. We ran through the building, knocking on classroom doors asking the students, 'Are you with us?'

"We left Central Junior with close to sixty students, crossed the football field where a one hundred more students and a teacher or two joined us. By the time we got in front of City Hall, we had well over a thousand students with us.

"The Kansas City Police Department (KCPD) followed us the whole time. They gathered some of our leaders and shuffled us onto school buses and transported us to a Catholic Church School called Holy Name. We were all packed into the basement of the church and told this was where we would get to say what we had to say. They even brought two local DJs from KPRS radio. One of the DJs had just taken the microphone on stage, when there was a large boom!

"The KCPD had fired a tear gas canister into the building through a window. Screams of panic were everywhere. We tried to find a way out, but all the doors were chained from the outside. The lights went out and we groped along the walls, trying to find an exit. We found a door, but it was chained from the outside. In frustration, we kicked and kicked until we knocked the door off its hinges . . . people began to pour through the small hole. I was almost run over by a car when I jumped from a small staircase to the street below. The police headed our way and hit us with clubs as more gas canisters went off. I took off running until I got home. After school the next day, the police, four cars deep, pulled up on us. They put us on the ground with guns to our heads, and put me under arrest for inciting a riot.

"It wasn't the first time I was considered to be a trouble-maker. Because I joined the Black Panther party and was their Minister of Information, the Kansas City School Board wanted me out of the school. One day, a security guard pushed me up against a wall and pulled a gun on me. Later, the principal told me, 'Vernon, we're not putting you out because you're a bad kid but because you have more control of the school than I do.' I was expelled from my all-black school, even though I was the student council president.

"A few years later, I was charged with armed robbery. I was innocent, but I went to the state pen for three years at the age of nineteen. While in prison, I decided to make the best of the situation. I worked in the prison library and taught older guys to read and write. To help pass the time, I wrote poetry like I did during my lonely times waiting for my mom to come home.

"One night, I got stabbed by a prison inmate and stabbed him in self-defense. When my girlfriend was not allowed to write to me because she wasn't yet eighteen, I started organizing again. I got together five hundred signatures on a petition to change the law. Under my leadership, we were successful. The law was changed.

"Much of my life, the powers that be wanted to destroy any potential I had as a leader. Eventually, it was proven that I didn't commit armed robbery. They had no choice but to let me go. Since there is no restitution for false imprisonment and I had little resources, I joined the Army.

"In the Army, I was harassed by officers. I fought back once and was shot in the leg. That was enough to turn me against the war, and from there, I turned to alcohol and drugs. I was in deep doubt of my purpose for living. Then I remembered what gave my life meaning—my writing.

"Because writing provided me comfort in my youth and I became good at it while I was in prison, I decided to become a professional journalist. I graduated from one of the nation's best journalism schools, the University of Missouri, and went to work for the *Kansas City Star*. While I was there, my activism cropped up again. I wrote an exposé about a mayoral candidate who owned an envelope company that was slated to become a bordello. I was beat up twice by people trying to convince me not to write the story. The article was pulled and replaced with a cosmetic ad. I began to see that publishing was all dictated by money. I left the paper and tried to get a job with the *Minneapolis Tribune*. I had a grade point average of three point seven, two years' experience, and references from the best writers in the country, but when they saw the color of my skin, I didn't get the job. I decided to end my professional journalism career.

"I became a cook and a part-time delivery man, so I could watch people in their daily lives and develop more ideas for my poetry. They were simple enough jobs, so I didn't have high levels of frustration and my creativity flowed. I also had more time to help out in my community.

"In '82, I decided to put twenty-five of my poems into a book. I put them inside a paper cover that Ginger, my wife and spiritual partner, made for me. I ran off twenty-five copies and began selling them. I just walked out the door and asked the first lady I saw if she would buy one. She gave me four dollars for two books. I've kept selling them that way since and have sold some thirty thousand copies of six books, all illustrated by Ginger.

"My writings and the way I choose to spend my time are central to my commitment to making the world better for others. A few years ago, some boys across the street were putting together a band but couldn't read music. They knew nothing about running a business. Ginger and I began working with them. We acquired an old library building and started to do shows with at-risk kids. We taught theater to some eighteen hundred kids. Half of them have gone back to school or found a job. We taught them what it means to have self-esteem, to have knowledge and ambition, to reach for something other than a bottle or gun, even if their neighborhood is infested with drugs and gangs. We've taught them how to have love in their hearts. In return, we have gained respect in our neighborhood. For example, one day, a group of youth drove by with a boom box blaring too loud. When they saw my wife and me on the front lawn, they turned the speakers down.

"After the Million Man March in Washington, DC, I began working with a Minneapolis group called the Men of March. We led the West Broadway march for social justice in North Minneapolis to try to get more opportunity for black men. That's hard to do in a city with racial attitudes.

"I get angry when the cops pull me over because I have a black face. We have ten times more blacks than whites in prison. A black kid gets busted for drugs, does a long prison term for simple possession. They've taken huge numbers of young black men and locked them up. It's another form of slavery.

"I was born optimistic. I always have hope. I want a community where kids can go out without worrying whether they're black, white, or green, and when they see each other they say 'Hi. How are you doing?'

"I want my poetry and social action to inspire hope in others, particularly kids. I write in the hopes that I never forget it has always been one man's or one woman's dream that brought about every major change . . . I have bullet holes in my legs and stab wounds. But I'm still here to dream."

People talk about many things
Sometimes they even like to sing
A lot of times they only dream
Of what they'd like to do
I've walked the streets of many lands
At times I've walked hand in hand
And I always thought I had a plan
But at times, I just don't know
White surf waters or deep blue skies
I'm looking for that natural high
A righteous way of getting by
Completion of the theme
This mental game of cat and mouse
Trying to build a solid house
Is the foundation Rock or Sand?
I just have the dreams of an average man.

"Against the ruin of the world, there is only one defense, the creative act."

Kenneth Rexroth

Questions for Contemplation:

1. Did one of your parents have to work so hard that she/he was hardly around? Were you lonely? If so, how did you cope? What did you do with your time? Did any of your current skills or talents emerge during this time?
2. What is your earliest memory of "standing up" over an issue? What happened?
3. What career or dream have you left behind in order to search for a more meaningful life? What were the results?
4. Vernon refers to his wife as a spiritual partner. What does that mean to you? Is there someone in your life whom you consider your spiritual partner? What does this person do to make you feel you are spiritually connected?
5. The ratio of black men to white men in prison is staggering. Vernon refers to this as slavery in a different form. What are your thoughts about this? What do you think should be done about this?

Resources for Reflection and Action:

Vernon Patterson's books of poetry: *Mellow Moods, Night Writings, Yesterday's Coffee* and *Dreams of an Average Man* are available by calling Vernon at 651-521-4418. About his works, Vernon says, "My writings speak from my deepest feelings and experiences of my tumultuous childhood, my civil disobedience and arrests, and my experiences with discrimination and chemical addiction. *Mellow Moods* is about friendship and love relationships. *Night Writings* deal with my experiences with racism and political action. *Dreams of the Average Man* is all about raising kids, family, and what black men, who have been pulled down so long, can do. *Yesterday's Coffee* speaks out against 'the garbage, the lies and the segregation' and the 'rich people sitting around over yesterday's coffee not realizing what they've done, and planning new strategies to hold back community.'"

Race and Culture in the Classroom: Teaching and learning through multicultural education, by Mary Dilg (1999). Describes and analyzes the significant challenges and joys at the heart of multicultural education with adolescents. Unafraid to address sensitive issues, the author shows how educators can treat questions of race and culture and points out that a multicultural approach to education is infinitely more complex than commonly acknowledged.

Off White: Readings on race, power, and society, edited by Michele Fine, Lois Weis, Linda Powell, L. Mun Wong (NYC: Routledge, 1996, new edition in press.) Making the claim that white is a color, Off White brings a much-needed analysis of the white racialization process to the multicultural discussion. Essays acknowledge that white identity, class, and sexuality are essential areas for studying racism.

Teaching Peace: How to raise children to live in harmony—without fear, without prejudice, without violence, by Jan Arnow (NYC: Berkley Publishing Group, 1995). For parents and teachers who want to encourage tolerance, respect, and self-esteem, and discourage hatred and violence, this book is a hands-on, down-to-earth approach that explains how to combat prejudice and reduce conflict.

The Caring Child by Nancy Eisenberg (Cambridge, MA: Harvard University Press, 1992). The study of children's altruistic, cooperative, and sharing behavior has a relatively short history. This book enhances our current understanding of the motivations behind prosocial behaviors and how these motives develop and are elicited in various situations.

Network of Educators on the Americas (NECA), PO Box 73038, Washington, DC 20056-3038. NECA is a national organization of K–12 teachers, parents, and community members that works with school communities to develop and promote teaching methods and resources for social and economic justice in the Americas. Phone: 202-238-2379. Email: necadc@aol.com. Website: www.cldc.howard.edu/~neca/.

Southern Poverty Law Center, PO Box 548, Montgomery, AL 36101. A nonprofit legal and educational foundation, internationally known for its *Teaching Tolerance* magazine and education program. Phone: 334-264-0268.

Mosaic Multicultural Foundation, PO Box 364, Vashon, WA 98070. Focuses on mentoring, rites of passage, and ways communities can use expressive arts to embrace cultural discord without resorting to violence. Phone: 206-463-9235. Email: mosaic@wolfenet.com.

Chapter 6

Peace Messengers

Teddy Copley, Lynn Elling, Jim Goodnow,
Rachel Hefte, Michael True

Armed with a powerful imagination, Peace Messengers not only have a dream, they share it with others and enlist them as partners in pursuing it. Committed to doing what they can to make the world a more peaceful place, they refuse to acquiesce to naysayers who believe that their efforts are ridiculous or futile. They overcome their own fears and the objections of others with convincing logic.

The Peace Messengers in this section have spent their lives working to make their imaginings become reality. Teddy Copley and Lynn Elling imagine a more peaceful world will result when children's and adults' environments become more peaceful. Jim Goodnow takes the unusual step of traveling cross-country, gathering signatures on a peace petition on which others have a chance to express their solidarity with the dream. Rachel Hefte and Michael True teach and learn as they travel across cultural and national boundaries, deepening their understanding of others in order to spread the message of connectedness and unity.

Peace Messengers remain surprisingly positive in the face of resistance from their peers, their government, and other obstacles in their way. Like the tireless force of running water, they seek not to squelch their opponents, but to redirect and sometimes to wear away resistance through their peaceful, ongoing actions, picking up support from all the people that join them along the way. Their inner strength and convictions provide the necessary power to continue to surge ahead in the world around them.

Disarming the Toy Box | TEDDY COPLEY

by Burt Berlowe

Created to be relentless war machines, the Commando Elite do not understand the meaning of "quit"—or "mercy." Experts in combat strategy and weaponry, these guys will stop at nothing to rid the universe of their enemy . . . Destruction, carnage, havoc—it's all in a day's work for the Commando Elite, the self-proclaimed heroes of the galaxy . . .

—From the Chip Hazard action figure package

The small soldier glared at Teddy Copley from behind the camouflage, pointing his rifle at her face and spewing his message of violence. Startled, she cringed, then became angry. She fought back in the only way she knew how.

It had all begun so innocently—a birthday party for her six-year-old boy, Dashel, complete with the usual children's games, cake, and giggles and shouts of delight as presents were opened. Then came a gift—the action figure called Chip Hazard from the movie *Small Soldiers*. This so-called "toy" assaulted Teddy's senses. Dressed in military attire, including assault weapons, hand grenades, and a "gutting" knife (according to the package), Chip Hazard was a symbol of destruction. Some moms would have let it go—after all, it was just a toy—but Teddy wasn't that way.

Teddy had never been afraid to speak her mind. She participated in a boycott of Nestlé products because of the company's actions in promoting infant formula in third world countries that resulted in malnourished babies. She protested outside of a store that ripped her off, demanding and receiving her money back.

She has always been what she calls "a political shopper," purchasing in a discriminating way, and using corporate ethics and manufacturing processes as a means of determining where to shop. Her credo: "I want corporations to be socially responsible."

Before she had children, Teddy studied the issue of male circumcision. She was repulsed by the practice. She went a step further, founding the Minnesota Chapter of NOCIRC (National Organization of Circumcision Information Resource Centers, which is an adamant opponent of the practice). "There hasn't been much info about how painful and risky the procedure is. I share the dangers of it and the myths surrounding the issue wherever I can.

"The American Academy of Pediatrics has finally admitted that routine circumcision of newborns is not medically necessary. Parents are allowing, and doctors are performing, what is essentially cosmetic surgery on nonconsenting, helpless babies in order to perpetuate a social custom. A male is circumcised every thirty seconds in the U.S. It is done to seventy-five percent of newborns in the Midwest (the national rate is sixty percent). We're the only country in the world that routinely circumcises baby boys for nonreligious reasons. Americans look in horror and disdain at cultures that practice female genital mutilation, but we refuse to look at what we do."

The slim, blonde suburbanite began as a lonely crusader in Minnesota on this issue. When bookstores and libraries refused to carry books on circumcision practices, she quietly slipped them onto their shelves. When she went to hospitals to assist with births, she left literature by the phones. She has a traveling exhibit replete with graphic images that she takes to conferences and conventions. She provides information to friends and relatives and works with nurse midwives, NOHARM (another anticircumcision organization) and Attorneys for the Rights of the Child.

At Dashel's sixth birthday party, when she read the words on the action figure package, Teddy didn't hesitate to make a decision for the rights of her child. "I told Dashel he couldn't have the toy." While Teddy continued to limit Dashel's exposure to violence, her ex-husband took their son to movies and bought him games that contradicted her message of nonviolence. The couple often argued about it and eventually they took the issue to a mediator, who drafted a letter of compromise, prohibiting Dashel from exposure to violent media and leaving toy purchases at the parent's discretion, "unless there was a problem." That solution frustrated Teddy. "Did that mean I had to wait until Dashel was shooting other kids in the school yard for there to be a 'problem?'" she wondered. Teddy went beyond her care and concern for her son and decided she didn't want any kids having the *Small Soldier* toys.

First, she found out that Burger King was putting the toys in their kids' meals as part of a promotion of the movie and that department stores had begun to carry assorted related items of clothing, lunch boxes, and so on. She wrote Burger King a letter, indicating that she would stop going there unless they removed the toys. When she called the toy manufacturer, she was told that the action figures were intended to help children "act out the movie." The movie was, after all, supposed

Photo by Todd Cota

Teddy Copley protests violent toys.

to be a satire of the military. Teddy didn't think it was funny.

She decided it was time to find help and contacted Women Against Military Madness (WAMM), which had done some war-toy protests several years before. She showed them a *Small Soldiers* pajama set made to fit a toddler, the Chip Hazard action figure, and a toy machine gun with darts. She told about watching the movie that was rated PG-13 with numerous acts of violence, noting that "the toys are made for small children who are too young to even see the movie."

Among those at the WAMM meeting was Deb Clemmensen, a child guidance worker and founder of Parents for Peaceful Play (PPP), an organization that successfully protested Rambo toys. Clemmensen had used a title for those protests: "Disarming the Toy Box." WAMM decided to help Teddy's campaign and to use the toy box name.

A few weeks later, on an August afternoon, Teddy and several WAMM members and recruits paraded in front of a Target Store that sold the war toys, the same place PPP had demonstrated in the '80s. The protesters carried signs and handed out literature to generally receptive patrons. At one point, Target officials ordered them off the sidewalk, but made no effort to stop them when they moved to the parking lot. When one unruly patron cussed at them and grabbed one of their signs, they simply told him, "Have a nice day."

Because of Teddy's initiative, WAMM formed a coalition of concerned parents, educators, peace and justice advocates, mental health experts, and others who believed that violent toys and other entertainment products could be damaging to children. They continue to work on this issue.

The following year, when Teddy sent out invitations to Dashel's seventh birthday party, she specifically requested that only nonviolent toys be given as gifts. One mother at the party commended Teddy for the request, saying she was grateful there were other parents trying to limit their children's exposure to violence.

Teddy explains: "It all goes toward making a more peaceful world and not inflicting physical or psychological harm on children. With so much violence in the media and toys, it's no wonder kids do what they do. If we don't become a more peaceful world, we are headed for self-destruction. I want to end exposure to violence so that the next generation will have a more peaceful society. I am trying to make an impact, one person and one corporation at a time. I hope to get the message out so others can have an impact, too."

Questions for Contemplation:

1. Do you think it's important to end young children's exposure to violence? Why or why not?

2. In war play of the past, children had to create the story and invent the script. They were free to experiment with the characters and take on a variety of roles. Researchers note that today's war play is narrowly scripted by merchandise-oriented TV and the multitude of products available to children with which to reenact the script. This takes away the children's original thinking about resolving conflict. Why is original thinking important? What TV shows, games, or activities do you think promote the development of children's original thinking? Why?

3. Very few people are all "bad" or all "good," yet children will say they are going to kill the "bad" guys. Next time you hear children say this, what kind of conversation could you initiate that would help children see the "bad" guys as complex people.

4. How could you help children move beyond "justified" retribution as the first solution in eradicating violence or "bad" behavior?

Resources for Reflection and Action:

Peace Begins with You, by Katherine Scholes (NYC: Little, Brown and Company, 1989). Award-winning author Katherine Scholes explains clearly and simply how and why peace has a place in all of our lives.

Boys Will Be Boys: Breaking the link between violence and masculinity, by Miriam Miedzian (NYC: Doubleday, 1991). A well-researched examination of the problem of male violence, exposing the ways in which we encourage violence in our sons, and offering specific, practical suggestions for change.

Who's Calling the Shots: How to respond effectively to children's fascination with war play and war toys, by Nancy Carlsson Paige & Diane E. Levin (Gabriola Island, BC: New Society, 1990). Examines the positive developmental needs served by dramatic play and contrasts them with the unimaginative, narrowly scripted play encouraged by today's TV and movie-based toys.

The War Against Parents, by Sylvia Ann Hewlett & Cornell West (Boston: Houghton Mifflin, 1998). The authors developed a parents' bill of rights stating that mothers and fathers are entitled to certain conditions, including a supportive external environment, honor, and dignity.

Raising Children with Roots, Rights, & Responsibilities: Celebrating the UN Convention on the Rights of the Child (Human Rights Resource Center, University of Minnesota, 229 19th Avenue South, Room 439, Minneapolis, MN 55455). An Early Childhood Family Education curriculum that uses the UN Convention on the Rights of the Child to provide the basis for twelve interactive sessions for parents and their children.

WAMM (Women Against Military Madness) 310 East 38th Street, Suite 225, Minneapolis, MN 55409. Phone: 612-827-5364. Website: www.worldwidewamm.org. WAMM is a nonviolent, feminist organization that works in solidarity with others to create a system of social equality, self-determination, and justice through the education and empowerment of women. WAMM's purpose is to dismantle systems of militarism and global oppression.

Concerned Educators Allied for a Safe Environment (CEASE), 17 Gerry Street, Cambridge, MA 02138. Phone: 617-874-0999. A national network of parents, teachers, and other advocates of young children working to promote antiwar toys.

Churches Against Violent Toys Organizing Packet. Available from Christian Peacemaker Teams, PO Box 6508, Chicago, IL 60680. Phone: 312-455-1199. Fax: 312-432-1213. Email: cpt@igc.org. Learn how to use nine criteria for rating each store in your community on a scale of one to ten, with ten indicating "toxic" access and availability of violent toys.

NOCIRC, Teddy Copley. Website: www.adbuster.org.

World Citizen | LYNN ELLING

by Burt Berlowe

Mere praise of peace is easy but ineffective. What is needed is active participation in the fight against war and everything that leads to it.
—Albert Einstein

Photo by Todd Cota

Lynn Elling

As evening settled over the South Pacific, the sound and fury of another day of World War II had temporarily subsided. A patriotic U.S. naval officer named Lynn Elling came ashore and strolled the beach of a tiny atoll called Tarawa, recently captured by the Americans after a ferocious battle with the Japanese.

A few years before, Lynn was what the Navy calls a "ninety-day-wonder," a green recruit who trained for three months as a midshipman right out of college. He had since been stationed on a ship in the South Pacific, isolated from the terror of the battlefields. He expected this stop to be just another confirmation of his ingrained dedication to America's armed forces.

But as he trudged casually through the warm sand, Lynn was unprepared for what he found. Though the battle for Tarawa was over, the spoils of combat remained. The usually busy island was empty and still. The remnants of village huts lay scattered and smoldering amidst leaves and branches from fallen palm trees. A faint smell of smoke lingered in the heavy, humid air. There was no trace of human life. Then, as he peered into some rubble, Lynn came across a bunker made of palm trees. He brushed aside the palms and looked down into the hole. There he found a pile of barely recognizable Japanese casualties. Upon closer examination, he noticed their soldier uniforms and the napalm burns that covered their bodies. The image seared his soul.

In a moment, Lynn's training and indoctrination crumbled. He found himself, for the first time, questioning the price of war. His imagination wandered far from the reality around him. He saw Tarawa like it once was: towering palms swaying in the ocean breeze; blue skies calm and clear; children playing safely in the sand; and families peacefully going about their business.

As his thoughts raced, he saw a Promised Land, a world without war. Tarawa represented this newfound vision. The words going through his mind surprised him: "Somehow, some way, the human family has got to learn to live in peace. I have a duty to my family and the rest of the human family to promote a peaceful, healthy world."

For years after the war, Lynn was haunted by

the question, "How can we abolish war, like we did slavery?" He constantly searched for a way to fulfill the commitment he made to himself at Tarawa. While working as an insurance agent, he attended a lecture on a phenomenon called "psycho-cybernetics" by Dr. Maxwell Moltz. He was particularly fascinated by what Dr. Moltz said about using imagination and visualization to get what you want. Lynn started to focus his imagination on creating a peaceful world.

He traveled to Europe and the Orient to learn about the past and imagine a new future. In 1964, he and his wife, Donna, visited Hiroshima, Japan. While there, they toured a war museum where he was appalled by a vivid depiction of the effects of the atomic bomb on Hiroshima. The displays showing people with flesh burned off reminded him of what he saw at Tarawa. "It was the absolute 'clincher' in my decision to promote a peaceful world. I thought, 'We've got the intelligence to put men on the moon, to fly rockets, and to make atom bombs. Why can't we have the good sense to come up with a formula to abolish warfare?'"

Lynn made another discovery in Japan that impacted his quest. Some two hundred sixty-seven cities had issued Declarations of Mundulization (derived from the Latin world "mundi" meaning "one world"). It called for people to recognize that they were all world citizens. Lynn attended a huge ceremony declaring Tokyo a world city. He walked out of there determined to introduce this concept at home.

When Lynn returned to Minneapolis, Minnesota, he and fellow activist Stanley Platt began to take action. They put together a Declaration of World Citizenship in 1968, the first of its kind in the country. He describes the unveiling event:

"We had an impressive ceremony on the steps of the Minneapolis City Hall. We had thirty-seven mayors there, along with a former governor and members of the city council, the county board, the bar association, the League of Women Voters, church groups, and so on, to sign the declaration. We flew a United States and a United Nations flag."

In time, many other cities endorsed the declaration, and Lynn took it to Russia, Italy (the Vatican), Lebanon, Iran, and Israel. He met with Father Felix Moreleon, who was the "Doctor Kissinger to the Pope," and sat down with top Egyptian leaders, with Yassar Arafat, and in India with Indira Gandhi. They all signed the declaration.

"In 1970, I wanted to visit with Marshall Tito in Yugoslavia about the declaration. Vice-president Hubert Humphrey wrote a letter to Tito, introducing us and saying that I wanted an interview. We got a letter back saying that it was impossible, that he was off on his island and wouldn't see anybody. Eventually, the American ambassador set up a meeting with Tito. We took the President's plane to his yacht and then out to the island, where we spent the day. He signed the declaration."

The groundwork Lynn did evolved into a groundswell. At last count, over two hundred cities around the world had issued Declarations of World Citizenship. "That became a credential for what we have been able to do since that time," he says.

In subsequent months, Lynn's career as a peacemaker took off. He was active in the World Federalists Association and chaired the United Nations Association, where he championed "world law with justice"—the right of the UN to keep the peace. But he soon became disenchanted with their inability to reach people, so he founded World Citizen, Inc. Its theme became: "Imagine a World without War."

With that theme in mind, Lynn focused on the building of a next generation of peacemakers. In the mid-1980s, he and his wife took a banner made by Sanford Junior High students with the words "Imagine a World Without War" on it to Hawaii, Fiji, New Zealand, Australia, Indonesia, Thailand, Greece, and Sweden.

"I had a chance to visit a lot of schools. Wherever we popped in, we were welcomed. Kids signed the banner and we videotaped it. We called the video, 'One World, One Family.' We previously had done one called 'Man's Next Giant Leap, World Peace through Citizenship.' Later we made others called 'Alpha or Omega,' and 'Spaceship Earth,' with the help of gifted and talented students at a Minneapolis, Minnesota, school. They helped write the script, telling how they intended to promote peace. We took them to Washington, DC. The Minnesota congressional delegation met with us to discuss the importance of quitting the arms race. Next, we took the kids to the United Nations to meet with Secretary General Kurt Waldheim. He couldn't believe how involved they were. He'd never experienced anything like it. They asked him, 'Why can't you get nations to quit fighting?' He was very impressed."

In 1987, Lynn met Louis Kousin, who had originated the concept of Peace Sites in New Jersey. Lynn took the idea and ran with it, setting up his first Peace Site in 1988 at Longfellow School near his Minneapolis home. Others followed in rapid succession. At last count, there were over seven hundred Peace Sites.

"Peace Sites provide one of the most valuable ways of effectively reaching young people," says Lynn. "Schools that become Peace Sites make a commitment to incorporate peace education into their curriculum. They hold dedication celebrations on a day of particular significance, such as United Nations Day, Earth Day, Martin Luther King Day, or Human Rights Day. Students and faculty seek ways to learn about and promote peace through music, poetry, artwork, and other participatory activities. Some schools give students awards for acts of kindness and respect. Others plant peace gardens, start conflict resolution training and classes on nonviolence, or find other creative ways to show their commitment to peace."

One St. Paul, Minnesota, Peace Site teacher summed up the program's impact by saying, "It's a feeling and attitude that extends to the playground, the classrooms, the halls, the lunchroom, even the bus."

Lynn adds, "Everybody, including janitors, kitchen staff, and engineers, is encouraged to take on the responsibility of finding a way to remind young people that they are part of the human family. The classroom is becoming a legitimate arena for engaging children in the process of peacemaking. As they understand and integrate peacemaking techniques, they can expand those lessons to address global issues. In so doing, they have taken an important early step toward making world peace a reality."

A prime example of Peace Site activity has taken place in Bloomington, Minnesota, where a consortium of schools involved over two thousand kids in getting a city park dedicated as a Peace Site and building a large replica of the world at the Mall of America. This "Build a Better World" project developed into an extensive educational experience. Students dressed up in hard hats and each took a piece of the world to study. The globe was eventually put, piece-by-piece, into boxes and taken to different parts of the world to be reassembled. Videos of these and other Peace Site events have been exchanged like pen pal letters around the world.

From somewhat humble beginnings, the Peace Site idea has become a worldwide movement. It includes schools, churches, mosques, synagogues, service clubs, an international airport in Cape Town, South Africa, and even a bridge between Norway and Sweden. Other sites include Elderhostels in Australia, Ecuador, Alaska, and Vietnam, the University of Peace in Costa Rica, the Club of Budapest, the Hungarian Culture Foundation, the President Jimmy Carter Center in Georgia, numerous YMCA and YWCA camps, various parks, and nature centers.

A poignant example of how Peace Site activity can build international bridges occurred on a recent spring day in South Minneapolis. A half-century after the bombing of Hiroshima, scores of school children joined some adults in dedicating the Lyndale Rock Garden and school as a Peace Site. The event was co-sponsored by the Hiroshima-Nagasaki Friendly Communities Committee as a way to promote healing and understanding between Japanese and American cultures. It was a colorful, cross-cultural, ceremony of music and narration, highlighted by the moment when a diverse group of children from urban, suburban, and rural schools stood together, holding up a drawing of the globe, while performer Larry Long sang, "Love Will Put Hatred down." (The globe has become the World Citizen logo.)

Lynn, seventy-eight-years old and walking with a limp, mounted the stage to christen the site. He was visibly moved as he said, "I am a dedicated peacemaker primarily because of three experiences in my life: firsthand exposure to war in the South Pacific during World War II, a visit to the Hiroshima and its Peace Museum, and learning how to successfully use my imagination in business as a peacemaker. I hope you take this day with you and make it part of your life . . ."

Watching Lynn at that moment, I was reminded of the first Peace Prize Festival held at Augsburg College, Minneapolis, Minnesota, in 1996. Approximately one thousand and students from thirty Peace Site schools took part. Each school adopted a Nobel Peace Prize laureate prior to the festival and came prepared to tell that peacemaker's story. The model for this event was a Nobel Peace Prize winning conference in the small fishing village of Pugwash in Nova Scotia, where scientists came together to discuss their role in preventing nuclear war and weaponry. The Augsburg Festival has since become an annual event sponsored by World Citizen, Inc., and has been joined by a Peace Prize Forum held each year at other Midwestern Lutheran colleges.

Lynn had emceed that first festival. In the gymnasium around him were displays from various Peace Site schools in the Twin Cities. In a nearby hallway, peace and justice groups were showcasing their work. The audience—a mixture of adults and children—watched from wooden benches that normally contained basketball fans.

Lynn finished his speech and left the stage. Walking across the gym floor, he paused frequently, visiting with the kids who were taking his dream into the future.

Questions for Contemplation:

1. What image has "seared your soul?" What has it caused you to question? Using your imagination, what can you see in its place? Describe it using all your senses—sights, sounds, smells, taste, and touch.

2. Do you believe it's possible to have a world without war? Why or why not? Would you like your school or workplace to become a Peace Site? Why or why not?

3. Whom would you invite to your Peace Site dedication ceremony? What events would you like to see planned for the day? How could your site keep a focus on peacemaking throughout the year?

4. What would make youth more capable of creating peaceful and just conditions? If you believe peace education is important, what do you think should be taught? How would you integrate peace education into the curriculum?

Resources for Reflection and Action:

Hell, Healing and Resistance: veterans speak, by Daniel Hallock (Farmington, PA: Plough Pub.,1998). Dozens of men and women veterans relate frank personal accounts about their journeys from guilt and confusion to peace and hope. Many of them came home from active duty feeling used, betrayed, and sidelined, swearing they'd never let war happen again to anyone.

Talking Peace: A vision for the next generation, by Jimmy Carter (NYC: Puffin Books, 1995). The first and only book written by a former president for a young adult audience. Carter sheds light on ways that every citizen, no matter what age, can contribute to the foundations of world peace.

Peace & Change: A journal of peace research (Blackwell Publishers, 350 Main St., Malden, MAA 02148). This journal presents scholarly and interpretive articles related to the creation of a peaceful, just, and humane society. Phone: 800-835-6770. Website: www.blackwellpub.com.

Peace Museums Worldwide, a United Nations Publication (United Nations, C115 Palisades Nations, CH1211, Geneva 10 Switzerland). At their best, peace museums are places where people can come together to understand that peace can't be imposed by law and order or institutions but is a process for which everyone is responsible. Although the idea of museums for peace is relatively new, there are already about sixty in the world. For a complete listing of peace museums, send for a free copy of this publication. Email: unpubli@unorg.ch.

World Citizen News, by NWO Publications (NWO, 113 Church St., Burlington, VT 05401). Started in 1972, *World Citizen News* is distributed gratis to all heads of state. It goes to members of the U.S. Senate, heads of embassies, chairpersons of U.S. Congressional Committees, four hundred nongovernmental organizations, and over three hundred media outlets worldwide. Website: www.together.org/orgs/wcw.

Hague Appeal for Peace, Inc., c/o IWTC, 777 UN Plaza, NYC, 10017. Seeks to sow the seeds for the abolition of war and the creation of a culture of peace. At the core of The Hague Appeal for Peace is the Hague Agenda for Peace and Justice for the 21st Century. This document—created through intensive consultation with hundreds of civil society organizations and launched at the Hague Appeal for peace conference in May, 1999—sets out fifty steps to creating a world without war. Website: www.hague-peace.org.

Global TeachNet listserv. Get global education information hot off the wires. Sign up for the free weekly announcements by contacting Anne Baker, Global Education Director at global@rpcv.org with your email address.

Calendar of Peace. Keep abreast of significant days and celebrations around the world. The UN Calendar of Peace is online. Website: www.un.org/Pubs/CyberSchoolBus/ and click on Events.

World Wise Schools Projects. A Peace Corps program that engages American students in an inquiry about the world, themselves, and others in order to broaden perspectives, and promote cultural awareness. Website: www.peacecorps.gov/wws.

World Citizen, Inc., 2145 Ford Parkway, Suite 300, St. Paul, MN 55116.

Peace Pilgrim Two | JIM GOODNOW

by Burt Berlowe

I shall remain a wanderer until mankind has learned the way of peace.

—Peace Pilgrim

With miles to go and promises to keep, white-haired Jim Goodnow hoisted the backpack on his aging shoulders and began to walk across America. It was a mid-summer day in 1996 in Los Angeles,California when the bearded former antiwar activist took his message of peace on the road and ultimately into the next century. In the process, he experienced profound twists of fate and inspiration that made his journey a unique American odyssey.

For Jim, the peace trek was a manifestation of a life journey. The searing images and experiences of his childhood propelled him north and south, east and west, through the thick and thin of U.S. civilization.

It was 1943. Jim was three-years-old. He would ride with his mother in her 1939 Ford, rumbling down the road, stopping often on the way to deliver Western Union telegrams to the grown-ups out on their front porches.

"She'd give them a telegram, and they would cry and shriek and fall down," Jim recalls now. "This was the way the government notified people of a friend or relative becoming a World War II casualty."

A few years later, Jim was in his kindergarten class during what they called a "duck and cover" drill, wherein everyone hid under his or her wooden desktop during mock airraid exercises. Jim was bewildered by it all. He said, "I could never figure out how those wooden desktops were going to prevent the A-bomb from ripping my classmates and me to smithereens."

Photo by Todd Cota

Jim Goodnow, with peace petition in hand, secures signatures.

At the age of six, Jim was sitting in a twenty-five-cent Saturday movie matinee at a local theater, watching the news of the day. "This huge fireball, followed by that ominous, sinister mushroom cloud, consumed the entire big screen. It was an image that burned deeply into my young tender mind. I still cry when I contemplate the senseless savagery of war. We were unknowing and innocent victims, or perhaps pawns is a better way of stating it, of the military propaganda machinery.

"Even at that young age, it made me think about and doubt the system. When I was older, I saw senseless commercialism and unnecessary violence and asked myself, 'Am I going to throw a brick at the TV, or am I going to do something about this?'"

Jim always had the wanderlust. Even when he was very young, he would hitchhike to different places. At fifteen, he ran away from home and began working on fishing boats in Fort Lauderdale, Florida. When it came time for him to be drafted for the Vietnam War, he joined the U.S. Coast Guard and was involved in missions picking up refugees fleeing from the Cuban revolution. He soon became a protester against the war. But it wasn't until years later that he began his campaign for world peace.

In the fall of 1995, Jim was sitting on the fourth floor of a hospital in Los Angeles, waiting to visit an ailing friend. Out of the blue, he remembered an affirmation of peace he had written for a global awareness class a few months earlier:

"We the people of the world envision a world at peace where all war has been permanently abolished from our home, Planet Earth. Therefore, we call upon the people of the world to live in true harmony and love. We believe peace will come—how soon is up to us. For this, let us hope and work and live peacefully."

Jim decided he needed to do something more with the affirmation. He turned it into a peace scroll, and, on August 14, 1996, at age 56, he set out to cross the country gathering signatures. His goal was to complete the trip for the beginning of the new millennium.

Since he didn't own a reliable vehicle, Jim planned to walk and hitchhike. Drawing on his seafaring experience to guide him, he wrote: "My thoughts are the rudder of my soul. My actions are the keel of my spirit."

As he prepared to leave, a Swedish couple from his apartment building volunteered to drive him out of the maze of California freeways. That, he says, was the first sign of what he came to call "the collective consciousness" that would accompany him on his otherwise solo journey. He tells of other such examples:

"After spending the first night in an open field under the stars, I hitched a ride in a pickup truck. I had no sooner gotten out of the truck than a lady in a passing car offered me a ride. She got out of her car dressed in what looked like a hospital-operating outfit with a badge on her dress. Before letting me ride, she asked me if was I carrying any knives, guns, or other weapons. I said 'no.' Then she started to frisk me. To me, that was further affirmation that we have to have peace in the world. During the ride, she told me she was a nurse in the military. I told her about my trip and the peace scroll. When we arrived at her work, she signed it.

"Eight days before I left on my trek, I received a fax from Doctor Robert Mueller, a former U.S. Assistant Secretary General and a chancellor for the University for Peace in Costa Rica. He had heard that I was starting out. He sent me a list called "Steps for Inner Peace" and the name and address of two Quakers, John and Ann Rush in Valle Vista, California, whom he suggested I contact during my journey.

"As soon as I was in their area, I called them. John arrived a few minutes later to pick me up. I felt an immediate bond with him. The most remarkable thing happened when we pulled into his driveway. I saw a 1977 Volkswagen bus with words painted on its side: 'Spirit of Peace.' When I had made up my initial list prior to leaving, indicating items needed for the trip, I had included 'a well-appointed RV vehicle that could be converted to a bus, and would be known as the Spirit of Peace.' I had been on the road less than four hours and there it was. When I saw it, the hair on my arms stood up and I got goose bumps. Before I left, I accepted Ann Rush's offer of the van as their contribution to my journey."

It was during that visit that Jim found out about Peace Pilgrim, the woman who had walked twenty-five thousand miles over nearly three decades for the cause of world peace. The Rushes had distributed four hundred thousand copies of her book. It has been translated into ten different languages and is published by the Friends of Peace Pilgrim organization. Jim adopted the Peace Pilgrim as a model for his own travels. "I felt tremendously guided by her. She became one of my key mentors, along with the Rushes and Mueller. It was a collective inspiration. I began to feel a part of the global family. From there, my journey became a flowing river with a course not to be denied."

Jim loaded up his new van with peace scrolls and acquired four hundred forty-eight pounds of Peace Pilgrim books written in English and Spanish and resumed his sojourn. He crossed the U.S. several times and ventured into Canada, stopping in big cities and small town churches, schools, shopping centers, picket lines, and so on. Each time, he solicited signatures and gave out Peace Pilgrim books. He gathered thousands of names in many languages on the affirmation scroll, including those of famous people like Congresswoman Maxine Waters, Arun Gandhi, Dr. Helen Caldicott, and Kermit Roosevelt (Teddy's grandchild), along with a one hundred one-year-old Ohio woman, a five-year-old in Santa Monica, a Navajo Indian girl, and many more.

Jim collected small donations or took odd jobs to pay for the cost of continuing his trip. He was often helped by the goodness of strangers who housed, fed, employed, and otherwise supported him. Once, after his van "blew up," he hitched a ride with a group of women who took him to a folk festival, where he washed dishes to pay for admission and secured more peace scroll signatures, including one from a festival performer—folksinger Peter Yarrow of Peter, Paul, and Mary.

Two things kept Jim going: his passionate commitment to his cause, and the inspiration of his mentors: Mueller, the Rushes, and Peace Pilgrim, whose presence he felt on the long and lonely highways, and who buoyed his spiritual faith. "There have been ups and downs," he says. "But I never wanted to quit. I am inspired to continue by a quote Dr. Mueller used from Peace Pilgrim: 'May God carry you on his shoulders when it becomes too heavy for you.'"

When Jim tried to drive south to Costa Rica to visit Mueller, he ran into his first resistance—a heavily armed patrol at the Nogales, Mexico, border. They asked him to put up a three hundred dollars bond to cross. He didn't have it. But then, he says, "a wonderful thing happened. They began signing the petition! Meanwhile, their boom box played John Lennon's song: 'Imagine.' I got goose bumps as I listened to the words:

Imagine all the people
Living life in peace . . .

"Out of the blue, a young woman, Marilu, helped me get the van through customs and gave me a signed copy of her poems and a one hundred dollar bill. A young man even came up to me and offered to get my border bail bond reduced.

"I spent the day in Nogales, Mexico, where I found the 'collective consciousness' to be evident again. I met an Episcopalian priest who let me use his church's parking lot for petitioning. I got signatures at WalMart, and the publisher of a periodical had Spanish words for Spirit of Peace painted on the bus." On the International Day of Peace in September of 1996, Jim sent two thousand eighty petition signatures to Robert Mueller—two hundred seventy of them in Spanish.

In a manner of speaking, Jim's journey will never end. "I am committed to everlasting peace," he says firmly. "I will remain active with global peace groups, teaching and speaking and being an ingredient in the collective consciousness. We have a wonderful opportunity to say yes to peace, not just talk about it but become part of it. We must all become part of the solution. We all have to want a peaceful world for our children and grandchildren.

"In a letter Robert Mueller sent me before I set out, he asked me to teach peace and tell stories to the children in my town. I told him that I intended to teach peace and tell stories to all children in all towns."

At the end of our interview, Jim extended a clenched fist and told about an eleven-year-old fifth grade girl he met while speaking at her school. She said, 'I have something I want to give you. It's my birthstone.'

'I can't take that,' I said. 'I would feel terrible.'

She replied, 'If you don't accept it, I'll feel even worse than you will. Please, I want you to have it.'"

Jim opened his clenched hand to show me the small blue birthstone. 'Keep the Spirit,' she told me. How could I ever give up? How could I ever quit on the children?"

Questions for Contemplation:

1. What do you think Jim means by the "collective consciousness?"
2. Have you had a "collective consciousness" experience? What happened?
3. What ideas do you have for achieving a world without war?
4. Why do you think so many people supported Jim's efforts? Would you? Why? Why not?
5. What is your earliest memory of questioning the way we humans live? What did you question?

Resources for Reflection and Action:

Peace Pilgrim: Her life and work in her own words, by Friends of Peace Pilgrim (Friends of Peace Pilgrim, 43480 Cedar Ave., Hemet, CA 92544, 1994). From 1953 until 1981 Peace Pilgrim walked for peace. Her words are those of a deeply sincere and devoted human being with a powerful vision.

Engaging the Powers: Discernment and resistance in a world of domination, by Walter Wink (Minneapolis, MN: Fortress Press, 1992). Winner of the 1993 Pax Christi Award. Walter Wink has biblically verified what more and more of us have come to realize intuitively—namely, that underneath and within the social, economic, and political crisis we face, there are profound spiritual realities which must be confronted.

No Ordinary Moments: A peaceful warrior's guide to daily life, by Dan Millman (H. J. Kramer Inc., PO Box 1082, Tiburon, CA 94920, 1992). Presents a peaceful warrior's way to turn our intentions into action, our challenges into strength, and our life experiences into wisdom.

A Theory of Everything: An integral vision for business, politics, science, and spirituality, by Ken Wilber. (Boston, MA: Shambhala Publications, 2000). A compelling blueprint for applying one of the greatest American philosophers' theories to our everyday lives.

Center on War and the Child, PO Box 487, Dept. F., Eureka Springs, AR 72632. Phone: 501-253-8900. Their research, education, and advocacy activities focus on the victimization of children by civil and international conflict.

Educators for Social Responsibility (ESR), 23 Garden St., Cambridge, MA 02138. Phone: 617-492-1764. Works with K–12 educators, students, and parents to introduce war and peace curriculums and global education into school systems. Sponsors conferences and provides speakers.

Physicians for Social Responsibility (PSR), 1101 Fourteenth Street Northwest, Suite 700, Washington, DC 20005. In addition to working on nuclear issues, they focus on ridding the world of toxic pollutants to safeguard our air and water and reduce easy access to firearms.

Planting Seeds of Peace | RACHEL HEFTE

by Burt Berlowe

. . . women of the town laundry
work and gossip and laugh at me
they don't believe I'll ever send them
the pictures I took . . .
. . . in the flash of the moment
you're the best of what we are—
don't let them stop you now
Nicaragua.

—Bruce Cockburn, February 1983,
On his album *Stealing Fire*

Photo courtesy of Rachel Hefte

Rachel Hefte poses with Nicaraguan child.

In early 1987, Rachel Hefte was busy preparing for a trip to Nicaragua. Kerin, a work colleague, had suggested he and Rachel join a coffee-picking brigade. Soon, they were accepted and preparing for a revolutionary, life-changing experience. Rachel's initial interest in this trip was piqued by stories and pictures of her cousin, LiAnn, who picked cotton there in 1984.

Rachel arranged time off from her work at a youth treatment center and raised funds to cover her expenses. As she studied the country and learned about the 1979 Revolution and Contra War, she also listened to music about Central America and tried to picture what her trip would be like. Bruce Cockburn's song intrigued her—why does he sing, "You're the best of what we are"? she wondered.

Two months earlier, for her Christmas greeting, Rachel had written a heartfelt letter to friends and family asking for emotional and financial support. She explained the risk she was taking, traveling to a country at war. "This is not a 'tour' or an easy vacation," she wrote. "I will be working and sweating side-by-side with my Nicaraguan hosts, experiencing typical Third World living conditions and eating beans, rice, and tortillas three times a day." She stressed her intent to learn, to contribute to a peaceful coffee harvest, and then to educate and create awareness upon her return to the states. She began the initial education lessons in that first letter:

"I often wonder why we in the U.S. are so patient and uncritical of the forty years of dictatorial rule by the Somoza family in Nicaragua. We now find our government is spending our tax dollars (one hundred million dollars was approved by Congress in 1986) to support an extremely dirty war against the seven-year-old Sandanista government. This is happening despite the popular support of the Sandanistas within Nicaragua, its friendly ties with our European allies, and its recognition by governments throughout Latin America. The Sandanistas have made gains in several areas such as combating widespread poverty, decreasing the illiteracy rate, and increasing land ownership by peasants, who now own ten times the land they owned under Somoza."

The response from family and friends was overwhelming. Rachel felt strongly supported as she embarked on her journey.

In the impoverished village just north of Matagulpa, Nicaragua, Rachel returned to the state farm after a long day of picking coffee beans with men, women, and small children.

The ravages of military conflict surrounded Matagulpa. The U.S.-supported Contras had infiltrated the countryside as part of their efforts to take over Nicaragua from the Sandanistas. Village residents, under the constant threat of attack, had an uneasy existence. Each day, a Sandanista soldier, armed with an AK-47 circled Rachel's brigade in the fields, in an effort to keep the group safe from the Contras. Volunteer brigadistas from Europe, South America, and the U.S. had arrived to help harvest the coffee, which was critical to their economic survival.

Living conditions were primitive and unrefined. Water was unfiltered and not safe to drink. Food was cooked over outdoor fires. The women cleaned their clothes on a rock and asked how the "white boxes" got clothes clean in North America.

Amid pervasive poverty and turmoil, the Nicaraguans were generous and hospitable to the volunteers living with them. Rachel was impressed with their resilience, gratitude, affection, and profound sense of family and community. She was inspired by their intense struggle to survive—how they organized at the grassroots level to ward off invading Contras and how, through it all, they continued to be open and friendly.

Rachel grew particularly fond of the village children. "The kids were so affectionate and loving, much like their parents. At the end of a long day of picking coffee beans, I remember playing with the children near their homemade wooden swing set and teeter-totter. There were war trenches surrounding the play area, but children still need to play, even if there is a war going on. These little kids were so much like three; four; and five-year-olds in this country, except for their distended, malnourished bellies. They would shout, giggle, and gaze in amazement when we blew bubbles."

The camaraderie of the villagers was a sharp contrast to the fear and confrontations in the countryside when the Contras were on the move. Rachel's journal contains the following description of one such frightening event:

"During our first evening in the mountains, we experienced a 'Contra scare.' We were told to line up and turn our flashlights off, to hand in our passports and follow each other up the hill. Men and young boys were carrying AK 47s to protect us.

"Word of Contras in the area spread quickly. A Brazilian brigadista came running down the hill yelling, 'Evacuation! Evacuation!' We [twenty-seven other North Americans and myself] were organized into squads and numbered off. We marched in silence... Where are we going? There are lots of coffee trees up here. That's what we're here to do: pick coffee. But where does one hide from the Contras? As we stumbled up a gravel road with all our bags, those first moments of confusion and fear flashed in my mind. This was serious. I wanted to turn on my flashlight. I panicked. 'Where was my buddy Kerin? Kerin?'

"We were on alert all evening, singing, learning revolutionary cheers, and talking nervously into a tape recorder. Kerin had a plan to hide the cassette under the bunk if something happened... We had to be escorted to the outhouse... Many remember hearing gunshots. Sandanista youth and peasant farmers held a vigil all night outside the building. How ironic, they stayed up all night to keep us safe from guns provided by our own country...

"Fortunately, we were kept safe during this Contra scare, but we learned the next day that a number of men, women, and children had been killed in a nearby village that same night..."

Another event sticks in Rachel's mind, "An ABC-News crew from the United States arrived one day while we were picking coffee. They wanted to interview the North American brigadistas. We kept saying, 'Interview the workers who live on his farm.' Though they had a Spanish-speaking translator, they refused to listen to or record the stories of the Nicaraguan people. They weren't interested in their stories."

The attitude of the ABC reporters impacted Rachel's perspective on the media. She became skeptical that standard news outlets were reporting accurate information.

"Those experiences affected me dramatically. I came back convinced that journalists and the government were worse than not accurate, they were perpetuating the war in Nicaragua by creating misinformation to justify U.S. involvement. I was determined to let others know the truth.

"When I returned home, I vowed to speak out whenever I could. Over the next two years, I spoke to over two thousand people in school, community, and church groups. Wherever I went, I spoke from the heart, hoping to move people to action, especially kids. The measure of my success was that many people heard my story and, as a result, were inspired to act on behalf of Nicaragua.

"Sometimes what I said ruffled conservative feathers. In my hometown of Fergus Falls, Minnesota, I was considered the 'pretty girl who came home to tell about her trip.' After I told my story at the Rotary Club, someone asked, 'Are you saying that the U.S. is lying?'

'Yes I am,' I replied.

Days later, an instructor at the local community college wrote a letter to the *Fergus Falls Daily Journal* saying that a daughter of Fergus Falls had come home with blood dripping from her hands, inferring that I was a Communist. The community wasn't ready to hear that our tax dollars were not helping other countries but were causing pain and suffering instead."

The Nicaraguan countryside and the village children are a long way from where Rachel currently spends her time in metropolitan Minneapolis. But intertwining paths of compassion and rebellion—roads she has traveled since her childhood days in Fergus Falls—inextricably connect the two.

"Growing up, my experience was not as idyllic as middle-class Kodak pictures might portray. While my work ethic was strong and the comforts of life were well provided, I questioned the inequities of the world. I expressed my opinions and experienced conflict with friends and family members. As a result, I felt different, like an outsider. I was very sensitive and had many upsets and problems. I didn't have a way to work them out, so I internalized them. I also realized that having money doesn't make you happy. I concluded that workaholism is an addiction that keeps us from being in the present and connecting with other people. I finally rebelled against the work ethic and my conservative background to find my own way.

"My parents encouraged me to attend Luther College, a Lutheran liberal arts school. They thought that a good education would answer my questions and get me a 'real job.' Instead, I got radicalized. Several religion professors influenced me, including one who said, 'Forget everything you learned in Sunday school.' A Peace, Bread, and Justice Class moved me to tears, then anger. I became disillusioned with the image of 'the great democracy,' the USA.

"A tour with the Lutheran Volunteer Corps to work in community, live simply, and work for social justice, furthered my radicalization. During a simulation as part of my orientation to work and live in the city of Baltimore, Maryland, I had my first direct encounter with the impact of class and race discrimination.

"The Lutheran Volunteer Corps gave us fifty cents and sent us out to role-play being homeless for a day. I was a homeless woman with a homeless boy friend. We went into a police station and asked about resources for homeless people. They yelled at us, 'Don't you have a place to stay?' It helped me understand what it is like to try to find resources without money or privilege. During that year, homeless people continually approached me, asking for money. Instead of giving them money, I took them out to eat and talked to them about their situation. One guy told me how he had lost everything: his family and his house—and he had his master's degree! I realized it was important to connect with homeless people and recognize them, not look past them or ignore them. Their stories matter.

"Because of where I live, I learned about segregation firsthand. My immediate neighbors were mostly poor and black. Just a few blocks away was a white, upper-class neighborhood. I didn't always feel safe. Sometimes, when I got on the bus, I was the only European-American. It just blew me away. It's one thing to read about segregation and feeling different—another to experience it. It became clear to me then that I wanted to work for its eradication and not be part of the problem.

"Compelled to do something, I returned to school to get my teaching certificate. After graduation, I began to teach world culture and social justice classes. But I wanted to do more than teach. I wanted to help improve the education system. I became a trainer for a conflict resolution program entitled Project CREATE. I researched alternative schools and experiential education, I taught controversial topics, and I questioned what was not in basic textbooks. In social studies classes, male teachers were preaching about wars, I was a young woman teaching about peace. I shared common people's history and questioned what had been written by privileged white men . . . Students came to me and said, 'Thanks for telling it like it is.'

"One of the most controversial liberties I took was teaching kids how to protest for social change. Still inspired by my memories of the activists I met in Namibia, Africa, who had fought against apartheid, I taught my students the nuts and bolts of organizing against policies that were not fair and/or healthy for people."

"In 1995, when I got back from Namibia (where I went on a Fulbright scholarship with a group of Minnesota teachers) I found out that some of my former students had organized a successful demonstration, complete with TV coverage, against school budget cuts. My celebration of their efforts came from a distance, however, because I already had left the school to find a place where my organizing skills and peacemaking passion could be utilized.

"I became a Violence Prevention Coordinator in Anoka County (Anoka, Minnesota) and conducted trainings on alternatives to violence for county workers. I also worked with school and community groups to promote projects and programs for peace. Eventually, I want to start a peace school, something like the famous Highlander School in Tennessee that has inspired so many great leaders. I believe sowing and nurturing the seeds of peace and justice in burgeoning peacemakers is one of the greatest needs of the peace movement."

Speaking of planting seeds, Rachel can often be found these days renewing and sustaining herself in the backyard vegetable garden behind the modest North Minneapolis home she shares with her husband Sean, a community organizer, and their two cats.

"When I was looking at this backyard trying to decide whether to buy this house," she muses, "it was as if the Earth spoke to me saying, 'Buy me. Take care of me. Plant a garden.'"

Questions for Contemplation:

1. If you were to act on behalf of another group of people, who would it be? Why?
2. A few people control much of our media. What are some alternative media and news sources you have found that tell things differently from the mainstream press?
3. Have you questioned your family's values? U.S. government policies? What have you questioned? What are your conclusions?
4. Rachel says her faith and spending time in her garden sustains and renews her. What renews and sustains you?

Resources for Reflection and Action:

Solutions to Violence High School Course, by Coleman McCarthy (Center for Teaching Peace, 4501 Van Ness St., NW, Washington, DC 20016). This book shows how to use nonviolent force—the force of justice, the force of love, the force of sharing wealth, the force of ideas, and the force of organized resistance to make change.

The Habits of Highly Deceptive Media: Decoding spin and lies in mainstreet news, by Norman Solomon. (Monroe, NE: Common Courage Press, 1999).

Culture Jam: The Uncooling of America, by Kalle Lasn. (NYC: William Morrow, 1999).

Abundant Life Seed Foundation, PO Box 772, Port Townsend, WA 98368. Each year, this group sends about eleven thousand free packets of open-pollinated seeds to places in need around the world. These seeds can be grown, then saved and replanted, or traded and distributed to others. They help communities feed themselves, rather than being dependent on outside aid. You can help by growing and donating your own seeds. Phone: 360-385-5660.

Peace Coffee. By purchasing Peace Coffee you support small, organic farmers. Phone: 612-870-3440 for a catalog. Website: www.peacecoffee.com.

Lutheran Volunteer Corps, 1226 Vermont Avenue NW, Washington, DC 20005. Phone: 202-387-3222. Fax: 202-667-0037. Website: www.lvchome.org

Nicaraguan Cultural Alliance, PO Box, 5051, Hyattsville, MD. Celebrating a poor land, rich in art and poetry, this group offers fine art materials from the paintings of Nicaragua artists. Current offerings include museum-quality Christmas and note cards, ceramic plates, hand-carved balsa figures, business cards, and boutique-quality T-shirts from the art of Nicaraguan artists who are paid a substantial annual fee. Phone: 1-800-746-1160. Website: www.quixote.org/nca.

El Puente Academy for Peace and Justice. This school is renowned for its work as a peace school. Website: www.usanetwork.com/functions/justone/puente.html.

Free the Children International, 1750 Steeles Avenue West, Suite 218, Concord, Ontario L4K2L7. Phone: 905-760-9382. Fax: 905-760-9157. Email: freechild@aol.com. Website: www.freethechildren.com. According to the International Labor Organization, there are more than two hundred fifty million working children. That's equal to the entire population of the United States. Craig Kielburger, a child himself at the time, started this organization to end child labor.

Teaching For Change. Website: www.teachingforchange.org/links.html. At this site you will be able to visit dozens of progressive organizations and publishers.

Adbusters. Website: www.adbusters.org.

The Peace Professor | MICHAEL TRUE

by Burt Berlowe

Those who don't go within, go without.
—Anonymous

The racially charged '60s were just beginning the day Professor Michael True walked into his North Carolina College classroom for the first time. As he gazed at the rows of students in front of him, he felt a surge of apprehension. Every young face he saw was black. Even though he had championed civil rights, this was his first real immersion in African-American culture. At age twenty-eight, and fresh out of graduate school, he wondered if he would be up to the challenge.

He didn't know it at the time, but the merging of his teaching and early activism would set him on a path of no return. In years to come, he joined the two in bold and unusual ways in his home and in many corners of the globe. In the process, he suffered the scorn of foes, colleagues, and neighbors, as well as the discomfort of prison.

Michael's interest in peace and justice had developed slowly. His father and two older brothers served during World Wars I and II, respectively, and he spent six months in the military during the late '50s. Although his immediate family wasn't politically active, his grandmother worked among the poor in Oklahoma City in the '30s.

"Grandma's commitment to the poor had a profound affect on me," he said. "Perhaps that's why I was so drawn to Dorothy Day, who founded the Catholic Worker movement. As a matter of fact, it was the *Catholic Worker* newspaper that stimulated my interest in social change movements when I began reading it as a grad student at Duke University.

Photo by Todd Cota

Michael True

"While I was at Duke, I saw racial prejudice all around me. In public places, whites and blacks used separate water fountains and toilets. A couple that lived across the hall from us in our duplex apartment was very prejudiced. Their father, the owner of the duplex, once threatened to shoot Sarah Boykin, the black woman who cared for our children.

"Blacks were only allowed to sit in the balcony of movie theaters, known as the 'crows' nest.' I joined other students from Duke and elsewhere to protest this policy. Black students, aware of the example of Martin Luther King and others on the Freedom Rides, were the principal organizers of the demonstration. They were impressive in their commitment to nonviolence. We carried signs calling for the integration of the movie theater while police lined the streets. Appointed demonstrators stood on alert at every corner to discourage any violent provocation.

"During this brief experience with nonviolent direct action, I learned effective strategies from the students, who were imaginative, brave, and intelligent in carrying out their plans. I learned on my feet—not only at my desk—what nonviolence is all about. It was a life-changing experience."

Upon moving his family to Worcester, Massachusetts, in 1965, Michael trained as a draft counselor and helped young men facing conscription make informed decisions about their futures. In April of 1970, he spent ten days in jail with students from Clark University for antiwar demonstrating at a local draft board.

"While a handful of us were in jail at the Worcester County House of Correction, the U.S. bombed Cambodia. At that point, two hundred sixty more Worcester citizens committed civil disobedience in an effort to close down the local draft board. After the killings at Kent State University, daily demonstrations involving students from the city's ten colleges, along with local citizens, turned

Worcester into a major center of antiwar activity."

The True home in Worcester became a place for extraordinary guests to call. On any given day, well-known peacemakers, in town for talks and conferences, sat at the True's kitchen or dining room table. Some familiar faces belonged to Daniel and Philip Berrigan, poets Denise Levertov and Robert Bly, David McReynolds of the War Resisters League, and Russell Johnson of the American Friends Service Committee, to name a few. Other visitors included Ammon Hennacy, "the one-man revolution," and Dorothy Day, who grew to admire Michael as much as he admired her. Occasionally, young men, AWOL from the Army, would stop by for military counseling or to ask someone to drive them to Canada.

The spacious three-story New England house also became a covert headquarters for an "underground church" made up of antiwar protesters and Catholic activists. On Sunday mornings, twenty or so clergy and laity gathered in the True living room. This "floating parish" was part of Michael's life from 1968 to 1978.

All this political activity around the True home provoked criticism from neighbors. "I often wrote to the local newspaper criticizing the draft and American foreign policy, particularly towards Southeast Asia," Michael recalled, "and the constant comings and goings of students and activists made our neighbors uncomfortable. Occasionally, even the children's teachers said hostile things to our kids or asked, 'What is your father up to now?' One woman accused us of making a ghetto of the neighborhood because we invited black people into our home."

These years were demanding and formative for Michael, his wife, Mary Pat Delaney, and their six children. Having a father who studied, taught, and wrote about key figures in the peace movement, led their oldest daughter, Mary Laurel, into active participation in demonstrations and civil disobedience against the Vietnam War and the nuclear arms race.

Michael constantly felt pulled to live on two parallel paths. One took him through the halls of academia as a peace study educator, advocate, and author of articles and books on peace and social justice. The other path led him into the streets, the halls of Congress (to testify against the draft), and occasionally to jail. Sometimes, the two paths intersected uncomfortably with each other.

"Blending activism and academia often gets one into trouble with both," Michael commented. "Academicians accuse you of not being 'scholarly' and activists accuse you of selling out to the establishment. A sustained movement for social change, however, must include a close association between study, research, and activism at every level. We have much to learn about effective strategies for social change from the tradition of nonviolence in the U.S. over the past three hundred years, as well as from Tolstoy, Gandhi, and others around the world.

"In a culture of violence, a teacher must recognize the structural violence in American education. To make the classroom nonviolent—that is, nonauthoritarian—I believe we need to respond to students' needs and interests. That takes a lot of work. Activism sometimes exposes the limitations of the campus, which some academicians regard as a haven or asylum from the larger community. Similarly, scholarship and research provide valuable insights for activists. Learning on the street as well as in the classroom made me more attentive to the conflicts between the values I profess and the way I live from day to day.

"When I proposed starting college peace studies programs, colleagues of mine thought I was crazy. Armed with Ph.D.'s earned from Catholic Universities during the height of the Cold War, faculty members were resistant to Peace Studies as an academic discipline and actually thwarted the efforts I made. In spite of considerable student interest, they accused me of trying to make activists out of the students. They called the courses we developed 'nonacademic.' Instead of providing a major or minor in Peace Studies, we were locked into offering occasional introductory courses. However, over the years, that situation has changed considerably through our sustained efforts. By 1999, there were some three hundred colleges nationwide offering majors in Peace Studies."

Michael has associated with the American Friends Service Committee, a Quaker organization, for over thirty years. Raised a Catholic, he celebrates that "Catholics have made a significant contribution to the peace movement." However, in 1995, he became an active member of the Quaker Society of Friends because Quakers are, in his words, "the true pioneers of nonviolence in the U.S." He particularly values their emphasis on meditation, their focus on peace, and their awareness of "God in every person."

"My experience living and teaching in China, North Korea, Japan, Australia, New Zealand, Hawaii, India, and Bangladesh allowed me to become more familiar with Asian religious traditions. Subsequently, I couldn't help but view Catholic ritual as narrowly Eurocentric, authoritarian, and exclusionary. I found it increasingly difficult to identify with the assumptions and top-down management of the institutional church, as well as its preoccupation with the belief rather than with faith and practice."

Two teaching experiences, in particular, left an indelible impact on Michael. The first of those took place when he was teaching in China during the democratic uprising that began at Tianamen Square in the spring of 1989.

"During my first night in China, I stayed at a university in Shanghai as students prepared banners and speeches for a huge demonstration the following morning. On the way to the train station for the six-hour journey west to Nanjing, we drove through huge crowds that filled Shanghai streets. Arriving in Nanjing, I joined one hundred thousand demonstrating students blocking the streets around the university.

"These students had learned effective nonviolent strategies on their feet. It was all very moving for me, watching and being there, as history was made. The demonstrators rocked the world and impacted their culture through their bravery and persistence in the face of great adversity."

The second experience occurred while Michael was a Fulbright lecturer in India in 1997 to 1998. He taught American literature at Utkal University in Bhubaneswar, and nonviolence at the Centre for Gandhian Studies, at the University of Rajasthan. His time in India coincided with the fiftieth anniversary of Mahatma Gandhi's assassination, and he met many of Gandhi's disciples and witnessed the consequences of his example and legacy.

Michael's sojourn into Gandhi's homeland was one of many intense associations with past and present peacemakers. "I'm inspired and excited by the peacemakers I meet and write about because they have stood against injustice and for humane values against enormous odds. Knowing them puts me in touch with the best people in the world. They are heroes and heroines for me as I try to understand the relationship between personal transformation and social change, as well as to learn peace from within and without."

Since his retirement from full-time academia, Michael has focused on political activism, along with speaking and traveling. In October of '98, he was one of eleven peace activists arrested for trespassing at Raytheon Electronic Systems in Andover, Massachusetts, a manufacturer of U.S. weapons used in the Gulf War against Iraq. In his testimony before the court, Michael spoke of the effectiveness of civil disobedience in ending slavery and promoting the rights of women, people of color, and workers. Found guilty, he and the other activists performed community service as an alternative to jail.

In 1996, the Consortium for Peace Research and Development (COPRED) named Michael "Peace Teacher of the Year." In 2000, he received the Peace Studies Association Lifetime Achievement Award.

"For it isn't enough to talk about peace. One must believe in it.
And it isn't enough to believe in it. One must work at it."

Eleanor Roosevelt

Questions for Contemplation:

1. What has impressed you, or been difficult for you, in your cross-cultural experiences?
2. Who is one of your peacemaking heroes or heroines? Why?
3. What forms of segregation are taking place around you?
4. Would you want to have a teacher who is a social activist? Would you want your child to have one? Why or why not?
5. It has been said that we are at the beginning stages of peace education, much like the bow and arrow stage was a beginning stage for the military. To advance our knowledge and skills, do you believe peace education and nonviolence should be taught in schools? Why or why not?

Resources for Reflection and Action:

An Energy Field More Intense Than War: The nonviolent tradition and American literature, by Michael True (Syracuse, NYC: Syracuse University Press, 1995). This book is about the literature of the United States and its social and political history. It centers on writers who imagined or projected a culture somewhat different from the one that has emerged. Their hopes and efforts are part of a complete story about what is and what might have been—as well as about possible choices for the future. True believes that the literary artifacts associated with a refusal to kill deserve more attention and reflection than historians and social scientists usually award them.

To Construct Peace, thirty More Justice Seekers, Peacemakers, Michael True. (Mystic, CT: Twenty-Third Publications, 1992).

Ordinary People: Family life and global values, by Michael True (Maryknoll, NYC: Orbis Books, 1994). Writing from his own family experiences, True explores how global values—a commitment to the Earth and a spirit of solidarity with others—can take root in the home. True shows how ordinary people can practice peace, nonviolence, social justice, and community in their families and in the world. Out of print, available from Growing Communities for Peace. Phone: 800-211-3971. Website: www.peacemaker.org.

Language and Peace, by Anita Wenden and Christina Schaffner. (Harwood Academic Publishers, Website: www.gbhap.com.). This book argues that language is a factor to be considered together with social and economic factors in any examination of the social conditions and institutions that prevent the achievement of a comprehensive peace. It calls for peace educators to include critical language education into their curricula and describes an approach for doing so.

Love in Action: Writings on nonviolent social change, by Thich Nhat Hanh (Berkeley, CA: Parallax Press, 1993). Nhat Hanh speaks in the tradition of Gandhi, King, and the Dalai Lama of the need for mindfulness, insight, and altruistic love as the only sustainable bases for political action.

Peace Calendar. (Available from Syracuse Cultural Workers, Box 6367, Syracuse, NY 13217. Phone: 315-474-1132. Fax: 877-265-5399). Helps you keep abreast of important dates and events for promoting peace and nonviolence. Guide includes talking points and activities for grades K–12. Includes extensive resources and a revised list of progressive educational organizations and publications.

Peacebuilder Partnership, 1819 H Street NW, Suite 1200, Washington, DC 20006. The Peacebuilders mission is to promote a systems approach to peacebuilding and to facilitate the transformation of deep-rooted social conflict. Receive the Peacebuilder newletter through membership. Phone: 202-466-4605. Fax: 202-466-4607. Website: www.imtd.org.

Chapter 7

Spirit Changers

Stacy Hersrud, Tom La Blanc, The McDonald Sisters, Shane Price, and Rita Steinhagen

Spirit Changers are compassionate rebels with a powerful presence. They come from a variety of spiritual and religious traditions but have a common bond: they have a deep faith that each person has a divine spark within, and they work to fan that spark to a flame. They call upon themselves and others to reach for their higher selves and manifest their own divinity.

Spirit Changers know that love heals and motivates, and are very good at loving themselves and others in spite of their challenges or even their failures. In fact, they seem to have an unlimited capacity for love, and they have faith that others do, too. Spirit Changers understand the power of spiritual transformation in overcoming the obstacles that can get in the way of our higher selves. Some work through the written or spoken word, and/or with other people to create events, rituals, or ceremonies in which people can experience new possibilities for themselves. They are willing to take leadership alone or to share power if it means something can take a turn for the better. Through their efforts, we are challenged to increase our heart capacities and let go of the boulders we so persistently drag along with us.

Some Leaders are Born Women | STACY HERSRUD

by Rebecca Janke

When Stacy was five, she cut out a quote in a magazine that said, "Some leaders are born women." She glued it to her baby picture. In third grade, she drafted her own version of a Bill of Rights that guaranteed justice in school.

"Until the age of sixteen, I thought of myself as magnificent. I loved to learn, got high grades, and was involved in many afterschool activities. I felt as if I were doing a joyful dance through the universe. However, though I was smart and could discuss interesting topics, I began to feel isolated from the other girls who mostly wanted to talk about boys. Boys didn't appreciate me because they felt competitive with me. They would yell at me and give me put-downs as I walked to school. Even the elders in my family held me at arm's length and didn't compliment me for my achievements—they thought I would get too big for my britches.

"My zeal for excellence and exploring the world stopped. I learned to distrust myself. How could I think that believing in my magnificence and loving the world and myself was the route to take when there were so many people telling me otherwise?

"I tried to transform myself from being bubbly and alive to being quiet, reserved, and ladylike. But I grew to hate denying my true self. With no place for a 'good girl' to go with such frustration, I went into a self-destruct mode. I started experimenting with drugs, developed an eating disorder, and was often suicidal. I even dabbled in shoplifting when I was unable to pay my bills and as a release for my unexpressed rage.

"I think the reason I didn't kill myself was because I truly wanted to live and really liked to learn and hoped that things would be better once I graduated from high school and entered college. However, when the time came, staying in college was in question because of my poor attendance due to chemical use. It was then that I learned about the power a single person can have. A professor from the University of Minnesota, with whom I interviewed, wrote me a letter of recommendation: 'Despite her record, I believe it does not reflect the greater part of herself.' Writing that letter was compassion in action. I studied political science, biotechnology, sociology, and women's studies, and went on to get a master's degree.

"College was an improvement over high school, but it was my work in battered women's shelters that really began to help me heal. I became convinced that living our lives in silence, self-hatred, and hatred of others does nothing to alleviate the suffering in the world. I could see how our internalized oppression perpetuated the very things we were trying to get away from. I became alive and myself again … and went to work as an activist. I was ready to speak out and create tools for removing obstacles that keep us down.

"I'm convinced social change becomes more effective when we begin to heal ourselves. It's hard to heal, however, when we are mired down with our resentments and memories of unjust acts that have been inflicted upon us. I began to ask myself some questions: 'How does an individual or a community of people move forward when there is so much baggage? How do we rise out of our emotional hellholes? I knew these questions were on other people's minds as well. The pain we experienced in our past is often an obstacle in the way of creating new lives.

"In trying to get beyond these forces that have such power over us, I came up with an idea for a community-wide forgiveness ceremony to promote healing within ourselves and with each other. I was so energized! I could visualize the whole thing in my head. As soon as I got home from work, I sat down and wrote out all the elements that I thought would work for this ceremony. It made sense . . . if we came together as people for healing perhaps the 'power of the people' could generate a force to unlock the prisons of the heart. I had never heard of this being done before but that didn't bother me because I had started to believe we needed to find a different way of doing things, that obviously many of the current approaches were not working, and we were paying the price in our lives and communities.

"I'm not a fool or a saint. I just believe in common sense. Common sense tells me that once we feel listened to, our pain is acknowledged, and we receive an apology, we become free to go forward. A new energy is born. Forgiveness becomes possible. I began to visualize what that energy would be like, hundreds of times multiplied by such a gathering.

"During the first twenty-four hours of looking at my notes, I had no doubt this could happen. But as many of us have experienced after a flash of light, we often do begin the doubting process, 'What was I thinking? Yeah, right, this could happen . . . in a million years! I don't even have a computer to design a flyer. I have no money to pull off such an event; musicians alone would cost a fortune.'

"However, I could not lay the matter to rest. I ran would-be conversations with nay-sayers in my head: 'We don't need a healing-forgiveness ceremony, we need to put these people in jail.' My silent response was, 'Yes, we need accountability but in many cases we also need to restore relationships because harm has occurred with people who are important to us such as parents, children, neighbors, co-workers, husbands, wives, and ex-husbands and ex-wives who are parenting children. Even if we decide to end a relationship, unresolved resentment shows up in new relationships. We need to get out of our vicious cycles.'

"No matter what nay-saying comment I could think of, I couldn't talk myself out of it. However, after dialoguing with myself about it for several more days and still not moving forward on it, I realized what internalized message I was hearing again, 'Don't draw attention to yourself.'

"'No! I will not stay quiet again,' the rebel in me screamed. I decided to ask others what they thought about this idea and see if they would be willing to lend their support. They loved the idea! Within a few days, one man called and said he had an old computer he didn't need anymore. 'Would that help?' he asked. A Native American drumming group and some dancers said they would volunteer their services. The agency I worked for, Genesis II for Women, said they would sponsor the event. I gave presentations to various members of the Minnesota Department of Corrections and neighborhood justice groups who were willing to help mobilize people to attend, as well as individuals and agencies to donate equipment, food, and music.

"People literally came out of the woodwork. I was amazed at how much positive energy there was. It seemed as if they were just waiting for some leadership to show up. I felt I had been handed a magnificent gift and opportunity, along with a responsibility to make this happen, which it did.

Photo courtesy of Stacy Hersrud

Stacy Hersrud

"At the ceremony, we shared our stories of pain and suffering, offered apologies on behalf of our ancestors and ourselves, experienced different cultural expressions of unity, sang songs of encouragement to go forward without violence to ourselves and others, and participated in a collective act of forgiveness. We went through a lot of Kleenex while releasing years of emotional tension, frustration, and bitterness.

"Whenever people become sarcastic and tell me it's hopeless to try to build a more peaceful world, I listen. I listen very intently, for in their complaint lies their passion in disguise. Instead of catering to their complaints–their lowest energy–I say, 'What do you think should be done about this?' After they tell me, I say, 'Use whatever privileges, talents, ideas, and resources you have, and get to work. Sarcasm is a luxury we cannot afford.' I believe it's my job to give their vision back to them. When people work on their visions, it leads to their magnificence and increases the light in the world."

Questions for Contemplation:

1. What internalized messages of negativity crop up when you contemplate providing leadership for a cause you believe in?

2. Think of a time you have expressed sarcasm. Is there an opportunity for social action lurking beneath the bitterness or frustration? Hidden in your sarcasm, is there an opportunity for growth and self-understanding?

3. What would help your healing process so that you are not trapped by your past?

4. Think of a time you have experienced someone else's sarcasm, perhaps in the form of a put-down. Instead of getting defensive and hurt, could you ask a question of the speaker that turns things around, such as, "What ideas do you have about addressing that?"

5. Share an action you have done that you think would contribute to peaceful or compassionate living. Ask others in your life to give you feedback on it. Are people resonating to your idea? If so, what can you do to make it a reality?

Resources for Reflection and Action:

The Compassionate Community: Strategies that work for the third millennium, by C.M. Harmer (NYC, Orbis Books, 1998). Harmer examines strategies that do and don't work in all parts of the world and includes a helpful resource list of community organizations.

The Power of One: Authentic leadership in turbulent times, by Sharif Abdullah (Stony Creek, CT: New Society, 1995). Breaks through feelings of despair, frustration, and alienation by prompting us to rethink our assumptions about power and leadership. Demonstrates how the new pioneers, people like us, can create a society based on love, compassion, sustainability, and authenticity.

Information on ending battering can be found at: menstoppingviolence.com (Men Stopping Violence), cpsdv.org (Center for the Prevention of Sexual and Domestic Violence), abanet.org/child (American Bar Association Center on Children and the Law), ncadv.org (National Coalition Against Domestic Violence).

Information on women finding their own power can be found at: womensnet.apc.org/beijing, mtsu.edu/~ccarroll/WOBIB.html, nawbo-sf.org (National Association of Women Business Owners).

From Blame to Forgiveness

by Julie Penshorn

It was a great sadness—a deep, immobilizing one. Sadness beyond the visceral kind that makes you feel like throwing up. My boyfriend's words, with their tone of finality, reverberated in my head: "We're really not compatible. It's nobody's fault. I can't live this way."

After a long, confusion-filled walk, I sat to clear my head. Alone with a retired park bench in a dilapidated, lakeside park, no one shared my burden. There was no healing ceremony in which to participate . . . I sat a long time. Much later, a story came. And then I knew it was somebody's fault—Grandpa Pete's.

Why did he have to die when I was so young? Why did he have to abandon me, leaving me with fears that loved ones can go at any time? Leaving me unwilling to give what my boyfriend needed?

How many times I remember hearing how Grandpa would stop at our house every Monday morning on his way to work. I was the "apple of his eye," they said. He lingered over breakfast with me, every Monday, until one day his visits suddenly ended. As a child, I couldn't understand that cancer had claimed him.

I've been allowing this trauma to be an excuse to stay fragile, to break at the slightest fear of abandonment, and to justify my defensiveness in intimate relationships. Finally, I realize I have no choice but to face the hard growth demanded by my lover who is asking me to be stronger. No false fronts of healthiness will suffice. Only the whole healing that comes from integrating the past, forgiving, and changing will do.

As I became aware of my wounds, I could almost feel them beginning to heal. I was grateful that I was able to discover where the pain was coming from after all these years of not being sure. I was grateful to realize, intellectually, if not emotionally, that I wasn't abandoned because I was inadequate or unlovable. Grandpa only abandoned me because he had no choice.

My boyfriend felt he had no choice but to leave. It hurt to be with me. My old wounds were projected onto him as I pouted or became sarcastic when I perceived his abandonment. When I felt abandoned, I blamed him.

He rebelled against the "Mr. Nice Guy" response he knew I wanted. It would have been much easier for him to leave or acquiesce. But he stayed and fought—tenaciously, lovingly, and painfully. Eventually, I realized that my fear of my inadequacy and my fear that I was not lovable, were not reflections of reality, but reflections of my past. He helped me dare to reach out and claim the love in front of me—take it, reciprocate it, and cherish it.

Leading Eagle | THOMAS LA BLANC

by Rebecca Janke

This is Our Law

Oh, Grandfather God!
Pity us, for we are a
Weak and lost people!
We ask only that our
Little ones and unborn
Be allowed to grow
Strong within the winds
Of their own directions!
For we look about us in these
Times and see children of all
Colors being abused, neglected,
Exploited and denied!
This we do not want amongst
Our circle, so,
This is our prayer,
This is our mind,
This is our law.

—Tom La Blanc

At age fifty-two, Tom La Blanc is a traditional Dakota orator who works to raise the self-esteem of Indian people. He hopes to serve as a unifying force to bring people of all races together. These efforts, coming from a man who has more reasons than most to be lashing out at the world, demonstrate how struggling to save one's own spirit can also heal the spirits of others.

Born to a single mother, Tom was taken from her at birth. Deemed "unfit," she was sterilized, and Tom was placed in foster care. He attached and bonded to no one in any of over one hundred places he lived. The longest time he ever stayed in one home was seven years, from the ages of four to twelve. By the time he was eighteen, he was bitter and utterly despondent.

"According to Erik Erickson, the noted psychologist, I should have remained a total wreck, since I had bonded to no one," Tom says, with his strong arms lovingly wrapped around his youngest daughter who was just awakening from a nap. "I almost proved Erickson right. As a young man, I was what they called incorrigible. Even Boys Town couldn't rein me in—I ran away. I felt I didn't fit anywhere and had no reason to live.

"Figuring the Vietnam War would be a good place to 'commit suicide,' I enlisted. When the woman who processed my induction papers heard my reason for going to 'Nam, she screamed, 'It should have been you, not my two sons who were killed in the line of duty!'

"Arriving in Vietnam, ready to end my miserable life, I was surprised to find a reason to live. It happened when I met the Vietnamese children who begged us [soldiers] for food. I was shocked and horrified to learn that the war was causing these innocent children to starve. Even though I wanted to die, I couldn't stand the thought that children were dying because of the war. 'My God,' I thought, 'They don't even have enough food.' At least I had food.

"To complicate matters, regarding my own suicide, I couldn't bring myself to shoot Vietnamese soldiers. Shooting even one man would perhaps leave a child an orphan. Knowing what happens to abandoned kids, my hand could not pull the trigger. Within days, I experienced the futility of war and began to think that we needed to invent something better to solve our human struggles. When the bullets began to fly around me and death was finally an opportunity, I found myself resisting death because I now knew I had a reason to live. For the first time in my life I began to think about . . . Who am I? Why am I here on this earth? What can I do with the life I have to help end the ways we destroy each other?

"Although I'm Dakota, I promised myself that if I got out of Vietnam alive, I would seek out the Chippewa tribe that had befriended me during a brief time in my early years and listen again to the spiritual truths they shared with me but that I had forgotten. Perhaps I could find the answers I was seeking.

"Soon after Vietnam, I sought and found the Chippewa, only to discover they were living lives of despair. Poverty had all but decimated their lives. However, their spirituality had remained strong. I was able to spend hours with wise, spiritual teachers. They told me, 'Even though we struggle to survive, no one can take away our spirituality. It cannot be denied or killed.'

"As much as I had been cut off from my Native spirituality as a youth, I now found it providing me comfort and giving me meaningful lessons that began to strengthen my spirit. The principle—all people are related—allowed me to finally have a 'family,' something that had been completely absent from my life. I slowly began to heal.

"It took me a long time, however, to be able to give the kind of love that is needed within one's immediate family. It's often easier to love people who naturally gravitate to you because of your shared values and interests. Within families, it's harder to keep focused on loving each other when differences arise. In my first marriage, I didn't know how to reach consensus with family members when our needs and wants were different from each other. Our marriage crumbled.

"I am fortunate that I got to be a father again later in my life. Through the years, I have developed a philosophy that allows me to be more at peace with others and myself. I look at my young daughter and know that I am her link and her children's children's link to creating a world where we use options other than war, racism, and classism to solve our problems.

"Although this is the most diverse nation on Earth, I'm heartened by our common denominators. As a matter of fact, we have so many, we can spend the rest of our lives working on them rather than letting our differences separate us. We're really not in positions of power, we're in a shared existence, and it's okay that we're struggling with each other. After all, we are undergoing one of the greatest racial and political experiments in creating this place called America.

"Sometimes we do the things we do simply because we have no other way of looking at life. Through my poetry and my one-man play, which I do internationally, I try to introduce new thoughts or perspectives. For example, I introduce the idea that our preoccupation with racial hatred and conflict may vanish like cannibalism. Look at Tiger Woods. We can't even tell his race. More and more children are being born with multiple racial backgrounds. Someday, we'll live in a world where the majority of people can no longer be prejudiced because several races will reside in each person. When I work with children in schools, they get this. All they have to do is look around them and know this is true.

Photo by Todd Cota

Thomas La Blanc embraces his daughter.

"It's important to give ourselves permission to experiment to create a culture of peace. I have found it to be much more effective to conduct these experiments and share ideas in small, rather than large groups. It's hard to find consensus, cooperation, and motivation for new ideas in a large group. When something is working well with a small group of people, it can catch on like wildfire. It's a good way to work to create change and actually get something done.

"In my poems, in various ways, I convey that we need to give peace a chance. We have given war a chance, many chances, and it has not brought us what we want. No one will be completely satisfied living in a culture of peace either, but we'll have a higher form of life, a better life. It's okay to fall and fail as long as we pick ourselves up and continue our quest. We can't constantly say 'no, no, no.' We have to say 'yes' to the greater part of ourselves and increase our capacity to work for the common good.

"Life is a great mystery. It is good when people work together to share what they know so we can see the bigger pictures and patterns, which hold more truth than the one piece within in our hand. Not one of us can know everything. So let us bump into each other and stumble and keep going. As we seek it out, we will find kindred spirits to hang out with. Maybe it will take several lifetimes to create it.

"Spirituality keeps me positive. It keeps me going when I feel I can't go on. Keeping my people alive also keeps me going. There is a high suicide rate in my culture among our young people—forty suicides in my community last year alone.

"Oftentimes, we do things because we think we don't have any other way of doing things. Kids do this, too. Teaching multiple-perspective-taking to them is an enormous step toward peace. We use it to save these kids' lives.

"Art is another key since it provides a way to communicate that often can't be said with words. It provides deeper insight into root causes of pain and suffering. Kids learn that dealing with root causes is far more effective than putting on a Band-Aid. Besides, we're not dealing with simple cuts. We're dealing with amputations. When people have been 'cut-off' from life-giving opportunities and nurturing support, they begin to hemorrhage.

"Another avenue my wife and I work through for reaching kids is improvisation. It teaches kids to find alternatives quickly and helps them understand there are different ways of getting one's needs met, as well as different ways to communicate which can create deeper understanding.

"The more I travel, the more I believe bad people are outnumbered. More people are doing good. We just don't hear about it. There's a part for everybody to play to create a culture of peace. I have faith that my daughter, her children, and her grandchildren will see what we've been doing. Peace is possible. When you think long and hard enough, you will know what to contribute—even if it is only a prayer."

"We're not dealing with simple cuts. We're dealing with amputations. When people have been 'cut-off' from life-giving opportunities and nurturing support, they begin to hemorrhage."

Tom La Blanc

Questions for Contemplation:

1. Tom gained new perspective on his emotional and spiritual struggles when he compared them to those of the Vietnamese children. Some of us close our eyes to the miseries of others so we can more easily continue to focus on ourselves. Thinking back to your childhood, what happened to you that was unjust or unfair? What have you done to work through your struggle(s)? Have you ever done something for others and discovered your own healing? What happened?
2. Sometimes when people are deeply wounded they seek to wound, or even destroy, themselves. Tom wanted to commit suicide in Vietnam. Others try to self-destruct with alcohol, drugs, or other methods. In what ways are you tempted to self-destruct when you feel unworthy? What do you do to overcome depression?
3. Tom believes that working with small groups is more effective than working in large groups to create change. What has your experience been?
4. Tom said it's often harder to be loving to members of your own immediate family than the people we pick as "family." Have you noticed this? How do you stay connected with family members when you find you have different needs and wants?

Resources for Reflection and Action:

Rediscovering Hope: Our greatest teaching strategy, by Richard Curwin (National Educational Service, 1252 Loesch Rd., Bloomington, IN 47404). This book gives specific, immediate strategies you can use to restore and enhance the sense of hope and the likelihood of success among all students—high-risk students in particular.

Reclaiming Our Prodigal Sons and Daughters: A practical approach for connecting with youth in conflict (National Educational Service, 1252 Loesch Rd., Bloomington, IN 47404). Offers the best research on positive youth development, a penetrating portrayal of the rootlessness of many of today's youth and a powerful, practical plan for reaching them. It makes a strong case that unless we nurture the spiritual dimension of our youth, we fail to meet all of their needs.

Reclaiming Youth at Risk: Our hope for the future, by Larry Brendtro, Martin Brokenleg, and Steve Van Bockern (National Educational Service, 1252 Loesch Rd., Bloomington, IN 47404). A classic in the field, this book integrates Native American child-rearing philosophies and Western psychology to provide a unique perspective on helping troubled youth.

Arts Approaches to Conflict, edited by Marian Liebmann (Bristol, PA: Jessica Kingsley, 1996). A rich resource of ideas, practices, and information, which explores creative ways to address conflict. It can be very effective in starting a process of change when other approaches have achieved very little.

Sister Act | THE MCDONALD SISTERS

by Burt Berlowe

An expectant hush falls over the standing-room-only crowd in the Minneapolis, Minnesota, courtroom as the tense drama of the trial of seventy-nine landmine protesters heightens to a climax.

Seated on the witness stand, Sister Jane McDonald has chosen a most unusual way to present her testimony. Leaning forward toward the audience, the white-haired nun lights a candle and places it on the armrest of her chair. As it burns, she begins to speak in a soft but powerful voice:

"When I was a little girl, my mother would light a candle and sprinkle holy water to keep us safe from storms. Now we're lighting this candle to show that we want to keep the children of the world safe."

Jane thrusts her arm upward, holding in her hand a child-size artificial leg. "This was once worn by a twelve-year-old Cambodian boy. He gave it to us and asked that we stop this violence." Then she begins to sing:

Take away the landmines.
All we want is to ban mines . . .

The lyrics drift past nearby jurors and into the gallery of spectators—several of whom quietly sing along in solemn harmony. At that moment, it becomes abundantly clear that these agonizing days in court have dealt with more than the legality of demonstrators' actions: They have put humanity on trial.

Photo courtesy of McDonald sisters

The McDonald Sisters, from left, Kate, Rita, Jane, and Brigid, with Margaret McDonald Boren, second from right, as they protest landmine.

The McDonalds: Jane, Rita, Kate, and Brigid, ranging in age from sixty-four to seventy-six, are sisters in two ways. They are actually related to each other. And they are all nuns who, for a half-century, have belonged to the Sisters of St. Joseph of Carondelet, a Catholic order of French origin that began in Minneapolis in the 1850s with a mission to serve the poor and downtrodden.

Individually, these sisters have their own distinct traits and charitable causes: Jane, the youngest, is a surrogate grandmother to neighborhood children and stray cats. She's an admirer of the Native American culture. She plays a Native drum, worships at a sweat lodge, and wears dreamcatcher earrings. Brigid, three years older, is spirited and prone to laughter. She has been a teacher and tutor in ESL (English as a second language) at a school in St. Paul, Minnesota, and serves on the steering committee of Women Against Military Madness. Kate, the second oldest, is a prim-looking former parochial school teacher who also tutors kids and is a women's advocate at a Catholic Charities drop-in center.

Rita, the most senior, has worked at halfway houses for drug addicts and battered women and is known for taking on anyone she believes is wrong, including judges in courtrooms.

Collectively, the sisters combine warmth, kindness, and spirituality with a feisty, unyielding commitment to social action.

Watching them at protests, it's hard to miss the sincerity and compassion, the sadness for the victims, as well as the anger at the injustices of random acts of war and violence. Even in their protest work, their hearts are filled with love, not hate; with welcome, not rejection. Their voices are strong, but never harsh. Their prayers and chants are not hollow, but transforming. They seek to touch others deeply—to change not only their minds, but also their souls.

These "rebel" nuns seem to be everywhere that peace and justice work needs to be done: at military bases, at landmine manufacturer Alliant Tech's fenced perimeter, at the School of the Americas, at the nation's capital, and even at the steps of the local Catholic cathedral.

There was little in the sisters' childhood to presage the maverick path they have taken. They grew up in the midst of the Great Depression on a one hundred sixty-acre farm in rural Minnesota. Their parents were devout Catholics and opinionated Democrats. Dinnertimes were often filled with political exchanges followed by family prayer.

Their father fought in World War I and had taught his eleven children the "just war theory"—that war was necessary to maintain democracy. Thus, when the Second World War came, the older children were anxious to get involved. Four of the brothers ran off to join the service, and Rita moved to Minneapolis and took a job cleaning and vacuuming B-25 bombers.

Farming struggles forced the family to send other children to live with relatives. In 1946, Rita shocked the family by deciding to join the Sisters of St. Joseph, and Kate, Jane, and Brigid followed suit. For several decades, they lived a semicloistered existence, dressing in traditional habits and teaching at Catholic schools or working in helping institutions.

Then some things happened that changed their lives forever. Kate explains: "It was a rumble of consciousness. We saw the funds dwindling at places we were helping out—while the military budget went up." Rita reacalls, "We also were getting lots of material on war resistance and began to read what it meant to do civil disobedience. The horror stories we heard about the Vietnam War also made us aware of grave injustices."

The sisters decided to take action. Rita says: "We were the pioneers. Very few from the Church would venture out at that time. There were a few active priests who demonstrated with us. But we mostly did it on our own. It wasn't easy at first.

Kate admits: "I'm basically a coward. I need a lot of support. Way back when I was really young, if somebody said to me, 'Would you go to jail for something?' I wouldn't have said yes. It was a thought process that had to develop." Rita adds, "We have ended up doing actions we never thought we could do or would do."

Rita discusses their first full-fledged demonstrations at Honeywell Corporation in Minneapolis, Minnesota. "We were protesting cluster bombs, which are antipersonnel weapons designed to explode into fragments that harm people but preserve structures. We had a prayer vigil every Wednesday morning and did some larger group protests. At the biggest one, we circled the building holding hands, singing, and praying. We didn't stop anybody from getting into the plant, but we made it inconvenient so they had to go around their usual route. When we were told to move, we didn't. Our goal was to shut business down for some time, and we did.

"We were arrested seven times at Honeywell and went to jail twice during the late '70s and early '80s. Once, we spent two days in solitary confinement when they didn't want to incorporate us into the prison work force. I didn't find it that hard.

"A lot of the women in prison were poor and black, and addicted to crack and cocaine, but we saw another side of them. We expected the best from them, and they gave it. They tried to take care of us and showed such tenderness and concern. I'm sure it was meaningful for them to do something for somebody and feel safe, knowing they didn't have to fear us."

In recent years, the McDonald sisters have been among the regular protesters at Alliant Tech (an offshoot of Honeywell), based in a suburb of Minneapolis, Minnesota. Alliant Tech is the biggest producer of landmine parts in the U.S. The sisters have been a potent team at these events: drumming, lighting candles, and displaying artificial limbs from landmine victims, reading prayers, singing soulful songs, and telling authorities, "We'll be back with many friends. This is like David and Goliath, and you know how that one ends."

One time, during a prayer vigil at Alliant, the sisters drew chalk images on the sidewalk, and left a child's shoe and crutch at the scene. "When we went up to the door of Alliant," Kate explains, "we were asked to leave. I said I would leave as soon as they stopped making cluster bombs and landmines. I was arrested."

When the Alliant protesters were brought to trial, the sisters were lead witnesses. They admitted trespassing at Alliant, telling the judge: "We felt it was our Christian duty—an obligation because of our faith and because international law demands it. To be silent is wrong. This is a moral and religious issue. Peace is rooted in truth, and truth is rooted in struggle. We want to resist preparation for war. Our voices are crying for peace and for justice. The whole world is watching."

Religious faith has remained a guiding force for the McDonald Sisters. "We must resist evil in whatever form it comes," says Rita. "That's part of our spirituality. We must speak for the voiceless—like children, who have no one to speak for them. We must increase the awareness of every person so they can see these situations with eyes of truth."

At the same time, the sisters have long since abandoned their nun's garb and with it their allegiance to many traditions and policies of the Catholic Church. Rita continues, "Traditional Catholicism is oppressive. I've gotten re-educated about spirituality. As our personal transformation grows, our lives have taken on new meanings and different purposes. We've sought out a path that gives us common homilies against oppressive Church policy. That's what keeps me from leaving the Church totally."

Jane adds: "Our prevailing theme is consistent railing against privileged classes and the resulting hierarchy, especially within our own Church. Who needs a privileged class papacy? Get rid of the ornaments, the collar, the clericalism, the Pope. Jesus would be the first to say 'no' to those things."

Photo by Todd Cota

Kate McDonald

Imprisonment and conflict with their Church are just a few of the hardships the McDonald Sisters have endured for their renegade activism. Once, when they were protesting against war toys, passers-by called them "old hags," and yelled, "get a life." At an Alliant protest, a stern-looking man in a business suit deliberately kicked the prosthesis the sisters had on display. Jane chased after him calling out: "I've never seen such a lack of respect. Don't you know this is a prosthesis a child has to wear because of what you make in this building?" The man turned toward her and yelled, "You're a moron." Her response was not a threat, but a barely audible, "God have mercy on your soul."

"We expect this kind of thing," says Rita. "It's a price we're willing to pay. We're willing to suffer to help eliminate the suffering of others."

Sometimes, the suffering cuts deep. A few days after an Alliant protest, Kate complained about how her wrists still ached from handcuffs that had been pulled especially tight during her arrest. Yet, she is fully willing to take on that pain for others. "There's no end to what we must speak out against," she says. "There's always some terrible injustice going on. For many people, their goal is to be comfortable. This work is not comfortable. You have to pay a price for justice, and go to jail if necessary to get what you want."

When will the sisters finally quit? "Every time, before we go to trial, we keep saying this will be the last time. But we know it won't be," says Rita. "Once your foot crosses that line, you can't go back."

The McDonalds have reached a point of no return in more ways than one. Theirs is a commitment deeper than religion, deeper than family, deeper than right and wrong. It's a commitment of the spirit. For them, peace can mean welcoming a new protester with a hug, holding a hand if someone is afraid of the police, or staying with someone who's been arrested. It is wielding a prosthesis as a staff of understanding with the hope that never again will a child wear it because of a so-called 'just war.' It is, in essence, finding and spreading humanity's compassion through rebellion.

"We're inspired by the work others are doing for peace and justice," says Kate, "and I assume others are inspired by our work. The affirmations we have received let us know that. Being active in peace and justice work is part of being spiritual. It is healthy for the soul."

Questions for Contemplation:

1. How might representatives of the world's religious and spiritual traditions enter into close dialogue with representatives of the world's military to:

   a. explore new paths toward peaceful resolution of conflicts?

   b. discuss the acceptability or unacceptability of the use of arms in the resolution of conflicts?

   c. discuss the criteria (if any) for a "just war?"

2. Can and should the military play a central role in conducting an ecological survey of the planet, as well as in the development and implementation of a comprehensive plan of stewardship for the Earth?

3. How can the world's military become an institution whose primary functions are related to universal service to humankind, i.e., meeting the challenges of natural disasters, famine, and epidemic?

4. The McDonald Sisters have rebelled within the Catholic Church despite the fact that they are nuns. Have you ever felt dissatisfied with your church's practices? What have you done to try to create change?

Resources for Reflection and Action:

In the Footsteps of Gandhi: Conversations with spiritual social activists, by Catherine Ingram (Berkeley: Parallax Press, 1990).

All Her Paths Are Peace: Women pioneers in peacemaking, by Michael Henderson (Colorado Springs, CO: Kumarian, 1994). Stories of women who substituted nonviolent conflict management methods for dysfunctional patriarchal, hierarchical domination methods.

Church and Revolution: Catholics in the struggle for democracy and social justice, by Thomas Bokkenkotter (NYC: Doubleday, 1998).

Catholics on the Edge, by Tim Unsworth (NYC: The Crossroad Publishing, 1996).

God in All Things: The spiritual exercises of Anthony De Mello, by Anthony de Mello (NYC: Doubleday, 1994). From his life as a Jesuit priest, psychologist, and spiritual gadfly, Anthony De Mello prods at our inner demons and illusions.

Here Comes Brother Shane | SHANE PRICE

by Burt Berlowe

Leaning across a dining area table in a North Minneapolis drug store is a tall, broad-shouldered man whose fiery, intense eyes blaze out from under his Kofi cap. His physique accounts for a small portion of his powerful presence, the ceremonial garb and air of wisdom do the rest. I feel as though I'm sitting at the table of an African chief. I wait while he eats some of his breakfast. Then Brother Shane Price looks up with his warm, penetrating smile and gives me his full attention.

He begins, "One night in 1994, I had the strangest dream. In it, I was standing in the middle of a grocery store parking lot near West Broadway—the main thoroughfare that bisects North Minneapolis. I appeared to be addressing a crowd. My hands were holding a megaphone to my mouth and I was barking out some sort of chant or command over and over again, although the words weren't exactly clear. For months afterward, I remembered and wondered about the dream. But I didn't understand what it meant.

"Several months later, however, following the Second Annual West Broadway March for Peace and Justice, I was looking through some photographs taken at the event. Suddenly, I stopped and stood in stunned silence staring at one of the photos. In it, I was standing in the West Broadway parking lot speaking through a megaphone. It was exactly the same image I had seen in my dream. It just blew my mind. I knew then that dreams can carry valuable information."

In some respects, Brother Shane has always been a dreamer. He grew up in Minneapolis amidst the struggles and high hopes of the civil rights movement. His mother was a leader in the move-

Photo by Todd Cota

Brother Shane Price

ment, and there were many meetings of black activists at his home. He listened to the powerful rhetoric of the time and developed an affinity for the spoken word. He fashioned himself as an orator or a radio broadcaster. But the assassinations of civil rights leaders in the '60s shattered his world. In the early '70s, he began to abuse drugs and alcohol. Shane's life went on that way for more than a decade.

Then one day in 1986, a seemingly routine event transformed Shane's life. He recalls it this way:

"I had taken my daughter to a carnival at the Phyllis Wheatley Community Center where a Latino evangelist was speaking. He asked if anybody in the community wanted prayer to be delivered from drugs and alcohol. I raised my hand out of spite. I didn't think he should make those claims. Inside I was saying, 'If you got it, I want it. If not, get out of here.' He prayed for me. The next day, the desire for drugs and alcohol completely left my taste buds. I no longer had any urge or desire to use. I became completely clean of drugs right then, and I've never gone back.

"Soon after that, I decided to share what he gave me by helping others. I kicked in the roots of my civil rights activism, became trained as a chemical dependency counselor, and created a social change organization based on faith and spirituality rather than bureaucracy."

In 1994, the year Shane had his mysterious dream, white men coming in from the suburbs and cruising the avenue looking for girls and gay guys, had given a North Minneapolis block the dubious distinction of being called "Hookers' Row." The johns would drive right past neighborhood children standing on the corner waiting for the school buses. Shane lived on that block, and his daughter was one of the kids watching the prostitution traffic. His doorstep became a refuge for students when the hookers and cruisers came by. The prostitutes and their johns were taking away the neighborhood.

Shane decided to take action. As a member of the Hawthorne Area Community Council, he put together a citywide coalition of several antiprostitution groups, social service organizations, and agencies. They called themselves the Unity Action Community Team. The team held a news conference to announce plans for a series of concerted actions designed to rid the neighborhood streets of the johns and their prostitutes. That led to a spontaneous community rally. He remembers it well:

"We took over eight city blocks. We knocked on doors, got on a local radio station, sent out flyers, and got church members to come and help. At night, we pitched a tent on a corner and roasted hot dogs and marshmallows. We told jokes and got to know each other. We sent foot soldiers around to check things out. We used chants and signs to empower the kids.

Our focus was on the johns. We videotaped their license plates. Later, we sent out 'Dear john' letters, informing them that they had been seen in the area. We got results. Wives of the johns called asking why we wrote that letter. That started a dialogue. Our goal was to send a message—this area was not open for that kind of traffic. This was to be a safe area for children to stand on their corners. There was a change right away. We took back our streets. The children could wait on the corner again. But we didn't stop there."

Even as the prostitution was being cleared away, West Broadway was still known as the drug center in the neighborhood. Shane and his cohorts decided to take back that street and their community "corner by corner," using the energy of the Hookers' Row success. In the aftermath of one of the most violent days in Minneapolis' history, when a four-year-old child was killed, they formed the "Gang of Good People" and planned the first West Broadway March for Peace and Social Justice. The activists went to the city for a marching permit, but public officials balked at the idea of shutting down a vital street like West Broadway. A huge political fight ensued as supporters wrote letters to city council members, making their case. The night before the event, they got the go-ahead to march.

With limited financial resources and only meager community donations, about five hundred participants trudged down the center of West Broadway, finishing the march at an area elementary school. Shane was there, leading the marchers. He recalls being "excited to have so many people in one place saying they were tired of the drug traffic and willing to stand up and say that peace was important enough to get up and march about."

The West Broadway March has become an annual event that begins and ends with neighborhood rallies. It has expanded in sponsorship, activities, and cross-cultural participation to include a job fair, voter registration, children's activities, forums on peacemaking and racism, recruitment of adoptive parents, information for people seeking a home or moving from welfare to work, and a food drive. It has led to the formation of the West Broadway Peace and Social Justice Foundation that raises money for community antiviolence projects and has played a role in the building of a new neighborhood school.

Shane has been a key organizer and speaker for each march. It was at one of them that he was first introduced with "Brother" in front of his name, and he has kept it ever since. At the rally preceding the '96 march, he stood on a makeshift stage near a West Broadway grocery store, posed like he had been in the dream, holding a hand mike and revving up the crowd—many of whom are wearing T-shirts that said, "Get Your Kuji On" (Kuji means self-determination).

"How many are here looking for peace?" he yelled. Hands went up throughout the crowd.

"How many are here looking for social justice?" same response.

At a concluding rally in a packed school auditorium after the march, Shane was presented with a special award for his role in organizing the event.

Gradually, the lines of marching feet on West Broadway have turned into circles of peace.

Shane, who administers a community social service agency, saw the limitations of the human services system. He decided to train with Native American circle leaders in the Yukon (Northwest Canada) to bring the restorative justice circle process to his community. Now, he facilitates circle discussion groups for families in trouble, providing transportation and child-care so they can come to the sessions. With people seated in a semicircle around him, he guides a frank and often emotional dialogue designed to resolve conflict and heal inner pain.

"We train circle groups in the neighborhoods where families need them so we can create a safe place to speak the truth. The circle is a place where they can minister to and serve their fellow man. It's a way to get with our humanity. It's a form of tough love.

"In the circle process, the perpetrator has to face the victim and community instead of a judge or a prosecutor. That's a different way to be. We're creating a new language that's changing people's lives. Community offenders are becoming good neighbors. The circle process is a beautiful way to build bridges."

The first time I participated in a circle was at a neighborhood meeting in North Minneapolis. Shane sat down at a small table containing a bowl, a jar of sweet grass, and an eagle feather. He called people together with a rhythm on a tall bongo drum. He then told the group, "The drum is a powerful tool of communication. We, as a people, have become accustomed to email, pagers, and cell phones, but the drum is the oldest means of communication. It has a way of calling people together. It is a way for us to look back to the history of humanity and help us in our relationships. The sweet grass is from the Native American culture and shows respect for the environment."

Shane passed around the feather during introductions. Each person held it as they told their name and shared a story about themselves. Eventually, difficult and unexpected feelings surfaced. A slender Jewish woman cradled a new baby and told how religious healing saved the child at birth. A mentally ill woman, abused by institutions, tearfully discussed the importance of "love" in the healing process, moving others to cry along with her. After everyone spoke, Shane ended with a reading from a book of meditations:

". . . a caring touch, a simple smile, may be all it takes to heal. . . In community, there is healing . . ."

On another occasion, Brother Shane demonstrated the circle process to a class of university students who were studying compassionate rebel stories. After setting out the usual items, he told the students that everything visible (he used a chair as an example) began in the invisible—as an idea in somebody's mind. He explained that the circle would take them to "invisible places where all the real work takes place, where the invisible begins to become visible."

Shane had requested ahead of time that the students each bring some items of special meaning with them to the circle. As they introduced themselves, they presented what they had brought and put it into a pile on a carpet next to Shane's ceremonial display. Some laid down chains given to them by family or friends. The classroom teacher set out his wedding ring. A school athlete left a medal he had won in sports. An English major took out a newspaper clipping about the murder of her mother. A classmate next to her presented a book of her own poems. She read one that had obviously been written during a time of despair. With each item, there was a story—of relationships, of teamwork, of joy or agony. These had been relatively quiet, reserved students up to now, but suddenly they were pouring out their souls, making what had been invisible into the visible. "Now," Shane told them, "I have come to know all of you better, and we can connect. Our stories are everything we are."

Shane carries his message from deep within. "We [in society] emphasize the body and the mind, but not the spirit," he says. "That can lead us to scary places. The spirit is where compassion takes place. The true worth of a man is the quality of his soul." He calls spirituality "a part of my work, my own personal deliverance. It gives me the ability to perceive a person beyond what he or she appears to be. I can look at a drug addict and see a sane and sober person. Then I can speak to the invisible person there and call him or her to a higher place. I will continue to push people to a higher spiritual level.

"Recently, we started working with a Puerto Rican family, including a fourteen year-old girl who was molested by her mom's brother. She's been meeting with us in circles for the last eight weeks. When I pass down her street and go by her house on my way home, she has a sense of who I am and what my values are. One time when I rode by, she and her girl-friend were sitting on the porch smoking cigarettes. Out my window, I could see her lips move, 'Here comes Brother Shane.' Then she put her cigarette out. That's the kind of accountability we expect and traditional social services can't provide."

In North Minneapolis, the words, "Here comes Brother Shane" have become a clarion call to organize and empower, as well as a mantra for peace, justice, and compassion. These words are recognition of the impact one man has had on a struggling neighborhood. They are evidence of how far Shane has come in turning his dreams into reality and making the invisible visible.

"Everything visible began in the invisable, as an idea in somebody's mind."

Shane Price

Questions for Contemplation:

1. Who has been a positive role model or mentor for you?
2. Have you ever had a strange dream that you didn't understand but that later manifested itself as a reality? What happened? What did you conclude?
3. Has your neighborhood ever had a march or rally promoting a particular cause? Did you participate? Is there a particular issue you think your neighborhood should rally about?
4. Restorative Justice is a fairly new concept in the United States. Would you like to see it become more prevalent in your community, school, or place of work? What are you willing to do to make it happen?
5. What are some things you have done to reach out to people?

Resources for Reflection and Action:

The Millionth Circle: How to change ourselves and the world, by Jean Shinoda Bolen (Berkeley, CA: Conari Press, 1999). Gives ideas for starting and sustaining circles, such as centering the circle; supportive rituals; how to nurture safety, equality, and respect for privacy; and ways to deal with conflict.

The FACTS Toolkit: Event planning for your family and community town supper (Wisconsin Clearinghouse for Prevention Resources, PO Box 1468 Madison, WI 53701). Phone: 800-248-9944. Website: www.wiclearinghouse.com. A tool for facilitating youth, family, and community development. Offers a structure so a community can mobilize its resources to create actions related to a community concern.

Stories of Transformative Justice, by Ruth Morris. (Toronto, Canada: Canadian Scholars' Press, Inc., 2000). A collection of stories from around the world on restorative justice, forgiveness, prison reform, and transformative justice at work.

About Juvenile Violence and Its Prevention (Bureau for At-Risk Youth, 135 Dupont Street, PO Box 760, Plainview, NY 11803). Phone: 800-99-YOUTH. Email: info@at-risk.com. Website: www.at-risk.com. Addresses the causes of violent behavior, danger signs parents should look for in children, and violence prevention techniques.

Citizen Circles. Website: www.renaissancealliance.org. Citizen Circles are open, emotionally safe forums in which people join together to not only expand their political awareness but to also take action to help make manifest the most compassionate society.

Peace Room. Website: www.Peaceroom.org. A model of a new social tool for positive evolution.

International Conference on Penal Abolition, 157 Carlton St., Suite 202, Toronto, Ontario, M5A 2K3, Canada. Challenges current approaches to criminal justice and works to transform the root causes of crime, bring power to communities, and heal victims and offenders. Conferences are held every two years. Phone: 416-972-9992. Website: www.interlog.com/~ritten/icopa.html.

Office of Juvenile Justice and Delinquency Prevention (OJJDP). Website: www.ojjdp.ncjrs.org. Provides grants and funding information, programs, resources, a calendar of events, statistics, and access to publications dealing with delinquency prevention, gangs, violence and victimization, and substance abuse.

Center for the Study and Prevention of Violence (CSPV) Website: www.colorado.edu/cspv/. Uses a multidisciplinary approach to violence and works to build connections between the research community, practitioners, and policy makers.

Jewels for Sister Rita | RITA STEINHAGEN

by Burt Berlowe

Don't agonize. Organize!

—Florynce R. Kennedy

Sister Rita Steinhagen stands by the window of her South Minneapolis apartment, welcoming the sunlight gleaming through the glass. She picks up a prism and moves it around so that colored patches of light reflect on her living room wall.

That moment takes the white-haired Catholic nun back to another time, not long ago, when she watched the sun's rays careen off the fence of a towering men's prison, next door to the Pekin, Illinois, women's penitentiary where she was confined. She remembers sitting in her tiny cell, experiencing the colors of that moment, and scribbling her impressions on a small note pad. She wrote:

The coils of razor wire
Like jewels in the morning sun
Belie harsh intent

She had been sentenced on her seventieth birthday, not for a major crime, but for standing up for peace.

Taking risks for peace has been Rita's forte ever since she joined the Sisters of St. Joseph of Carondelet some fifty years ago. Along with the McDonald sisters, she has been arrested numerous times. However, this time when Rita was arrested for trespassing at the School of the Americas in Georgia, she became an international hero and discovered a new cause: prison reform.

It was 1997, and Rita was among some two thousand protesters who committed nonviolent civil disobedience at SOA. They marched in silent procession to the slow cadence of a drum, carrying

Photo by Todd Cota

Rita Steinhagen shares her story.

white crosses with the names of SOA victims. Rita and six hundred other demonstrators crossed onto the school's property past the sign that says, 'Welcome to Fort Benning Military Base.' They all were arrested. She recalls:

"We were put on a bus and asked to give up all our 'lethal weapons,' such as ball-point pens, nail files, and nail clippers, and any pins we were wearing. Then we went to a big field and stood in line with plastic bands around our wrists and got patted down by the military and photographed. Twenty-five of us repeaters were later sentenced to six months in federal prison and fined three thousand dollars. The eighty-nine-year-old judge who sentenced us is the same one who sent Martin Luther King to prison and released Lt. William Calley (who led the Mai Lai massacre in the Vietnam War)."

What Rita saw and felt in prison appalled and outraged her:

"I was in a cubicle about nine by eleven feet, which held one metal bed for me and one for my cell mate, a small desk, and two short metal lockers. The beds were one yard apart. There were four wings (called alleys) to the building, each housing thirty-two women. There were also two small dorms, each with six bunk beds in them. For me, the noise was the worst thing—that, and the lack of privacy. You could walk down the center of an alley and look in all the cubicles, and since there was nothing soft to absorb the sounds, it echoed like a drum. You could hear anyone laugh, snore, holler, clomp down the hall, or bang their locker.

"People would walk on the floor 'clomp clomp clomp,' open up a metal locker 'bang bang bang bang.' The girl across the hall wanted something—'clomp clomp clomp.' The guards were coming—'clomp clomp clomp.'

"We were counted five times a day during the week. Two prison guards with their big key chains clanging walked between the rows of us standing by our beds at the 4:00 p.m. count. The other counts were taken at night with flashlights shining on us. A sixth count was taken in the visiting room. When the guards shouted 'count time,' we stood in a line against a wall to be counted—like cattle.

"The prison experience is punitive, intimidating, and demeaning. There is nothing there to rehabilitate anyone. It simply warehouses people. Everyone worked to make twelve cents an hour. I was assigned to correct papers in a class. Even though it took only a short time to do the task, I had to sit there for seven hours a day. It wasn't a place for questioning or discussion. If you caused any problems, you were sent to a maximum security jail in Peoria, Illinois and that was an even more terrible place."

To maintain her sanity, Rita kept a journal and wrote Haiku poetry, turning her experiences and feelings into pearls of wisdom and gifts to others. One poem, "Counting the Humans," was about the demeaning process of being counted. She also wrote about the beauty of a sunrise and the irony of the sun reflecting on razor wire. Sometimes she would express the joy she continued to find in small things:

Fluffs of cottonwood
Sailing upward in blue sky
In prison but free

Rita was appalled by the long sentences many of the women in the prison were serving for nonviolent crimes, such as first-time drug offenses. In a letter from jail that appeared in the Sisters of St. Joseph's *Rita Watch* newsletter, Rita aired her feelings about this issue:

"... I feel anger rising; and my anger includes another target besides the SOA and my harsh prison sentence. It now includes the sentencing laws and the prison system. I am appalled at the length of sentences many of the women have been given. Five to ten years is common, and there are some who are facing a ten to twenty-year sentence. Many of these women have small children who live far away and they may not see for months. Some haven't had visitors in three or four years. I fail to see the need to have these women walking around this circle for years, especially when there is little or nothing to prepare them to earn a living wage when they leave. And there is no private place for them to go to cry—no counseling. It's hard to hang on to hope ..."

Rita reached out to those women, shining some light into their lives so that they could find the jewels locked within their souls. She became a heroine not only to them but to her friends in the outside world. She received regular visitors and twenty to forty letters a day from fourteen countries. One such letter from Zapatistas in Mexico addressed to all of the SOA prisoners said: "In serving jail time for your actions, you have become heroes to us all."

Rita says she got her social conscience from Catholic Worker pioneer Dorothy Day, whom she had met a couple of times. "Day put her actions where her mouth was. She lived it," says Rita, who has done the same.

Rita's active involvement began in the '70s, when she founded a Free Store, the Bridge for Runaway Youth, and the St. Joseph's Home, a refuge for women and children. She particularly recalls her experiences with vagabond kids: "Initially, those youth would come into the Free Store. One day, a youth asked me, 'Why don't you find us a place to stay?' We found a boarded up house, unboarded it, moved the runaways in, and later got it staffed and licensed." The Free Store and the Bridge still exist, though now in other parts of Minneapolis.

Perhaps the biggest turning point in Rita's activist career came during her stay in Nicaragua and Guatemala during the Contra War in the '80s. While in Central America, she worked in the fields, lived with the common people, and listened to their stories. At the time, she was working for Witness for Peace, an organization that documented Contra attacks on civilians and hosted groups coming to Nicaragua to see for themselves what was going on. Often, her personal security was in danger:

"There was so much tension. You didn't know when you went down those roads if you would be ambushed or hit a landmine."

It was during her time in Nicaragua, Rita says, that she first saw the devastation caused by the Contras and came to believe that they were directed and armed by the CIA and trained at the School of the Americas.

"I met a man from El Salvador who told me he had been a medium-ranking officer in the Army. One day, he was handed a list of villages with names of residents to exterminate. He knocked on one door and a man came out with a small child sitting on his shoulders and his pregnant wife standing beside him. He turned to his commanding officer and said, 'I can't do it.' So, the officer shot the man in the doorway. Both the officer that did the shooting and the top commander had been trained at the SOA."

What keeps Sister Rita going is what brought her this far in the first place. "I'm sustained by the Gospel," she says. "Specifically, the life of Jesus. He was a radical who bucked the authorities, and they got him for that, just like they got me. My spirituality is basic, absolutely basic."

Evidence of that spirituality and what it has wrought pervade Rita's apartment and keep her constant company. During our interview, gospel hymns softly float from an old-fashioned radio perched on a small table. In her study next to an open Bible is a small hanging crucifix (Salvadoran made) and a picture of four church women who were assassinated in El Salvador by SOA graduates. Mementos and artifacts of her social activism adorn her walls and fill filing cabinets.

On a windowsill is that prism that captures sunbeams streaming in and turns them into sparkling jewels of light—gifts of freedom Rita will carry in her heart wherever she goes.

"They can jail the resister, but not the resistance."

Anonymous, found on a bumper sticker

Questions for Contemplation:

1. Rita is disgusted with the U.S. prison system. Do you agree that reforms are needed? What do you think needs to be done?
2. Have you ever known or visited anyone in prison? If so, what do you know about his or her experience?
3. Do you believe we should continue the War on Drugs by giving long prison sentences? Why or why not?
4. We spend over fifty billion dollars a year on the War on Drugs and still haven't succeeded in having a drug free America. How do you think we should be spending our money?
5. Do you think good prison rehabilitation services will encourage down-and-out people to commit crimes to access such services that are otherwise out of reach? Why or why not?

Resources for Reflection and Action:

Prison Moratorium Project, c/o DSA, 180 Varick St. 12th Floor, NYC, 10014. A youth-led, grassroots organization dedicated to ending prison construction. Phone: 212-727-8610 ext. 23. Website: www.nomoreprisons.org.

Prison Activist, PO Box 339, Berkeley, CA 94701. Builds action networks among educators, activists, prisoners, and prisoners' families; exposes human rights violations and challenges the expansion of the prison-industrial complex. Phone: 510-893-4648. Website: www.prisonactivist.org.

The Sentencing Project, 514 10th St. NW, Suite 1000, Washington, DC 20004. A national leader in the development of alternative sentencing programs and in criminal justice policy reform. Addresses racial and economic disparity in sentencing. Phone: 202-628-0871. Website: www.sentencingproject.org.

The Garden Project, Pier 28, San Francisco, CA 94105. Empowers inmates to transform themselves and their communities through organic gardening, tree planting, and transitional employment. Phone: 415-243-8558. Website: www.gardenproject.org.

American Friends Service Committee, 1501 Cherry St., Philadelphia, PA 19102. A Quaker organization that advocates prisoner rights, promotes alternatives to incarceration, offers training in nonviolence and restorative justice, provides support groups for friends and families of inmates, and campaigns for abolition of the death penalty. Phone: 215-241-7000. Website: www.afsc.org.

Families against Mandatory Minimums Foundation (FAMM Foundation), 1612 K Street NW Suite 1400, Washington, DC 20006. Phone: 202-822-6700. Fax: 202-822-6704. Email: famm@famm.org. Website: www.famm.org.

Chapter 8

Sally Chapeau, Betsy Raasch Gilman, David Miller, Vincent Rush, Mary Shepard

Truth Seekers question. They do not settle for "apparent" or even what some might call "obvious" truth; they seek absolute truth. They defy experts and deny professional opinions. Truth Seekers are so committed to their quest, they risk ridicule, ostracism, and alienation.

Sally Chapeau ignored what the teachers and other "experts" said about her son in favor of a more comprehensive understanding. Betsy Raasch Gilman sought to revolutionize American society by going beyond societal conventions at home and in her politics. David Miller took great risks by speaking up against what he believed were government lies and participating in antiwar activities. Vincent Rush challenged the Pope and sacrificed his opportunity to become a bishop, and Mary Shepard travels and studies, seeking firsthand knowledge and facts, rather than believing what the mainstream media says.

Ignoring the Experts | SALLY CHAPEAU

by Julie Penshorn

"We moved in the spring of my son, Adam's, tenth grade year. Adam was mad. He didn't want to go to a different school—didn't want to make new friends. I felt he had a right to have an opinion about where we lived because, at seventeen he had an established life. It wasn't fair for me to tell him he had to leave his friends, but yet, Adam's stepfather and I wanted to move from the city to a place in the country. To solve our dilemma, I agreed to drive Adam back to the city every day for school. Since I worked near his school, it wasn't too inconvenient.

"Within days of moving, we faced our first problem. Adam didn't want to come home with me! He wanted to hang out with his friends after school. Fortunately, our fights about this lasted only a couple of months until the school year ended. He then moved into an apartment with a friend for the summer.

"School had always been a touchy subject with Adam. He was difficult to have in class. Though he didn't lack for brains, he could be disruptive. In second grade they attributed this to immaturity, and his dad and I decided to keep him back. As it turned out, this was a poor solution. He was still disruptive, and, after being held back, he was bored to boot! As the years went on, we had no shortage of challenges with school, friends, behavior, and so on. Now he was seventeen, and on his own for the summer.

"The plan was that he would continue staying in the apartment with his friend and then resume school in the fall. But during the summer, I began to worry about Adam. On many occasions when I called him at noon, he'd still be sleeping. I had no faith that in the fall he'd make it to classes if he continued living with his friend. Plus, I was dealing with guilt. In some ways, I felt I had abandoned him in my quest to live in the country. After much reflection and discussion with my husband and extended family, I decided to get an apartment near his school to share with him, until he graduated. I felt it was critical to support my son's education. I believe parenting is a lifelong commitment and was grateful for my husband's support, even though this meant a drastic change in our lifestyle.

"Adam had been a sickly baby and whiny. While he was still a toddler, his dad simply rejected him, and within a very short period of time our marriage collapsed. Now that he was toddling off into adulthood, I felt I couldn't reject him. I believe in not giving up on a child—no matter how challenging they may be—and Adam certainly was a challenge!

"I was frustrated with the schools because it seemed they offered no support for a person with Adam's temperament. I had a conference with one teacher who inadvertently revealed that my son was the subject of staff lounge discussions—very negative ones. He said, 'I heard Adam was an incorrigible student, so I took it on as a challenge. We get along famously. He participates in class, he's doing fine.' So I said to the teacher, 'You mean you sit around in the staff lounge talking about my son and the other kids?' He was silent. I concluded that teachers were whining and commiserating with each other about having to deal with troublesome kids, not trying to find solutions.

"One time when Adam was in junior high, we had a meeting with the viceprincipal, a counselor, and a couple of teachers to address some concerns. It was obvious that Adam had been labeled and that everyone had a prejudiced, negative view of him. However, when the counselor brought in his report card, everyone's mouth dropped open. They had no idea he had such good grades . . . all As and Bs.

"Still determined that Adam would graduate, when September came, I followed through on my plan to live with him. Some people thought I was nuts. Others were convinced I was leaving my husband.

"I took him to school every morning and dropped him off right at the front door. When I got his report card, I realized he'd been going in the front and going out the back door! His grades were fine. He had all Bs. But he had been absent 40 days that quarter!

"'What was the point of making this sacrifice?' I wondered. I wished I could put him somewhere and they would let him out when he was done—sort of like cooking a batch of cookies! But I guess I was the baker, so there was no one else to do the job.

"We had the apartment for six months when Adam began his overt rebellion. He was repeatedly in trouble, and both of us were called into the office. I knew most of it was happening because Adam wanted respect and thought he should be treated as an equal. He wasn't getting respect from the teachers. Teachers would get so irate with him . . . He could have reported them for their bad behavior.

"At one meeting, a teacher got so worked up, he stood up and yelled until the veins in his face popped out. He had to leave the room. The principal apologized for his behavior.

"When a teacher suspected Adam was high in class and reported it to the office, I was told he needed to be drug tested. We could appeal this decision, during which time he'd be suspended. I put the school officials on the line and said, 'Did you catch him smoking pot? Did you find it on him? Or was this just more discrimination because he was a difficult kid?' We decided to appeal, but Adam dropped out of school before our appeal went to the board.

"I thought this was the end of my son's life. However, he studied for and took his GED, and passed with flying colors. All the 'experts' believed he should finish high school and not be allowed to test out. I was okay with letting him get his GED, but I insisted he had to try to get into a college if he passed. I didn't want taking the GED to be an easy out for him. I just wasn't going to let him go into idle mode.

"Adam was accepted at St. Cloud State, his college of choice. He's now in his second year and getting more and more serious about studying. With everybody off his back, he's taking on his own responsibility.

"What I've learned from all this is that standard procedures don't work for every child. Don't give up. Trust your instincts. Find a way to work with your kid even if it means taking an alternative route. The experts don't always have the answers."

Photo by Julie Penshorn

Sally Chapeau and her son, Adam, spend some time fishing.

Questions for Contemplation:

1. Have you been in a situation where you felt the teacher(s) were not on your side? What made you feel that way? What could they have done differently to support you?
2. What did your parents do to show you support and to help you be accountable?
3. When you didn't follow a mainstream path, what did your parents do? Was it helpful or not? Why?
4. Many kids claim to be bored in school or don't want to go to school. What do you think causes this? What do you think needs to change? What will it take for this to happen? What might be your role?
5. Sally picked up on the fact that her son was being talked about negatively in the staff lounge. Do you believe that when we talk negatively about someone it becomes a self-fulfilling prophecy? Do you talk about someone in a negative way? What could you be saying instead?

Resources for Reflection and Action:

The Myth of the A.D.D. Child: Fifty ways to improve your child's behavior and attention span without drugs, labels, or coercion, by Thomas Armstrong, Ph.D. (NYC: Penquin Putnam Inc., 1997). Armstrong believes that many behaviors labeled as A.D.D. are in fact a child's response to complex social, emotional, and educational influences. By tackling the root causes of these problems, parents can help their children experience positive changes in their lives.

Kids are Worth It: Giving your child the gift of inner discipline, by Barbara Coloroso (NYC: William Morrow, 1994). By encouraging kids to like themselves, to think for themselves, and to solve their own problems, Coloroso believes that children will grow into adolescents armed with the fortitude to survive and prosper.

Parenting Toward Solutions: How parents can use skills they already have to raise responsible kids, by Linda Metcalf (Paramus, NJ: Prentice Hall, 1997).

On Their Side, by Bob Strachota (Greenfield, MA: Northeast Foundation for Children, 1998). Helps us learn how to become an advocate and ally to our students, and how to be "on their side" rather than constantly being stuck in opposition.

Teenage Liberation Handbook: How to quit school and get a real life education, by Grace Llewellyn, (1997).

Tips and Tools for Getting Thru to Kids, by Phillip Mountrose (Sacramento, California: Holistic Communications, 1999). This book shows parents and educators how to heal themselves so they can more effectively help children. It offers a unique combination of emotional intelligence and healing love.

The Challenge to Care in Schools: An alternative approach to education, by Nel Noddings (NYC: Teachers College Press, 1992). Noddings asks us to seriously question some of our most deeply entrenched ways of thinking about education. She argues that we need a radical change in both curriculum and teaching to reach all children, not just the few who fit our conception of the academically able.

Understanding Temperament: Strategies for creating family harmony, by Lyndall Shick (Seattle, WA: Parenting Press, 2000).

Growing a Revolution | BETSY RAASCH GILMAN

by Burt Berlowe

It was 1978. Within the rickety confines of a farmhouse/retreat center in the midst of a Kansas cornfield, a noisy crowd had gathered to plant the seeds of radical social change.

The occasion was the seventh meeting of a revolutionary organization with a bold name: Movement for a New Society (MNS). Among those attending was twenty-six year-old Betsy Raasch Gilman, who came from the Twin Cities of Minneapolis/St. Paul, Minnesota. The Kansas cornstalks were new to Betsy, but social action was not.

Born in St. Paul in 1952, Betsy grew up amidst the political turmoil and rapid social change of the '60s, a time she recalls with fond clarity:

"I got into the peace movement because of my mother. She took me to my first antiwar march in 1965, a march to protest the landing of U.S. Marines in Vietnam. A handful of us marched around downtown Minneapolis holding signs—two-by-two—and spaced several yards apart so that the group would look larger than it was. I was in the eighth grade."

The next summer, Betsy attended a week-long peace camp in Iowa sponsored by the American Friends Service Committee. Betsy and her peers discussed the Middle East conflict, civil rights, and the Vietnam War. She read a book called *In Place of War* that laid out a form of nonviolent, civilian-based defense.

"Civilian-based defense," Betsy explains, "means the U.S. populace would refuse to cooperate with invading forces. Citizens would preorganize, preplan, and drill themselves in actions that would make it impossible for an enemy to successfully conquer the country. They would do things to cause confusion, such as turn street signs around and disconnect telephones and electricity. The idea of noncooperation with an opponent is the linchpin of nonviolence. We can't avoid the violence aimed at us by an opponent, but we can reduce it when we are not violent ourselves. With such clear alternatives to armed conflict, I became a pacifist.

Photo by Todd Cota

Betsy Raasch Gilman spends time at home with her cat.

"During high school, a group of friends and I were involved in the antiwar and the black justice movements. As a white person, I tried to find ways to be an advocate for black students. They wanted black history to be taught at the school, along with practical courses like business law instead of Latin. Sympathetic white students, like me, found it hard to give them the support they needed because the students influenced by Black Nationalism distrusted white students. They thought we would take over and run things.

"I believed black and white students could come together over student rights. We all disliked the way we were treated as students. We felt like prisoners. The administration conducted periodic searches of our lockers, St. Paul Police patrolled the halls, and we had no voice in the Parent/Teacher Association. Through our protest activities, we finally gained inclusion in the PTA. It became the Parent/Teacher/Student Association. Our requests, including classes in black history, business math, and car mechanics, became available my senior year."

"During the Vietnam War, Grinnell was probably the 'hottest' protest area in Iowa," Betsy recalls. "After the mining of the Haiphong harbor, we had a three-day fast. We adopted a chapel as our headquarters and had candlelight vigils and marches—with support from faculty and townspeople. When Salvador Allende, the socialist Chilean president, was overthrown in Chile, we marched through the streets of Grinnell by candlelight. Once, when Senator Bob Dole spoke in support of U.S. war policy, we protested. We surrounded the building, singing and giving our own speeches. I remember wondering what on earth was I was doing in this little college town when so much was happening all over the world? It seemed like all we needed to do was shout a bit and occupy a building and the system would change—snap! It took me years to realize that social change usually happens much more slowly."

While attending Grinnell College in Iowa, Betsy became an active feminist. She helped integrate women's writings into American Studies classes and was also a founder of the Iowa Women's Political Caucus that encouraged women to run for public office.

Returning to St. Paul after college, Betsy immediately got involved with Women's Advocates, which had just opened its doors. This was the first shelter in the country for battered women, and it posed some tough ethical dilemmas for Betsy. "Some of the victims came in with scars, broken bones, and so on," she says. "I was a pacifist. But what could I say to those who wanted to take karate or other self-defense classes? Mostly, we housed women and children fleeing from abusive husbands and boyfriends, though some were from state institutions for the mentally ill and developmentally disabled. I listened to them, went to court with them, took them to the welfare office, answered phones at the shelter, stayed there overnight, helped residents get their possessions from their apartments, and played with the children. Since domestic violence was such an unknown issue then, we all did public speaking about it. The battered women's movement was unstructured. There was no training for it. We taught ourselves as we went."

Around this same time, a number of Quaker activists came together to form the Movement for a New Society. MNS was a network of small collectives that sought to combine struggle for radical change with personal sharing, support, and training. Members worked together on what was wrong, determined how they would like to change it, and developed a strategy for getting there. The ultimate goal of MNS was to create a democratic, ecologically sustainable culture through ending corporate capitalism and social oppression. We used nonviolent direct action and adopted a simple, economically secure lifestyle compatible with nature while emphasizing community. In Betsy's words, "Values of individualism, competition, maximum production and consumption, bigness, complicated and unnatural technology, and elitism were replaced by collectivism, cooperation, smallness, simple and natural technology, equal conditions for people, and democracy."

The best example of the MNS was the Philadelphia Life Center (PLC)—a multigenerational support community. It began in 1971 with about thirty-five people but grew to over one hundred residents of seventeen communal households. Activists from all over the world came there for training and often stayed a year or more. Life Center trainers also visited other locations to give workshops, which led to MNS branches in many other American cities.

Betsy attended a workshop on nonviolence led by PLC/MNS trainers in St. Paul in 1977. "It was fabulous for me, a terrific, life-changing experience," she says. "We camped out and cooked together for four days in a Quaker meeting house. Every day, we had three large workshops and discusses topics like meeting facilitation, conflict resolution, sexism and racism, creating intentional communities, and self-run study groups. I was enthralled.

"It was after that workshop that I joined MNS to continue learning how people can work at the grassroots level: planning and organizing demonstrations, kicking off events, writing press releases, dealing with the media, and keeping demonstrations peaceful. It was strong grounding for me in the skills of political activism."

Betsy turned her six-bedroom St. Paul house into an intentional community, where she lived with other MNS members. "By sharing a house, we could live simply and work part-time for bread labor," she explains. "The rest of our time was devoted to activism. We supported one another practically and emotionally. Everyone shared chores: cooking, cleaning, childcare, and the like. We even shared cars sometimes. It could be stressful, but it also provided me with lots of long-time friends, and many children that feel like my own."

Through MNS, Betsy took part in a number of campaigns in the '70s and '80s. "We had a great impact because of our training programs," she says.

"We hooked up with the Nuclear Freeze campaign and the antinuclear-missile movement in Europe. We started women's peace encampments at military bases and factories. I helped start a campaign locally against the deployment of Cruise and Pershing missiles. Many of us went to Central American countries as nonviolent escorts for activists threatened by oppressive governments. We helped improve the food co-op movement nationally. And MNSers organized 'Take Back the Night' marches in several U.S. cities, where women paraded through pornography districts to show they wouldn't be intimidated by male violence. We kind of threw ourselves into every issue, all the movements, all at once. We were active in Three Mile Island, the saving energy movement, the Persian Missile campaign, and Trident Submarine demonstrations.

"We were also trying to have egalitarian, meaningful relationships with our loved ones, raise our children to be free people, and develop ourselves spiritually. And we put lots of effort into unlearning our own oppressive attitudes and behaviors, especially around sexism and classism. It was an all-or-nothing, whole-life commitment."

Because MNSers believed that everyone in the community should help raise the children, Betsy took in two boys who were orphaned because their father murdered their mother and then killed himself. At first, Betsy recalls, "It was hell, sheer hell. The boys screamed and cried, 'I hate you! I won't live with you! My mother would never want me to live here!' The boys stole, swore, smoked, sulked, refused to be hugged, and generally appeared ungrateful. Counseling wasn't helpful. The kids regarded it as punishment: 'My dad shot my mom, so I have to go to counseling.' It went on like that for several months."

Betsy's family eventually adopted the two boys and she says, "Things are better now." In her expanded household as well as in out in the world, she has found ways to quell violence and distress.

"What we did at MNS was tremendously important to me, better than any school I ever went to. I am thankful for the leadership skills I developed. I've hoped some phoenix like it would arise from the ashes, but one hasn't appeared. I regret that eleven years of my life in MNS didn't bring widespread transformation. We had a reunion in 1996. It was terrific. Fifty people showed up. Many are still working on social change issues."

Betsy and other former MNSers founded a training collective called Future Now that teaches social change skills to grassroots organizations. She sees Future Now as a continuation of MNS work. "I'm still building a revolution," she says. "To the extent that MNS had a strategy, we saw three beginning stages: cultural preparation for a major shift of power, building strong people's movements, and actions for revolutionary reforms. Those three processes might go on for years before a fourth step becomes possible: massive nonviolent rebellion against the social order. That's what you think about when someone says 'revolution.'

"Future Now is working at two of those first three steps. For instance, I did training for the board of directors of residents' organization in a low-income housing complex in St. Paul, Minnesota. They're learning how to organize and operate a resident-run organization. Their first steps have given me real hope. One thing they've done is make a library in the apartment complex with books and computers for the kids.

"In many ways, I don't think of myself as a peacemaker," she says. "I'm a justice-maker. Making peace is not necessarily making justice. It's the other way around. I do everything I can to be as peaceful as possible, but I'm a troublemaker, an activist interested in justice. If that means rattling a few cages, I'll do it in a nonviolent way. Social change won't happen without conflict. The challenge is to resolve conflict in a way that builds relationships without losing track of justice."

Questions for Contemplation:

1. Betsy first got involved in peacemaking or, as she says, "justice-making," through her mother. What peacemaker has influenced you? How were you influenced?
2. Betsy believes that cultural changes are more likely to happen through a revolution by the people. What are your thoughts? What ideas do you have for people's voices to be heard?
3. What role have you played in raising children that are not your own?
4. What ideas do you have for creating a sustainable, democratic culture?
5. What do you think would reduce or prevent domestic abuse?

Resources for Reflection and Action:

Powerful Peacemaking: A strategy for a living revolution, by George Lakey (Gabriola Island, BC: New Society Publishers, 1987). Presents a bold and comprehensive approach to creative social empowerment and global transformation in the quest for a peaceful and just world.

The Fabric of the Future: Women visionaries illuminate the path to tomorrow, edited by M. J. Ryan (Conari Press, 2000). Each woman offers insights into how we can navigate from chaos to clarity within our times.

Grassroots Grants: An activist's guide to proposal writing, by Andy Robinson (Oakland, CA: Chardon Press, 1995). Information on who's got the grant money and how to write a proposal that can get it.

Moving Toward a New Society by Susanne Gowan, George Lakey, William Moyer, Richard Taylor (Gabriola Island, BC: New Society Press, 1976).

Life Is a Miracle: An essay against modern superstition by Wendell Berry (Washington, DC: Counterpoint). Berry says we must ask ourselves: How does one individual act, sensitively and compassionately, without doing irreparable damage? Provides compelling advocacy of the worth of every individual creature, the importance of accurate language, and the deep advantages of living in a community.

Action Coalition for Global Change, 55 New Montgomery St., Suite 219, San Francisco, CA 94105. Phone: 415-896-2242. Fax: 415-227-4878. Email: acgc@igc.apc.org. Website: www.idaho-web.com. Membership group of over sixty nongovernmental agencies. They have formed a global network to promote peace, a just global economy, a healthy environment, and human rights.

Global Education Associates, 475 Riverside Dr., Suite 1848, NYC, 10115. Phone: 212-870-3290. Fax: 212-870-2729. Email: gea475@igc.apc.org. Website: www/igc.apc.org/gea. A network of people in over ninety countries committed to promoting global systems that advance a more just and peaceful world order.

Peace Behind Bars | DAVID MILLER

by Burt Berlowe

Nonviolence is not cowardice. In fact, nonviolence is a very active endeavor using our brain, our cunning, and our humor. It's our ability to stay calm, to size up the situation, while observing all that is going on at the time and coming up with some kind of action that retains the life, health, and dignity of the person(s) who oppose or attack us, while maintaining our own dignity and integrity. Nonviolence takes more effort and courage than violence.

—Board Member Al Bostelmann
of Pax Christi Twin Cities

Clang! Clang! Clangggg!

The banging of the iron cell doors echoes through the long hallways, shattering the tense silence at the Faribault, Minnesota, State Prison. It is a defining sound, signaling that order and harmony have prevailed—at least for the time being.

Most of the time, this penitentiary is the last place you'd look for any signs of peace. It is home to hardened criminals for whom violence has been a brutal and seemingly indelible fact of life—the only solution to frustration and rage. Many have little hope of leaving. Even in moments when the prison seems peaceful, violence is merely locked in the minds and memories of inmates, ready to escape at the slightest provocation.

But on this day, as David Miller strolls the corridors of the correctional facility, something unusual is taking place. Inside their tiny cubicles, several smiling convicts wave self-made signs that read:

"This is a violencefree zone."

"Alternatives to violence practiced here."

Photo courtesy of FNVW

David Miller

"Avoid the path of violence and stay on the path of truth."

In one cell, a prisoner is helping a fellow inmate learn skills for nonviolence.

David stops to greet and congratulate them for their efforts and ask about their progress. Earlier that year, he and some cohorts spent a weekend at the prison as part of the Alternatives to Violence Project (AVP) training for inmates, run by Friends for a Nonviolent World (FNVW).

At the time of our interview, David is the director of the FNVW office in Minneapolis, Minnesota. It is the latest of his many stops on a rocky road strewn with the debris of a violent home, youthful rebellion, and brash, controversial efforts at social justice.

David's upbringing prepared him for confrontation with a hostile world. He was raised in upstate New York in a Jewish family during the tumultuous '60s. His father was a brusque, working-class man who taught by example the language and behavior of the streets. The Miller household teemed with physical and sexual abuse, as well as with drug addiction.

"My brother was physically abusive as well. I was younger and smaller than he was, so I learned wrestling to defend myself. But mostly, I used wit and humor to deflect him. It was the first realization I had that one could use nonviolent techniques to protect oneself.

"From the age of eight, I was attracted to the culture of rock music and the concept of nonviolence. I was never tolerant of injustice or abuse. Whenever I could do something against either one, I did. I first committed civil disobedience in the sixth grade. Girls at my school were not allowed to wear pants to class. To protest, I wore a miniskirt to school. They kicked me out, but they changed the rule.

"By the early '80s, I was a full-blown activist. I joined the nuclear freeze campaign to promote unilateral disarmament and conversion of weapons to peaceful uses. I helped build a model of the Trident submarine to use in the campaign and did leafleting at a naval base. As we handed people flyers, they would ask us, 'What do you do?'

We said, 'We want to change the world.'"

At about this same time, David joined a collective, intentional community located in New York, known as the Knolls Action Project, where, he learned nonviolent activism related to issues like military tax resistance and the struggle for empowerment in El Salvador and South Africa.

"As the years went on, I had some friends and neighbors that got hurt by muggings and shootings," he recalls. "My whole approach to street violence became one of firmly, but nonviolently, asserting power—saying, 'It stops here.' I sought allies to make a better neighborhood. We did a pledge of resistance and cleaned up a park that had been trashed. We were forever giving something to the community.

Never one to stay put too long, in 1983, David moved to Alaska. A relationship with a woman who worked at a battered woman's shelter led him to start a counseling center for male abusers.

"While in Alaska, I also did direct action at Trident sites and counseled conscientious objectors. Counseling and aiding anyone resisting the draft was a felony that could lead to up to five years in prison and a ten thousand dollars fine, but I took the risk anyway.

"Because of my various kinds of protest work, my phone was tapped and my mail opened. It was frightening. My parents were worried, too, and pressured me to stop. I got great advice from war resisters. They cautioned me that using only direct resistance was to put myself in a goldfish bowl. To avoid too much visibility, they suggested I find other ways to speak truth to power.

"I decided to get a doctorate degree in psychology. After working on it at Temple University in Philadelphia, Pennsylvania, I moved to Minnesota to write a dissertation. It didn't take long, however, before I realized that power and money were seducing me. I knew I would turn into a Frankenstein if I went around calling myself a doctor. I never wrote my dissertation. I realized that if I were going to help change others, I had to be true to myself and get back to grassroots nonviolent social action activities. I believed my place was working with people on the streets and in prisons.

"That decision led me to this job, Director of Friends for a Non-Violent World. In our Alternatives to Violence workshops, people do a lot of role-playing of real-life situations that evoke typical violent, knee-jerk responses; but instead of acting on that, participants are asked to create and use an alternative to violence strategy instead. It's quite amazing what solutions can be found when we take the time to look for the nonviolent ones.

"All of what we do at FNVW is rooted in nonviolence," says David. "Having good organizing skills is a part of nonviolence, as is speaking truth and equality and respecting the integrity of others. Our biggest challenge is to work to promote nonviolence without taking on too much."

When David wants to be at peace with himself and the world, he meditates or does Tai Chi, which he learned from studying Buddhism in Albany, New York. Sometimes, he goes for a swim. "If someone is swimming next to me and they want to go faster, I actually slow down instead," he says. "To be at peace, you can't rush. Sometimes, I want to do more, but I know I need to do less.

"I do have anger in me. I have to realize that I'm not always as perfect or gentle as I would like to be. So I need to be more compassionate with myself and not expect perfection. We have to be able to laugh at ourselves and make peacemaking fun. I've come to a place where I know I can do it imperfectly and celebrate it and give others hard feedback in a loving, nurturing way.

"To be a peacemaker, you have to take care of yourself. We also have to honor people for who they are, not just what they're doing. The process is more important than the result."

David has recently moved on to become the Executive Director of the Western North Carolina Aids Project whose mission is to help people affected with HIV/AIDS achieve the best possible quality of life and to educate the community about HIV/AIDS.

Questions for Contemplation:

1. What alternatives-to-violence stories do you know? What alternatives-to-violence strategies have you used when faced with anger or rage?
2. What do you remember as being unfair or unjust when you were in school? What did you do about it?
3. David was cautioned to not always put himself in a goldfish bowl. What behind-the-scenes ways have you discovered in order to create change?
4. What have you found to be effective in seeking deeper, more intimate dialogue with loved ones?

Resources for Reflection and Action:

No Alternative? Nonviolent responses to repressive regimes, edited by John Lampen. (Available through the Pendle Hill Bookstore, 338 Plush Mill Road, Wallingford, PA 19086.) Phone: 800-742-3150 ext. 2. Collection of essays examining the field of alternatives to a violent response to repressive regimes.

Changing the Bully Who Rules the World: Reading and thinking about ethics, by Carol Bly (Mpls., MN: Milkweed, 1996).

Lighting Candles in the Dark, by the Friends General Religious Education Conference Committee. (Available through the Pendle Hill Bookstore listed above.) Inspiring stories from Quaker history about people who showed courage as they dealt nonviolently with difficult situations.

Organize Now. Website: www.organizenow.net. Provides technical tips for activists, as well as a comprehensive, updated library of links to web resources on technology and social change. Anyone can subscribe to the email list by sending a blank Email message to: org-c-subscribe@topica.com.

Center for Partnership Studies, PO Box 51936, Pacific Grove, CA 93950. Phone: 408-626-1004. Fax: 408-626-3734. Website: www.partnershipway.org. Based on Diane Eisler's research, the center's goal is to develop opportunities for men and women to live in partnership in all parts of the globe and foster equitable relationships—whether intimate or international.

Delancey Street Foundation, 600 Embarcadero St., San Francisco, CA 94107. Phone: 415-957-9800. Foundation founded by Mimi Silbert. Provides housing, training skills, and work for ex-convicts and people with drug and alcohol problems—transforming society's outcasts into responsible citizens.

Search for Common Ground, 1601 Connecticut Ave., NW, Suite 200, Washington, DC 20009. Phone: 202-265-4300. Fax: 202-232-6718. Email: scmarks@sfcg.org. Website: www.sfcg.org. An international, nongovernmental organization that pursues new ways of thinking about conflicts and new approaches to finding cooperative solutions.

Daddy

by Rebecca Janke

As I sat listening to the expressed rage, sadness, and worry of the thirteen men in Faribault Prison, whose wives and girlfriends weren't bringing their children to visit, I thought of my own dad. He was never sent to prison, but he lived in a prison of his own, created by the trauma of World War II.

His job in the war was to bag dead bodies to be shipped home for burial. He viewed all life as sacred and knew that he was sending home, not a dead solider, but a dead husband, dead son, dead brother, or dead nephew. He suffered a "nervous breakdown" and was sent home with a military discharge.

His way of coping was to become a workaholic and stay so busy that he wouldn't need to deal with his emotions. He provided for us but remained distant, not wanting to play, go on vacations, read us stories, or roast hot dogs, like we saw other fathers doing with their children. We knew he loved us but often didn't feel his love in concrete ways—he was too "busy."

The week before I went to the prison in Faribault, Minnesota, to help prisoners learn alternatives to violence, I came upon some letters my dad had written to my mother years ago when we were on vacation without him. The tears began to flow as I sat on the couch and read how much he loved and missed us. I was surprised because, in my mind, I had thought he would be relieved we were gone so he could get his work done. In those letters, I felt him reaching out to me in ways I never understood when he was alive. Even though he died several years ago, he was very present—embodied in the letter I held in my hands. It was good to "hear" his voice again and be told that I was missed and loved.

During the workshop at the prison, I witnessed one father after another lament, and many sobbed, over severed relationships with their children. They felt they would never be able to impact their children's lives in a positive way. I shared with the prisoners how much it meant to me to be able to "sit on the couch" with my dad again through his letters.

I know the status quo is in favor of letting prisoners suffer for the harm they have caused others, but I also know there is a kid on the outside that wants to know his/her daddy's love. I was broken-hearted at the thought of the children not having contact with their dads and offered the following suggestion:

Keep writing letters to your children, sharing your love and the wisdom you have found and wish your children to know. If your wives, ex-wives, or girlfriends won't let the letters go through, put them in a safe deposit box. Make instructions through an attorney that your children will be notified when they are eighteen that the letters are waiting for them and they can "sit on the couch" with you.

Daddy Do You Love Me?

Song, by Julie Penshorn

Daddy do you love me?
Did you ever want to know me?
Was I ever in your heart?
Did you ever even hold me?
You know that I don't know you
And sometimes I don't care
To meet the man who left us lonely
And wasn't ever there.

Chorus:
But, we're all children of a daddy.
We're all children of a son.
We're all children of a daddy,
And daddy for me, you are the one.

We'll always be related
Doesn't matter where you're hid,
You'll always be my daddy
No matter what you did.
Aren't I important?
Don't I mean even a bit?
Do you think that it's been easy
Understanding why you quit?
What do you want to tell me?
What have you learned so far?
Can you share a bit of wisdom
From where you are?
You could write it in a letter,
You could send it through the post.
You could send it to my grandma—
Guess she sees you the most.
Mom won't talk about you.
She doesn't want to hear
Anything about you.
It breaks her down in tears.
Now daddy, you're a human,
You must feel pain like me .
So send me just one letter,
It would mean so much to me.

Bones and Soft Tissue

by Julie Penshorn

I've been accused of being stubborn when I'm in a conflict. People think that's the trait that compels me to persist—to push the conflict to a resolution—even though the conflict might end sooner if I would just shut up. But I think it's my sense of justice that causes me to insist that my perspective, or the point I'm trying to make, be understood. To me, it seems essential for reaching truth.

The fact is, if I don't get a turn to clearly express my feelings, I feel bullied. Also, I believe if we take the time to dialogue or even argue—if that's what it takes—enough to understand each other, we'll do better in future conflicts. We'll both have a better understanding of the other person's point of view, and we'll be capable of long-term solutions.

Which brings me back to my struggle. I feel very angry and powerless when I'm dealing with someone who curtails the conflict resolution process prematurely by using the conflict as an opportunity to separate. I mean, this person probably is not talking with me and/or is choosing a solution unilaterally. I believe that's unfair. But more frustrating to me is that it takes away any opportunity I might have to give the gift of perspective. It halts the search for workable, real solutions and curtails our ability to uncover and reveal deeper truths.

Deeper truths don't come easily. In our search for them, we may go around and around pushing and pulling on each other, but in the process, we may find some new ground and begin to see with new eyes. Rebecca, co-author of The Compassionate Rebel, *has started workingout. Her personal trainer pushes her. "Don't quit now. Take it to a new level. Break through the barrier," he says. I told Rebecca that's just what she does to me! Pushes me to develop new psychological muscles!*

Rebecca says her trainer will sometimes give the weights she's struggling to lift just a little boost so she can go further than if she were doing it by herself. She says even though he pushes her, she knows he's there to give her support. She does the same thing to me. She always celebrates my change efforts and tiny improvements as a compassionate rebel, and she never allows me to believe I'm hopeless. It's paid off. After seven years of working together, I've learned a lot about myself and a lot about pushing without attacking.

When I teach horseback riding, I often find I have to push my students to get them to overcome their fears. "Don't let that horse bully you! He's trying to show you he's the boss. He wants to make all the decisions. You need to let him know that's not okay. You are in this relationship, too!" If the horse is the only one who gets to offer an opinion, the person is often bullied. Few horses are as generous as the storybooks say! Most would take the first turn back to the stall, their buddies, and food. Thus, if you have a different idea, you must let them know you have something to say.

Many of my young girl students are experts at self-pity when the horse expresses a contrary opinion. "I can't do it (sob sob)! This horse doesn't like me!" I say, "So what! Right now, she doesn't have to like you, she just needs to know what you have to say. You have a right to an opinion!"

As women, we have learned that we should never challenge or confront contrary opinions. I believe that's wrong. In fact, I believe it keeps us in superficial relationships that rob us of intimacy and our full humanity. But we must also be ready to be pushed. There is a balance between the soft, supportive kind of love that we need with its cuddling and closeness, and the tough love we need. Rebecca gives me so much positive feedback that I feel safe and supported when she pushes me. I'm able to listen to all her thoughts. She speaks truth. Similarly, when we work with horses, we help them feel safe and create a kind environment for them so they aren't afraid and can listen.

"Being a compassionate rebel is knowing when to be in your bones and when to be in your soft tissue," Rebecca said. Translated, she meant knowing when to be strong and firm, like your bones, and when to be loving and supportive, like your soft tissue.

So, after much soul-searching, I've concluded that my anger at those I love is the fuel to keep me in my bones—to keep me brave and energetic enough to continue to push through barriers and give the compassionate gift of perspective and empowerment. The more I use my soft tissue and connect with my loved ones–the more I'm positive, encouraging, patient, and observant with them–the better prepared they are to listen when I rattle my bones!

The Rebel Who Loves Freedom | VINCENT RUSH

by Rebecca Janke

Freedom is the beginning of everything. If there is any way that we are made in the image and likeness of God, it is in being free.

—Vincent Rush

It was 1968. As an ordained priest, Vincent Rush was facing a moral dilemma that would forever change his life. The spiritual foundation on which he became a priest was beginning to crack. He was willing to give up years of preparation, accumulated academic honors, and his standing in the community, rather than be part of the destruction of the Gospel which he believed the Church's "rule of law" was perpetrating.

The seeds for daring to be a critical thinker were actually planted by some of his philosophy, theology, and ethics professors who exposed him to the rigors of logic and to logic's dependence on experience. Those seeds matured in his intelligent, inquisitive mind and he began to think beyond where most human beings think—when it becomes too confusing, uncomfortable, or too unsettling.

He had come to believe that the rule-oriented legalism, which permeated so much of Catholic thought of that time, wasn't scripture-based. He resolved to have a more flexible and compassionate outlook as the vision of his ministry. It was this that led him to tell people that the two most important words in making a moral decision were "it depends."

"I was impressed by Aristotle's saying that you should never ask from a discipline certitudes it can't give. We do not have certitudes about how God is going to act in any given situation because we don't know what God sees. All we can know for certain is our own intent. Intent is everything in determining morality. Good intentions are not always enough, but without them we have nothing.

"Take the situation of three different people responding to a drunken man lying on the curb of a street asking for a handout. The first person gives him a ten-dollar bill and thinks, 'What a good-for-nothing, lazy person,' and goes on his way. The second person responds with a ten-dollar bill and thinks, 'This makes me feel good about myself. All these people here will witness what a generous person I am.' The third person gives him a ten-dollar bill and thinks, 'There but for the grace of God go I. I wonder what conditions brought him to this place? I wonder what I could do to help alleviate the problems of homelessness?'

"For those of us watching this situation, we would all have seen the same thing—three different people giving the man ten dollars. What was different was the intent. Why we do the things we do is the question. It's not about rules, it's about being a compassionate, loving person.

"In 1968, the Vatican was prohibiting medically accepted methods of birth control. People were being told that if they used the pill, they would go to hell. I knew that the intent for some people to use artificial birth control was the same as their intent for natural birth control. They were trying to better take care of the children they already had, prepare livlihoods before becoming parents, protect their security, or not wanting to add to a growing world population. To damn their souls to hell was an emotional crisis for them–and for me. I knew I could not get in the pulpit and support this ruling. I was distraught and could find no way to comfort myself.

"I went to visit another priest and then walked the streets until 2:00 a.m., convinced I had no choice but to leave the church. I then drove to a friend's house and because of the warmth and trust that defined our friendship, I was able to hear him when he said, 'Vince, we need priests like you who challenge us to think. If you are distressed about the Church now, what will it become if you leave?' It was at that moment that I decided to stay but only on the condition that I would speak freely. If the Church couldn't handle it, they would have to let me go. I became the King's loyal opposition.

"That Sunday, I told the parishioners, 'Follow your conscience. You know your circumstances best. You shouldn't feel you are forbidden to practice artificial contraception.' Not only did I say it for them, but I said it to save my own integrity. The next week, a woman who had heard about my comments the previous Sunday came to talk to me.

"'Father, is it really true that last Sunday you said it was up to us to decide to use the birth control pill?' she asked me. 'I have ten children and have had numerous miscarriages in my seventeen years of marriage. My psychiatrist has told me that I should not have any more children since I'm on the verge of having a nervous breakdown. My husband's wages are being garnished to pay back hospital bills and my check is going to support our family. When I told my husband we had to stop having sex, he said he would go to the red-light district.'

"She felt her only solution was to go on the pill, so she discontinued participating in communion. Her older children were very upset with her for not receiving communion and told her if she couldn't go to communion, they were not going either—and they were going to stop going to church altogether. The lady concluded her story to me by saying, through her tears, 'Since I started taking the pill, I have believed I would have to go to hell to keep my children in church.'"

Even though this took place over thirty years ago, Vince still cries softly when he thinks what the "rule of law" was doing to this woman and her family. "I told her she would not go to hell and to start participating in communion. 'Thank you, Father,' she said as she walked away, drying her tears."

For Vince, this was the straw that broke the camel's back. He was determined to preach and teach publicly the supremacy of conscience over Vatican teaching, which is in accord with the teaching of the Catholic Church. The Dignitatis Humanae-Vatican II document states: "because they are persons . . . endowed with reason and free will . . . they are bound to adhere to the truth." He began to point out publicly beyond Sunday mass just where he thought the Vatican was in error.

"Laws are just guides," Vincent told me. "It's good to know that the sign says, 'Slippery When Wet.' But to make moral judgments, we need to know the circumstances and we need to know intent. I like the quote from the play, *A Raisin in the Sun* by Lorraine Hansberry, 'You're so busy thinking about what's right, you don't know what's

Photo by Todd Cota

Vincent Rush

good.' When we know we are free to take account of ALL the circumstances, and we look at our intent, we have a much better chance at being a moral person.

"Fortunately, I've never gotten into trouble with my views because the people who are ready to hear what I have to say take it in and are glad to be set free and become responsible for their own morality. The people who aren't ready, ignore me or think of me as a small fish and not that much of a threat. However, I was not promoted to bishop, though I had all the credentials."

What started with pastoral experience of people not feeling free to follow their conscience because of some law, has led Vincent to a life of preaching and teaching the primacy of moral virtue. His book *The Responsible Christian* and his more recent twelve-hour video series were his attempts to spread the information to a wider group than his immediate audiences. He really believes it when he says: "Being free is what makes us most in the image and likeness of God."

So You Say You Want Peace

by Julie Penshorn

So you say you want peace?

But you're not gonna rock the boat.

Gonna take anything,

Poison with no antidote.

Don't rock the boat.

So you say you want peace?

There's a landmine in the ground.

You gonna take anything?

Even lies and a runaround?

Because you want peace?

Don't follow the leader, though the leader is strong.

Do your own thinking—learn what's really wrong.

Peace is more than silence,

Peace is taking a stand.

Peace is standing up for truth,

Standing up.

Stand up.

If you really want peace.

Questions for Contemplation:

1. What have you done to form your conscience?
2. What have you questioned? What has happened with your struggle?
3. Think about your history classes in high school. Were they taught from all points of view of those involved, or were they presented as fact from one ethnic/class/gender point of view? How can we be encouraged to think beyond mainstream culture?
4. Have you ever had an experience where more than the "rule of law" should have been looked at? What happened? How do you think it could have been handled differently?
5. Have you ever sought to be right and ignored what was good? What happened?
6. Who has helped you with a spiritual struggle? How were they helpful?
7. What is your reaction to the "being in your bones and your soft tissue" concept?

Resources for Reflection and Action:

The Responsible Christian: A popular guide for moral decision-making according to classical tradition, by Vincent E. Rush (Chicago, IL: Loyola University Press, 1984).

How to Make a Moral Decision, by Vincent Rush, Ph.D. (Bar Enterprises, Inc., PO Box 16653, St. Paul, MN 55116-0653). A twelve hour video series which outlines an approach for examining moral dilemmas. This series is designed to assist in clarifying one's thinking, and provides a consistent method for analyzing and resolving the difficult problems one faces in the course of living.

Between Eden and Armageddon: The future of world religions, violence, and peacemaking (NYC: Oxford University Press, 2000).

Imagine: What America could be in the 21st century, edited by Marianne Williamson (NYC: Rodale, 2000). In the realm of highest possibilities, what could America look like in fifty years? What kinds of changes would have to occur in order for that to happen? How can an individual or an institution best contribute to such change? Ms. Williamson posed these questions to forty of her well-known contemporaries. This book is their collective response: a powerful, provocative, and compelling vision and a prescriptive call to action.

Sowers of Justice, Office for Social Justice, 328 West Kellogg Blvd., St. Paul, MN 55102. Phone: 651-291-4477. This membership organization for Catholics is committed to changing hearts and changing structures on behalf of justice. Call to subscribe to their quarterly newsletter.

Center for Theology and the Natural Sciences, 2400 Ridge Rd., Berkeley, CA 94709. Phone: 510-848-8152. Fax: 510-848-2535. Website: www.ctns.org.

John Templeton Foundation, 2 Radnor Corporate Center, 100 Matsonford Rd., Suite 320, Radnor, PA 19087. Phone: 610-687-8942. Website: www.templeton.org. Established by renowned international investor Sir John Templeton to encourage progress in life's moral and spiritual dimensions, this foundation works closely with scientists, theologians, medical professionals, philosophers, and other scholars. The Templeton Prize for Progress in Religion is awarded annually to an individual of any religious tradition or movement whose ideas or research contributes to our spiritual knowledge.

World Conference on Religion and Peace, 777 United Nations Plaza, New York, NY 10017. Phone: 212-687-2163. Fax: 212-983-0566. A global movement with chapters in more than thirty countries, this group engages in peace initiatives and peace-related activities throughout the world. Works with U.N. agencies and vigorously promotes multireligious cooperation to resolve conflicts, encourage sustainable development, and further human rights.

Peacemaker Community. Website: www.peacemakercommunity.org. This interfaith community trains, empowers, and connects peacemakers around the world.

Standing Up to Power | MARY SHEPARD

by Burt Berlowe

As Mary Shepard and her travelling companion strolled casually down the Kingston, Jamaica, street, they were hardly prepared for what lay ahead.

A Jamaican woman came towards them, holding an infant in her arms. In a moment, she was right in front of them, and they paused to listen. Then, the young mother thrust her child towards Mary and her friend. In a quiet voice, she begged: "Please, take my baby. I can no longer feed him. Please, take him with you."

The two American women were stunned beyond belief. They wanted to help, but they knew what they had to do. They gently told the mother they couldn't take her baby. They continued on their way, trying to forget what they had just seen. But its impact refused to go away.

For Mary, the shocking event on the Kingston street would become a catalyst of her peace and justice work—a lifetime of committing her ample resources to defending the less fortunate as they struggle against potent forces. Nowadays, years and miles removed from Jamaica, Mary is still speaking truth to power and taking the time to tell about it.

There is something inherently peaceful and prosperous about Mary Shepard's home—situated among woods and fields in the serene Twin Cities suburb of Mendota Heights, Minnesota. On this late winter day of our interview, patches of snow cover the ground beneath leafless trees and the air is free of the din of city noise. The spacious two-story rambler home sits at the end of a long driveway in its own private wilderness. At first glance, this would seem to be a place of respite and perhaps cozy retirement—hardly the setting from which to wage energetic and contentious campaigns for peace and social justice.

But even as she seems secluded from core civilization, this eighty-year-old daughter and wife of corporate wealth remains in close touch with the world as a peacemaker and advocate for those in need.

Mary was born on the Upper East Side of New York City right after World War I. Her parents were well-to-do liberal children of clergy. Her father was a lawyer for J.P. Morgan, who worked on Wall Street. Neighbors and friends were all part of the ruling class. Mary was brought up as one of five church-going, protected daughters. She attended Vassar but left after her sophomore year in 1939 to marry a business executive and move to Minnesota.

There was nothing in Mary's early years that suggested peacemaking tendencies. "Looking back on it now, our family was instrumental in the way the war was run," she told me, seated at her dining room table framed by a window displaying her scenic backyard. "I recall my father, talking by phone to a brother-in-law in England who was directing the bombing of civilians in European cities, saying he could hear the bombs dropping. It seemed natural to me to hear my father talk that way. Later, my husband served in the Navy in World War II. I wholeheartedly believed in what they were doing.

"I began to think more deeply while I was at Vassar. I heard a Czechoslovakian describe what was happening to the Jews in the Holocaust and slowly began to realize that something was terribly wrong. Later, when I was in England with my father, a friend said to us, 'I don't like what Hitler is doing to the Jews. But he's awfully good for business.' I thought that if Germany could do that to Jews, we could do awful things, too."

However, the real turning point in Mary's peacemaking career came during the Vietnam War, while she was a homemaker, raising four children in her Mendota Heights house.

". . . I would sit and watch TV, and my friends would tell me that the war was winnable—that we were doing the right thing. My children were subject to the draft, so I found out everything I could. I was a Republican who chaired the platform committee plank on Vietnam at the 1968 convention. We deliberated for months. The horror was revealed. We came up with a good campaign plank that said we should get out of Vietnam. We pointed out that Vietnam always wanted to be a democracy and what we were doing didn't make any sense. But when I introduced the plank to the convention, I was practically booed off the stage, and the plank was eventually defeated.

In the meantime, I had seen poor kids being drafted and sent to Vietnam while our friends' (more affluent) kids were being kept out by proper colleges and medical deferments. Friends who had children subject to the draft helped in the peace movement for a while, but after their personal crisis was over, they walked away. I was disillusioned."

Rather than give up, Mary organized. In the early '70s, she and many close friends formed the Urban Concerns Workshop, a nonprofit organization that went into community centers, churches, and high schools to teach kids how to work within the political system on the issues they cared about. The program included creation of a TV documentary and a handbook.

In 1979, as the Iran Hostage crisis exploded, Mary traveled to that country with members of Clergy and Laity Concerned (CLC) to meet with the students who were holding more than fifty Americans hostage in the capital city of Teheran.

"We put together forty people of all walks—professors, cleaning women, phone operators, union organizers, blacks, Indians—the most amazing conglomerate of people. We went to Iran to find out what the U.S. did that made these students so angry that they would raid our embassy and hold hostages.

"Clergy members arranged for CLC leader Karen Lehman and me to visit the U.S. Embassy while we were there. We weren't able to see the hostages, but we did talk to many of the students in and around the complex. That visit had a tremendous impact on me. It made me realize that Iran shouldn't get all the blame for the hostage situation—it was partly due to U.S. policy toward that country. At the same time, we tried to tell those students that their actions would be used as an excuse for the U.S. to increase its arms buildup.

"Although the hostages were not released at that time, we had begun to raise awareness of the larger issues in our relationship with Iran. I began to take people to Iran and other countries to increase their awareness. Karen and I also spoke at churches, to community groups, and wherever we could, explaining why the students had seized the embassy and how the U.S. should share some of the blame for that incident. People who refused to believe in or accept what we were saying met us with skepticism and anger. They couldn't see the truth. But I now work in the peace movement without any illusions about the way that we conduct our foreign policy. I realize our country is not going to let go of the economic power grip that has caused our militarism."

Photo by Todd Cota

Mary Shepard finds solace in her office retreat.

Mary has traveled to Brazil, Nicaragua, Russia, Vietnam, Israel, Grenada, and Jamaica on peacemaking ventures, often going to areas where clergy and social workers were trying to help the oppressed. In Jamaica, she came "face-to-face with women who didn't have enough food to feed their babies. "Each time we were there, we visited the American embassy and discussed what we had seen. The ambassador said everyone in oppressed countries was happy and all they had to do was pick fruit from their trees if they were hungry. My visits with the American ambassador were always a shock. I would find myself so angry, I redoubled my efforts."

The work she did in Central America led Mary to direct involvement in the formation of Women Against Military Madness (WAMM), an organization she credits with helping to forestall American involvement in Central America during the early years of the Reagan administration. WAMM provided a vehicle for effective antiwar work. Subsequently, she found a way to get at the injustices she perceived in American foreign policy:

"I organized tours for people to the Pentagon, World Bank, and State Department. I wanted to show them that if you want to do something for other countries, you have to start with the policymakers at home and understand what they're doing. We got lots of citizens involved.

"Many people who traveled on my Nicaraguan tour began to question America's commitment to democracy. By the time we were done with the tour, the change in attitudes of our group was stunning. Almost every person that went with us came home and did something within the peace movement. They were incredibly motivated.

"We splintered into many different movements that have recruited hundreds of thousands of new people. I've seen it explode in numbers. There used to be six of us at demonstrations, then the Gulf War demonstration filled a huge college auditorium. We had an antiwar rally for Clergy and Laity, and cars were lined up for miles. It's amazing to me that we grew so fast.

"The anti-Vietnam War demonstrations petered out after Americans no longer feared being drafted. There was a long period of inactivity between that time and the Persian Gulf War. Those were discouraging times because there was still so much to do.

"Unfortunately, the church groups I worked with weren't as active in the peace movement as I would have liked them to be. I worked for Clergy and Laity Concerned for about fifteen years as a fund-raiser and church organizer. To my surprise, they weren't at all interested in the religious foundations of antiwar organizations. Generally, churches were a disappointment. People never got out of the pews to do anything.

"One time, I went with members of an Episcopalian parish, seeking a meeting with the archbishop to ask him to help stop the war in El Salvador. The archbishop refused to talk to us. Our group sat in the Cathedral and demonstrated for weeks. Many fasted. We then asked our Christian brothers and sisters to sit with us, and we filled the church. The police were summoned and arrested us. We were all piled into paddy wagons and eventually went before a judge. He just laughed us off.

"My peace and justice work is faith-based, so the reluctance of churches to act has been difficult for me. I'd have little hope and wouldn't care so much if it weren't for my faith. Many in the peace and justice movement have become contemptuous of the religious establishment. Most were brought up to go to church, and they became bitter and disillusioned by the Church's attitude toward them.

"The peace and justice community may have given up on established church organizations, but they have been finding spiritual grounding for their work elsewhere. I used to go to an Episcopal church during the Vietnam War but was not happy there. I was part of the movement to disinvest in South Africa. I watched friends from Wall Street on the church's board of trustees decide to invest in South Africa. So I quit the church and wrote a letter to the archdiocese. Board members responded with a letter to the church saying I was a traitor. I went looking for another church."

Locating Mary Shepard's new church requires a real leap of faith. It doesn't have a building of its own, a minister, or a traditional congregation. To get there each week, Mary enters the People's Center building on the West Bank of the University of Minnesota and walks down a winding hallway to a single doorway with the name—Holy Trinity of St. Angsgar inscribed on it.

Behind the door is a unique church founded during antiwar days by a radical priest named Bill Teska, who later used it as a sanctuary for Salvadoran refugees. Teska has long since moved on to other parishes, but some of his original followers, including Mary, have stuck together.

"There are twelve of us at the most," Mary says. "We have a social Christian community that isn't a geographical community. We meditate on Saturday morning and worship at 10:00 a.m. every Sunday morning. We read the Gospel if it moves us and discuss what it means to us. The core of our worship is the liturgy of the Episcopal prayer book, although we have changed the language to make it more inclusive and have incorporated variations contributed by such people as Native Americans and the creators of the New Zealand prayer book. We're part of the Episcopal Church at-large, but we don't have a priest, except those who visit. We have no money. We struggle to pay the rent each month. This is our second space on the West Bank, and we know that we could be homeless at any time."

It seems fitting that Mary's church is just down the street from KFAI, a leading community-run radio station that offers alternative news and viewpoints. In WAMM circles, Mary is specifically known for her work in supporting media that provide a liberal option to the establishment.

Mary claims that "the mainstream media is

used by the corporate establishment to maintain power. They're great propagandists of the status quo. They say lovely words about democracy even as they squash it all the time."

Mary's answer to this dilemma: "If you don't like what's out there, find an alternative." She started and financially supported *The Collective Voice*, an upper Midwest peace and justice magazine that was published for a few years during the past decade before running out of money. Calling radio "the instrument of every revolution," she has been an advocate for KFAI-like stations and programs around the world. "I know," she says with confidence, "that I can do something to keep the media's feet to the fire and expose the truth about economic policy."

Whether it's finding alternatives to war, church worship, or establishment government and media, Mary has used her wealth and privilege for the benefit of things and people she believes in.

"I know that my money has saved human lives and made a difference in other ways. I put it to good use. But I feel I can do more than give money. I also am committed to taking action in other ways.

"It's a difficult struggle. A huge majority of human beings have to fight each other for the crumbs left over, while policy-makers laugh all the way to the bank. The public at large has lost its innocence. The American dream is not there. What troubles me is that people go from innocence to cynicism without anything in between—huge numbers of people.

"We can change the system. We need to turn it upside-down and reward generosity, sharing, and inquisitiveness. We have to believe that the system can be made to work. It's possible there will be peace. We'll have it when enough people want it, and, instead of keeping their power and money, will redistribute their wealth. Without that kind of justice, there can be no peace.

"Communities of caring people are very powerful if they work for the well-being of the whole group rather than themselves—such as when faith communities in Latin American churches joined together. There were no priests as leaders. They formed co-ops. They shared everything they had. The co-ops were the most threatening thing the dictators had ever seen. They did everything to break them up.

"I don't care what you call it—whatever the boundaries are—this kind of community can unite those who care about each other. People can come to each other's aid when needed. Wherever you are, organize everyone you can to find out where the power structure is infringing on you, and strategize some way to stop it.

"To get our bearings, we need to dip deeply into the well of the collective consciousness of the human race . . . We must be humble enough to heed the old prophets, to regain our sanity, and save ourselves."

> "Human beings are so made that the ones who do the crushing feel nothing; it is the person crushed who feels what is happening. Unless one has placed oneself on the side of the oppressed, to feel with them, one cannot understand."
>
> *Simone Weil*

Questions for Contemplation:

1. Why do so many people leave their values and ethics behind when it comes to decision-making about their investments or spending their money?
2. What are the root causes of poverty in your community? What can be done to reduce or eradicate it?
3. What alternative media source(s) do you use? Why?
4. What does your church do to demonstrate its commitment to peace? Is it enough for you? How could you influence your church to do more?

Resources for Reflection and Action:

The Habits of Highly Deceptive Media: Decoding spin and lies in mainstream news, by Norman Solomon (Monroe, NE: Common Courage Press, 1999).

Manufacturing Consent: The political economy of the mass media, by Edward Herman and Noam Chomsky (Basic, 1993).

Robin Hood Was Right: A guide to giving your money for social change, by Chuck Collins and Pam Rogers. (NYC: W.W. Norton, 2000). The authors argue we should carefully choose ways to put our contributions to work, to help build the kind of world in which we want to live. Instead of spending "just pennies a day" to feed one starving child in Guatemala, for example, we might have more impact by giving that money to projects that focus on building up Guatemala's local economy. Rather than buying a few toys for poor kids once a year at Christmas, we might choose to fund organizing for a living wage, so that the children's parents could afford to buy Christmas presents themselves.

The Impact Project, 21 Linwood St., Arlington, MA 02174. Phone: 617-548-0776. This nonprofit organizes support groups for people with financial surplus (earned or inherited) who are seeking a more just and sustainable world. In addition, they offer individual counseling, workshops, a money workbook, and a quarterly newsletter (*More than Money*). Their work assists people to clarify their values around money and use their resources effectively to help make the world a better place.

Center for Media Literacy, 4727 Wilshire Blvd., Suite 403, Los Angeles, CA 90010. Phone: 800-226-9494. Fax: 213-931-4474. Email: cml@medialit.org. An educational and membership organization that develops projects and materials to promote critical thinking about the media. The center's clearinghouse offers books, videos, and teaching materials for use in schools, parent education, community centers, or for any group interested in the media literacy movement.

National Institute on Media and the Family, 606 24th Avenue South #606, Minneapolis, MN 55454. Phone: 888-672-5437. Website: www.mediafamily.org

Foundation for Ethics and Meaning, 26 Fell St., San Francisco, CA 94102. Phone: 415-552-6336. Fax: 415-575-1434. Website: www.members.aol.com/pomeaning. Michael Lerner began this national movement for a "politics of meaning." The foundation organizes annual conferences and study groups and develops policies to show how a society might work if based on caring, meaning, and spiritual sensitivity.

Global Exchange, 2017 Mission St., Room 303, San Francisco, CA 94110. Phone: 415-255-7296. Fax: 415-255-7498. Website: www.globalexchange.org. An education and advocacy organization dedicated to linking North Americans with grassroots groups working for social justice, human rights, and sustainable development around the world. They also operate stores that give fair profits back to developing world artisans.

Chapter 9
World Workers

Marianne Hamilton, Don Irish and Marjorie Sibley, Arthur Sternberg, Lois Swenson, Jody Williams

World Workers have stepped outside of the boundaries of their own country to work for change in another part of the globe. Their efforts are devoted to making their adopted place in the world safer and/or more just. World Workers believe that what affects one, affects all.

World Workers look deeply at themselves and at infrastructures. They seek to be consistent in beliefs and actions. They are convinced that preaching change is useless without looking at one's own contribution to the problem and, if necessary, changing oneself and/or working to make the necessary political changes. Sometimes this comes at high cost to themselves and their loved ones.

Bringing the Buddha Home | MARIANNE HAMILTON

by Burt Berlowe

From where the Buddha sits, the world below looks a lot like home.

Perched atop an elevated bookcase, the porcelain figurine from Far Eastern civilization poses in meditation. Nearby, other symbols of Asian culture and universal peace spread across the sunlit high-rise apartment. There are books on Buddhism and Hinduism, travel guides on Southeast Asia, photo albums full of pictures taken in and near Vietnam, and gifts of peace and friendship from abroad. These are more than just physical objects from faraway lands. They are a compendium of Marianne Hamilton's universe.

If, as tradition says, the Buddha represents wisdom, enlightenment, and inner peace, then Marianne is its personification. At the age of eighty, she has logged over a half-century of peace and justice activism around the globe and, in the process, has found the way to her own inner tranquillity. Her journey has been challenging and often risky. She has felt the sting of mace and gas in her nostrils, and the gnawing isolation of a locked jail cell. She has stood in battlefield trenches and ducked bombs and bullets in a foreign country, harbored fugitives in her home, and chastised her own country's government and her Church—all for the sake of nonviolence and world order. Once an aspiring actress, Marianne has played a key role in the real world of global conflict. And, despite her advancing years, she keeps coming back for encores.

Marianne grew up with actress ambitions during the '30s and '40s, hosting her own radio program that also appeared on locally syndicated TV. But the event that most shaped her destiny was her husband Norman's participation in World War II. "I supported the war until I joined a Mortimer Adler group in Chicago," Marianne says. "Adler said, 'I've seen the horrors of war. There's got to be a better way. Go find the peace movement.' I followed his advice."

With her husband at war, Marianne was left alone to raise their two children on a limited income. Angered by that situation, she wrote a letter to the local newspaper complaining about the problems war wives were having with insufficient financial support. After receiving the letter, the newspaper called her and said they were going to organize a meeting of war wives. Marianne attended and found the place jammed with some twelve hundred women. She subsequently helped form a wives' support group that met until the end of the war.

In the mid-40s, at the age of twenty-six, Marianne and her husband joined the United World Federalists, an organization advocating for a strong United Nations. She recalls, "Most of the Federalists were older than I was. I had the youthful enthusiasm that I notice in others now. When the civil rights movement started, I became active in my church and democratic ward club, and later in the movement against the Vietnam War."

During the tumultuous 1968 Democratic National Convention, Marianne, a Eugene McCarthy supporter, ran headlong into the massive antiwar demonstrations taking place near the convention hall. With her fourteen-year-old son at her side, Marianne was soon swept up in the protest. She remembers it this way:

"We walked a couple of blocks beyond the line of the National Guard, which had bayonets trained on us, and went up Michigan Avenue. I noticed that I was older than others in the demonstration. When I saw the blocks of young national guardsmen advance with their bayonets, I stood there and said to them, 'You should be ashamed of yourself!' and we pushed through the line. We hauled kids away from mace and looked up at Vice-President Humphrey's window, hoping he was watching the horrible things going on. His aide came to the window and pulled the shade down. Police in cars ran people against walls and jumped out and beat them. Anybody that had long hair and looked the least bit radical really got it from the police. Young people yelled at me: 'You saw it ma'am, tell it like it is.'

"Whenever I felt discouraged with my protest work, I knew we couldn't give up. I remember saying to my children, 'There's a whole big world out there, we've got to do something.'

"Another time, we flew to Washington, DC, for a peace demonstration. I met an old Federalist friend there who suggested that we show President Nixon that middle-class Americans were against the war. We bought expensive fur hats, put them on, and marched by the White House. Soon, police, for no apparent reason, sprayed mace and tear gas on us. The next day, I read in the paper that Nixon had said the marchers 'looked like a bunch of Bolsheviks.' When we got back on the plane, the stench of tear gas on our clothing was still so strong that we were making stewardesses sick!

"Once I was taken to the police station during a peaceful antiwar demonstration in front of the Federal Building in Minneapolis. Someone put up a Vietcong flag. Suddenly, the riot squad came roaring around the corner, shields in front of them. We kept singing and praying, but they broke up the demonstration and took people away. I was older than most of the others, so they didn't know what to do with me."

Marianne's antiwar activity went well beyond peace marches to broader work within the Catholic community. She organized a group of Catholics from around the country to go to the Vietnam Peace Talks in Paris and meet with delegations from North and South Vietnam to find out what was really going on. "I do organizing to get at the root of problems," she says. "That's what small committees can do." She also led a Catholic delegation into Hanoi, Vietnam, in 1972 and secured release of some POWs that had been tortured.

"I traveled around North Vietnam at night in a jeep with no lights. One evening, the jeep broke down and we began walking along a country road. A woman walking behind me, a South Vietnamese reporter, was terrified. Bullets began to fly overhead, and we ran into the trenches on the side of the road. We got to the Red River Bridge and found it was bombed out. A ferryboat of strangers came and took us across the river. They told us Jane Fonda had been there just before us.

"Our efforts to free prisoners was hard work. We wrote hundreds of letters. Sometimes we'd feel ineffective and want to quit. Once, when I was working on prisoner liberation with another woman in our little office, she fell to the floor. I asked her, 'What's the problem?'

She said, 'I can't do this anymore. I've had enough of this.'

I said, 'Get up and try again. Were not going to free any prisoners that way.'"

Photo by Todd Cota

Marianne Hamilton

Marianne ended up behind bars herself for obstructing justice during a post-Vietnam War peace protest:

"I saw what prison was really like and how guards treat women like children, ordering them around. One woman in solitary confinement screamed all the time. I asked the guards to do something. They didn't do a thing.

"I went to jail to make a point. All of us protesters did that. Most of the prisoners there were prostitutes and drug users. They didn't understand why I just didn't pay my fine and get out. I didn't think anything of going to prison, but when they locked those doors, I got a real unstable feeling. Knowing you can't get out is claustrophobic."

Marianne's reputation for antiwar activity made her a target for government surveillance. She was convinced CIA agents were monitoring her and her family. Marianne also stirred up attention by helping young men who refused to fight in the Vietnam War and harboring some of them in her house. "By the time the war finally wound down, I was tense and worn out," she says.

However, the end of the war wasn't the end of Marianne's activism. In late 1981, she placed an urgent phone call to her friend and fellow peace activist Polly Mann. She was increasingly concerned about the international nuclear buildup that had accompanied the coming of the Cold War, and the effects it was having on Americans during a supposedly peaceful time.

"People were building bomb shelters in their basements. It was getting ridiculous. So I called Polly and told her, 'Things are so bad I think we should start an organization.' We got together for lunch and discussed it. We got others interested and had a party of about sixty women on Christmas Day of '81. That led to the founding of Women Against Military Madness (WAMM). We got everyone to pledge one hundred dollars so we could rent an office. I was the first director, along with Pam Costain. Women came forward and formed empowerment groups. For some of those women, doing demonstrations was something new and risky. WAMM members from the wealthy Minneapolis suburb of Edina, for instance, would stand behind their protest signs so no one could tell who they were.

"When WAMM started, we thought it would be a global organization that would get people to stop war. But WAMM has changed with the times. Lately, it has been asking questions such as: 'Why is the U.S. keeping its military all over the world? Is it for the sole purpose of protecting corporate globalization and privatization? What are we doing about fiscal development and poverty in developing nations? More and more people are now saying that social, military, and globalization issues are all one. My upbringing in parochial schools taught me about the interconnectedness of humanity—that we can't separate one from another. That's my personal motivation. And it seems to motivate a lot of people."

In recent years, Marianne has become disillusioned with the institutional Church. The Catholicism she was raised with considered her peace activities "immoral and unpatriotic." Now she no longer attends church regularly. Once, she walked out of a service at the Basilica of St. Mary's church in Minneapolis, "after the priest said we were at peace when we were bombing the hell out of Vietnam." For a long time, people and organizations she belonged to, because of her antiwar activity, ostracized her. Gradually, that changed and, in the mid-1980s, the League of Catholic Women presented her with a special peacemaker award—an engraved pitcher—and made her a lifetime member.

Recently, Marianne has found some new ways to attain inner peace. "When I was in Paris," she says, "I watched a group of Buddhist monks meditating in a circle. There were Catholics there, too. One was a priest offering mass. At first, I thought that Buddhism was primarily a philosophy. But Asian Buddhism is way of living. It has equanimity about it that I admire. In Vietnam, I worked with Buddhists who were pacifists—not the kind of pacifism that doesn't do anything—but pacifists working for peace. Actually, I'm not a total pacifist. I believe that people are entitled to defend themselves."

Marianne uses a method of meditation that helps her concentrate and be peaceful. She does both sitting and walking meditation regularly at home and also attends group sessions. "It gets my mind and body in harmony. I have become wiser and more compassionate about all living things in the world. It has changed my whole life. It's perfect for organizers. We organize because we're angry. Meditation helps calm and direct that anger. It makes me realize that we can't change the world overnight and keeps me focused on my compassion for all people.

"I am at peace with myself. Being at peace with myself makes me realize that what happens is the way the world is. But I couldn't be at peace with myself if I weren't working for change or if I just sat back and watched others do it."

Whenever she has doubts about whether change is possible, Marianne turns to the mini-world in her apartment and finds evidence of what can be done. One of her favorite places to look is into a Vietnamese conical hat. When she turns the hat toward streaming light, she can make out a Vietnamese word inside which, in English, means "peace."

Questions for Contemplation:

1. What do you feel called or compelled to do?
2. Imagine yourself at some future event celebrating some aspect of what you feel you are called to do. Dream backward from the future to the present. What steps need to be taken to attain your vision?
3. How does your proposed action better the life of your community members, family, or fellow workers?
4. Marianne called her friend Polly and started the WAMM organization. Who would you like to call to start an organization? What kind of organization do you feel is needed? What existing organization do you feel merits your support and involvement?

Resources for Reflection and Action:

Economic and Social Justice: A human rights perspective, by David Shirman (Human Rights Resource Center, University of Minnesota, 229 19th Avenue South, Room 439, Minneapolis, MN 55455). This curriculum treats economic and social rights as inalienable human rights, putting them in both local and global perspective and illustrating the interdependence between social/economic rights and civil/political rights. Intended for adults and young people.

Insight and Action: How to discover and support a life of integrity and commitment to change, by Tova Green and Peter Woodrow with Fran Peavey (Gabriola Island, BC: New Society Publishers, 1994). Presents three valuable processes for overcoming periods of doubt, indecision, and discouragement.

Field Guide to the Global Economy, by Sarah Anderson, John Cavanagh, Thea Lee, and Institute for Policy Studies (NYC: New Press, 2000). Illustrated throughout with charts, graphs, and political cartoons, this book makes the international economy understandable to everyone while revealing the harmful effects of corporate-driven globalization. Describes how the global flow of goods, services, money, and people affects communities, workers, the poor, and the environment.

Ploughshares Fund, Fort Mason Center, San Francisco, CA 94123. Phone: 415-775-2244. Fax: 415-775-4529. Email: ploughshares@igc.apc.org. Website: www.ploughshares.org. Public and grant-making foundation founded by Sally Lilienthal, with the purpose of building "global security in the nuclear age."

State of the World Forum, The Presidio, PO Box 29434, San Francisco, CA 94129. Phone: 415-561-2345. Fax: 415-561-2323. Email: forum@worldforum.org. Website: www.worldforum.org. An educational foundation with no political, economic, or partisan affiliation; the forum is a global network of individuals seeking solutions, with a multidisciplinary approach, to the challenges facing humanity in the twenty-first century.

The Global Fund for Women, 425 Sherman Ave., Suite 300, Palo Alto, CA 94306-1823. Phone: 650-853-8305. Fax: 650-328-0384. Email: gfw@globalfundforwomen.org. Website: www.globalfundforwomen. This grant-making foundation provides flexible, timely, financial assistance to women's groups around the world.

Partners in Courage |

DON IRISH AND MARJORIE SIBLEY

by Burt Berlowe

Courage is the price that life exacts for granting peace.

—Amelia Earhart

There's a bitter subzero chill in the air on this January day. Don Irish is in a crowd of three hundred men, women, and children, trying to stop a plane preparing to haul military supplies from Minneapolis, Minnesota, to Central America for use in the Contra War. Their goal is to sit in front of the plane to prevent it from taking off. They are scaling a fence and heading toward their waiting target, well aware of the cadre of national guardsmen chasing them.

As Don climbs a hinged ladder on the inside of the fence, icy water from the Guardsmen's hoses suddenly strikes him, its full force stinging his back. He stumbles and falls, landing on his shoulder on the frozen ground. Within seconds, it seems, he is being hauled away, along with a dozen or so others. They are taken to a National Guard post, then released to walk half a mile back to waiting cars. Don's clothes are frozen to him like armor. Later, when he returns home, he is unable to remove his coat without help. The deformation in his shoulder remains a constant reminder of that day.

Being in harm's way for peace is not unusual for Don. He has been doing it for half a century in the U.S. and Central America, putting himself in danger to keep others safe. His reason sounds simple: "We need to risk for peace, not for war."

Don's has had two intimate partners in courage. Betty, his first wife of forty-two years, was at his side during most of his activist ventures. For the past decade, he has been married to an Illinois farm girl named Marjorie Hedrick (Sibley), who has also given much for the cause of peace. They were wed—the second marriage for both—when each was about seventy years old, and have since traveled together through the minefields of social action.

At the time of this interview, Don and Marjorie reside in a white-collar St. Paul neighborhood where single family houses are perched on hills above the street. Their brick 1920s house sits at the top of a winding concrete staircase. Inside, in their front room, stacked on eight shelves, is an extensive peace library, full of books and magazines they have accumulated over the years.

Seated at a table in their dining area, Don and Marjorie alternately relate their peacemaking stories. Don wears a T-shirt that says "Paz por Justicia," which is Spanish for "Peace Through Justice."

Raised in a conservative Methodist family, Don's "radicalization" began early, when, as a member of a church youth movement, he was associated with several religious activists and conscientious objectors. He eventually became a conscientious objector himself during World War II, and by 1951, had become a Quaker. Don and his first wife, Betty, worked together on three major ventures. They helped Japanese-Americans find housing and employment in Chicago, co-directed the American Youth Hostel Meredith Country School and Camp, and established a scholarship fund for youth of the Lummi tribe in the Pacific Northwest. Don particularly remembers the prejudice he witnessed against the Lummi: "For instance, if an Indian tried on a hat in a store, he had to buy it because 'it was contaminated.'"

Don and his family participated in the Civil Rights movement in the South from 1958 on, while he taught in universities in North Carolina, Mississippi, and then Louisiana. They joined others in desegregating restaurants, picketing theaters, and registering voters. Their daughters helped with desegregating schools and swimming pools.

Don's plunge into the volatile South was an early signal of his special type of courage. Time after time, even while working as a university professor in Minnesota, he would risk and incur personal trauma and injury to stand up for a cause. Sometimes, these actions happened close to home, like the time he was arrested on trespassing charges after a sit-in at the office of a Minnesota senator.

"Four of us stood trial for the whole group and were convicted as expected," he recalls. "We were given three choices: pay a one hundred ten dollars fine, do community service, or spend five days in jail. As a retired Hamline University faculty member, I could have paid the fine, but thousands of others in this world are unable to afford to stay out of jail. I was already doing community service, so I told the judge, 'Why should I buy my way out just because I have the money?' I took the jail term, a good learning experience for any privileged person.

"In jail, I was stripped and dressed in prison garb. They took everything away—my money, my razor. I didn't shave again until I got out. They denied me my own books, including one I was preparing for publication. I was in the same cell with four young black men, learning new card games and gaining other insights about their culture. In a meeting with a social worker, chaplain, and the warden, I was asked if I would do a similar protest again. I said, 'As long as U.S. policy is what it is, I will continue to do what I'm doing.'"

Most of Don's peace work has taken place abroad, where he has used his relative affluence and organizing skills to help those less fortunate. His most profound and dangerous work happened in Latin America during the Contra War, as a team member of Witness for Peace in Nicaragua and Peace Brigades International (PBI) in Guatemala. His time was spent hiking through the mountains and jungles of Eastern Nicaragua as part of an unarmed bodyguard protection program for local activists whose lives had been threatened.

Marjorie Hedrick was born in 1920, following World War I, the fourth of ten children in a Midwest farming family. Upon graduating from high school, a craving for higher education prompted her to leave the farm to attend college at the University of Illinois. There, she became a confirmed pacifist and member of the University Peace Club, working with faculty and students to oppose World War II underway in Europe. After Pearl Harbor, some of the club members changed their position; but Marjorie remained firmly against the war. During that time, she took a course from Professor Mulford Q. Sibley, an outspoken pacifist. They were later married and stood together as social justice activists for forty-seven years. "We did everything: public speaking, rallies, churches," Marjorie says. "We spoke truth. Those in power didn't like that."

Photo by Todd Cota

Don Irish and Marjorie Sibley

During the '60s and '70s, as American public opinion about the Vietnam War vacillated, the Sibleys became known for their unshakable opposition to the war and their willingness to speak, write, and organize against it. A letter that Professor Sibley wrote for a student newspaper brought a fervent response. In it, he defended students' rights to express widely diverse views about the war or other issues. After Mulford debated the issue with a St. Paul City Councilmember, the Sibleys received many threatening telephone calls and letters, some suggesting they 'get out of town.' Someone burned a cross on a neighbor's lawn that was meant for the Sibleys. Later, Mulford was denied entrance to

Canada for a speaking engagement.

While Marjorie was often by Mulford's side, she also found her own niche: working on behalf of feminists. She helped start a Women's Studies program at a college where she was employed and worked to improve the salaries of faculty women—challenging deans and presidents on such issues as tenure, diversity, and other policies and practices. She also participated in an international peace conference in Crete in 1990 and traveled in Eastern Europe, Mexico, and Central America.

A Quaker since the early '50s, Marjorie has hung on to what she calls an almost absolute pacifism. "I believe you should react to war but with nonviolent methods and that you have to believe totally in the sacredness of life," she says. "For example, you can't be against war and for capital punishment. It also means that you don't abuse your spouse or your child, or use hateful words, such as calling police 'pigs.'

"There are very few absolute pacifists, those who wouldn't cooperate with authorities even in prison and would have to be force-fed. I don't think I would go that far. But no one knows how he or she would react in certain situations. We all hope we would respond in a nonviolent way. But if I had a starving kid at home, I might put my fist through a window to steal a loaf of bread."

For most of their adulthood, Don and Marjorie took separate though similar paths. They were both academics and political activists and were members of the same Quaker Meeting for many years. Their families knew and often visited each other. "It was a long relationship and shared values that brought us together," says Don. After losing their first spouses, they were married in 1990.

It didn't take long for the new couple to become companions in peacemaking. Two weeks after their wedding, Marjorie accompanied Don to Nicaragua, riding lumber trucks with Witness for Peace. They later joined Guatemalan Indians as Witnesses for Peace during a 1991 commemoration of a recent massacre of civilians in Santiago de Atitlan. Army personnel at a nearby base had fired on an indigenous demonstration against military violations of human rights and killed many of the ten thousand Indians present. Don described the profound event this way:

". . . As a gesture of solidarity with the people of Santiago de Atitlan, a throng of U.S. citizens and indigenous adults and children walked together to the edge of town. The delegation was racially and geographically diverse, wide-ranging in age, and varied in occupation and religious faith. All together, we numbered more than a thousand. We handed flowers to those without them, conversed pleasantly with those near us, and greeted residents watching the procession from their doorways and windows. We hiked on a high and wide pathway alongside the Atitlan lake and beside a rising mountainside. Below were women washing clothes on rocks at the lake's edge and clusters of fishing boats and dugouts resting upon the banks. We assembled under a shady canopy of trees encircling an open area. A small band with guitars and percussion instruments played and accompanied our singing.

"Following the ceremony, conducted in three languages, we walked back to the church. The sanctuary was packed. Every bench was full of people. Indigenous colors were everywhere. Indian women reached out in every direction seeking our hands. We felt truly accepted and valued.

"Just before the close . . . a white dove flew down from its perch in the high rafters and landed on a speaker-amplifier nearby. Perhaps this symbol of peace came forth to indicate a new era dawning in Santiago de Atitlan. Later, we found out the military had decided to close its base."

Don and Marjorie have become inseparable participants in the peace movement. "We didn't get married at age seventy to be apart," says Don. "We have traveled, marched, and picketed together with our separate families and together as one large family. We believe that values are more effectively caught than taught."

In recent years, another, younger member of the Irish-Sibley clan has continued the family tradition: Marjorie's daughter, Muriel. She was the only Canadian member of the International Gulf Peace Team at the Iraq-Saudi border in January 1991. In 1994, she participated in a mass demonstration against lumber-cutting of virgin timber on Vancouver Island.

Recent health problems have limited Marjorie's activities and resulted in the couple moving from their St. Paul house to an assisted living facility. But Don shows little sign of slowing down. He made his third trip to the School of the Americas protest in 2000 and has been speaking on international issues. And while not able to accompany him on some trips, Marjorie has remained a supportive partner.

Though now in their 80s, neither has any intention of stepping back from their commitment to peace. You don't stop because you're old," Don exclaims. "You do what you believe in as long as you can. One of the insights I learned in Latin America is that the peasants do not retire. Retirement is a luxury of the affluent and privileged. We haven't retired from peacemaking or from being active citizens. I'm not one that could play golf and let the rest of the world go by."

Marjorie adds: "I couldn't do anything else. For us, nonviolence is a way of life."

Don Irish's long-time commitment to social justice earned him a 1997 Twin Cities International Citizen Award. In addition, a special award has been established in his name at Hamline University to recognize exceptional faculty, staff, and student activists.

How to Hang in There for the Long Haul

by Don Irish

Young people who are committed to peace and justice sometimes ask their elders how they have been able to continue such efforts for so long. We need to gain and retain the talents, energies, and early commitment of these youth. What guidance can be given them? Here are some suggestions:

Recognize that those who plant trees may not live to enjoy the fruit.

Everybody/everything is connected to everybody/everything. A holistic approach to life is more effective, comprehensible, and satisfying.

You can't do everything—but you can always do something.

Remember that the world does not depend upon you alone for needed changes.

Redefine success in your endeavors for societal change. To prevent a situation from becoming worse is success. To gain a portion of what is attempted without retreat from one's goal is success. To be among the first to initiate a movement for peace and justice that brings its achievement decades later is success. To keep hope alive during dark days is also success.

Realize that persons who are alone rarely manifest courage. You need to find others of like mind so you can provide support for each other, enabling all to withstand the societal pressures that will be brought to bear against nonconformity.

Develop a faith that can sustain you.

Adopt a nonviolent philosophy as a way of life. Try to make it applicable to all your behaviors and attitudes.

Find joy and satisfaction in small gains because those are usually what you will get!

Focus your challenges on issues/problems, not attacks on persons. Avoid demonizing opponents, for hate will not resolve conflicts or reconcile the parties. People are what they are for reasons that need to be understood, though not necessarily excused.

Know that a majority is not needed to bring significant changes.

Believe that at times, "They also serve who only stand and wait." We cannot always stop mounting tragedies midstream, especially if we are "outsiders." Ultimately, the parties in contention must be willing to resolve their problems together. Then, we can assist.

Know that there are many ways and means to bring change nonviolently.

Remember that means and ends are inextricably linked. The means used predetermine the ends attained.

Respond to those who question the efficacy of nonviolence. Turn the question around: "How effective have violence and war been?" There is growing literature on the successful use of nonviolent means to resolve conflict and injustice.

Observe that serious structural problems will not be resolved by middle-of-the-road" measures. Radical changes may be needed for dealing with the root causes.

Learn from the long experience of others. For instance, indigenous peoples have much to teach and demonstrate to us about the nature of sustainable societies.

Retain a sense of humor.

Don't expect leadership for major, structural societal changes to come from the top. Political courage is rare and tends to follow growing grassroots sentiment. Laws tend to follow societal changes in attitudes and conditions, not anticipate them. So the grassroots work has to precede, and build pressures for, change.

Recognize that there really are no absolute dictators. Even they must keep their ears to the ground, are affected by world opinion and actions, and eventually must modify their positions to maintain control. Their legitimacy can be undercut by many nonviolent forms of resistance and noncooperation from within and without.

Accept that you will have "psychic pressures," ambivalences, uncertainties, and perhaps some "cognitive dissonance."

Operate from hope, not fear or despair; from possibilities not futilities; and organize, not immobilize, others.

Read, view, and hear a wide variety of sources of information, for knowledge is power!

Frequently appraise your views and behaviors in relation to chosen role models that share your values and principles.

Without compromising your basic orientations and not seeking absolutes, weigh regularly your integrity with regard to consistency and wholeness.

Seek diversity in personal relationships that enable you to understand different perspectives held by those of other cultures and experiences.

Discern the humanity within one's opponents—the human being in military uniform, the perspectives of corporate functionaries, the rationales of government officials, the experiences of police.

Avoid the either/or, black/white, good/evil polarizing approaches to discussions and solutions. There are always alternatives, and some of them needed may be radical. Idealism may be the ultimate realism, given where the so-called "realists" have brought us!

Recognize that even when one has done all he or she has felt able to do, the human race may still collectively fail to change its ways sufficiently and in time to avoid its own created catastrophes. However, one can still live with integrity, work for justice and peace, and feel secure with whatever reckoning the greater cosmos may render. If you, others, and I persist, we may even find that we have helped bring about a new more humane, sustainable society!"

Questions for Contemplation:

1. Don believes we may not be able to do everything, but we always can do something. What is one issue or concern you have and what is one thing you could do about it?
2. To avoid burnout, it is important to find respites. What gives you a sense of relaxation and an opportunity for renewal? How often do you feel you need to do or have this to keep your balance? What have you done to assure that this time is set aside for you?
3. What is your reaction when Don says, "Serious structural problems will not be resolved by middle-of-the-road" measures and that radical changes may be needed? What nonviolent extreme and urgent actions have you seen or read about that did create change?
4. Since it is important to maintain a sense of humor when working for social change, what makes you laugh?
5. Marjorie says, "Nonviolence has become a way of life." Has nonviolence become a way of life for you? Why or why not?

Resources for Reflection and Action:

New Internationalist Magazine. (New Internationalist, PO Box 1143, Lewiston, New York 14092). Won the award for "Best International Coverage" six times in the past ten years. It brings together a stimulating variety of news and analysis from a radically different perspective (Alternative Press Award Winner).

The Steps of Nonviolence, by Michael Nagler (Fellowship of Reconciliation, PO Box 271, Nyack, NY 10960. Phone: 914-358-4601, 1999). An eloquent and persuasive presentation of the seven steps of principled nonviolence. Shows both the personal and social power of the nonviolent way of life.

A Force More Powerful, Video by Films for the Humanities and Sciences. Phone: 800-257-5126. Website: www.films.com. Acclaimed documentary filmmaker Steve York tells the stories of six nonviolent movements, making the case for the validity, importance, and unique power of this strategy for creating change throughout the world in our century.

Unarmed Bodyguards: International accompaniment for the protection of human rights, by Liam Mahony and Luis Enrique Eguren. (West Hartford, CT: Kumarian Press, 1997).

The Politics of Nonviolent Action, by Gene Sharp. (Boston, MA: Porter Sargent Publishers, 1973). Includes three volumes—*Power and Struggle: The methods of nonviolent action, Political Jiu-jitsu at Work, and The Dynamics of Nonviolent Action.*

Nonviolent Activist. The magazine of the War Resisters League, Lafayette Street, NYC, 10012. Email: wrl@igc.org.

Global Nonviolent Peace Force. Website: www.nonviolentpeaceforce.org. The Global Nonviolent Peace Force is forming to mobilize and train an international, standing peace force. They will be sent to conflict areas to prevent death and destruction and protect human rights, thus creating the space for local groups to struggle nonviolently, enter into dialogue, and seek peaceful resolution.

Witness for Peace, Box 29497, Washington, DC 10017. Phone: 202-269-6316.

Peace Brigades International, 4722 Baltimore Avenue, Philadelphia, PA 19143, (215) 727-0989.

The Global Nonviolent Peace Force, c/o Peaceworkers, 801 Front Ave., St. Paul, MN 55108 (651) 487-0800. Website: www.nonviolencpeaceforce.org. The objective of this organization is to mobilize and train an international standing peace force that will be sent to conflict areas around the world.

Center for Ethics and Economic Policy, 2512 9th St., Suite 3, Berkeley, CA 94710-2542. Phone: 510-549-9931. The center offers values-based economic training and leadership development to organizations wishing to further their own goals of social change.

Center for Popular Economics, PO Box 785, Amherst, MA 01004. Phone: 413-545-0743. Email: cpe@acad.umass.edu. Through their publications and workshops, they teach economic literacy to activists and educators, with the goal of preventing social issues from being distorted by economic jargon.

Social Venture Network, PO Box 29221, San Francisco, CA 94129-0221. Phone: 415-561-6501. Email: svn@wenet.net. Website: www.svn.org. Social Venture Network is a membership organization of successful business and social entrepreneurs dedicated to promoting a more just, humane, and sustainable society by changing the way the world does business and by supporting progressive solutions to social problems.

Long Distance Runner | ARTHUR STERNBERG

by Burt Berlowe

The FOR [Fellowship of Reconciliation] has been in the forefront of the nonviolent struggle for peace and justice. It stands for a courageous dedication to the liberation of humanity from the triple evils of poverty, racism, and violence.

—Coretta Scott King

It's was a chilly January evening in 1947. Inside the St. Paul, Minnesota hotel, a well-dressed black man approached the front desk to check into the room reserved for him several days before.

The fair-skinned desk clerk in charge for the evening nervously waited on the approaching customer. "May I-I help you?" he stammered, surprised that an African-American would be in the whites-only hotel.

"I'm Doctor Bayard Rustin," the black man responded. "Some friends of mine from Hamline University reserved a room for me here for tonight."

The clerk furtively scaned his guest register, then, without looking at Bayard, quickly said: "I'm sorry, but all of our rooms are taken."

"But mine was reserved," Bayard said.

The clerk repeated his statement.

Bayard turned and walked to the hotel phone and placed a call to some of his Hamline friends, who, in turn, called others they knew. One of those in the phone tree was a lanky thirty-five-year-old executive secretary of the Fellowship of Reconciliation (FOR) named Arthur Sternberg. In what seemed like minutes, Arthur and his Hamline cohorts joined Bayard in the hotel lobby. One of them told the clerk why they were there.

"We're here to support Bayard. He's in town to speak at our college, and we had reserved a room for him. He tells us you won't let him have the room. We're going to sit in your lobby until you change your mind."

Photo by Todd Cota

Arthur Sternberg advises a young peace worker.

Receiving no response, they carried out their threat. They quietly, steadfastly sat in the lobby through the night and into the next day. Finally, after some twenty-five agonizing hours, the hotel broke its rule and gave Bayard his room. He spends the next two nights at Arthur's house, but a major victory for civil rights had been won.

As Arthur drove Bayard to the train station following his visit, the famous guest and a friend, Wally Nelson, hatched a plan for a Journey of Reconciliation—a trip through Southern border states to further promote equality for African-Americans, a risky venture given the climate of the times. It was just the beginning of Arthur's long social justice journey.

Arthur Sternberg is now ninety years old. He has spent three-quarters of that time resisting war and injustice here and abroad and helping others to do the same. Despite advancing age that has bent him over a bit, the retired publishing house attorney is as well-preserved as the natural woodwork in his West St. Paul home. As he verbally traces the steps of his marathon run through the twentieth century, his recollection is a bit labored at times but is remarkably clear in detail.

"My involvement with the peace and justice movement started in 1935 when I came to St. Paul, Minnesota. I discovered the Worker's Defense League (WDL) that was assisting small unions in getting started. A primary example was the Southern Tenant Farmers Union serving African-Americans in cotton growing areas. There were very few unions in the South. An organization of that type had a real struggle to exist. In more recent years, they have been involved in other types of activity, such as immigrant problems and injustices in the workplace.

"I became interested in labor unions through my work with WDL and the Socialist Workers' Party. I particularly recall an incident with people involved in the violent 1934 Minneapolis truck driver's strike. Some were Socialist Workers' Party members and were convicted under the Smith Act, which prohibited conspiracy to overthrow the government. Some eighteen were convicted. They were the first people prosecuted under the Smith Act. I played a role in assisting their appeals to federal court. Their appeal was turned down, and they went to prison and served their time . . ."

In 1938, Arthur became one of the early supporters and board members of Co-op, Inc. of St. Paul, which began with one grocery store and expanded to four in the Twin Cities. "Members of FOR (the Twin Cities chapter) came to Co-op, Inc., wondering what they could do to help," he recalls. "In the spring of 1942, I attended my first FOR meeting in St. Paul and became a member. I have been involved since.

Arthur also joined the brand new World Federalist Organization (WFO). They campaigned for military disarmament, world government, and United Nations reform, specifically to get the United Nations Assembly to eliminate veto power that might immobilize the National Security Council.

Arthur's biggest footprint is found in the doorway of FOR, founded at the onset of World War I when he was three years old and now the oldest and largest interfaith peace and justice organization in the world.

"In the early '40s, there were a limited number of peace organizations compared to today," Arthur says. "The only other one was The Women's International League for Peace and Freedom (WILPF). My wife became a member of that organization then and remains one today."

During World War II, Arthur was a conscientious objector (CO). After the passage of the 1940 draft act, the Quaker, Mennonite, and Brethren churches developed CO camp programs that were supported by FOR.

COs were assigned to one of the camps, through a cooperative framework of churches. They participated in various projects, mostly environmental—a smoke-jumping project, putting out forest fires, planting trees to prevent erosion, and the like. "I thought I would be in a public service camp as a CO," Arthur says. "But when I went to get my ticket to the camp, I was given a deferment from service.

"Between World War II and the Vietnam War, there were numerous demonstrations and annual Easter marches in opposition to the draft," he recollects. "In the mid '50s, FOR sponsored antinuke marches, including a long one in Minneapolis on a chilly day before Easter. I remember being on a platform in Loring Park emceeing and speaking against the war.

"In the summer of 1967, many organizations were involved in big marches as part of the national mobilization for a nuclear freeze. We had a local committee, not a great number of people. It was called SANE/FREEZE. That was during an interim period when the U.S. wasn't involved in any wars, but there were grounds for antinuclear weapons activity. People were making bomb shelters. FOR built shelters for the shelterless."

There have been major transformations in the peace movement since Arthur was most active. "The peace movement as a whole does not have the antiwar activism that it had in earlier years," he muses. "That's because of the end of the Cold War. We no longer have Russia (or anyone else) as an enemy. That's had an effect on the peace movement. It now has to work on local issues."

Now that his long peacemaking journey is winding down, Arthur is helping a younger generation begin theirs. He co-founded World Citizen, Inc., with Lynn Elling, which has become the developer of Peace Sites in schools and elsewhere throughout the world.

Through his membership on the Dayton Avenue Presbyterian Church Social Action Committee in St. Paul, Arthur was instrumental in having the church designated as a Peace Site. "We're not an antiwar church," he says, "but we have become a Peace Site through World Citizen to show our commitment to peace. We fly the peace flag that shows a picture of earth from space. The first ones we flew were torn down. We're now on our fourth flag. We also maintain a peace literature table at the church, and we promoted a high school essay contest. The day the church was dedicated as a Peace Site, the winner read portions of her essay."

Arthur is humble in assessing his impact on the most violent of our centuries. "I hesitate to list anything as accomplishments. I have continued to be an antiwar person because it is the right thing to do. I have to rebel against the destruction it causes to humanity, property, and the land. The things I've done were things that needed to be done by people who cared about them. I cannot say categorically that certain things I was involved in averted a more disastrous result—but they may have.

"I have never been one to have great goals or objectives. I have tried to participate in activities that I felt were important. I have had hopes but not expectations of great results. I also haven't felt great disappointment. It's that kind of disposition that has enabled me to stay involved as long as I have."

Whether working globally or locally, Arthur has continued to practice the philosophy of nonviolent resistance that stood up so well in that hotel lobby years ago. "I feel that violent ways of resolving conflict situations are hardly the way to do it," he says. "There must be peaceful ways of resolving disputes at any level—with employer and employee, parent and child, constituent and local government. I have tended to influence people to be peaceful by example rather than word. To be a peacemaker, I say, 'Be at peace with all people and follow wherever that leads.'"

Questions for Contemplation:

1. Arthur says that not feeling great disappointment has kept him an active peacemaker for so long. What do you do when you are disappointed? Does your response to disappointment keep you strong? How could you increase your fortitude?
2. Who have you stood up for? What were your reasons? What were the results?
3. How can business and commerce bring its collective experience and strategies for innovation into partnerships with groups and organizations—such as nongovernmental organizations (NGOs)—now working for peace, justice, interreligious understanding, and ecological sustainability?
4. What can schools do to make nonviolent strategies accessible to students?
5. Arthur is one of the longest active members of FOR. What organization have you supported the longest? What organization(s) has your family supported? What do these organizations do that make you or your family want to continue to support them?

Resources for Reflection and Action:

The Long Haul: An autobiography, by Myles Horton/Judith and Herbert Kohl (NYC: Teachers College Press, 1997). A major catalyst for social change in the United States for over sixty years, the Highlander Folk School has touched the lives of many activists, including Jane Addams; Reinhold Niebuhr; Martin Luther King, Jr.; Rosa Parks; Eleanor Roosevelt; and Pete Seeger. Filled with disarmingly honest insight and gentle humor, *The Long Haul* is an inspiring hymn to the possibility of social change.

We Make the Road by Walking: Conversations between Paulo Freire and Myles Horton, edited by John Gaventa, John Peters, Brenda Bell (Philadelphia, PA: Temple University Press, 1991). A dialogue between two of the most prominent thinkers on social change.

The Road Less Traveled and Beyond, by Scott Peck (NYC: Simon & Schuster, 1997). "When we think simplistically about everything, we set ourselves up to always expect simple solutions, obvious answers, and clear results even in complex situations," says Peck. When trying to solve problems, this is a good reference book to learn how to steer away from quick fixes.

World Federalist Association, 418 7th Street SE, Washington, DC 20003-2796. Phone: 202-546-3950. Fax: 202-546-3749. Email: wfa@wfa.org. Website: www.wfa.org. WFA is a nonprofit citizens' organization working for a democratic world federation achieving positive global goals that nations cannot accomplish alone. Check their website for important world documents, periodicals, brochures, booklets, books, videos, and special action alerts.

Choosing Peace: A Handbook on War, Peace and Your Conscience, by Robert A. Seeley (Central Committee for Conscientious Objectors, 1515 Cherry Street, Philadelphia, PA. 19120. Phone: 800-NO JROTC. Website: www.libertynet.org.ccco).

Democratic Organizing for a Democratic Society, by Roni Krouzman. (Order through rkrouzman@hotmail.com, 1999). Concrete suggestions, including a section on how to go about emergency decision-making.

The Power of the People: Active nonviolence in the United States, edited by Robert Cooney and Helen Michalowski (Gabriola Island, BC, New Society Publishers, 1987). Contains a history of FOR and war tax resistance.

The Fellowship of Reconciliation, Box 271, 521 N Broadway, Nyack, NY 10960. Phone: 914-358-4601. Email: FOR@forusa.org. Website: www.nonviolence.org/for/fellowship.

Publishes the *Fellowship* magazine at the same address.

War Tax Resistance, Peace Tax Campaigns, 2121 Decatur Place NW, Washington, DC 20008-1923. Phone: 202- 483-3751. Email: peacetaxfund @igc.org. Website: www.nonviolence.org/peace tax.

The Sheep Lady | LOIS SWENSON

by Burt Berlowe and Rachel Hefte

The flutter of a butterfly is felt around the world.
—Anonymous saying posted in Lois Swenson's home.

Lois Swenson says she first brought a sheep to her house in North Minneapolis in the spring of 1991 because of her dislike of lawnmowers. "They pollute the air and use up a nonrenewable source of energy," she said. She quickly learned that her "grass mower" came with additional benefits. "Mow," as he was appropriately named, also brought the curious out of houses and cars to get a closer look, both while he was in her yard, and when she took him on walks. "Kids started to call me the 'Sheep Lady,'" Lois chuckled as she told me her story. Mow helped connect neighbors, and his popularity gave Lois a forum to discuss community issues. Some friends insisted that Lois bring Mow to their house and leave him for a while, so they could meet and talk with their neighbors!

While Mow was a "hit" in the inner city, the "baa, baa, baa" sound from the garage and the constant care in the city was restricting Lois' freedom since she also likes travel and attending conferences and community gatherings. Thus, Mow was returned, after his brief urban tour, to a farm in Wisconsin to live out the rest of his sheep days.

Lois uses a more conventional type of lawnmower now and enjoys her freedom to volunteer to promote social justice; invent a creative approach to build community; connect people of diverse economic, social, and ethnic backgrounds; and lobby for the planet's health.

Early in the morning, you might find her combing the alleys to find "treasures that others have thrown out." New immigrants, refugees, and friends are often the happy recipients of these treasures of furniture, warm clothes, and other household items. Many roommates who have lived at Lois' house through the years have also enjoyed the fruits of Lois' dumpster-diving. They've also learned numerous ways to live more simply.

After a light breakfast and coffee, Lois reads her recycled newspaper (she has convinced neighbors to share the paper to spare a few trees), and then she picks up the phone to call her local and state representatives on issues that she cares about deeply. Hunger, poverty, environmental issues, and refugee issues are concerns that Lois has concentrated on during the past twenty-five years. Now, she spends much of her time educating people about food, farmers, and the farm crisis.

On some days, Lois, a retired teacher, goes into the schools to speak about sweatshops or conduct an activity about recycling. Other days, Lois hops a bus to volunteer at the Resource Center for the Americas or at WAMM (Women Against Military Madness). She knows every bus route in the metro area, so she can move freely without driving. Listening to speakers and attending community meetings fill the other hours of her days. Lois also spends time talking with young people and urges them to travel abroad since her travels and experiences learning from people who live around the globe have had a profound effect on her life. She also visits friends, reminding them that we are consuming far more than our share of the world's resources. "They wonder that I don't want new things. I tell them we have too much. They know if they're around me that I'm probably going to discuss issues that they normally wouldn't think about."

When Lois was an elementary school teacher in a mostly white Minneapolis suburb, her desire for adventure and learning about other cultures peaked. When she finally got the chance to travel in the early '70s, she went to Africa.

"I choose to go off the beaten track, joining a group traveling overland on a camping safari. There were thirty of us, all white folks: North Americans, English, Australians. We spent fourteen weeks crossing from Kenya in East Africa to the Sahara Desert, and then to London, England. We lived in a tent and traveled in a land rover. It was during the time of the Biafra War and famine. I knew nothing about the political situation. I had no idea that a war was going on. I just thought it would be an exciting adventure to travel across the continent. We spent a week camped in a city park in Uganda where Idi Amin had just come to power. Desperate people begged as we came through. I developed a real love and concern for the people that we met.

"Later, under the auspices of the Third World Institute, Lois traveled to Guatemala. I had a profound experience with the farmers in Guatemala," she says. After walking for ten miles carrying tools, they were standing on a mountainside preparing to dig out fishponds to farm fish and increase protein in their diet. Then, some military planes flew overhead. It was absolutely insane that we were giving military equipment to their government to be used against these desperately poor people. I knew we had to educate the North Americans about what was going on. I came home and did numerous speaking engagements.

"That whole experience was the beginning of a

drastic change in my life. I officially joined a group studying the causes of world hunger, which led to traveling throughout Guatemala again, as well as Honduras. I learned, firsthand, the effects of U.S. foreign policy of giving military aid to dictators. I came to realize that because the U.S. policies were supporting foreign dictatorships, my own country had inadvertently become a root cause of hunger and starvation for people far and wide. The impact was much more significant than I thought. When I got back home and asked friends to help end these atrocities, they thought I'd gone crazy. They said, 'This is just a phase. She'll get over it.' But I didn't.

"The year after I came back from Guatemala, I started a course for teachers on the root causes of hunger. It was one of the scariest things I ever did because a lot of the teachers disagreed with me on the issue. They thought ours was a model country, saving the rest of the world. I was saying we had soiled fingers. This point of view was received with total rebellion, and they didn't want to hear anything about it."

"Much later, after my early travels in Africa, I became increasingly interested in the political situation there. I came to know Oromo people from the horn of Africa. They invited me to their gatherings where I met leaders of their liberation movement. One of them asked, 'Why don't you come and visit us?' With that, I went to Sudan in '84 when the famine was just beginning to reach the media. I realized that we weren't being told the whole story. I saw people starving because they couldn't farm. The war was all around them. What few crops managed to grow, the government burned right before the harvest. The people knew if they spoke out, they would

Photo courtesy of Lois Swenson

Lois Swenson connects with a young Oromo refugee.

be thrown in prison.

"There was a lot of political posturing, and food was sent, but the food was being sent to areas controlled by the government and used against the people. I got call after call from people who wanted to send food, but nobody wanted to deal with what was causing the problem. I received a lot of harsh criticism from faith-based groups that had strong connections to the Church in Ethiopia.

"I went back again in '85 to Sudan, to some liberated areas of Western Ethiopia, trying to learn more about what was going on and relate it to policy issues. It was the government against its people. A small group (the government) was subjugating the largest group in the country (the people). The whole issue of Africa is so misunderstood."

Lois resigned from teaching at the age of 52, a move that coincided with other lifestyle changes she embraced as a result of her travels abroad. She explains:

"These trips have been life-changing experiences. When I went to the homes of the peasants, they invited me in. They apologized because they didn't have my favorite coffee or any sugar. In Mexico, I sat on dirt floors in houses with one light on the ceiling, with beautiful people, warm and wonderful. The poorest are the ones that are most generous.

"The first time I was in Guatemala, I watched beautiful air conditioned buses taking groups of tourists into the mountains. They could afford it. But the local people were walking, often barefoot, with huge loads on their heads or back. Once you've been to a poor country, you realize you don't need the things you've needed before. When people have no shoes, it suddenly doesn't matter what color your shoes are.

"There is enough food for everyone in the world. We have people starving because governments deny them access to it, and we support such governments!

"I think part of my job is increasing awareness, and the rest is reducing what I, as one individual, consume. I want to develop a bumper sticker that says: 'He (She) who drives the oldest car is the most successful,' or 'He (She) who wears the most patched clothing.' Currently, it's just the opposite. Success means driving the biggest car or wearing the latest fashion.

Lois lives simultaneously in two different worlds. For over twenty-five years, she has owned a home in North Minneapolis so she can be in the midst of a diverse inner-city neighborhood. The rest of the time, she occupies a cozy shack next door to her family farmhouse in Southern Wisconsin, where she raises organic, free-range chickens, and vegetables, much like her family has always done.

"We all had been organic farmers, before farm chemicals were available. Mother stored foods. Everything came off the farm. One day, my brothers came home from Ag class, pleading to use fertilizers because everybody else was starting to do it. It took a lot of talking before they became convinced of the dangers of the chemicals to the land and to us. Now, both my brothers are farming organically."

In recent years, Lois has become acutely aware of America's farm crisis—more and more small farmers going out of business—when crop prices hit rock bottom. "Farm issues are justice issues," she says. "Farmers are neglected because they work in the dirt. They are victims of a whole globalization system that is all out of whack. We are building our military budget while our farms are neglected. Urban sprawl is taking away farmland. Where will our food be grown?"

A primary problem, Lois continues, is that U.S. farmers are being asked to feed the world when that isn't necessary. "We should be eating locally and seasonally. I've been out in the fields with the farmers that grow the vegetables. Other countries can grow whatever we can. And we can grow more of our own food and have less need for shipping from Mexico, for instance. That would save on energy consumption. Who are we as North Americans that we have a right to keep consuming and consuming? Mexicans should be eating their own food, not providing it for us. We need to educate people to buy and sell locally grown products." One of Lois' projects is to get community gardens going in her northside neighborhood. She calls the gardens "great community-builders that bring people together."

Ever since she first encountered an interracial world, Lois has worked to build international bridges through her own travel and continuing education. More recently, this has led to a unique project where she has become a different kind of tourist guide:

"It's funny how doors open in various places. What seems like a really big risk can lead to something exciting. I've made connections with some wonderful Mexican people concerned about social issues. Now, I go to Mexico every winter to work on a project, trying to find ways to get tourists off the beaches and into the barrios. There are all these millions of people who go to Mexico who don't know what's going on politically. I'm looking at this project as a subversive way of teaching people. Things aren't going to change unless we reach additional people. I do a lot of sitting around in hotels and making conversation with people. I tell them that Mexico is in a terrible state nationwide. You only have to go a few blocks off the beach to find where the hotel workers live in tarpaper shacks. Meanwhile, the people who run the tourist industry go around in polished uniforms in their big cars. I also try to increase their awareness that the tourist industry is destroying the natural habitat on the beaches."

Like other international activists, Lois has many reminders of her work scattered around her home. One of her most poignant examples is a poster on a wall of some Oromo children she worked with in a refugee camp who were survivors of Ethiopian atrocities.

"I worked with them on building a school," she says wistfully, glancing at the photo from her dining room chair." "Once, I remember, we were drawing on a blackboard and needed an eraser. One of the children ran to the other classroom to find something, and came back clutching a tiny rag. Under horrible conditions, these were caring people who would do anything for me, their guest. We can learn from that."

Questions for Contemplation:

1. What places or people in the world do you want to visit?
2. What humanitarian role could the U.S. military play when a country is experiencing civil strife?
3. Do you have a viewpoint on a topic that is not well-received? What makes it hard for others to hear what you have to say?
4. What ideas do you have for ensuring a safe and sustainable food supply in the U.S.?
5. What ideas do you have for eliminating hunger in the world?

Resources for Reflection and Action:

Finding Solutions to Hunger: Kids can make a difference, by Stephanie Kempf (KIDS, PO Box 54, Kittery Point, ME 03905. Phone: 207-439-9588). Uplifting, engaging, interactive, and challenging lessons for middle- and high school students on the roots and solutions to domestic and international hunger.

Economic Apartheid in America: A primer on economic inequality & insecurity, by Chuck Collins and Felice Yeskel with United for a Fair Economy (NYC: New Press, 2000). Details the growing gap between those who are prospering in the global economy and those who are not, and the failure of large numbers of Americans to speak out or act against it.

Threshold 2000: Critical issues and spiritual values for a global age, by Gerald O. Barney with Jane Blewett and Kristen Barney (Arlington, VA: Millennium Institute, 1999). It points the way to a new dialogue—amoung religions and the other guiding institutions—about the future of the Earth and the human community.

Race, Poverty & the Environment: A journal for social justice and environmental justice. Urban Habitat Program, Box 29908 Presidio Station, San Francisco, CA 94129-9908. Phone: 415-561-3333. Fax: 415-561-3334.

Land Stewardship Project, 2200 4th St., White Bear Lake, MN 55110. Phone: 651-653-0618. Website: www.landstewardshipproject.org. Their mission is to foster an ethic of stewardship for farmland, to promote sustainable agriculture and to develop sustainable communities.

Community Food Security News, CFS Coalition, PO Box 209, Venice, CA 90294. Website: www.foodsecurity.org.

National Organic Directory, PO Box 363, Davis, CA 95616. Phone: 530-756-7857. Community Alliance with Family Farmers—policy and education.

Ecology Action/Bountiful Gardens. 18001 Shafer Ranch Road, Willitis, CA 95490. Phone: 707-459-6410. How to grow lots of healthy food in a very small space.

Mothers and Others, 870 Market St., Suite 654, San Francisco, CA 94102. Phone: 415-433-0850. Consumer guides, advocacy, and education.

Pesticide Action Network, 49 Powell St., Suite 500, San Francisco, CA 94102. Phone: 415-981-1771. Putting the bugs back into biodiversity.

Food First, 398 60th Street, Oakland, CA 94618. Phone: 510-654-4400. Preeminent food and social justice think tank, publishes books and newsletter.

Oxfam America, 26 West St., Boston, MA 02111. Phone: 617-728-2594. Oxfam America is an advocate for the world's impoverished people. Its triple mandate is to create awareness of their plight, educate people about the underlying social and political reasons for it, and take action to change it.

Ordinary Hero | JODY WILLIAMS

by Burt Berlowe

> *What's beautiful about grassroots political movements is that people who are viewed as being dispossessed, as being powerless, as being ignorant, as being outsiders—suddenly . . . tip the balance, . . . change the means of exchange of the coin of the realm. Suddenly, we become people who define what humanhood is and what power is, and then the world turns over.*
>
> —Barbara Smith, *Visionary Voices*

Inside the busy Cambodian clinic, a dark-skinned boy with one leg is leaned on a crutch, waiting his turn in a long line. Every so often, he hopped forward, trying to steady himself before pausing to rest again. His sad young face reflected the pain and awkwardness of his every move. He was bewildered by what had happened to him and yet realized that his life had changed forever.

Just a few months before this was a happy child, playing in a field near his home as he had many times. Suddenly, without warning, he stepped on a landmine, setting off an explosion that ripped apart his left leg. The extent of the damage caused the doctors to amputate his leg just above the knee. He had come to the prosthesis clinic to be fitted with a new limb and afforded the chance to walk again.

As it was on many other days, the clinic was filled with amputees of all ages in wheelchairs, on crutches, or sprawled out on cots and mats. There were children injured while at play, grandmothers blown apart while collecting firewood to make a family meal, and men and women whose tilling hoe struck one of the deadly metal objects planted in the soil. They were all victims of Cambodian landmines.

On a summer day in 1991, the clinic had a special visitor—an American peace activist named Jody Williams. Until then, Jody had only heard and read about the damage done by landmines. Witnessing these examples firsthand, her empathy swelled and her anger boiled. As she watched the one-legged boy and the other patients still to be treated, she knew she couldn't just stand on her two capable legs and do nothing. She left the clinic that day, dedicating herself to a compelling cause—one that would ultimately earn this unpretentious small-town girl the world's most prestigious peace prize.

Photo by Todd Cota

Jody Williams

Jody's desire to help society's victims was learned at an early age. Born at the dawn of the '50s, she was raised in a log cabin in the placid, church-filled hamlet of Putney, Vermont. The scant population of twelve hundred included her mother who worked in public housing projects and her father who was a county judge. She learned early on to be a humanitarian by defending her handicapped brother from frequent tormentors. At the same time, she recalls being "a good, conscientious student who never bugged anybody and always did my homework before it was due. Then came college, and I didn't know what I wanted to do with myself. I had a series of boring and irrelevant jobs and kept going to school and getting more degrees in search of something better."

As she was working toward a masters degree in international relations, Jody found an issue that energized her. "The Vietnam War was my transformation," she says. "I opposed it and did some marches at the University of Vermont. I thought it was wrong for the U.S. to be in a region we didn't know anything about."

Her interest in Vietnam eventually led Jody to developing countries. "One day in 1981, I was waiting for a train in a Washington, DC, subway station. An organizer was leafleting people as they got off the train. I was handed a leaflet that read, 'El Salvador: Another Vietnam.' What interested me was it had 'Vietnam' in the title. I eventually became involved with the Nicaragua-Honduras Education Project, which was raising awareness of American policy in Central America. For eleven years, I worked to stop U.S. intervention in Central America and to direct medical aid to El Salvador. I got a firsthand look at the ravages of war.

"I remember that, during the Pakistani missile crisis, I would hide under my desk in fear of possible nuclear fallout. Little did I realize then that there was another type of fallout that was doing mass destruction. Landmines were contaminating seventy countries around the world. Organizations like Human Rights Watch and Handicap International and others had reported millions of landmines in the ground in countries like Cambodia, Angola, and Ethiopia. I found out that a landmine injures someone every twenty-two minutes. That had a lasting impact on me.

"During a trip I made to Egypt, the army took me to El Amin where there had been a battle in the desert in World War I. There were two hundred seventy-four thousand square kilometers of land that had seventeen million landmines. Since World War II, they have removed less than forty percent of them. That's land that once was a breadbasket and can no longer be used.

"I went with some army officers to look at the area. We drove three and a half hours into the desert on a little, skinny road, then turned off onto the unmarked, landmine-infested desert. Since I didn't want to risk being blown up, I stayed in the tent and watched squads trying to remove the mines. I sat there looking at the expansive desert around me, knowing that no one could walk there, that the people were being denied their own land.

"In Cambodia, landmines cover fifty percent of the territory. The eighty-five thousand refugee families from the war, now repatriated in their country, don't have enough land to grow sufficient rice. So much land was contaminated by landmines that only twelve hundred families got land. All the rest got a one-year supply of rice and fifty dollars. That's an example of the long-term impact of landmines.

"In 1991, the Vietnam Veterans of America Foundation (VVAF) opened a prosthesis clinic in Cambodia, in an area where landmines still remained from the Vietnam War era. Virtually every amputee at the clinic was there because he or she had stepped on a landmine. The Vets' Foundation thought it wasn't enough to just put limbs on people. They had to go to the root cause of the problem. I made a commitment to help them.

"The veterans' group invited me to run a fledgling organization, the International Campaign to Ban LandMines (ICBL). While there were assorted grassroots organizations working against landmines, there was no coordinated strategy."

Under Williams' leadership, a handful of anti-landmine organizations with human rights roots came together in New York in October of 1992 to coordinate their efforts. "It began with three of us sitting around a table," Jody explains. "We agreed to host a conference for nongovernmental organizations (NGOs) the following year. In May of '93, the first international conference on landmines drew forty NGOs and began to build support for the ultimate goal: a worldwide ban on the use, production, trade, and stockpiling of landmines."

From this inauspicious beginning, ICBL grew rapidly into a coalition of over thirteen hundred human rights, humanitarian, children's, peace, disability, medical, veterans, development, arms control, religious, environmental, and women's organizations, working together in more than seventy-five countries. In October of 1996, a conference of 50 NGOs, observer states, and others, met in Ottawa, Canada, and agreed to sign a treaty banning antipersonnel mines. In December of 1997, more than ninety countries, not including the United States, gathered in Canada—this time to formally sign the treaty into law. As of this writing, the number of treaty signers is at one hundred thirty-one.

Jody Williams was down on her farm when she received the news that she had become an international hero. She had unceremoniously turned forty-seven the day before and was relaxing in the Putney, Vermont, house where she had spent most of her younger years. She was there when the phone call came congratulating her on winning the Nobel Peace Prize for her crusade against landmines.

Hours later, Jody walked out of the farmhouse to greet the press. She was barefoot, wearing jeans and a tank top. This may not have been customary dress for a Nobel recipient. But it was vintage Jody. As her accomplishments and plaudits have grown, she has remained true to her natural self: "I'm just an ordinary person," she says. "I shop at Safeway. I vacuum rapidly. I haven't changed. This was one small way to contribute to making life better for a few. We didn't set out to change the world. We didn't set out to be heroes. We certainly didn't set out to be recognized by the Nobel committee. We set out to banish this one weapon that is illegal under international law."

The ICBL's historic impact was made in a remarkably short amount of time against enormous odds. The major superpowers: The U.S., Russia, and China were against the treaty, and there was general resistance from the diplomatic community. "One of the things we've seen out of the landmine campaign," says Jody, "is that a lot of governments are very uncomfortable with this model because they don't want civil society to have an ongoing voice, especially on security issues. Typically, governments and NGOs have been seen as adversaries. The 'men in suits' do not want to have their process disrupted by having open dialogue with civil society. That undercuts the behind-closed-doors way of diplomacy.

"A key element of our campaign has been the willingness of the middle and smaller powers of the world, in conjunction with the NGOs, to step out and set an agenda and come together to move this issue forward, sometimes with the direct opposition of the big powers. We spoke with authority, standing in every door of every government that was interested in people having a role in civil society. This campaign was a breakthrough because some governments took the risk of allowing us in the room. Ultimately, we did end up changing the world on this one tiny issue We showed how ordinary people working together can accomplish extraordinary things."

While proud of the campaign's accomplishments, Jody believes that "there is a lot more to be done." She is determined not to let up until every nation signs and conforms to the international treaty. She has been particularly critical of the United States, which insists on leaving its landmines in Korea for several more years, and won't sign a treaty that doesn't allow for that exception. Removing the millions of landmines that currently exist, making sure that countries who have signed the treaty comply with its regulations, creating an international criminal court, halting the use of children as soldiers, and slowing the spread of firearms, are some of the tasks Jody and the ICBL are advancing.

The antilandmine crusade has taken its toll on Jody. In early 1998, she decided to give up day-to-day coordination of the campaign (three people were hired to take her place), prompting rumors that she had been dismissed from ICBL. Actually, she became an international ambassador for the campaign, focusing on ensuring treaty compliance, mine clearance, and victim assistance. Her travel schedule, as she puts it, is "horrifying at best." The day she spoke at the Nobel Peace Prize Festival in Minneapolis, I was able to corner her for only a hurried interview. Although obviously weary from the hectic pace, she told me that she "would be going home for about six seconds," before taking off on another trip to several foreign countries.

Jody's motivation for continuing her frenetic and often difficult campaign is simple but powerful. It hearkens up memories of defending her brother, of funneling medical aid to the poor, and, primarily, of the Cambodian clinic and the boy without a leg. "What keeps me going," she says, "is the conviction that it's the right thing to do. It makes me feel good every day that I'm doing something that makes a difference for someone else."

Questions for Contemplation:

1. What have you witnessed firsthand that makes your anger boil?
2. Were you considered to be a "good" kid? If so, what motivated you to be that way? If not, what do you think motivates kids to be "good?" What are the advantages and disadvantages of being a "good" kid?
3. Since it infringes on civilian's lives and prohibits land use for decades to come, do you think it should be illegal for the military to plant landmines? How can government at all levels assist in the development and nurturing of cultures of peace throughout the world and, in particular: a) eliminate the use of landmines and government sales of arms, and b) support the development of peace studies and peace action programs?
4. Jody started her work with two other people. They eventually developed a worldwide effort. Who could you invite to join you in a neighborhood, statewide, or worldwide cause?
5. When you are having trouble giving to your family or loved ones because of extra stress in your life, what works for you to reconnect with them?

Resources for Reflection and Action:

The Art of Peace, edited by Jeffrey Hopkins (Ithaca, New York: Snow Lion Publications, 2000). Nobel Peace Laureates discuss human rights, conflict, and reconciliation.

Peace Within Our Grasp: Making the dream a reality, by CR Dale Kline (Available from Dale Kline, 820 Hampton Ridge Dr., Akron, OH 44313). This book delves into the roots of behavior to find the causes of war and suggests ways to prevent wars.

Doing Democracy, (Journal) by the Center for Living Democracy, RR #1, Fox Farm Rd., Brattleboro, VT 05301. Phone: 802-254-1234. Website: www.Americannews.com. The Center for Living Democracy believes that "doing democracy" is a learned skill and one best carried out at the grassroots level. The center believes that ordinary citizens have a vital role in solving public problems, and that in so doing they are creating a growing "democratic revolution" in our country.

Peace Education News (PEN), Publication of the Canadian Peace Educator's Network, PO Box 839, Drayton Valley, Alberta TOE OMO, Canada. PEN supports and promotes balanced and responsible formal education about peace and security issues.

In the Tiger's Mouth: An empowerment guide for social action, by Katrina Shields (Gabriola Island, BC: New Society Publishers, 1994). A readable and practical manual for dealing with obstacles to individual and organizational effectiveness.

Resource Manual for a Living Revolution, by Virginia Coover, Ellen Deacon, Charles Esser, and Christopher Moore (Gabriola Island, BC: New Society Publishers, 1978). A classic sourcebook on group process and other skills useful to those involved in social change through nonviolence.

Alternative to the Pentagon, by Franklin Zahn (Fellowship of Reconciliation, PO Box 271, Nyack, NY 10960. Phone: 914-358-4601, 1996). The author provides an imaginary account of an invasion of the United States and illustrates how it could be defeated nonviolently. Outstanding photos of nonviolent campaigns.

Interhelp, PO Box 86, Cambridge, MA 02140. This is an international network of people who share their deepest responses to world conditions that threaten human life and the Earth. They help people within their own communities to move through feelings of isolation and hopelessness to empowerment. They offer community gatherings and training in despair and empowerment, deep ecology, and personal support systems.

International Campaign to Ban Landmines. Phone: 202-547-2667. Website: www.icbl.org. Email: cblAicbl.org.

Act For Change Website: www.actforchange.com. ActForChange.com is Working Assets' online activism site. They keep in touch with hundreds of advocacy groups and post those actions they think you'll find most valuable. Then they connect you directly to decision-makers that can influence the outcome of important events. With a click of your mouse, your voice will be heard.

Sharing My Cereal

by Julie Penshorn

I've been hearing a lot of complaints from my family lately about work taking over my life. My boyfriend and son don't believe I'll ever get through this busy time and think we'll always have to work from sunup to sundown with no time to play or relax. Thus, when I need their help the most, they are becoming less motivated to help out. As I was working on Jody's story, I wondered if she had a family and how they were dealing with her schedule of flying back and forth all over the world.

What does a compassionate rebel do when life presents financial hardships, an overwhelming workload, family conflicts, or all of the above? How does someone break free of the hurtful status quo responses designed for self-protection?

If I want to make a compassionate rebel response, where do I start? And how do I keep the issues from my past from rearing up within me and blocking my compassion?

That shame monkey has been with me for quite awhile. I first felt its sharp claws as a child when I was told I was "bad" or "wrong" to try to remedy injustices. I remember hearing, "That's just the way it is," and "You can't change the world."

Neither of my parents knew quite how to deal with me, but it was hardest for my mother. She loved me and recognized my intelligence and independence, but she wanted me to "fit in" and be a "good girl." My parents were trying to protect me from the expected consequences of my rebellious nature. Though I thought they were wrong intellectually, emotionally, they had a powerful grip; their approval was very important. I remember feeling angry that they couldn't just support me, even stand up for me to my teachers and others when I rocked the boat. I also remember my self-doubt. I often thought, "If they think I should be different, and fit in better, perhaps they are right."

Of course, when faced with parental disapproval, a child can get very scared of abandonment. "If I don't fit in my own family, where do I fit?" and "I wonder if they'll throw me out if I persist with my ways." Thus, I developed an impatient, angry attitude that I thought would defend me from experiencing criticism—to which I was deeply sensitive, since it meant disapproval. My terror of abandonment was so strong, I couldn't even identify it. I didn't know I was scared. I thought I was justifiably angry that people wouldn't support me. I would reply defensively to any small hint of disapproval or even a legitimate question.

It took years of personal reflection and searching, and then years of acceptance and support from my business partner, Rebecca (who dialogues with me as I struggle with my dilemmas) to begin to loosen the grip of my shame monkey. I remember telling Rebecca more than once, "I know what I need to do, I just can't do it."

She would say, "There must be a good reason for you not to do it. What is it?"

Sometimes I would just choke. I couldn't figure it out. Other times, I would get mad at her, "Just drop it. That's enough!" I'd cry.

Finally, her gentle persistence paid off. I began to recognize that I was okay—even if I did something unusual, extraordinary, weird. The shame monkey loosened its grip as I got a very different feeling from my anger. It was much less frightening, much less negative. It didn't come with fear of abandonment. I recognized my ideas were valid, my rebellion was necessary, and I had an important voice.

Then, came the idea of "The Compassionate Rebel." In fact, it was the rebel in me who helped discover the concept. I knew in my heart the importance of the voice of dissent. I knew, because of Rebecca's response to me, that some people would appreciate my perspective and not abandon me. They would see that I had a gift to offer. I also knew that I had to stop delivering my gift by shoving it down people's throats! Sometimes it was too much for them to swallow! So, I finally realized that it's not the rebel that's the problem, it's the lack of compassion. It's hard to be compassionate and gentle when you are frightened or angry.

Horses turn their rear ends toward a threatening

situation, person, or other horse. So do people! To help people stay open to my insight or my thought, I had to make it less threatening, more palatable. It took me forty years to understand this!

My journey is just beginning. Every intimate relationship reminds me that my old habits are still entrenched. Every perceived rejection opens the door to my lifelong fear of abandonment—the true root of my shame. But instead of expressing my anger and hostility in a vain effort to protect myself, now I am learning to pause and breathe, pound the dirt, play my guitar, and quell my initial shame-based reaction, remembering compassion for myself and others, remembering I'm not alone, remembering I'm okay.

A big component of remembering compassion is forgiveness. My parents, grandparents, teachers, and others were all doing the best they could. In fact, I was particularly blessed by a very supportive family. But, even though they were great, I still had to forgive them for questioning me and not knowing what I needed. And, I needed to forgive myself. Now, my task is to forgive my son and my boyfriend and accept that everyone is doing their best. When I do that, the compassion stays.

Recently, one of my kindergarten students in the artist-in-residency I was doing as Peacemaker® told us how her parents calm down when they are fighting. She said, "Well, they go to separate rooms to sleep, and then in the morning they share their cereal. They link arms and she puts a spoonful in his mouth, and he puts one in hers." My interpretation of that is: calm down before speaking or acting in anger.

I've learned to accept that my path, though it considers my family, is mine. I can't expect others to the do the same amount of overtime I am. Even as I go through this challenging time, I must give my family my love freely and reconnect with them by supporting their dreams and accepting their doubts rather than fearing their abandonment. They shouldn't fear that I will abandon them, either.

I have to recognize that my feelings come from within. They are remnants of my history and don't present an accurate picture of the present. I must look up, smile, and value myself. Then, I can share my cereal.

Sometimes You Wouldn't Even Know that I Love You

By Julie Penshorn,
for Mom and Dad

Sitting here in the darkness,
Only my mind can see.
Thinking 'bout my friends who love me, and my family,
Loving me from head to toe, loving me.

I've walked a path of contention,
Speaking out when silence prevailed,
Fighting against stupidity, despair, and misery.
You were there if I succeeded or if I failed.

Bridge:
With you, I practiced working for justice.
You demonstrated right and wrong.
You gave me the spirit deep and strong.

Sometimes it must be scary,
Watching me take fall after fall.
Trying your best to help me out, and knowing my path's my own.
You give everything you can—you give it all.

Chorus:
You are the first I pushed away.
You are the last to see me celebrate.
I want to say I'm sorry for what I've put you through.
Sometimes you wouldn't even know that I love you.

Chapter 10
Torch Carriers

Eddie Rustin, Hannah Nelson-Pallmeyer, Edwin Holmvig-Johnson,
Marika Staloch, Chris Carroll, and Jesse Lecy

We dare not forget today that we are the heirs of that first revolution. Let the word go forth from this time and place, to friend and foe alike, that the torch has been passed to a new generation of Americans.

—John F. Kennedy, Inaugural address, 1961

Many of us, who were adolescents and young adults in the '60s, spent time protesting. Perhaps our cause was racial injustice, the Vietnam War, or equal pay for women and men. As we began to have families of our own and pursue our livelihoods, it may have looked as if some of us had abandoned of our causes and succumbed to the lure of the mainstream.

Perhaps that's true . . . Or, perhaps we directed our energies toward our children through our social-justice parenting and grandparenting. Our babies are now young adults, and the world is seeing the fruits of this quiet labor. Young activists are popping up all over the country to join those with more history as social activists. We call them Torch Carriers. Their organizing and networking skills position them to be taken seriously by the powers that be. They have maintained their individuality and yet know how to develop a sense of community with others in order to work together on a common cause.

Torch Carriers, now in their teens and 20s, are showing how they are different from their predecessors. Some are very much a part of mainstream America. You wouldn't recognize them by the clothes they wear, the way they talk, or the way they comb their hair. Others' outward appearance is more obviously "counterculture."

These activists are prepared to act at a moment's notice. Many believe you don't need to drop out in order to make change in the world . . . you just need to be present when needed.

Martin's Legacy | EDDIE RUSTIN, HANNAH NELSON-PALLMEYER, EDWIN HOLMVIG-JOHNSON

by Burt Berlowe

One of the reasons our culture is falling apart is because we're going into therapy instead of becoming social activists.

—M. Bray Pipher, in *The Shelter of Each Other: Rebuilding our families*

It's six a.m. Dawn is revealing a steel gray sky. In his South Minneapolis home, thirteen-year-old Eddie Rustin is preparing to meet the emerging day. School classes are still three hours away, but he has another, vital appointment to keep.

As he does nearly every Wednesday morning around this time, Eddie joins friends and family at the doorstep of Alliant Tech, the Hopkins, Minnesota, manufacturer of materials for landmines. For an hour or so, he prays, protests, and sits in front of the corporation, doing his part to promote peace. Then he heads home to catch the bus that takes him to Risen Christ Catholic School and a more normal existence as a sixth-grader still learning the ways of the world.

Eddie isn't alone as a youthful protester. The Community of St. Martin has several families with children that routinely meet to protest Alliant Tech's products. Though barely into puberty, these children are veteran activists.

Eddie's visits to Alliant Tech began in the summer of 1996 and have continued on a regular basis. "When we first started going to Alliant Tech, the workers would give us the finger. Now they don't. I march around with banners and signs, but I haven't sat in front of the doors. My mom wouldn't let me get arrested. I'm a little young, you know."

The Community of St. Martin, a residential section of twenty to thirty households covering about a mile radius near a Mennonite church and Montessori school in Minneapolis, Minnesota, is a close-knit group. It is named after five Martins: Martin of Tours, a fourth-century Roman soldier turned pacifist; Martin Luther, the sixteenth Century Christian reformer; Martin Luther King, Jr., a leader in nonviolent protest; Martin De Porres, a Spanish-Indian healer who served the poor in Peru in the 1600s; and Martin Niemoller, a German pastor imprisoned for his nonviolent resistance to Nazis during World War II. The focal point of the community is St. Martin's Table, a restaurant and bookstore that has a strong emphasis on peace, spirituality, and social justice.

The St. Martin's children learn and practice social action at an early age. At the age of ten Eddie, along with his toddler sister, Molly, and a neighbor girl, sold Kool-Aid for Rwanda in the parking lot, of a neighborhood grocery store. "In one day, we raised about ten dollars to help supply food and medicine to Rwandan citizens," Eddie told me.

Another time, Eddie joined in a demonstration at Toys 'R Us, a national toy-selling retailer. "My family and several other families stood in the parking lot asking people coming out of the store if they had bought Ninja Turtles war toys, and, if so, to put them in our bucket to take them out of circulation. We wanted to build consumer awareness about war toys."

Several of the St. Martin's children are School of the Americas (SOA) protesters. They have ridden with the St. Martin's cavalcade to Fort Benning, Georgia to join with demonstrators from all over the country.

Eddie said, "I missed two days of school when I went to SOA. We rode for twenty-eight hours straight through. We stayed at a cheap hotel next to the base so we could walk from there to the place where we protested. On the day before the big protest, we drove into the base and went right by the School of the Americas. It's a big, beautiful building that has half an earth globe on the top. But it's a torture camp. It teaches people from Latin America ways of torture and military techniques that they can use on their own people. It could be used for a regular school, not to teach such awful things.

"Some friends and I planted crosses along the way. The security cops made us pick them up. Then we protested nonviolently outside the gates with our signs and had a vigil. Some people made speeches. Many got arrested and handcuffed because they crossed the line onto the base. Our country shouldn't be doing stuff like this."

Eddie carried his experiences and viewpoints back to his classroom. He told teachers and other students about his activities and became known as an advocate for peace. "I decided that I'm a pacifist like Jesus. There's always an option other than war.

I had a debate with one of my teachers about justified war. He's not opposed to war.

"I gave a report on the School of the Americas to a sixth grade class, and a student came to me and said, 'Well, that's in another part of the world. How does that affect us?' My response was that this is one world that needs to work together, like the parts of your body. If you cut off one part of your body, it won't function as well. He thought about that. Others are beginning to share my point of view. One friend, in particular, wants to go to a protest with me and bring two others."

Because of his reputation in school as a peacemaker, Eddie has been assigned to monitor and mediate any disagreements that might erupt among the students on the bus.

Eddie wants to help heal growing divisions between people and bring more compassion and understanding to his neighborhood and the rest of the world. He said, "There's a lot of stereotypical stuff going on around us. I walk down the street, and I've seen elderly women grasp their bags closer to their sides. It makes me feel bad. I try to be polite to people when they walk by, and say 'Hi.' I said, 'Hi' to an elderly woman on the street the other day. I hope it changes her outlook on things. I want to continue to be a peacemaker when I grow up. I'll stay along the line of being an activist my whole life. That's my calling."

Hannah Nelson-Pallmeyer, daughter of St. Martin's author and professor Jack Nelson-Pallmeyer, is trained as a manager in the RAP

Photo courtesy of Peace Village

Hannah Nelson-Pallmeyer, right, and friend Molly at Peace Village camp.

(Resolving Arguments Peacefully) program in her school. When students have a fight, she helps them resolve the conflict. Hannah has even given a presentation, including two role-plays on conflict resolution, to faculty at St. Catherine's College in St. Paul, Minnesota. When she was just eight years old Hannah played the role, based on a true story, of a twelve-year-old boy who was a victim of the child labor system. He was bound to a loom and forced to work eighteen-hour days. Once freed, he set out to tell the world what happened to him–until friends of his former captors gunned him down.

Recently, Hannah was becoming a documentary movie producer. She was working with classmates on a film about Minneapolis' debate over a proposed new professional baseball stadium—doing the interviewing, filming, and final production. She hopes to use the film to convince the powers that be that a stadium should not be built with public money.

Edwin Holmvig-Johnson was just five weeks old when his parents took him to demonstrate against military aid to El Salvador, and fourteen months old the first time he went to an Alliant Tech protest (when the company was still called Honeywell).

Edwin was eventually arrested for his protesting at Alliant Tech. "The police used handcuffs on us and put them on tightly. One man's wrist was turning blue. We were taken on a bus to the municipal Ice Arena and processed there. My dad waited outside the door the entire five hours I was inside. One of the police sergeants screamed that he would take us to jail. Some of the protesters were rude, but I decided to be polite. I was prepared to go to trial if I had to.

Photo courtesy of Peace Village

Eddie Rustin shares information about landmines to a group of younger kids.

"My mother was active in the overground railroad that brought people from Central America to the U.S.," said Edwin. "My dad is a Vietnam combat veteran and is determined to raise his children to be pacifists. He took me to watch and pray for my mother when she was being arrested. Our work takes us near and far. We went to a rally at the Minnesota State Capitol the other day, and we visited Peace Trees Vietnam in Dong Ha last summer to see the reforesting of places that used to be littered with landmines.

"I have crossed the property line at Fort Benning, Georgia, twice but wasn't arrested. I might do it again. I would be glad to have this on my record. They don't usually arrest minors. But if they do, the record isn't given to employers, just to the military. That would establish me as a conscientious objector if there were ever a draft."

Edwin's penchant for activism is being passed down to his younger siblings. Sisters Svea and Bessie first joined the family trips to Fort Benning when they were eight and four years old respectively, and lately, baby brother Vinh has been going along, too. By Edwin's standards, infancy is hardly too young to begin making peace.

In the summer of 2000, Eddie, his sister, Crissy, and Edwin, along with four other St. Martin community members, took a trip to Guatemala, where they stayed at a children's orphange. When he returned, Edwin gave the following account of the venture and its affect on him on a youth radio news program produced by St. Martin youth:

"We were seven gringos from middle-class America who saw small children and their caretakers that had virtually nothing—all sorts of ordinary people with extraordinary generosity—people who make less than three dollars a day. We saw a marred and torn place finally putting itself back together.

"It was an amazing trip that opened up my eyes to the plight of developing nations. It amazed me to see the results of our foreign policy. Most of all, it rocked the foundation of my belief system. Upon my return to the U.S, I felt thankful for the opportunities here and for what I have. I felt a little disconcerted, however, at Dayton's (department store), my place of employment, to see some of the prices in the oval room—nineteen hundred dollars for a Chanel suit, more than the average Guatemalan makes in a year. That's an amazing feat that you can spend three times someone's annual income in the time it takes to swipe a MasterCard.

"It is difficult to balance living within our culture and our country with trying to withdraw from it completely. I reject the notion that complete cultural withdrawal is necessary. I choose to believe that a balance between enjoying the good things about our culture, its openness, diversity, and democratic ideals, while resisting excessive consumerism and violence, is possible. Now I just need to find this balance."

Photo courtesy of Peace Village

Edwin Holmvig-Johnson, far right, joins his fellow peacemakers at Peace Village camp.

Questions for Contemplation:

1. What do you think about exposing young children to protesting?
2. Teachers may be chastised when they take public political positions, yet some argue that when teachers are silent, it endorses the status quo, which also is a political position. What do you believe teachers' responsibilities are to their students when it comes to teaching social action and democratic citizenship?
3. Ask a child in your life to share a "little worry" and a "big worry." What he/she says provides opportunities for meaningful social action. How would you help a child work on what he or she sees as worrisome or wrong with the world?
4. What are some ways to be an activist besides being a protester? Which ones personally interest you?
5. If you could wave a magic wand over the world, what one thing would it have the power to change? What do you need to do to become the wand?

Resources for Reflection and Action:

Teaching for Social Justice, edited by William Ayers, Jean Anne Hunt, & Therese Quinn (NYC: The New Press, 1998). Features a unique mix of hands-on, historical, and inspirational writings on topics including education through social action, community building, and adult literacy. Includes an extensive teacher file, resource section, and list of activist-oriented websites.

Tug of War: Peace through understanding conflict, by Terrence Webster-Doyle (Ojai, CA: Atrium Publications, 1990). Includes creative stories and activities on how to resolve conflict in peaceful ways. Designed for young people.

Making the Peace: A fifteen-session violence-prevention curriculum for young people (Oakland, CA: Oakland Men's Project, 1997). This book is a practical approach to conflict resolution that helps teens not only to reflect and dialogue about various forms of violence they experience but also learn about becoming allies, healing hearts, and taking action to improve conditions in their lives and the lives of others.

Peacebuilding for Adolescents: Strategies for educators and community leaders, edited by Linda Forcey & Ian Harris (NYC: Peter Lang, 1999). The authors promote a humane response to aggressive and acting-out school children. They do not advocate tougher criminal justice measures to deter youth from crime. Instead, they believe we need to teach young people to value peace, to learn to manage their own conflicts, and to live more peacefully.

Peacemaker's ABCs for Young Children: A guide for teaching conflict resolution with a peace table, by Rebecca Janke & Julie Penshorn Peterson (Shop online at www.peacemakers.org). Helps teachers initiate a peacemaking classroom and a simple conflict resolution process for children ages three to eight. Website includes many other peace education resource materials.

We Can Solve it Peacefully, by Julie Penshorn Peterson (Scandia, MN: Growing Communities for Peace, 1995). Supports the Peacemaker's ABCs curriculum with fourteen songs and short dialogues with kids. A fun, toe-tapping tape. Stands alone.

The Co/Motion Guide to Youth-Led Social Change, by Leigh Dingerson and Sarah Hay. (Alliance for Justice, 1998). Introduces young people to tools, skills, and strategies to work for change in their communities. This hands-on-training manual outlines the dynamic processes of strategizing and action planning, and includes how-to information on conducting research, campaign planning, organizing meetings, coalition and community building, making and meeting a budget, working with the media, and evaluation. The manual is infused with stories of young people making a difference in their communities through service, advocacy, and organizing.

Devon Green, at the age of five, started a metal recycling firm and at the age of nine has over eighty clients. With her father's help, Devon collects about five thousand pounds of aluminum, brass, stainless steel and copper a year, including eighty-three thousand cans, mostly from businesses. You learn more about how to do this in your community by logging on to her website. Website: www.fl1.com/healthe-world.

Revolution From Within

A prelude to Marika Staloch and Chris Carroll

I seek no backward voyage across the sea of time. I will ever press forward. I believe that the present should be better than the past and the future better than the present.

—Inscribed on the statue of Archbishop John Ireland in the courtyard of the University of St. Thomas in St. Paul, Minnesota.

At first glance, The University of St. Thomas in St. Paul, Minnesota, resembles a medieval English courtyard. It's solid tradition of Catholicism and conservatism is portrayed in its stone, sixteenth century-style buildings with Latin inscriptions, its landscaped courtyards, and its manicured walkways.

Beneath this stoic facade, a revolution has been brewing that is chipping away at the university's solid foundation. It is being led—not by outside agitators—but by some of its most loyal students and faculty. They've brought justice and peace studies into the school's curriculum, and with the help of the campus ministry, have gone on to organize and participate in the Student Coalition for Social Justice (SCSJ). Professors David Smith, Jack Nelson-Pallmeyer, and Marv Davidov, and many of their students are putting social justice theories into action both on and off the campus. Their goal is to transform St. Thomas into a more progressive, social justice-minded institution.

We interviewed two of the coalition's recent leaders: Marika Staloch and Chris Carroll. They both chose to tell their stories in unique ways. Marika added a speech she had presented at a peace conference. Chris asked that, instead of actually telling his story, we use samples of poetry and songs he wrote during his years at St. Thomas. We also are including a poem submitted by SCSJ activist Jesse Lecy.

Finding a Soapbox | MARIKA STALOCH

by Burt Berlowe

> *. . . one-time sources for inspiration and empowerment, such as the Church, have now become silent baths in which the status quo is baptized.*
>
> —Chris Carroll

Marika Staloch walked the plush environs of St. Thomas University alone, hurrying her step to avoid her classmates' pressure to be one of the crowd. As usual, she had chosen not to join the churchgoing students flocking to regular afternoon mass. As she scurried away from the beckoning voices, she once again became a campus anomaly; a questioning Catholic daring to challenge the status quo.

This type of incident had happened to Marika frequently during her many trips through the corridors, courtyards, and commons of St. Thomas. At any time, she could have taken the easy route and given in to the calls for silent noncompliance. Instead, she had chosen to stay on a more difficult path—one that continued a childhood trek in search of something called "a soapbox."

This journey began for Marika in an unlikely place. She grew up in a white, rich, and conservative Minneapolis, Minnesota, suburb, where social and economic justice were rarely issues of public debate. Her parents, however, were exceptions to the rule. Her dad, for instance, was almost kicked out of high school for protesting against the Vietnam War. Following in her father's footsteps, Marika began at an early age to express her opinions and work for justice.

By the time she was in junior high, Marika had begun expanding her awareness to the needs of people beyond her immediate environment. She volunteered at an inner-city church that helped mentally ill people, served as a peer helper, organized retreats, and helped coordinate a children's fair for Earth Day that brought together city and suburban youth.

Marika went off to college at the University of St. Thomas, intent on continuing her social activism. What she saw and felt there angered and frightened her.

"My first year at St. Thomas was horrible," she recalls. "I grew up Catholic, but found it to be too limiting. I questioned many of its traditions. When I chose not to attend mass at St. Thomas, I was ostracized for it. Students would pressure me to attend. All that did was make me more determined not to be part of it.

"Once I helped a gay friend who had come out of the closet and was verbally harassed by homophobic students. I became discouraged by the lack of tolerance and willingness to be hurtful. At that point, I decided to be a justice and peace studies major.

"As part of my major, I took a class from Jack Nelson-Pallmeyer and learned, much to my relief, that religion can offer more than just theology. It can be a source of justice and peace. Jack talked about how his life had changed when he dedicated it to justice and peace. He was a huge spiritual influence, just when I needed it.

"What I was learning also affected how I invested some money my grandpa gave me. Since I now understood, through class discussions, how investing in large corporations can promote the downfall of small corporations, I invested my money in a small justice-oriented group.

"Through Jack Nelson-Pallmeyer's class, I also learned about the School of the Americas (SOA). Thousands of peasants, including children, have been killed (in several countries) by people trained at this school.

"In the fall of '98, when I heard about the opportunity to go to a protest march to object to the actions of the SOA, I decided to go as a college reporter and planned to share the story in our college newspaper when I returned. Originally, the school supported those of us who wanted to go and was willing to give each of us one hundred dollars to help cover expenses. At the last minute, they withheld the funds due to a complaint they received. Not only was I disappointed that the administrators withdrew their support, but it smacked of hypocrisy to me. 'How can we claim to be a Christian University and not raise our voices to stop the slaughtering of innocent people?' I wondered.

"We held our own fund-raiser and were able to raise enough money to go to the SOA. Seven thousand people from all over the country showed up to protest. I attended a nonviolent training session for those who wanted to cross the line and risk arrest and was delighted to see a Catholic priest, Father Roy Bourgeois, speak out. That was a beautiful moment for me because he asked us to make a group pledge of nonviolence. He told and showed us how religion really should be: people working for peace and justice, not just talking about it.

"One of our hotel rooms was set aside for young people to pray. Many struggled with how they would tell their parents if they chose to be arrested. I decided not to be arrested because I didn't want my camera confiscated. I figured I would be more effective if I took good pictures to go along with my story.

"Two thousand protesters decided to cross the

line. It was amazing to watch so many people—kids and adults—stand up for SOA victims who couldn't stand up for themselves. It was a transforming experience.

"When I got back to school, I wrote the SOA story. Even though I knew that the editors were not used to leftist thought in the school newspaper, I still had hopes the school administrators would show support of our SOA efforts. Generally, there was little response at all to my article. People were good at keeping silent when they didn't want something to get attention. However, it did offend one of our administrators, and I noticed the tension between us immediately. It hurt me to get such resistance. That's when I got into the Student Coalition for Social Justice."

As Marika continued her peace studies education, she yearned to find out more about other cultures. Her desire became reality when she was able to travel with other students to Guatemala to study Economic Ecology.

"I noticed that the Guatemalan people were impoverished in American terms, and their village was segregated: Latino versus Mayan and rich versus poor. Yet, there was much joy in their lives. They laughed and joked with each other all the time. They asked me, 'Do you laugh more with us or with your family at home?' I said I laughed more with them. It was good for me to come back home realizing that laughter is such good medicine. That has been important to me ever since.

"I was fortunate to be able to stay with a Mayan family for a week. I was amazed at the way they took me in and allowed me to get to know them, even though I hardly knew their language. They taught me how to make tortillas, slice a pineapple, and wash my clothes by hand. They laughed (good-naturedly) at me for not knowing those little things. It made me realize how little I knew about their everyday living.

"When I didn't see any grown men in their house and asked where their father was, the mother and daughter said he had been murdered while he was out in the fields. They thought it was a government-sanctioned political murder. I knew the United States' position was to support the Guatemalan government, and I was horrified to think the U.S. may have had a role in his murder."

Photo courtesy of Marika Staloch

Marika Staloch carries a Guatemalan child.

Marika returned to St. Thomas from her Guatemalan visit better prepared to finish what she had started—transforming the college into a bastion of social action. She plunged into SCSJ activities, including a peace camp on campus where people spoke out against the bombing of Kosovo. She also initiated a letter opposing U.S. sanctions against Iraq. She told everyone she could that it was hypocritical to have the ROTC on campus and suggested requiring ROTC students to take justice and peace classes.

To provide a tool for public dialogue regarding critical issues, she became a co-founder of the alternative newspaper on campus, called the *Soapbox*. It was published by the Student Coalition, which she also helped organize. The *Soapbox* gives students a forum for expressing opinions that might not otherwise be heard.

"One of the hardest things about graduating from St. Thomas [in 1999] was leaving the *Soapbox* behind," Marika says. "It was hard to let it go. It was my baby."

"The soapbox concept went beyond the coalition newsletter. The SCSJ also sponsors regular Soapbox Live events where students have a chance to say their piece on any issue.

"The purpose of the coalition is to radicalize our conservative college and develop a revolutionary student movement," Marika muses. "I made efforts to change the minds of people on campus. I'm glad I had the chance to work with a budding justice and peace community. I feel like a pioneer having helped to build it.

"My initial stereotype of the peace process was that it was hippies trying to save the world. I didn't think that it could be people like me doing it. Now I realize that peace can be exciting and intense when you allow yourself to question the status quo. It has made me a stronger person."

A few months after she graduated from St. Thomas, Marika found another soapbox, writing and delivering the following speech at a peace conference:

"The most frequently asked question to me from people not involved in the peace movement is: 'How do you care so much about that stuff?' (The 'stuff' being politics.)

My answer is cliché, but to the point, 'How do you not?'

"But I've been forced to think about that question when deciding the path I want my life to take now that I've graduated. If they were to push the question further, I think I would answer: 'Because I'm mad.' Or perhaps, 'Because I'm sad.' And a lot of it has to do with the fact that I'm scared.

"I can envision peace:

I envision myself, female, not needing to be constantly aware of that.

I envision myself American, not needing to be embarrassed of it.

I envision myself a concerned citizen, but not being in a minority because of it.

I envision myself a white person who does not have any more power because of it.

I can envision little things like being able to go to any large city and breathe the air, taking midnight walks without having to be afraid; being able to buy something, knowing that what I purchased isn't contaminated or the product of unfair labor conditions.

I can envision peace.

"So why am I scared?

"I'm scared because I don't understand how the power works in this world. I'm scared when I see the media and the politicians and the general public shutting their eyes to protesters, activists, and strikers. I'm scared that even if we do care a hell of a lot about the world and get a revolution going, it may only be the tip of a very huge undertaking.

"And I'm scared because our society tells me my career should start soon. That I should sell my daylight hours so I can be productive and make use of the degree I just earned. I will become mature, responsible. And when I have a career, I'll have to give up silly notions of taking off three days to listen to talks on peace.

"But I did and here I am. And during these three days, I've remembered that I'm female, I'm American, I'm an activist, and I can change the world. And I'm part of a very strong family of people who care.

"And now I'm not so scared."

Questions for Contemplation:

1. In what kind of town did you grow up? Was it a mixture of cultures or a monoculture? Did you have an opportunity to meet people of other cultures?
2. Did you have a religious upbringing? How did it affect you? Have you followed its tenets or retreated from them? Why?
3. Did you fit in well at the school(s) you attended? Were any of your views not accepted? If so, how did you feel? What did you do about it?
4. Have you ever gotten on a "soapbox" about an issue? Would you like to? If the thought scares you, what would be the worst thing that could happen? What do you need to do to overcome your fear?
5. Like Marika, do you think there needs to be an avenue for alternative ideas to be heard? What ideas do you have for providing such a forum? What would it take to make it happen and with whom can you connect to make it be a reality?

Resources for Reflection and Action:

Student Coalition for Social Justice, University of St. Thomas, 2150 Summit Ave., St. Paul, MN. Phone: 651-962-6598. Email: msvertin@stthomas.edu. The *Soapbox* newsletter is published by the Center for Service Learning and Social Action.

Consortium of Peace Research, Education, and Development (COPRED), c/o ICAR MSN 4D4, George Mason University, Fairfax, VA 22030-4444. Phone: 703-993-2405. Email: copred@gmu.edu. Website: www/gmu/edu/departments/1CAR/copred. In addition to publishing a peace research journal and conducting conferences, they have published the "Global Directory of Peace Studies and Conflict Resolution Programs" which is available for sale via their webpage.

Overseas Development Network (ODN), PO Box 1430, Cambridge, MA 02238. Phone: 617-868-3002. A network of college activists working on Third World issues.

Sojourners, Box 29272, Washington, DC 20017. Phone: 202-636-3637. A magazine for staying abreast of peace and justice issues.

Seeds of Peace: A catalogue of quotations, complied by Jeanne Larson and Madge Micheels-Cyrus (Santa Cruz, CA: New Society Publishers, 1987). Designed for easy use with pages tabbed by subject, this book is an invaluable resource for speechmakers, sermon writers, and newsletter editors.

When Students Have Power: Negotiating authority in a critical pedagogy, by Ira Shor. (Chicago, IL: The University of Chicago Press, 1996). After twenty years of critical teaching, Shor unexpectedly found himself faced with a student uprising. How Shor resolves this student rebellion, while remaining true to his commitment to power-sharing and critical pedagogy, is the profound learning of this book.

Human Rights Here and Now: Celebrating the universal declaration of human rights, edited by Nancy Flowers. (Available from the Human Rights USA Resource Center, 229 19th Avenue South, Suite 439, Minneapolis, MN 55455, 1998).

The Kid's Guide to Social Action, by Barbara A. Lewis. (Minneapolis, MN: Free Spirit Press, 1991). Contains real stories about kids and teens that are making a difference at home and around the world. Provides step-by-step guides to social action power skills. Provides addresses, phone numbers, and websites for other social action groups, federal and state government offices, and awards and recognition for kids.

Social Action Biblography, by Rebecca Janke. Available from Growing Communities for Peace, PO Box 248, Scandia, MN 55073. Phone: 651-257-2478. Contains hundreds of resources for social action ideas for children ages three to twelve. Website: www.peacemaker.org.

I'll Fix It Tomorrow | CHRIS CARROLL

by Burt Berlowe

Unless you are dirt poor or filthy rich, life is a series of compromises. Try to remain true, and when you falter, try to remain honest.
—Chris Carroll

"The experiences of my college years as a justice and peace studies major at the University of St. Thomas, in St. Paul, Minnesota, have formed within me a critical consciousness and a dedication to live my life in service and solidarity with the poor and marginalized of society.

"Two of the outlets I have begun cultivating for expressing my observations as I live the life I have chosen are poetry and song. What follows are some examples.

Photo by Todd Cota

Chris Carroll (far right), hosts a St. Thomas student production.

Lost in the Margins

When she was a child
She could wish upon a star
When she was a child
Life didn't seem so hard
Now she is lost in the margins
She can't even read a word
The pious offer blessings
But no book's gonna save her
She is lost in the margins
She can't even read a word
She's living paycheck to check
To dream would be absurd
She is lost in the margins . . .
When she was a child
She would wish upon a star
When she was a child
Life didn't seem so hard
When she was a child
She could believe in angels
But belief is a luxury
That she just can't afford.

I'll Fix It Tomorrow

CNN and the media circus
Spinning lies through a closed circuit.
You thought the Gulf War had ended?
It's not over 'til the sanctions are lifted.
We're worshipping the TV screens
We're reading the wrong magazines
We're in the driver's seat
Turning our keys
"No Blood For Oil"???
We're in the driver's seat
Turning our keys . . .
My car has broken down
Ruining my day
The bombs keep coming down
Turning night into day
In the time it takes
To walk
To the gas station
For a pack of cigarettes
Ten more children
Have drawn their last breaths.
I walk back home
Little blister on my foot
Tired little child
Makes a bed of soot.
"Who still speaks of the American genocide?"
(Adolph Hitler, 1941)
Who will speak of the sanctions in 2021?
Who will speak of the horror today?
Starvation continues
Disease continues
Bombing continues.
My car is still broken down.
I'll fix it tomorrow.

"We cannot wait for the world to turn, for times of change that we might change with them, for the revolution to come and carry us around its new course. We ourselves are the future. We are the revolution."

Beatrice Breuteau, philosopher

Questions for Contemplation:

1. This piece is unusual because Chris doesn't really tell his story, choosing instead to share his poetry. Based on what you read, what do you think you know about Chris? How might this poetry relate to his activism at St. Thomas?

2. Have you ever felt in solidarity with any individual or group of lesser means? If so, what was that like? What did you do to show your solidarity?

3. Have you ever felt "lost in the margins?" What did you do about it?

4. What is your opinion of the U.S. sanctions in Iraq? What ideas do you have for resolving this dilemma?

Resources for Reflection and Action:

Bridging the Global Gap: A handbook to linking citizens of the First and Third Worlds, by Medea Benjamin and Andrea Freedman (Washington, DC: Seven Locks Press, 1989). This book is the first major work on the growing internationalist movement that is focusing national attention on the interdependence of nations and on the connections between local and international struggles. Representatives of unions, schools, churches, community groups, and local governments have joined to search for nonviolent ways to wage world peace and end poverty. They are traveling across the globe to discover concrete ways of supporting their Third World counterparts.

Comprehensive Peace Education: Educating for global responsibility, by Betty Reardon (NYC: Teachers College Press, 1988). Reardon addresses the need to help educators and citizens alike understand what peace education is, why it is needed, and how it should be pursued. She investigates the root causes of the violent conditions facing society today, so that we can better understand how education can be used to interrupt the cycle of ever-increasing world violence.

Peace Education, by Ian Harris (Jefferson, NC: McFarland & Company, 1988). This book defines peace education, discusses current activities, presents key issues and topics, describes obstacles, suggests educational approaches for different age groups, discusses new ways of thinking, explains how to construct educational programs that will provide information about the impact of violence upon human communities, addresses fear generated by the arms race, and presents alternatives for resolving conflict nonviolently.

Institutionalizing Peace: The conception of the United States Institute for Peace and its role in American political thought, by Rhoda Miller (Jefferson, NC: McFarland & Company, 1994). This book traces the historical development and reasons for institutionalization of the concept of a Department of Peace and analyzes the institute that resulted from the federal legislative process, comparing it with the Arms Control and Disarmament Agency. The role of peace education, peace research, and peace action in shaping the institute is also presented.

Peace Organizations Past and Present: A survey and directory, by Robert S. Meyer (Jefferson, NC: McFarland & Company, 1988). In a day when the media are filled with accounts of international disputes, this author takes a look at a different dimension of the international scene—a dimension filled with ordinary people who are concerned about the level of violence on which our world is poised and who have done something about their concerns. They have organized scores of different groups, each group having as a common thread the promoting of peace.

Global Kids, 561 Broadway, 6th Floor, New York, NY 10012. Phone: 212-226-0130. Global Kids prepares urban youth to become community leaders and global citizens. Academic and leadership programs help young people become aware of world issues and cultures, develop critical thinking, and develop communication and leadership skills.

Twin Cities Campaign to Lift Sanctions Against Iraq, c/o Marie Braun. Phone: 651-962-6598.

Committee in Solidarity with ANDES (COSANDES). Promotes partnership with El Salvador, 2940 16th Street South, Room 305, San Francisco, CA 94103.

Vision

By Jesse Lecy,
St. Thomas student and
SCSJ member

Used with permission

Open your eyes—
Don't you see
The hunger in mine
That cannot be quenched with flesh and fruit?
Look again—
Don't you see
The sky painted every morning
By the rising sun?
Try real hard—
You can see
The children's need to be touched and taught;
You can see
The power in smiles and laughter—
The language without words.
Don't you see
The mountains trying to reach heaven,
Stars falling to find the earth,
And the hope in hearts that the two places can be the same?
Don't you see
The poor man's struggle,
The rich man's poverty?
Don't you see
The simple pleasure in leaving
Your sweat and blood in the earth you've plowed?
Close your eyes
And try harder
To see the things you can change.
Feel the humanity you are a part of,
Listen to the life all around you;
All the passion and pain, laughter, and sorrow.
Smell the musty stench of struggle in the air
And try to taste the sweet
Victory man knows
When he looks at the world for the first time
With his heart.

It's happening! The Compassionate Rebel *Revolution*

There is a new, different kind of revolution stirring in our land. You can find it anywhere: next door, down the street, even in your mirror. It is easy to join and understand, deeply personal yet universal, and fueled by anger and love. Its millions of members share a common name: "Compassionate Rebel."

To many people, the word "revolution" means overthrowing a government or system, often in a violent or subversive way. The Compassionate Rebel Revolution isn't about that. It does promote drastic change but in ways that are peaceful, positive, and uplifting; ways that build up rather than destroy. It is a revolution of hope for a better world.

The Compassionate Rebel Revolution is about big and small issues and actions. Most often, it consists of smaller scale acts that happen everywhere, every day, committed not just by seasoned activists, but by ordinary people. It is out of these individual acts that larger movements are made. For example, it took one angry voter complaining about a confusing ballot to rouse the masses in protest of a questionable count in the year 2000 U.S. presidential election. Throughout history, it has only taken a handful of citizens to weave a revolution.

Virtually every significant movement or action in our history has had one thing in common. It began with someone telling a story—to a friend, relative or stranger, before a small or large audience, around a campfire or in a community circle. The culture of storytelling permeates our society: from books, TV, music, and movies to church sermons, political campaigns, and family get-togethers. Stories entertain and inform, preserve and share history, bring people closer together, and call us to action. The civil rights movement, for instance, was steeped in a tradition of African-American storytelling. A story someone told about a voting problem in Florida became the catalyst for a new post-civil rights movement. There is no doubt that stories can change the world.

Storytelling also changes the teller of the story by opening new doors to the past and inner self, as well as expanding and deepening interpersonal relationships.

We have discovered the power of storytelling in our work with the upcoming generation of compassionate rebels we refer to as "Torch Carriers." In camps and classrooms, students have read chapters from this book and met the people they read about. Afterward, they have told us how much that experience moved them and helped them realize that they can make a difference in the world. As one young man said, "It was like reading a fairy tale then meeting the heroes."

Whatever your age, being a compassionate rebel is an integral part of the human experience. It basically asks these questions: Can you acknowledge and nurture the rebel part of yourself? Are you ready to look at the world with your heart? And will you share your story with others? We believe that anyone can find compassionate rebel traits and stories inside of themselves and others if they look hard enough. If that is the case, the Compassionate Rebel Revolution is a lot bigger than we have ever imagined and a lot smaller than it can become.

We invite you to embrace your compassionate rebel persona. Send us your compassionate rebel story or vignette, telling us about yourself, or someone you know. Describe your "rebel moment," (that sudden epiphany of chance or opportunity when you moved from innocent bystander to taking action). You never can tell. You just might make history.

For more information on the Compassionate Rebel Revolution and availability of the featured compassionate rebels as speakers, visit our website at www.peacemaker.org, or contact us by email at peace@peacemaker.org. Our mailing address is: PO Box 248, Scandia, MN 55073-0248.

A Fable on Peace

—Adapted from "The Weight of Nothing" (February, 1995). From the Link, newsletter of Congregations Concerned for Children, Minneapolis, Minnesota

"Tell me the weight of a snowflake," a coal mouse asked a wild dove.

"Nothing more than nothing," was the answer.

"In that case, I must tell you a marvelous story," the coal mouse said. "I sat on the branch of a fir, close to its trunk, when it began to snow . . . Since I didn't have anything better to do, I counted the snowflakes settling on the twigs and needles of my branch. Their number was exactly 3,741,952.

"When the next snowflake dropped onto the branch—nothing more than nothing, as you say—the branch broke off . . ."

The dove, since Noah's time, an authority on the matter, thought about the story for a while and finally said to herself, "Perhaps there is only one person's voice lacking for peace to come about in the world."

Index